CAMBRIDGE STUDIES IN
MEDIEVAL LIFE AND THOUGHT

Edited by M. D. Knowles, Litt.D., F.B.A.
*Fellow of Peterhouse and Professor of Medieval History in the
University of Cambridge*

NEW SERIES VOL. 2

TAVISTOCK ABBEY

TAVISTOCK ABBEY

A STUDY IN THE
SOCIAL AND ECONOMIC
HISTORY OF DEVON

BY

H. P. R. FINBERG

M.A., F.R.Hist.S.

CAMBRIDGE
AT THE UNIVERSITY PRESS
1951

CAMBRIDGE
UNIVERSITY PRESS

University Printing House, Cambridge CB2 8BS, United Kingdom

Cambridge University Press is part of the University of Cambridge.

It furthers the University's mission by disseminating knowledge in the pursuit of
education, learning and research at the highest international levels of excellence.

www.cambridge.org
Information on this title: www.cambridge.org/9781107453715

© Cambridge University Press 1951

First published 1951
First paperback edition 2014

A catalogue record for this publication is available from the British Library

ISBN 978-1-107-45371-5 Paperback

PREFACE

THE region with which this book is concerned has been strangely neglected by historians. Devonshire is the third largest county in England, and it is also one in which old habits tend to persist, sometimes for generations after they have been modified or given up in less conservative shires. Hence it abounds in subject-matter of historic interest. Yet until recently very little had been done to elucidate the character and chronology of its early occupation by the men of Wessex; and archaeology has yet to reveal what sort of life the Britons of Dumnonia were leading when the English colonists first moved into their midst. The prehistoric mining industry of Cornwall has attracted much attention: the mining records of Devon remain virtually unexplored. No monograph has been written on the cloth trade of the peninsula; and as for agriculture, all that current textbooks have to say about it is that the open-field system was not practised in this part of England: a statement which turns out to be demonstrably incorrect.

It is clear that sooner or later Devonshire will have to be fitted into the mosaic of English social history. In the following pages an attempt is made to supply one or two of the missing fragments. I have called the book a study in the social and economic history of Devon, because it deals less with the monastic life as such than with the agrarian, industrial, and administrative life of that part of Devon in which the estates of Tavistock Abbey lay. A Benedictine community is primarily a body of men devoted to a life of prayer; and the daily round of liturgical offices in the choir of the abbey church is apt to leave few traces in the records. As a rule we hear about it only when the monks excite remark by neglecting their essential function. But regarded from the outside as an economic unit, a property-owning corporation, a producer and consumer, every great abbey provides material for social history; and the further we look back into the so-called middle ages, the greater importance does that material assume.

It must be confessed at the outset that the present study

labours under severe limitations. The period of nearly three hundred years that elapsed between the English occupation of Devon and the foundation of Tavistock Abbey can receive only superficial treatment. Further, most of the estates with which this book deals lay in the western half of the county; and they have to be studied by the light of records which are not by any means complete. The great register of the abbey, from which Dugdale printed some important excerpts, vanished in the eighteenth century. If the monks of Tavistock ever wrote a chronicle of their house or drew up a custumal of their manors, these too have disappeared. No extant court roll, and only one account roll, precedes in date the fourteenth century.

On the other hand, the abbey was an ancient royal foundation, established nearly a hundred years before the Norman Conquest. It was the richest monastic house in Devon, and the only one that held its lands in chief of the Crown by knight service. Its economic interests embraced fisheries, mines, fairs, markets, and agriculture. From the twelfth century onwards the borough outside its gates was directly involved in the tin-mining industry of Dartmoor; and later it became an important centre of the cloth trade. Altogether it would not be easy to find an institution more closely linked with the economic activities of its neighbourhood.

Moreover, the available materials, though deficient in the respects noted above, are far from scanty. Some account of them is given at the end of the book. Here it is enough to say that the public records, printed and unprinted, especially Domesday Book, the Pipe Rolls, and the Rolls Patent and Close, provide the background for information extracted from such documents as the episcopal registers of the diocese of Exeter, and above all from that portion of the abbey muniments which passed at the Dissolution into the hands of John, Lord Russell, and now belongs to his descendant the duke of Bedford. The collection includes a small cartulary that forms an invaluable bridge between Domesday Book and the later records. There are also court rolls of several manors; over a hundred and fifty account rolls; originals or transcripts of a dozen manorial 'extents'; and more than a thousand classified deeds, ranging in date from the twelfth to the sixteenth century, many of them executed by persons of quite modest station.

Like most great monastic houses, the Abbey of Our Lady and
St Rumon of Tavistock was endowed partly with ecclesiastical
benefices and partly with territorial estates. It will be advisable
to begin with a short history of this aggregate, describing the
gradual accumulation of churches and manors, the fluctuations
of loss and gain, the slow recovery from the impact of the Norman
Conquest. Next, the physical background will require examina-
tion. Here the eighteen square miles of the ancient parish of
Tavistock will serve as a microscopic specimen of the agrarian
landscape. Taking account of the evidence from place-names, an
endeavour will be made to reconstruct the pattern of settlement
in this part of England. Turning then from the soil to the tillers of
the soil, we shall inquire into the condition of the serfs and the
free peasants before and after Domesday. These investigations
will pave the way for a detailed study of the arable and pastoral
husbandry practised by the monks of Tavistock on their demesne
lands. The subject of sheepfarming will lead on naturally to the
trade in woollen cloths; and having now set foot in the industrial
field we shall not leave it without paying some attention to the
other great local industry, tin-mining. Other sources of revenue,
such as markets, fisheries, and courts, will claim their share of
notice; after which a chapter on the management of the estates
will gather up all these threads, enabling us to see how the abbey
made the most of its resources, or at times failed to do so, in the
effort, renewed from century to century against varying obstacles,
to discharge its obligations to the public and to its own community. By way of epilogue, the story will be continued for a few
years beyond the Dissolution.

It will be obvious to every reader how deeply I am indebted to
the duke of Bedford for the generosity with which he allowed me
access to his muniments. Without this privilege the book could
never have been written. A labour of research prolonged over
several years has been rendered easy and pleasant by the courtesy
and active goodwill of the staff of the Bedford estate offices at
Woburn, Bloomsbury, and Tavistock, particularly Mrs A. M.
Osborne Samuel, Mr W. Corbett, Mr T. S. Bliss, Mr W. M.
Finnie, Mr R. G. Chapman, and Mr F. T. Nowell. I have to
thank Mr G. F. Kingston, head of the agricultural department,

Seale-Hayne College, Newton Abbot, for his care in reading and commenting upon the manuscript of Chapters IV and V; the Rev. M. D. Knowles, Litt.D., F.B.A., F.S.A., professor of medieval history in the University of Cambridge, for criticism and advice on the manuscript as a whole; and the Leverhulme Trustees for a contribution towards the expenses of research. Others who have kindly assisted in various ways are the president of St John's College, Oxford (Dr A. L. Poole), the provost of Oriel (Professor G. N. Clark), Mrs M. C. S. Cruwys, Miss Cecily Radford, the Rev. W. M. M. Picken, Professor M. M. Postan, Messrs G. J. Abell, J.P., John Benson, Eric V. Kingdon, Hugh A. Lomas, Edward Miller, and R. Hansford Worth. To my wife, and to my friend Dr W. G. Hoskins, I am especially grateful for their constant encouragement and the invaluable help they have given at every stage of the work.

H. P. R. F.

CONTENTS

ILLUSTRATIONS

LIST OF ABBREVIATIONS

BM	British Museum
CCR	*Calendar of Close Rolls*
CFR	*Calendar of Fine Rolls*
CPR	*Calendar of Patent Rolls*
DA	*Devonshire Association, Transactions of the*
DB	*Domesday Book*
DCNQ	*Devon & Cornwall Notes & Queries*
Dugdale	Dugdale's *Monasticon Anglicanum* (1817–30)
EHR	*English Historical Review*
ETC	'Some Early Tavistock Charters' (EHR LXII)
FA	*Feudal Aids, Inquisitions and Assessments relating to*
K	Kemble, *Codex Diplomaticus*
L & P	*Letters and Papers, Foreign and Domestic*
N. S.	New Series
Oliver	Oliver's *Monasticon Dioecesis Exoniensis*
PND	*The Place-Names of Devon*
PRO	Public Record Office
PRS	Pipe Roll Society
Reg.	*Episcopal Register*
TPR	*Calendar of the Tavistock Parish Records*
VCH	*Victoria County History*
W	Woburn Abbey muniments

CHAPTER I

THE ENDOWMENTS OF THE ABBEY

I. THE TEMPORALITIES

No Celtic twilight shrouds the beginnings of monastic life at Tavistock. The abbey was an Old English royal foundation, one of those established by king Edgar and his ministers in pursuance of their grand design for covering England with a network of Benedictine houses. It seems likely that political considerations had their part in this plan. The monasteries were indeed designed to be, above all, centres of piety and learning, but they were also to be landowners in close dependence on the Crown. As such, they would make for cohesion in the body politic. The unity of the English realm, so lately achieved, and still so liable to sudden fissure, needed every prop that statecraft could devise.

So far as Devon was concerned, the royal scheme was fulfilled in 968, when the old monastery at Exeter was revived under abbot Sideman. Cornwall, however, required special treatment. Its ecclesiastical traditions were of Celtic mould, and its monks had lived under a rule very different from that of St Benedict. With great prudence, therefore, the government determined that a new abbey, dedicated to Our Lady and the Cornish saint Rumon, should be established not in Cornwall itself but just across the Tamar, at a point directly in line with the main road from Bodmin and Liskeard.

Tavistock at this period lay within the royal hundred of Lifton. From a reference in Alfred the Great's will, and from later documents, it appears that a substantial portion of the king's demesne in Cornwall was attached to Lifton for administrative purposes, under an officer who bore the rank of high-reeve.[1] In 974 this important bailiwick was in the hands of Ordulf, the king's brother-in-law. To him therefore fell the task of supervising the beginnings of the new house. His also was the privilege of supplement-

---

[1] DA LXXVIII, 1946, pp. 268 sqq.

ing its endowments from his patrimonial estate. In later centuries the abbey was always, and justly, considered as a royal foundation; but the first place among its 'founders' in the monastic sense of the term, meaning its chief benefactors, was reserved for Ordulf, and the second for Ordulf's wife Ælfwynn.

By 981 the abbey was ready for its charter. This document was issued in the name of the boy-king Ethelred. Its effect was to confer upon Tavistock, as the seat of the abbey, the status of a privileged 'book-land'. Within its boundaries the abbot would enjoy seignorial rights previously vested in the king. The obligation of providing armed men in wartime and of contributing towards the upkeep of bridges and fortifications was not lifted, but from all other national burdens Tavistock was henceforth to be exempt. The abbey lands were to be held in perpetuity; on no account might they be sold, exchanged, or granted away.

A list of the original endowments is given in the narrative prefixed to the great register of Tavistock. It is evidently drawn from very ancient records, if indeed it is not transcribed directly from the charter of 981.[1] Twenty properties are named. Eight of them, namely Tavistock, Milton Abbot, Hatherleigh, Burrington, Romansleigh, Downeckney, Linkinhorn, and an unidentified estate which Dugdale read as "Chuvelin," are ascribed to Ordulf. The others form a composite list, in which no distinction is made between the benefactions of Ordulf's wife and those attributable to other members or friends of the family. A group of four estates which heads this second list, namely Abbotsham, Worthygate, Orleigh, and Annery, may safely be ascribed to Ælfwynn, for they are all in the vicinity of Alwington, that is, Ælfwynn's *tun*, a village in the far north of Devon which bears her name. Three others, Colebrook, Leigh, and Woolston, cannot be identified with certainty, for their names are shared by several places in Devon and Cornwall. Thornbury and Panson lay in the hundred of Black Torrington. Sheviock and Rame on the south coast, and Stoke Climsland on the Tamar, were important Cornish manors.

The same narrative refers to a special voluntary contribution made by Ælfmær, abbot of Tavistock, towards the Danegeld levied in 994. The abbot is said to have given "a pound and a half

[1] See Appendix B, p. 280.

by weight for his demesne lands in Devonshire: to wit, 21 man-
cuses for Tavistock, as much again for Hecfelda and Burrington,
and 60 pence by weight for Thornbury."[1] This passage has several points of interest. For one thing it seems to bear out the statement in the so-called Laws of Edward the Confessor, that ecclesiastical demesnes were not originally charged with Danegeld. Had
they been liable, there would have been no special merit in
Ælfmær's contribution.[2] Then again, it seems unlikely that he
would have paid anything for Heathfield, the waste land to the
north of Tavistock: yet no other "Hecfelda" or "Hetfelda" is
named in connection with the abbey. Finally, why was nothing
paid for Abbotsham or Hatherleigh, to name but two of the other
Devon manors? Here the answer may well be that Ordulf had reserved a life-interest in some of the property. He is known to have
lived until 1005, and the language of Ethelred's charter—"concessa sunt vel concedenda"—hints at some form of posthumous
benefaction.[3]

In 997 the abbey was burnt down by Danish raiders.[4] This
seems to have had no more than a passing effect on its fortunes.
Lyfing, who was abbot until 1027, raised it to a new height of
prosperity. His benefactions are described by William of Malmesbury as "multa et spectabilia", but no particulars are given.[5] It
was probably during his term of office that the unfortunate prince
Eadwig, younger brother of Edmund Ironside, earned for himself a place in the list of founders. Exiled by Cnut's order soon
after his exclusion from the throne, he wandered restlessly by sea
and land; then, falling sick, crept back to lay his bones at Tavistock, bequeathing to the monastery, as a last gift, his manor of
Plymstock.[6]

[1] Dugdale, II, p. 495.
[2] The passage is not one of those examined by Round in his discussion of
the subject (*Domesday Studies*, I, pp. 92 sqq.).
[3] In the same way his contemporary Æthelmær, the founder of Cerne
Abbey, gives the township of Cerne "postquam ego . . . hoc saeculum
relinquam" (K 656*).
[4] *Two Saxon Chronicles*, ed. Plummer, I, p. 131.
[5] *Gesta Pontificum*, p. 201.
[6] Florence of Worcester gives a different account of Eadwig's fate, and has
been followed by most historians; but reference should be made to Freeman's criticism (*Norman Conquest*, I, p. 700) and to DA LXXVIII, 1946,
pp. 265, 266.

On Lyfing's promotion to the see of Crediton he was succeeded by Ealdred, the future archbishop of York. Ealdred's abbacy lasted from 1027 until 1042 or the following year, when he received episcopal consecration, apparently in order that he might act as Lyfing's coadjutor in the diocese of Worcester, which Lyfing now held in plurality with Crediton.[1] The post of coadjutor bishop was unendowed, and provision seems to have been made for Ealdred at the expense of the monastery he was leaving. Two manors, Denbury and Coffinswell, of which we now hear for the first time, remained in his possession until 1066 and probably until his death in 1069, after which they reverted to the abbey.[2]

Lyfing and Ealdred were among the foremost statesmen of their time. Ruled by such men, the house could scarcely fail to prosper. Sihtric, the next abbot, was not their equal, but he was a forceful character, and energetic in promoting the interests of his monastery. This was the more necessary because under the house of Godwin no churchman's property was safe. Godwin's daughter Edith became queen in 1045, and Lifton hundred, with its Cornish appurtenances, was settled on her for her lifetime. It was administered by a certain Ordgar, a descendant it would seem of Ordulf and Ælfwynn. On one occasion Ordgar freed a number of slaves in the vicinity of Tavistock, including one from Stoke Climsland, a manor which, as we have seen, had formerly belonged to the abbey.[3]

Ordgar left a son named Ordulf, living in 1066, at which date he appears in Domesday Book as lord of nineteen manors in Devon, two in Cornwall, and one in Somerset. A man of great strength and gigantic stature, Ordulf was also passionately fond of the chase. One of his favourite hunting-grounds was Horton, in east Dorset, where a small monastery, of recent foundation, attracted his notice and secured some benefactions from him. It is said that he expressed a wish to be buried there; but one day, while hunting upon Dartmoor, he lost his way and perished of exposure. After this it was inevitable that his body, when found, should be interred at Tavistock beside his ancestors. In accordance with the custom of the age, Ordulf had assigned one of his

[1] K 772, 784, 912, 916.
[2] DB IV, pp. 166, 167. For a similar transaction later in Ealdred's career, see William of Malmesbury, *Vita Wulfstani*, pp. xxviii, 19, 20.
[3] DA LXXVIII, 1946, pp. 271, 272.

manors for a 'soul-scot' or gift to the church in which he should be buried; and of this manor abbot Sihtric now took possession. It was Antony, in Cornwall, a desirable acquisition both for its own sake and as adjoining the lands given by Ordulf's forebears in Sheviock and Rame. In the course of the Domesday inquest the abbot of Horton put in a claim to Antony, but failed to convince the royal commissioners.[1]

At the beginning of 1066 the abbey held lands in three counties, assessed for Danegeld as follows.

DEVON		hides	virgates
Tauestocha	Tavistock	3	2
Mideltona	Milton Abbot		2
Lideltona	Liddaton in Brentor		2
Hadreleia	Hatherleigh	3	0
Tornebiria	Thornbury	1	0
Hama	Abbotsham	2	0
Wrdieta	Worthygate in Parkham		2
Bernintona	Burrington	3	0
Liega	Romansleigh	1	0
Hundatora	Houndtor in Manaton		2
Plemestocha	Plymstock		2
		16	0

CORNWALL		hides	virgates
Savioch	Sheviock	1	0
Rame	Rame		2
Tregrenon	Trewornan in St Minver		2
Pennehalgar	Penharget in St Ive[2]		$\frac{1}{2}$
Talgar	Tolcarne in North Hill		$\frac{1}{2}$
Treiswantel	Trewanta in Lewannick		$\frac{1}{4}$
Heli	Illand in North Hill		$\frac{1}{4}$
Trenuwit	Trenowth	2	0
		4	$1\frac{1}{2}$

[1] This account of the transaction rests upon a combination of evidence derived from William of Malmesbury (*op. cit.*, p. 203), the Exon Domesday, and oral tradition first written down in the seventeenth century. It is more fully discussed in DA LXXVIII, 1946, pp. 272 sqq.

[2] Not Penhawger in Menheniot, as stated in VCH *Cornwall*, II, p. 67. In 1306 it was referred to as "Chirleton" (FA p. 206); and Chirleton, now Charaton, was a tithing in the parish of St Ive which included Penharget (DCNQ XXIII, 1948, p. 202).

B

DORSET		hides	virgates
Oscherwille	Askerswell	3	0
Powrtone	Poorton	2	0
		5	0

Total 25h. 1v. 2f.[1]

To the Devonshire list must be added a small property at Way in Bridestowe;[2] Orleigh, which was not a manor, and therefore does not appear in Domesday Book; and Annery, which was attached to Worthygate.[3] In Cornwall, Illand and Trewanta had been purchased by abbot Sihtric, who had also bought up the reversion of two virgates in Boyton and two in Tribicen *alias* Trebihan (Trebeigh in St Ive).[4] We have seen that Antony, another manor rated at two virgates, was acquired soon afterwards.

It is evident that notwithstanding the clause in Ethelred's charter forbidding alienation, a number of the original estates had been sold, exchanged, or lost. By 1066 Leigh, Panson, Colebrook, Downeckney, Linkinhorn, and Woolston were in other hands; no more is heard of "Chuvelin"; Stoke Climsland now belonged to Harold. Harold, like his father Godwin, is known to have enriched himself at the expense of many churches. There is no direct record of his despoiling Tavistock, but it is hardly probable that after snatching Topsham from the bishop of Exeter, and land at "Tretdeno" in Cornwall from the canons of St Petroc, he would have been content to leave Tavistock unscathed.

To the countess Gytha, Harold's mother, such encroachments were a cause of acute distress. Gytha was an intensely pious woman. On one occasion she refused to eat food grown on land which had been taken from a monastery. After the battle of Hastings she came down to Exeter, anxious no doubt to undo, so far as possible, the misdeeds of a son who had come to so disastrous an end in this world, and to secure prayers for his salvation in the next. At some date between October 1066 and the capitulation of

[1] DB IV, pp. 163-8, 38, 39; I, p. 78 c.
[2] *Ibid.*, IV, p. 265.   [3] Reichel, *Hundreds of Devon*, p. 578.
[4] They were however assessed at 1 virgate and 1 ferling respectively. Sihtric's purchase of Boyton and Trebeigh is recorded in the list of *Terrae Occupatae*, but the Exon Domesday names Alnothus and Osulf as in possession TRE. It may be inferred that what Sihtric bought was a reversionary interest. For the identification of Heli with the Elent of the *Terrae Occupatae*, and of both with Illand, see DCNQ XXII, 1942, p. 95.

Exeter in the early spring of 1068, she conveyed to abbot Sihtric her large estate of Werrington, consisting of approximately nineteen square miles in the Cornish hundred of Stratton and seven in Black Torrington hundred, on the Devonshire side of the Tamar. The political situation being what it was, any sort of traffic with a member of the fallen dynasty involved some measure of risk; but if, as has been suggested here, the abbot had a good claim for restitution of property seized by Harold, he might feel reasonably safe in accepting such compensation as Gytha had it in her power to offer.

In point of fact, no one demurred to the transaction. Sihtric remained in undisputed possession of the manor until his death in 1082. He seems often to have had surplus funds at his disposal, and to have employed them in buying out impoverished thegns. By this means he acquired Leigh and Liddaton in the neighbourhood of Tavistock, and enlarged his property at Burrington by adding to it Northcote and some land in the adjacent parish of Roborough.[1] The purchase of a virgate at Raddon, near Thorverton, gave him a foothold in east Devon. By lending money to a burgess of the cathedral city, and taking a mortgage on the borrower's house, he acquired a residence in Exeter. Irresponsible gossip, repeated in the next generation by William of Malmesbury, accused him of piracy.[2] The fact behind this accusation may be that he accomplished some successful police-work at the expense of the Channel pirates. As lord of Sheviock and Rame he was particularly well placed for keeping watch over the Tamar estuary, and more than one churchman at this period undertook a special responsibility for coastal defence. It is an undoubted fact that the Scilly islands, a favourite haunt of sea-rovers, presently became the seat of a dependent priory colonized from Tavistock.[3]

[1] DCNQ XXIII, 1948, p. 241. Leigh, in Milton Abbot, may have been the "Lege" of the original endowment (*ante*, p. 2). In 1066 it is said, like Panson, to have been in other hands; but is it quite certain that the Domesday jurors, after a lapse of twenty years, never mistook an undertenant for the owner?

[2] *Gesta Pontificum*, p. 204.

[3] See below, p. 15. It was the abbot of St Benet's, Holme, who watched over the East Anglian coast (Freeman, *op. cit.*, III, p. 717). In later centuries the abbot of Tavistock was more than once called upon to guard the south coast, e.g. in 1377, 1383, and 1404 (CCR 1374–7, p. 497; 1381–5, p. 270;

These activities of its last English abbot gave Tavistock, for the first few years after the Norman Conquest, a delusive appearance of prosperity. But the impact of the conquest was to be not less disastrous for having been delayed. The Norman magnates, whenever they could find a pretext, enriched themselves at the expense of the house. Baldwin, sheriff of Devon, took the small property at Way. The Conqueror's half-brother, Robert, count of Mortain, helped himself to Boyton, Trebeigh, Illand, and Trewanta. He also acquired Trenowth, but as nothing is said of usurpation here, we must either postulate an omission in the record or suppose this large and valuable manor to have changed hands by legitimate means.

Far more serious were the losses due to the introduction of knight service. It is generally agreed that when the Conqueror exacted military service from bishoprics and abbeys, as he did in 1070 or soon after, he introduced a new principle of tenure. There had been military tenants of a sort before the conquest, such as the four thegns who in 1066 were settled at Tavistock, holding between them a considerable portion of the manor. But the Normans who took their place represented feudalism fully fledged. Unfortunately for Tavistock, there was no other monastic house in the peninsula sufficiently well endowed to support the burden. Perhaps for that reason a disproportionately heavy quota was exacted from the abbot of Tavistock, who was called upon to maintain fifteen knights, while St Albans, a vastly richer house, provided only six.[1] It is probable that Sihtric, like some

CPR 1401–5, p. 353). The Cornu family, successors in title to one of the Domesday knights, held the inland manor of Thornbury on the express condition of coming with the lord abbot to defend the coast whenever called upon to do so.

[1] Professor Stenton considers that "the theory of a political discrimination between one abbey and another becomes less probable the more closely it is examined" (*Anglo-Saxon England*, p. 627). Professor Knowles thinks the assessment was based on the actual number of men-at-arms retained at the moment (*The Monastic Order in England*, p. 610); in which case Tavistock may have suffered from Sihtric's patriotic zeal. After the destructive raid on the south Devon coast which the sons of Harold carried out in 1069, he may well have kept on foot an exceptionally strong defensive force. While agreeing with Professor Knowles in his explanation of the assessment, I have given reasons elsewhere for believing that he attaches too much importance to Malmesbury's gossip about Sihtric (EHR LVIII, 1943, p. 195). It is possible that the chronicler picked up some tale of piracy at Sherborne Abbey, to which Horton was annexed *c.* 1118. No doubt the loss of Antony

other churchmen in the same plight, contented himself with hiring mercenaries, for in later documents the organization of the Tavistock knight service in its permanent form is always credited to Geoffrey, the first Norman abbot (1082–8).[1] By 1086 territorial endowments had been carved out of the abbey lands for most if not all of its fifteen knights. The picture of these holdings given in the Exon Domesday may be summarized as follows.

KNIGHT	FIEFS	VALUE IN 1086[2]		
Ermenald	Sheviock, Antony, Rame, Trewornan, Tolcarne, Penharget; ½ virgate in Tavistock	£12	3	4
Ralph	Thornbury; ½ virgate in Hatherleigh; ¼ virgate in Tavistock	3	15	10
Hugo	¼ hide ⅓ virgate 1 ferling in and near Tavistock	2	1	8
Robert	1 virgate 2 ferlings in Tavistock; 1 virgate 1⅝ ferlings in Romansleigh	1	19	7
Ralph de Tilio	¾ virgate in Tavistock		12	6
Geoffrey	1 ferling in Tavistock; ½ virgate ½ ferling in Hatherleigh; 1 virgate in Burrington; Liddaton	2	18	6½
Nigel	1½ ferlings in Hatherleigh; 2 virgates 2¼ ferlings in Romansleigh	1	11	0½
Grento	Coffinswell (2 hides)	4	0	0
Walter[3]	2¼ virgates in Hatherleigh	1	17	6
Rainald[3]	Houndtor (½ hide)	1	0	0
		£32	0	0

still rankled. But all that is certainly known about Sihtric in his later years, apart from his acquisition of Werrington, is that on Whitsunday 1068 he attended Queen Matilda's coronation at Westminster, and that he died on the 6th of April 1082, still in possession of his abbacy (Davis, *Regesta Regum Anglo-Normannorum*, p. 6, no. 22; Bodleian MS. Digby 81, fo. 86).

[1] ETC VI, VII, XII.

[2] Domesday Book sometimes gives only a collective valuation, as when the six fiefs in Tavistock are said to be worth 100s. all told. In such cases the value of each one has been computed by treating its geld assessment as an index of proportionate value. On this reckoning a ferling was worth 4s. 2d. at Tavistock, 3s. 9d. at Hatherleigh, and 2s. 6d. at Romansleigh.

[3] Not expressly named as a military tenant. Walter's is the largest fief in Hatherleigh, and may therefore be identified with Broomford (see below, p. 13). In subsequent lists Broomford and Houndtor both appear as knights' fees, as also does Liddaton, which Geoffrey is described as holding "of the abbot's demesne".

It is known from later records that some of these fiefs were expected to provide for more than one knight. Ermenald's, for instance, was always reckoned as four knights' fees.[1] In all probability, therefore, the ten military tenants named in Domesday Book accounted between them for the whole service of fifteen knights.

It was a cardinal principle of the Domesday inquest that no transfer of land effected since the death of Edward the Confessor should be recognized as valid unless the holder could produce a charter from king William or show that he had been put in possession by the Norman sheriff. Under this rule all the lands that Sihtric had acquired after 1066 were liable to forfeiture. Northcote, Liddaton, Leigh, and Antony were saved by their conversion into knights' fees. Raddon was leased off to William, the king's usher, and the land in Roborough, near Burrington, to a still more powerful magnate, William Capra.[2] Only Werrington remained in hand; and a brief note in the Exon Domesday shows how the Domesday commissioners dealt with it. "The abbot's predecessor held this manor, and the abbot was seised of it when king William sent his barons to inquire into the lands of England. He was disseised by them because the English testified that it did not belong to the abbey on the day king Edward was alive and dead."[3] As Werrington had belonged to Gytha, it was turned over to the sheriff Baldwin, who farmed all that remained of her property in Devon. He forthwith annexed the manor to his own shire, thereby depriving Cornwall of some nineteen square miles and creating an anomalous boundary which has puzzled mapmakers ever since.[4]

Werrington was valued at twenty pounds a year. The forfeiture of this great manor, and the usurpation of the Norman mag-

---

[1] Or, what comes to the same thing, six and a half 'small fees of Mortain' (*Testa de Nevill*, p. 394).

[2] These were civilian tenures. The annual value of Raddon was 5s.; that of Roborough 20s. In the twelfth century Raddon was held of the abbot by the Fitz-Ralphs at a yearly rent of 2s. and a wax candle weighing three pounds (ETC xi).

[3] DB iv, p. 165. But for this note in the Exon Domesday we should know nothing of Sihtric's transaction with Gytha. The Exchequer Domesday gives no hint of it. How many other changes of ownership lie concealed under the terse formulas of the official record?

[4] Finberg, 'The Early History of Werrington', EHR lix, 1944, pp. 237 sqq.

nates, completed the havoc wrought by the imposition of knight service. Thanks to king William and his followers, the abbot and convent found half their property gone. By the end of 1086 the land under their immediate lordship, and cultivated either by themselves or by their non-military tenants, had dwindled to the following estates.

DEVON	hides	virgates	annual value		
Tavistock	2	0	£12	0	0
Milton Abbot		2	8	0	0
Leigh with part of Liddaton		2	3	0	0
Hatherleigh	2	0	10	0	0
Abbotsham	2	0	5	0	0
Worthygate		2	1	0	0
Burrington	3	0	7	0	0
Denbury		2	2	0	0
Plymstock		2	2	0	0
A house in Exeter					
CORNWALL					
Nil					
DORSET					
Askerswell	3	0	6	0	0
Poorton	2	0	2	0	0
	16	2	£58	0	0

To this must be added an unknown extent of glebe-land, and two Cornish acres at Trewrickle in Sheviock, given to the abbey by Ermenald and his wife Deintedosa.[1]

Ten years later there came another turn of the wheel. The Conqueror was now dead, and Baldwin had been succeeded as sheriff by his son William. In the spring of 1096, when the government was busy raising money for a Norman loan, abbot Wymund seized the opportunity of reviving his claim to Werrington. Doubtless he knew better than to approach William Rufus empty-handed. What sum of money changed hands is not known, but it satisfied the king, and no opposition seems to have been made by the new sheriff. Since abbot Wymund is known to have

[1] ETC xxxix, xli. The Cornish acre might be anything from fifteen to three hundred English acres. For the glebe-lands, see below, p. 18.

had a brother William, who may be identified conjecturally with
the sheriff's brother-in-law William Fitz Wymund,[1] it is possible that the transaction had been prearranged in family council. What is certain is that Rufus handed to the abbot, in token of
renewed seisin, an ivory knife which he was holding at the time,
and shortly afterwards the royal "gift" of Werrington was proclaimed by formal charter.[2]

If Wymund's family was indeed connected with the sheriff's,
his next action becomes all the more intelligible. He now created
a sixteenth knight's fee, and settled it on his brother William.
This fief consisted of two submanors, Cudlipp and "Roborough",
the latter being apparently another name for what is now called
Morwell, on the western side of Tavistock.[3] Apart from its possible use in persuading the sheriff's family to relinquish their
hold on Werrington, the abbot could justify this step by pointing
out that many of his fellow barons had found it advisable to endow additional knights. The motive was to ensure against defaults. If any knight failed to attend the muster, it was the baron,
his feudal overlord, who was called to account; and this might
happen at any time to one who maintained only his exact quota.
The same argument was doubtless invoked when Panson was recovered by the abbot and promptly made over to a military tenant. But in the following reign such transactions were disallowed.
On two separate occasions Henry I issued writs commanding the
restoration of Cudlipp, Roborough, and Panson, and prohibiting
any increase in the number of military tenants above the fifteen
endowed by abbot Geoffrey.[4]

The great king's order seems not to have been carried out, for
at the close of his reign (1135) sixteen fees were still held of the
abbey.[5] As in 1086, they were distributed among ten knights. In
the following table an attempt is made to identify them by reference to the Domesday list and later fee-lists.

---

[1] DB IV, p. 272.
[2] Dugdale II, p. 497; Finberg, *op. cit.*, and 'The Devon-Cornwall Boundary', DCNQ XXIII, 1947, pp. 104 sqq.
[3] DA LXXVII, 1945, p. 158.   [4] ETC VI, IX.
[5] *Red Book of the Exchequer*, p. 250.

RICHARD DE ALNETO (i.e. Daunay)   4 fees
  Sheviock, 1 fee; Rame, 1 fee; Trewornan, 1 fee;
  Tolcarne and Penharget, *alias* Chirleton, 1 fee with
  Antony and part of Tavistock (probably Taviton).[1]

ROGER CORNU   2 fees
  Thornbury, $\frac{2}{3}$ fee;[2] East Pulworthy in Hatherleigh,
  $\frac{1}{4}$ fee;[3] Nutley in Tavistock, $\frac{1}{12}$ fee;[4] West Liddaton in
  Brentor, $\frac{1}{4}$ fee;[5] Romansleigh, $\frac{3}{4}$ fee.[6]

RALPH DE OSKEREUILLE   2 fees
  Askerswell, $\frac{1}{2}$ fee; Eggerdon near Askerswell, $\frac{1}{2}$ fee;
  Poorton, $\frac{1}{2}$ fee;[7] Broomford in Jacobstowe, $\frac{1}{2}$ fee.[8]

WILLIAM DE TRIBUS MINETIS (i.e. Tremenets)   2 fees[9]
  Coffinswell and Daccombe.[10]

REGINALD DE LIDDINTONE   2 fees
  ? East Liddaton in Brentor, $\frac{1}{2}$ fee; ? Northcote in
  Burrington, $\frac{1}{4}$ fee; ? Langabear and Marshford in
  Hatherleigh, $\frac{1}{4}$ fee; ? Quither, $\frac{1}{4}$ fee, Foghanger and
  Poflet, $\frac{1}{4}$ fee, Youngcott, $\frac{1}{8}$ fee, all in Milton Abbot.[11]

---

[1] FA pp. 205, 206; ETC XLI; p. 69 below.

[2] *Testa de Nevill*, p. 781; FA pp. 327, 357, 407.

[3] *Testa*, p. 781; FA pp. 327, 409. [4] FA p. 402.

[5] *Testa*, p. 781; W. D Bdle 45, no. 4 (quitclaim, 18 June 1289, by William le Cornu to the abbot and convent, of the whole land of West Lydeton, held by him as $\frac{1}{4}$ knight's fee).

[6] *Testa*, p. 781 (Copener); W. D Bdle 84, no. 22 (list of knights' fees preceding an Extent of Hurdwick, 1387: Robert Cornu, two fees in Thornbury, Romanyslegh, Poleworthy, Lydeton, and Nutleghe).

[7] *Testa*, p. 425; W. D Bdle 34, no. 6 (extract from an Extent of Askerswell, 1292: John de Oskereswell, deceased, held $\frac{1}{2}$ fee in Oskereswell, $\frac{1}{2}$ fee in Pourton, $\frac{1}{4}$ at Ekerdon, and $\frac{1}{2}$ in the county of Devon).

[8] Extent of Hurdwick, 1387: John Oskereswill, $\frac{1}{2}$ fee in Broomford. In 1242 William de Legh was the undertenant (*Testa*, p. 781).

[9] In Hearne's edition of the Black Book of the Exchequer, p. 118, this knight is erroneously credited with three fees.

[10] The heiress of Tremenets married Richard Speke (*Collectanea Topographica et Genealogica*, I, 1834, p. 62, no. 28), who held these two fees in 1162 (PRS, v, p. 6). His descendant conveyed them to the abbot of Tor (Oliver, p. 184; *Testa*, p. 781).

[11] The constituents of this fief appear to be in the main identical with those retrospectively attributed, in the 1387 Extent of Hurdwick, to Geoffrey de Northcote, who is said to have held two fees in Northcote, Odam, East Liddaton, Langabear, and Marshford. From *Testa*, however, it appears that he held Odam through a mesne lord (p. 781). For Northcote, Langabear,

GEOFFREY DE LEGE $1\frac{1}{2}$ fees
    Leigh in Milton Abbot, 1 fee;[1] (Odam in) Romans-
    leigh, $\frac{1}{2}$ fee.[2]

WILLIAM GURDET $\frac{1}{2}$ fee
    Chillaton in Milton Abbot.[3]

HUGH DE WICHA (i.e. Week)   1 fee
    Week in Milton Abbot; Ogbear and Hasworthy in
    Tavistock.[4]

ROBERT DACUS (i.e. le Deneys, or Dennis) $\frac{1}{2}$ fee
    Houndtor in Manaton.[5]

WILLIAM DE CREUEBERE $\frac{1}{2}$ fee
    Crebor in Tavistock; Fishleigh and Hannaborough in
    Hatherleigh.[6]

                                          16 fees

A comparison of this table with its Domesday counterpart (p. 9 above) shows that Ermenald's fees had descended entire to the Daunays, Ralph's to Cornu, Rainald's to Dennis, and Grento's to Tremenets. Hugo's fief is almost certainly identical with that of Hugh de Wicha, and Geoffrey's may have passed intact to Reginald de Liddintone. At other points the two lists do not correspond. Since 1086 the lands in Dorset had been converted into knights' fees, and some of the older fees had evidently been redistributed. It is unnecessary to pursue the history of these estates through later fee-lists. They brought no

---

and Marshford, see *Testa, ibid.,* and FA pp. 370, 408. East Liddaton must be the "Estdatun" in Tavistock hundred afterwards held as $\frac{1}{2}$ fee by Laurence de Wike (FA p. 322). The remaining $\frac{3}{4}$ fee can only be conjectured. References to Quither, Foghanger, Poflet, and Youngcott occur in FA pp. 322, 372, 404, 451. Even with these additions, $\frac{1}{8}$ fee is missing; but this was also the case in 1242, when, according to *Testa,* the Devon fees amounted to $10\frac{3}{4}$, making, with 4 in Cornwall and $1\frac{1}{2}$ in Dorset, $15\frac{7}{8}$ in all.

[1] Geoffrey's grand-daughter Alice, who married Robert Champeaux, held Leigh in 1242 (ETC XLII; *Testa,* p. 781).

[2] In 1346 John Oskyswyll held $\frac{1}{2}$ fee in Romansleigh in succession to Thomas Champeaux (FA p. 408).

[3] *Testa,* p. 781.   [4] *Ibid.;* FA, pp. 322, 404.   [5] FA, p. 339.

[6] W. D Bdle 9, no. 1 (quitclaim, *c.* 1238, by Margery, daughter of Richard de Crewabeara, of all her right in land at Crewbeare, with appurtenances at Fishlega and Hanaburga); *Testa,* p. 781.

profit to the abbot, except an occasional relief, wardship, and escheat: windfalls due to him as feudal overlord. The lands themselves had passed out of his demesne.

In 1114 Henry I made a formal grant to the abbey of all the churches and lands in Scilly which in times past had supported a group of hermits. From a charter of confirmation by Reginald, earl of Cornwall, it appears that this territory consisted of four islands: St Samson, St Theona, St Elidius, and Rentemen or St Nicholas; that is, Samson, Tean, St Helen, and Tresco.[1] Richard de Wicha, constable of Scilly, gave another island, called Nurcho, apparently the modern Bryher, with three 'bescates' in Eumor and two in Agnas (St Mary's and St Agnes), a bescate being the amount of land that can be dug with a spade in one day;[2] and earl Reginald granted the right of taking sea-wrack throughout the isles, with reservation of whales and entire ships.[3] In order to manage these remote possessions, a dependent cell or priory was established on Tresco. But the situation of the isles, constantly exposed to piratical descents and barely tenable in wartime, detracted much from their value.[4]

Throughout his reign Henry I did his best to safeguard and promote the welfare of the abbey. A strong hand was needed, for one of the outstanding characteristics of the twelfth century was the ease with which lay barons could encroach upon Church property. Roger de Nonant, a powerful Devon magnate, took possession of Denbury and held it until a peremptory royal writ commanded restitution.[5] During the troubles of Stephen's reign

[1] Dugdale, II, p. 501.

[2] ETC LI. Oliver, p. 95, misprints *bescata* as *boscata*, thereby creating a ghost-word which has crept into the *Medieval Latin Word-List*.

[3] In 1302 the exceptions were stated to be whales, gold, scarlet cloth, and ermine (*Placita de Quo Warranto*, p. 110).

[4] On the 8th of May 1209, a hundred and twelve pirates were beheaded on Tresco (DCNQ XXII, 1945, p. 250). Towards the close of Edward I's reign the abbot and convent declared that in time of war they had little power to do justice on felonious mariners. They proposed therefore to surrender their temporalities in Scilly to the Crown in exchange for lands in Devon of the same value, namely, sixty pounds a year. They added that there was anchorage for a thousand ships, and that the harbour was much frequented by ships from France, Normandy, Spain, Bayonne, and Gascony. An inquiry was ordered, but nothing came of the proposal (PRO Ancient Petitions, S.C. 8, 3720; cf. also CPR 1301–7, pp. 348, 538).

[5] ETC II.

the late king's charters respecting supernumerary fees in Panson, Morwell, and Cudlipp, were set aside under pressure from two knights.[1] Thus by the accession of Henry II the original fifteen fees had been increased to seventeen and a half. It appears that Robert Postel, abbot from *circa* 1147 to 1155, sometimes granted charters of feoffment without consulting his fellow-monks.[2] Doubtless he acted under strong compulsion, but such grants were legally void, and might be revoked in a more favourable season.

To offset these losses, the small manor of Ottery was acquired from the Albemarles, apparently in Henry I's reign.[3] Parochially it belonged to Lamerton, which at that date extended so far north-eastward as to include that famous landmark, the extinct volcano called Brentor. On the summit of this conical rock a small church, dedicated to St Michael the Archangel, was built early in the twelfth century by Robert Giffard, lord of Lamerton and Whitchurch, who gave it to the abbey with some acres of surrounding land. As a result of this transaction a new manor came into existence, called Holeyeat, which connected Liddaton and the Milton group of manors with Tavistock. Thus the hundred of Tavistock, separated from Lifton in 1116 by decree of Henry I, took shape as a continuous territory over which the abbot exercised wide powers of civil and criminal jurisdiction.[4]

At the beginning of Henry II's reign Walter, a monk of Winchester, was appointed abbot, with a special mandate to recover the possessions alienated by his predecessor. In this arduous task he was encouraged by archbishop Theobald.[5] Some deeds of restitution were procured, most of them in return for cash; but depredations continued under the less forceful abbot Baldwin (1174–84). A typical loss was that of Passaford, in Hatherleigh, which a certain Robert Fitz Baldwin Fitz Gervase confessed to having extorted from the abbot "through the power and pressure of my uncles Roger Fitz Reinfred and Master Walter of Cou-

---

[1] *Red Book, loc. cit.*   [2] ETC XVIII.   [3] *Testa*, p. 757; cf. ETC III.

[4] Dugdale, II, p. 496; for the date, see DA XLVII, 1915, p. 376. The same Robert Giffard also gave or sold Thorntor and Moortown from his Whitchurch demesne; and his son Walter several farms in Whitchurch and Lamerton, including Hecklake, Wastor, and Langford (ETC XIV, XXXVIII, XLIX, LIX).

[5] ETC XVIII.

tances, keeper of the royal seal".[1] Herbert, the next abbot, found it expedient to procure a papal bull of confirmation and protection. This bull, issued by Celestine III on the 29th of May 1193, carefully enumerated the possessions of the house, including those settled upon military tenants; but apart from these, the list of temporalities reduces itself to the nine Devonshire demesne manors of 1086 (p. 11 *supra*), with the additions of Ottery, Holeyeat, the Scilly isles, and Werrington.[2]

The Domesday manor of Tavistock, already dismembered by the conversion of its thegn-lands into knights' fees, came to an end at some date between 1105 and 1185, when one of the abbots, most probably abbot Walter, created a borough outside the monastery gates. For manorial purposes the name of Tavistock was thenceforth limited to an urban district covering about half a square mile. Outside its boundaries lay a rural district known as the manor of Hurdwick, so called from the abbot's *heordewic*, or demesne-farm. This comprised the residue of the original manor. The abbey itself, though lying geographically within the borough, was accounted an *enclave* of Hurdwick. With the establishment of the borough, Hurdwick became the seat of the abbot's barony, and its court the centre of his feudal and hundredal jurisdiction.[3]

For the next two and a half centuries the territorial position remained substantially unaltered. Some land in Cornwood, given by Adam de Middleton in 1280, was the principal new acquisition.[4] Though still liable for their knight service, the abbots managed by steady perseverance to recover one by one the old thegn-lands in and near Tavistock. Abbot Baldwin gave back Trewrickle to the Daunays in exchange for their Tavistock fief.[5] Crebor escheated to the abbot in 1238, when the family which had held it so long died out in the male line.[6] In 1262 Sir Thomas Archdeacon gave or sold Morwell back to the abbey.[7] The process was interrupted by the Statute of Mortmain, passed in 1279 with the ostensible object of preventing the conversion of military into civilian tenures.[8] Henceforth no monastic house could take possession even of its own fiefs without first applying for a special

---

[1] Dugdale, II, p. 499.
[2] *Ibid.*, p. 498.
[3] DA LXXIX, 1947, pp. 129 sqq.
[4] Dugdale, II, p. 499.
[5] ETC XXXIX, XLI; p. 69 below.
[6] W. D Bdle 9, no. 1.
[7] DA LXXVII, 1945, pp. 161, 162.
[8] Stubbs, *Select Charters*, p. 451.

inquest "ad quod damnum", and thereafter purchasing from the Crown a licence to alienate in mortmain. This procedure was followed in 1289, when Sir Odo Archdeacon restored West Liddaton to the abbey, with the consent of William Cornu, its overlord, for the purpose of endowing a yearly distribution of shoes and clothing to the poor.[1] It was followed again in 1310, when Robert David, on behalf of the abbot, purchased Ogbear from Walter de Wike.[2] In 1352 John Dabernon, sheriff of Cornwall, bought up Week, the last of these knightly submanors, and gave it to the abbey in exchange for free quarters within the abbey precincts during his lifetime, and a chantry in the parish church after his death.[3]

II. THE SPIRITUALITIES

From a very early date, perhaps from the foundation of their house, the abbot and convent owned a number of parish churches. Many of these possessed glebe-land, and all were entitled to certain dues from their parishioners, of which the chief was tithe, a levy of ten per cent. upon the fruits of husbandry. It was a form of property which brought the owners into very close touch with every branch of rural economy.

When the English first occupied the south-western peninsula, they found it dotted with churches and chapels of Celtic origin. A good example of such old foundations is the church of St Paternus at North Petherwin. This lay some three miles west of the new English settlement at Werrington, but nevertheless kept its place as the ecclesiastical centre of the district. As such, it served an area of nearly thirty square miles, including the three

[1] Dugdale, II, p. 497; W. D Bdle 45, nos. 2–7; *Rotuli Parliamentorum*, I, p. 63a; CPR 1281–92, p. 364.

[2] W. D Bdle 41, nos. 7–16; PRO *Lists and Indexes*, XVII, p. 123: CPR 1307–13, p. 325. Leigh and Foghanger were already in the abbot's hands; Nutley was probably recovered with West Liddaton. W. D Bdle 38, no. 6: grant by Robert, son of Roger Champeaux, to the abbot and convent in frankalmoign of all his lands in Leigh, with all other tenements and fees which he held of them (N.D., c. 1260). Bdle 35, nos. 2–4: quitclaim to the abbot by Stephen, son and heir of Stephen Stoyl, of all his rights in Wyk Stoyl (Stilesweek in Tavistock) and Foghanger (1284). Nutley reverted to the abbot between 1284 and 1346 (FA pp. 327, 402).

[3] W. D Bdle 47, no. 11; Dugdale, II, p. 501; W. D Bdle 53, no. 137.

modern parishes of North Petherwin, Werrington, and St Giles on the Heath.[1]

The early English colonists can have had little leisure for church-building. From time to time, if the ancient church were too far off, they would gather round a wayside cross, where a visiting priest would say Mass and preach to them. But as settlement became more widespread, lords of manors found it convenient to set up churches on their own land. A lord who did so would assign his tithe, or a portion of it, to the new foundation. Old English law, solicitous for vested interests, forbade him to give more than a third, but it was plainly reasonable that the assets of the mother-church should be reduced in proportion to its liabilities. Moreover, the building of a church, like the building of a corn-mill, involved an outlay for which the owner felt he had a right to expect some return. He therefore bargained with his priest on whatever terms he thought fit, sometimes reserving to himself a portion of the revenue. Many a parish became territorially coextensive with a manor.

It is not known how many churches the monks of Tavistock built or acquired before the Norman Conquest. Domesday Book omits all mention of them. From another source we learn that abbot Geoffrey, when he gave up his Cornish manors to the knight Ermenald, reserved the ownership of three churches, those of Antony, St John, and Sheviock.[2] A charter drawn up between 1155 and 1160 shows the abbot handing over the endowments of these churches 'in farm' to a certain Andrew, dean of Petherwin, who in the presence of the bishop takes an oath to administer them faithfully. He is to hold them until his death or—what comes to the same thing in legal eyes—his retirement into a monastery, and is to pay the abbey thirty shillings yearly in three instalments, at Candlemas, midsummer, and St Rumon's feast (30 August). The surplus remaining after this and other necessary expenses have been met will of course go into the dean's own pocket.[3]

It was a prime object of the reforming party in the Church to abolish lay control of tithe, and to substitute for the mass-priest

---

[1] Possibly Virginstow as well. This parish paid 2s. yearly to the abbot and convent, who from 1279 onwards were also patrons of the benefice.
[2] ETC vii.   [3] Ibid., xv.

holding office at the will of the lord an incumbent instituted by the bishop. Legislation to this effect was enacted by the first and second Lateran councils (1123, 1139). In consequence church-owning laymen found themselves compelled to resign their spiritualities into the hands of persons in holy orders, called 'parsons' or rectors; and monastic corporations, if they wished to retain their churches, had to seek episcopal consent. The same Robert Giffard who gave St Michael's, Brentor, to the monks of Tavistock also gave Lamerton church, with its glebe-lands at Thele and elsewhere.[1] Elias Coffin relinquished a ferling of glebe belonging to St Peter's, Monk Okehampton, but "in recognition", as he says, "of this beneficence" he made the abbey give him twenty shillings in cash and a silver casket worth another fifteen shillings, with a bezant for his wife Matilda and a silver buckle for William his heir.[2] Meanwhile the abbey, to secure possession of its churches, was obtaining one charter after another from former lay owners and from the bishops of Exeter. Bishop William Warelwast (1107–37) confirmed their rights in the three churches of the Sheviock fief, as also did his two successors and archbishop Richard.[3] Bishop Robert (1155–60) appropriated the church of St Constantine, Milton Abbot, to the sacristan and the almoner of Tavistock, but stipulated that a "sufficient" portion of the revenue should be assigned to a perpetual vicar instituted by the bishop.[4]

This is the earliest known English reference to the office of parochial vicar. There is a widespread but erroneous belief that the impropriation of churches deprived the parish priest of something to which he had a right. He had indeed a right to such portion of the endowment as would provide him with a living wage, but tithes were not paid only for the support of the clergy. They constituted a general fund, applicable to such objects as the repair of the church fabric, the relief of destitution, hospitality to travellers, and indeed any recognized Church purpose. The history of the Lamerton endowment illustrates this very clearly. After some controversy with the guardian of the infant William

---

[1] ETC XXIV, XXV, XXXI, XXXVIII, XLV, XLVI.   [2] *Ibid.*, XXX.
[3] *Ibid.*, VII, X, XV, XXXI.
[4] *Ibid.*, XVI, XVII; confirmed by archbishop Baldwin (1185–90) to the sacristan, without mention of the almoner (XLIII).

Giffard, the right of the abbey to Lamerton church was upheld by a mixed jury of clerics and laymen, and confirmed by bishop Bartholomew, who defined the vicar's portion as one half of the tithes, offerings, legacies, burial fees, and produce of the glebe. Out of this income the vicar was to meet all parochial expenses. The other moiety, free of all charge, was to go to the abbot and convent. Soon afterwards the abbot and convent assigned their share of the glebe-corn and tithes to John, vice-archdeacon of Cornwall, on the understanding that they should inherit one-third of his goods and chattels. By 1191, the vice-archdeacon being dead, they were free to use their moiety for other purposes. Abbot Herbert, with the consent of the vicar and bishop John of Exeter, decided to endow a new charity. He and his monks had been accustomed to provide food and drink for three poor men daily during Lent. They now resolved to do this every day throughout the year, and the Lamerton revenue was devoted to this object in perpetuity.[1]

Just as the modern rate-payer knows his rates will be expended partly by the local authority for its own purposes and partly by the county, so the tithe-payer, though doubtless grumbling at having to pay so much, had no special grievance if a portion of his tithe was spent outside the parish. In the instance just given, the rector's half was used first to subsidize a diocesan functionary who had no official income of his own, and afterwards to make better provision for the poor, while the other half supported the vicar and maintained the parish church. In 1287 the stipend of all vicars in the diocese of Exeter was fixed at one-eighth of the parish revenue.[2]

St Helen's church at Abbotsham was appropriated at first to the sacristan with the special object of providing the abbey church with lights. In 1246, when the sacristan had acquired an income from borough rents, abbot Alan gave this endowment to the prior and convent, with a proviso that in future they, and not the abbot, should supply the refectory, cloisters, and infirmary with hand-towels and table-napkins.[3] The infirmary was main-

---

[1] ETC XLV, XLVI; DCNQ XXII, 1945, p. 285; White Kennett, *Parochial Antiquities*, II, p. 35n.
[2] Snape, *English Monastic Finances*, p. 82.
[3] ETC XXVI, LVIII; W. G Bdle 1, no. 2.

C

tained out of the revenues of St John the Baptist's, Hatherleigh.[1]
From Clement III the abbey obtained the privilege of appropriating the whole revenue of their churches during vacancies preceding the appointment of new vicars.[2] In 1193 Celestine III
confirmed them in possession of all the churches above-named,
and, in addition, those of North Petherwin, Burrington, and
Denbury.[3]

Tithes were a frequent subject of contention. At one time the
constable of Scilly believed that he was under no obligation to
pay tithe on the conies taken in his island rabbit-warren. He was
undeceived by a peremptory letter from Bartholomew of Exeter.
The bishop sent him an order from the royal justiciars, and backed
it with a threat of excommunication. As the culprit was at that
moment smarting under a fine of forty marks inflicted on him for
an offence against the forest laws, he was in no condition to brave
the combined powers of Church and State. He went at once to
Tavistock, and there, before St Rumon's altar, took his gospel
oath that in future the spiritual lords of Scilly should have all the
rabbits due to them.[4]

The decentralizing process by which new parishes had been
created was now at an end. Sometimes the lord of a manor would
set up and endow a chapel, only to find himself worsted in conflict with the rector of the mother church. Thus, in the time of
bishop Bartholomew, a jury of three clerics and three laymen upheld the rights of abbot Baldwin, as rector of Milton, against William de Legh's claim to nominate a chaplain of his own. The dispute ended in a compromise by which the vicar of Milton found
himself obliged to celebrate at Leigh on Wednesdays, Fridays,
Saturdays, and Sundays.[5] In the vast manor of Werrington there
were two chapels, dedicated to St Martin and St Giles. They are
now the parish churches of Werrington and St Giles on the
Heath; but it was long debated between Tavistock and Launceston Priory whether they were daughter chapels of Launceston or
North Petherwin. Finally Launceston secured a portion of the
tithes and offerings on condition of paying fifty shillings yearly
to the abbey.[6]

[1] ETC XXXVII, XLIII, LVII.   [2] *Ibid.*, XLVII.   [3] Dugdale, II, p. 498.
[4] ETC XXXII, XXXIII.   [5] *Ibid.*, XXXVI, XLII, LIV.
[6] *Ibid.*, L. Dugdale, II, p. 500, gives the text of an agreement by which
abbot Walter, *c.* 1164, recognized that Plymstock was a chapelry of Plympton.

In the disturbances of Henry III's reign the rights of the abbey were rudely shaken. Walter Bronescombe, bishop of Exeter (1257–80), was a prelate of high reputation and an energetic administrator, but his dealings with Tavistock were arbitrary, to say the least, and there is reason to believe that he was egged on by subordinates who, under cover of the civil war, aimed at feathering their own nests. In 1265 he cited abbot John Chubb to show by what right the monastery held the appropriated churches of Tavistock, Lamerton, Milton, Brentor, Abbotsham, North Petherwin, Hatherleigh, and the chapel of Monk Okehampton, with yearly pensions from Burrington, Werrington, Denbury, and Antony, and certain tithes from Sheviock and Rame.[1] The abbot's right was indisputable, but for some reason at which we can only guess he did not put in an appearance. Bronescombe then sequestrated all the revenues, and instituted one Robert de Trello as rector (not vicar) of Hatherleigh. This ecclesiastic did not venture near the place himself, but his proctor came down, escorted by the earl of Gloucester's steward and some five hundred of the earl's retainers, threatening to burn down the whole village. Livestock valued at £22 1s. 4d. was seized, and the tithe-corn was sold off by the bishop's steward. One of the abbot's men who tried to prevent this robbery was killed. Werrington, Abbotsham, and Monk Okehampton were similarly plundered. The damage was stated by a local jury to be incalculable. Meanwhile the abbot was at loggerheads with some of his monks. This gave the bishop a handle against him, and when Chubb brought an action against the bishop's minions in the civil court, Bronescombe retaliated by deposing him on the ground that his administration had been intolerably wasteful![2]

It may have been during this contest that someone at Tavistock set to work and fabricated a charter dealing with seven of the appropriated churches. This document purports to have been drawn up in the preceding century. It states that having regard to the poverty of Tavistock Abbey, Bartholomew, bishop of Exeter, with the assent of his cathedral chapter, confirms abbot Herbert

[1] *Reg. Bronescombe*, p. 266. The pension from Burrington was 7s.; from Denbury 3s. 4d.; from the Werrington chapels 50s.; from Sheviock 3s.; and from Rame 2s. 2d.
[2] *Cal. Miscellaneous Inquisitions*, I, p. 129; *Reg. Bronescombe*, pp. 266 sqq.; CCR 1268–72, p. 101; DCNQ XXII, 1944, p. 194.

and his convent in possession of the churches of Tavistock, Lamerton, Milton, North Petherwin, Hatherleigh, Abbotsham, and Brentor, "as the writings of our predecessors more fully testify". It is quite true that, with one exception to be noted presently, all these churches, and others besides, had been appropriated to the abbey by Bartholomew or earlier bishops. Consequently the charter must have been concocted, not in order to create rights where none existed, but as a comprehensive title-deed which would be particularly useful if the originals should fall into an enemy's hand. First published in 1284, it was accepted as genuine by Bronescombe's successor, and later by Pope Boniface IX. What brands it as spurious is its reference to abbot Herbert, whose term of office did not begin until some fifteen months after Bartholomew's death.[1]

The one church of which no earlier record has come to light is the parish church of St Eustace at Tavistock itself. That the town had from the first its mass-priest is not in doubt: John, "chaplain of Tavistock", is among those who witness the settlement of the controversy over Leigh chapel *circa* 1177.[2] But the bull of Celestine III alludes only to the abbey church and to the parish "chapels". Had a parish church existed in 1193, it would almost certainly have been mentioned by name like the others. About fifty yards east of the main abbey gateway there was a small chapel dedicated to St Matthew, which the monks believed to be more ancient than the abbey itself.[3] This may well have served the needs of the lay population until the close of the twelfth century. Then or soon afterwards St Eustace's was built on its present site, but the earliest authentic reference to it occurs in 1265.[4] The right of the abbot and convent to the rectorship of Tavistock was a prescriptive right. They may have relied on this and neglected for some time to seek episcopal confirmation.

---

[1] Dugdale, II, p. 498; *Reg. Bronescombe*, p. 376; *Cal. Papal Letters*, v, p. 426; DCNQ XXII, 1944, pp. 175, 186. The chronological slip is all the more striking in that the interval between Bartholomew's death and Herbert's election is clearly indicated in the contemporary Annals of Tavistock (Bodleian MS. Digby 81, fo. 87b).

[2] Morey, *Bartholomew of Exeter*, p. 157.

[3] DCNQ XXII, 1942, pp. 56 sqq.

[4] In the citation by bishop Bronescombe, *supra*, p. 23. The change of title from chaplain to vicar occurs at Totnes *c.* 1216 (DA LVII, 1925, p. 274).

In 1358 bishop Grandisson ordered provision to be made for the vicar of Tavistock as follows. He was to have a house, garden, and stable rent-free; firewood to the value of 6s. 8d. yearly; the same daily allowance of bread, ale, and meat or fish as a monk of the abbey; twelve quarters of oats annually for his horse, and a tithe of the hay grown on the Lamerton demesne; an allowance of 13s. 4d. yearly for his clothing; a taper worth sixpence every year at Candlemas; a penny every Sunday and threepence on each of the principal feasts; the offerings of one chapel in the parish church; half the customary marriage fees; tithe of the best garden in Tavistock at his own choice; one good calf, one pig, one cheese, one keg of butter, one lamb, one goose, and one fleece, to be selected by himself out of the whole parish.[1] No better arrangement could have been devised for embroiling the vicar both with the abbey and with his parishioners. After much intermittent friction, the matter was reviewed in 1514 by archbishop Warham and bishop Fitzjames of London, the parties having agreed to accept their arbitration. By their award the vicar kept his vicarage-house and became entitled to all burial offerings, but had to give up the other perquisites in return for a fixed salary of twelve pounds a year. The arbitrators expressed the hope that he would be able to attend to the cure of souls with all the more freedom of mind now that the trouble of collecting parochial dues was transferred to the abbot and convent.[2]

After the violence and rapine of Bronescombe's episcopate, order had gradually been restored. Bronescombe himself in 1277 confirmed the appropriation of Lamerton, and subsequently instituted rectors of Denbury and Virginstow on presentation of the abbot and convent.[3] His successor restored Hatherleigh in 1284.[4] Antony was re-appropriated in 1296,[5] and Burrington in

---

[1] *Reg. Grandisson*, p. 1196.

[2] W. D Bdle 78, no. 4. From the Hurdwick account rolls it appears that notwithstanding this award the abbey continued to provide oats for the vicar's horse. In 1539 the Court of Augmentations found that the yearly value of the vicar's emoluments, in cash and offerings, amounted to twenty pounds, and that the abbot and convent kept the vicarage-house in repair (Oliver, p. 93). The other vicarages had been settled at various dates: North Petherwin and Abbotsham in 1269 (*Reg. Bronescombe*, pp. 20, 211); Antony in 1309; and Burrington in 1310 (*Reg. Stapeldon*, pp. 32, 91).

[3] W. D Bdle 84, no. 18; *Reg. Bronescombe*, pp. 132, 189.

[4] *Ibid.*, p. 376.   [5] CPR 1313–17, p. 271.

1304.[1] In 1351 abbot Richard Ash obtained permission to appropriate St Andrew's, Whitchurch.[2] During the episcopate of Stafford (1395–1419) the abbot and convent presented to nine vicarages and two rectories.[3] The right of presentation, however, lapsed to the Crown whenever the abbacy was vacant.[4]

At Antony the glebe-land constituted what was sometimes called a manor, though it does not appear that any courts were held there. The system of farming out glebe-land and tithes was given up after the twelfth century, but direct administration did not always yield better results. In 1348 bishop Grandisson complained that through the folly of abbot John de Courtenay the tithes were being sold for half their value.[5] Two surviving accounts of tithe-corn sales in the years 1429 and 1438 exhibit wide variations in detail, though the totals are not far apart.

	1429			1438			
Hatherleigh	£14	12	8	£5	9	8	
Antony		16	4	12	10	6	
Burrington	11	7	8	5	12	6	
N. Petherwin	26	13	6	22	7	2	
Tavistock				10	2	2	
Milton Abbot				12	10	2	
Lamerton	38	11	6	6	5	0	£48 11 2
Whitchurch				11	15	10	
Ottery				7	18	0	
	£92	1	8	£94	11	0	

Tavistock was better endowed than any other monastery in Devon and Cornwall. Yet by national standards it was far from wealthy. In the middle of the fourteenth century the English Benedictines taxed themselves at the rate of a penny in the pound

---

[1] *Reg. Bronescombe*, p. 404.

[2] *Reg. Grandisson*, p. 1107. For earlier transactions affecting Whitchurch, and abbot Robert Champeaux's abortive scheme for establishing a chantry there under an archpriest and three assistant priests, see *Reg. Stapeldon*, pp. 402 sqq., and DCNQ xxii, 1946, p. 346.

[3] Tavistock, Whitchurch, Milton Abbot, Lamerton, Hatherleigh, North Petherwin, Abbotsham, Burrington, Antony (vicarages); the rectories of Denbury and Virginstow.

[4] CPR 1216–25, p. 435; 1367–70, pp. 161, 184, 207.

[5] *Reg. Grandisson*, p. 1057.

to meet the expenses of their provincial chapter. Bury St Edmunds and Glastonbury headed the list, Bury paying £8 13s. 2¼d.
and Glastonbury £6 11s. 8d. These contributions indicate that
the two richest houses were assessed at £2,078 10s. and £1,580
respectively. Tavistock was charged 17s. 4d. on an assessed income of only £208. Of sixty-five houses in the list, twenty-four
were poorer than Tavistock, but its resources were plainly not
commensurate with its responsibilities as the most important
monastery in the south-west.[1]

During the episcopate of William Brewer (1224–44) the finances of the abbey were found to be in a deplorable state.[2] Matters were not improved when the abbacy fell vacant four times in
six years (1257–62), for each vacancy involved a heavy payment
to the Crown.[3] In 1333 it was feared that some of the monks
would have to go begging for their daily bread;[4] and in 1351
abbot Richard Ash declared that owing to various misfortunes,
including the Black Death and the devastation of the Scilly
Isles by pirates, the house was nearly bankrupt.[5] When the
abbots got into debt, as happened more than once, their bishop
accused them of wanton extravagance; but the charge was never
supported by concrete particulars, except in 1345, when bishop
Grandisson reproved his own nominee John de Courtenay, an
abbot of noble birth and fond of the chase, for keeping a pack of
hounds.[6]

For a monastic house labouring under financial difficulties,
impropriation of parish churches was the recognized panacea. As
we have seen, it was in constant request at Tavistock. But it was
never carried so far there as at Plympton, where the Augustinian
priory, the second richest house in Devon, owned eleven parish
churches and nine chapels, besides drawing pensions from eight
other churches. The combined income from these sources was
almost exactly equal to that brought in by the temporal possessions of the house. At Tavistock the proportion between spiritu-

[1] *Chapters of the English Black Monks*, ed. Pantin, 1931–7, III, p. 158.
There was a supplementary tax of one farthing in the mark, which gives the
same result. Cf. *ibid.*, pp. 174, 178.
[2] ETC LVIII.
[3] CPR 1247–58, pp. 560, 573, 602; *ibid.* 1258–66, pp. 22, 35, 84, 87, 91,
219; CCR 1259–61, pp. 294, 447; *ibid.* 1261–4, p. 132.
[4] *Reg. Grandisson*, p. 716.   [5] *Ibid.*, p. 1107.   [6] *Ibid.*, p. 997.

alities and temporalities was roughly one to three and a half.[1]

After the appropriation of Whitchurch the complaints of poverty ceased. In 1462 abbot John Dynyngton, who had backed the Yorkist side during the wars of the Roses, was favoured by Edward IV with a grant of Cowick Priory and all its possessions.[2] This priory, situated in a suburb of Exeter, had been a dependency of Bec, the great Norman abbey, but had been confiscated during the French war. Its temporalities consisted of the manors of Cowick, Exwick, and Christow, with scattered properties elsewhere in Devon, and Hawkwell in Somerset. The priory also possessed the churches of St Thomas, Christow, Spreyton, and Okehampton, and pensions from Meeth and Whimple. These acquisitions enabled the abbey to spend its last three-quarters of a century in something like affluence. In 1535 its possessions were valued at the respectable total of £902 5s. 7½d., one sixth of which was made up of the Cowick properties.

---

[1] In the valuation of 1535 the spiritualities of Plympton are valued at £454 7s. 2½d., and the net temporalities at £443 13s. 5⅝d. The total therefore should have been given as £898 0s. 8¼d., that for Tavistock, reckoned in the same way, being £902 5s. 7½d. By an error in the reckoning, however, the gross temporalities of Plympton were mistaken for the net. This gave a false total of £912 12s. 8¼d. (*Valor Ecclesiasticus*, II, pp. 375 sqq.).

[2] CPR 1461–7, pp. 222, 273.

CHAPTER II

THE AGRARIAN LANDSCAPE

D EVON belongs to the western highland zone of Britain. It is a land of abrupt alternations, of wide moorland expanses interspersed with huge tors, and of downs broken up at frequent intervals by deep and narrow gorges. The prevailing wind is westerly. Clouds blown inland from the Atlantic encounter the moorland heights and discharge themselves over the surrounding country in frequent downpours. Each of the main rivers is fed by countless tributaries.

Bounded on the west by Celtic Cornwall, and on the north and south by the Bristol and English Channels, Devon is connected with the mainland by a frontier only thirty-six miles wide, about half of which, until modern times, was flood-land. Travellers who made their way into the county had good reason to curse the narrow lanes that climbed steeply uphill and downhill over boulders and through deep mud, so that, as Hooker grimly remarked, "be they ever so well monted upon theire fyne and deyntie horses out of other countries, after that they have travelled in this countrie but one journey they can forbeare the second."[1] The natives lived for the most part confined to their own little valleys and the immediate vicinity. If an inhabitant of the Tavistock district had business at Exeter, he must either brave the mists and mires of Dartmoor or take a circuitous route, first northward to Okehampton, then eastward between the moors. The great prehistoric trackway sometimes alleged to have traversed Dartmoor in a direct line from Exeter is regarded by most competent authorities as mythical.[2]

[1] Hooker, *Synopsis Chorographical of Devonshire* (*c.* 1598), printed in DA XLVII, 1915, p. 336.
[2] It is dismissed by Grundy ('The Ancient Highways of Devon', *Archaeological Journal*, XCVIII, 1941, p. 136). Hencken, while believing that a trackway ran from the west of Cornwall past Bodmin towards Callington and Tavistock, is more than doubtful whether it continued directly eastwards to Exeter (*Archaeology of Cornwall and Scilly*, pp. 128, 179, 180, 197). Some writers, who begin by assuming the existence of this "great central track-

Altogether it was a landscape apt to encourage local idiosyn-
crasy and to retard the pace of social change. Pent up in semi-
isolation from the rest of England, Devon naturally acquired a
strongly marked regional character. Down to the nineteenth
century it went its own way, still talking its ancient dialect, cling-
ing to old usages, remote, provincial, and self-satisfied. It has
always been thus. About the year 1174 a dispute between the
abbot of Tavistock and Richard Coffin, lord of Alwington, concerning the bounds of their respective properties, was settled by
arbitration, and the boundaries, as determined by twelve local
jurors, were put on record "before the whole county" in the shire-
court at Exeter. A bi-lingual document was then drawn up, after
the fashion of a pre-Conquest 'land-book', the boundaries being
described in Old English vernacular, while the preamble and
conclusion were in Latin, from which, however, the new-fangled
word *manerium* was carefully excluded, for what the rest of
England had learnt to call a manor was in Devonshire still called
a book-land.[1]

The county had its own system of weights and measures. Tin
was weighed by the 'long' hundredweight of a hundred and
twenty pounds.[2] The Exeter cornmarket used a bushel of ten
gallons in place of the statutory eight.[3] At Tavistock a stone of
cheese or butter weighed sixteen pounds, and there is reason to
believe that the pound weighed eighteen ounces.[4] In many parts
of Devon the acre was 5,760 square yards, as against the 4,840 of
the statute acre. Hence in 1318 the vendor of an "English acre"
at Pixon in Tavistock was at pains to mention that while it conformed to the national standard of forty rods in length by four
rods' width, it was measured with a rod of eighteen feet, not the

---

way", have attempted to plot its course over Dartmoor by piecing together
several east-west tracks that can be found on the moor, in some cases miles
apart (DA XXI, 1889, pp. 431 sqq.; LXI, 1929, pp. 343 sqq.; LXXIX, 1947, pp.
187 sqq.); but the greatest living authority on Dartmoor, Mr R. Hansford
Worth, has declared that over a great part of its alleged course there is no
visible sign of its existence.

[1] ETC XXIX.   [2] Lewis, *The Stannaries*, p. 252.
[3] W. Beveridge, 'A Statistical Crime of the Seventeenth Century', *Journal
of Economic and Business History*, I, 1929, pp. 503 sqq.
[4] The manorial account rolls testify to the large customary stone, but do
not reveal the size of the pound, for which see Vancouver, *General View of the
Agriculture of the County of Devon*, p. 231.

statutory sixteen and a half.[1] In studying the cultivation of the Tavistock demesnes, this fact of the large customary acre must be kept well in mind.

At the close of the eighteenth century Marshall declared that a native of the Midlands or the North "might travel through all the countries of Europe and not find practices more foreign to his own than those of Devonshire".[2] In a region so tenacious of local usage the question naturally arises: How far were its distinctive agricultural methods inherited from Celtic times?

Three memorial stones preserved at Tavistock date from the Celtic era. One of them, inscribed to the memory of "Nepranus, son of Conbevus", was found in West Street, Tavistock. Its lettering is Hiberno-Saxon. The other two were brought from Buckland Monachorum. They commemorate "Sabinus, son of Maccodechet" and "Dobunnus the smith, son of Enabarrus". Part of this last name, Enabarr, is repeated on the edge of the stone in Ogham characters, a species of script invented in southern Ireland. The name Maccodechet occurs in Anglesey, and also in Kerry, Cork, and Kildare.[3] In addition to these monuments, there are two Celtic habitation-sites in the vicinity of Tavistock. The first, Walreddon, is situated on the 400-foot contour, two miles south of Tavistock. It is not mentioned by name in Domesday Book, but first occurs, as Welradden, in an undated document of *circa* 1235.[4] Its name, Weala-ræden, signifies a 'community of Welshmen'.[5] The other site is an irregularly planned earthwork, enclosing a space of some two and a half acres within a rampart four to six feet high. It stands about a mile north-east of Tavistock, on the 425-foot contour, near the spot where the Tavy is joined by a stream significantly called the Wallabrook or Welshmen's brook. The earthwork itself is first mentioned in 1387 as "a parcel of land called Trendle", but its original character is established beyond any doubt by recent finds. An edge-tool, and a brooch and brooch-pin, all of bronze, and of late Celtic manufacture, afford proof enough that here was

[1] W. D Bdle 23, no. 5.
[2] *Rural Economy of the West of England*, I, p. 188.
[3] Bray, *Traditions etc. of Devonshire*, I, p. 373; *Archaeologia Cambrensis*, 1874, p. 333; Brash, *The Ogam Inscribed Monuments of the Gaedhil*, p. 350; Macalister, *Corpus Inscriptionum Insularum Celticarum*, I, pp. 467, 471, 472.
[4] W. D Bdle 39, no. 5.   [5] PND pp. xxiii, 248.

once a Celtic hamlet.[1] If still in occupation when the English reached the Tavy, it was probably deserted soon afterwards. The name Walreddon, however, if the accepted interpretation of it is correct, implies that a group of West-Welsh maintained their own distinctive settlement for some time after the invasion. As a highland people, the Britons of the south-west avoided heavy soils and thickly wooded valleys; they preferred the open ground and light soil of the foothills. In this respect both Trendle and Walreddon are typical of the sites favoured by the West-Welsh, and left alone, for a while at any rate, by the invaders.

It would be rash to assume that the native Celts had made no attempt to clear the valleys; but the truth is that hardly anything is known of pre-English husbandry in Devon. During the fifth and sixth centuries Britons from the south-western peninsula migrated in large numbers to the opposite shore, where they laid the foundations of modern Brittany. It has been surmised that after these migrations Devon was but sparsely populated, until the English began to settle there.[2] Whether or not this was the case, it is a fact that barely one per cent. of Devon place-names is pre-English.

One feature of agrarian practice, which used to be regarded as distinctively Celtic, was the cultivation of the outfield. This involved the division of the arable into two unequal portions. The infield, or portion nearest to the hamlet, was manured with household or farmyard refuse and subjected to intensive tillage. The outfield consisted of the wild heath, furze, and moorland that lay outside and usually above the hamlet. Part of this was broken up at long intervals, cropped for two or three years in succession, and then abandoned to the furze and rough grasses which quickly resumed their hold; after which the process might be repeated on another division of the moor.[3]

The infield of a hamlet community would be tilled commu-

---

[1] Worth, 'Prehistoric Tavistock', DA LXXIX, 1947, p. 125. Trendle (Extent of Hurdwick, 1387) is the OE *trendel*, meaning circle or ring; cf. Chisenbury Trendle, the great Wiltshire earthwork. Rowtrundle, "the rough trendel", is a hut circle in Walkhampton, Devon. The editors of *The Place-Names of Devon* erroneously state that Wallabrook is not an old name. Its lower waters pass Indescombe, *alias* Endescombe or Yentelescumb (1316); hence it was sometimes called Endlesbrooke (1310) or Entesbrok (1319), but the form Walabrok can be traced back to 1345 (W. D Bdle 53, no. 32).

[2] PND pp. xix, xx.   [3] Gray, *English Field Systems*, pp. 159, 170.

nally; but the system was not operated only by communities. On many farms in Devon and Cornwall the infield was called the in-ground; the enclosed pasture middle grounds; and the furze, moor, or down, the out-ground.[1] Quite frequently portions of the out-ground, not required for common pasture, or not used as such throughout the year, were annexed to particular farms. Thus a ferling of land in Whitchurch, given or sold to Tavistock Abbey *circa* 1130 by Robert Giffard, is defined in the confirma-tory charters of his descendants as half a ferling at "Tornator" and half a ferling *super montes*.[2] A number of tenants at Milton Abbot held a ferling each, or a multiple thereof, on Ramsdown. One of them, Robert de Medwille, *circa* 1245, quitclaimed to the abbot and convent all his right "in monte de Hramlegdun", so that they might cultivate that portion of the down whenever they chose; at the same time reserving fuel for his own hearth and pasture for his flock "outside cornfields and meadows".[3] Nearly six hundred years later, Vancouver notes that "a considerable part of the anciently cultivated lands, now called the moors, belongs exclusively to particular estates."[4]

A little earlier Marshall found that in many places the cultiva-tion of the waste was controlled by the lord of the manor.[5] This was evidently the case at Tavistock. In 1252 the abbot and con-vent, while granting out a tenement at Butworthy, reserved the right to enclose, let, or otherwise use their whole waste of But-worthy except the common pasture of Langstone Moor.[6] An un-dated thirteenth-century grant of a ferling at Blackmoorham gives the tenant right of common for his cattle over the whole waste of Whiteborough Down "when it lies untilled; but it shall be lawful for the abbot and convent to cultivate the said waste whenever they shall think fit."[7] That this right was not suffered to lie dormant is proved by a note in the 1387 survey of Hurdwick,

[1] N. J. G. Pounds, 'Lanhydrock Atlas', *Antiquity*, XIX, 1945, pp. 20 sqq.
[2] ETC XIV, XXXVIII, XLIX. The word used in these charters is not *ferlingum* but *sillingum*, as to which see the note on XIV *ibid*. Tornator is a lost name; but a reference in 1310 to "the great rock called Thorntorr" (W. D Bdle 27, no. 3) locates it in the field called Great Rock Park, between Taviton and Whit-church Down (Nat. Grid 20/495741).
[3] W. D Bdle 38, no. 1.   [4] *Op. cit.*, pp. 290, 291.   [5] *Op. cit.*, I, p. 32.
[6] W. D Bdle 4, no. 3. Butworthy is near Cudlipptown. On the Ordnance map Langstone is misnamed Launceston Moor.
[7] W. D Bdle 3, no. 1.

mentioning that Simon Porteioye (a witness to parish documents between 1349 and 1361) formerly took two ferlings of White-borough Down at a rent of seven shillings; "now it is in the lord's hand, unlet." Again, in 1310 two and a half ferlings at Newton were granted with common pasture for all the grantee's cattle that could winter upon Luscombe Down "when the said waste lies untilled and not let off".[1] In 1347 four acres on Heathfield were let for cultivation at a penny each.

These references are too few and brief to determine how sys-tematically the outfield was cropped. Part of the common may have been ploughed all over for a year or two, and afterwards left under grass for an indefinite time; or some of it might be divided into sections, each ploughed regularly in its turn, a new section being broken up each year; or small patches may have been tilled almost at random. In later centuries the custom varied from parish to parish. At Great Torrington a hundred and sixty-three acres of the common were known as 'tillage lands', in which the lord of the manor and certain tenants yearly exercised the right of growing spring corn and excluded their fellow-commoners un-til the corn was harvested. At Okehampton some two hundred and fifty acres of common were set apart in the same way, but here winter corn might be sown.[2] A court roll of the manor of Farway, dated 1619, records that "divers of the tennants did about forty-six years since plow and put in tillage" all that part of the common called Knowle Hill: an operation which custom per-mitted, and which they repeated in the following year.[3] Similar

---

[1] W. D Bdle 21, no. 3.

[2] Alexander and Hooper, *History of Great Torrington*, p. 80; Vancouver, *op. cit.*, pp. 275, 289.

[3] BM Add. Ch. 13858. I owe this reference to Dr W. G. Hoskins. Marshall noticed extensive marks of cultivation on the Blackdown Hills in East Devon. So also in the west of the county: "The better parts of these open commons have evidently heretofore been in a state of aration, lying in obvious ridges and furrows, with generally the remains of hedgebanks corresponding to the ridges" (*op. cit.*, i, p. 32; ii, pp. 46, 48, 132 sqq.). Vancouver describes the "ancient moorlands" of North Devon as "bearing evident marks of a former cultivation, their surfaces generally having been left under ridge and furrow" (*op. cit.*, p. 274); and he found traces of the same practice in the Okehampton district (pp. 290, 291). In 1742, when one of the Milton Abbot tenants began to enclose his ferling on Ramsdown, a local agent of the Bedford estate wrote: "They say the plot he is enclosing is called Slemans Corner, and there is old banks round it as if it had formerly been enclosed.

customs are on record in other highland regions, Cornwall included; but they are also found in the eastern and midland counties.[1] Evidently they have nothing to do with racial characteristics. They may represent a stage in the evolution of agrarian technique, but if so, archaeology has yet to decide whether that stage had been reached in Devon before the coming of the English.

The English conquest of Devon began in the second half of the seventh century. It was completed long before the close of the eighth, by which time the men of Wessex had also occupied east Cornwall. From time to time the natives took up arms and tried to resist, but for the most part they looked on with sullen acquiescence while land which they had not cultivated themselves was gradually cleared and occupied by the newcomers. Some laws of Ine (689–726), regulating the conditions upon which a well-to-do settler might take up a grant of land and plant his dependants on it, would seem to imply a colonizing movement directed and controlled by the government of Wessex.[2]

It was largely an occupation of still uncleared valley sites. Most of the larger rivers bear pre-English names. In several instances these names were at first applied also to the surrounding country. Thus the Tavy gave its name to two distinct settlements, one on each bank, and it was not until the thirteenth century that these two places were distinguished as Marytavy and Petertavy, from the dedication of their churches to St Mary and St Peter. A string of manors, nine in number, lying along the Clyst, are named after that river, each with some distinguishing addition; and at least two manors on the Otter only acquired distinctive names after the Norman Conquest.[3]

There is likewise old banks on other places of the Down which looks like enclosures as well as that, and have formerly been ploughed, as appears by its lying ridge and furrow, and are called by other names. I desired him to desist from enclosing any further till I could hear what his Grace's pleasure is" (Bedford Office, Bloomsbury, Devon Letters 1738-63: Jarvis Knight to R. Butcher, 19 Jan. 1742).

[1] For Cornwall, see Pounds, *loc. cit.*, and for Scotland, Randall, *History in the Open Air*, p. 84. Cf. M. W. Beresford, 'Lot Acres', *Economic History Review*, XIII, 1943, p. 75, and J. Saltmarsh and H. C. Darby, 'The Infield-Outfield System on a Norfolk Manor', *Economic History*, III, 1935, pp. 30 sqq., for examples from the counties of Norfolk, Suffolk, Nottingham, and Warwick.

[2] Hodgkin, *History of the Anglo-Saxons*, 1935, I, pp. 316, 318.

[3] PND p. xxviii.

In Devon charters of the eighth and ninth centuries place-names compounded from bases indicating physical features, such as *-ford*, *-well*, *-ridge*, *-wood*, *-lake*, *-combe*, *-down*, *-hill*, *-moor*, far outnumber all the rest. Habitation-bases, such as *-ton*, *-cote*, *-worthy*, appear infrequently at first, and are still the minority in documents of the tenth century, although by that time the proportion has increased.[1] It seems clear that the effective occupation of Devon was a very gradual process, begun in the seventh century and continued down to the Norman era, when it may have been somewhat retarded by the operation of the forest laws. If so, it was resumed with fresh vigour after the disforestation of the county in 1205. Fully three-quarters of the existing farm-names are on record before 1350.

Many Devon place-names reflect the social and economic stratification of the early settlers. The thegn, whose life, in virtue of his gentle birth, is valued at six times as much as that of the richest peasant, obtains a land-book, or charter of seignorial privilege, and his 'book-land' figures on the map to-day as one or other of a dozen Bucklands. Charlcombe, Charleton, and Charlwood, among other names, commemorate the *ceorl*, or free peasant, and scores of *-cotes* his lowly neighbour the *kotsetla*. The *gafolman*, or peasant distinguished from his neighbours by payment of a money rent, is to be found at Galmpton, Gammaton, and Galmington.[2] Only the slave leaves no trace at all, because he neither owns land nor cultivates it on his own account.

It will be worth while to dwell a little on these distinctions, for they lie at the root of the social system we shall be examining in later chapters.

The slave of the Old English period is either descended from servile forebears, or, if born of free blood, he has been forced into slavery by crime or poverty. A lower value is set upon his life than upon that of even the poorest freeman. He cannot implead his master in the public courts, and cannot hold any property in his own right. So long as his bodily strength endures, he is employed on the lord's home-farm. He is fed from his lord's table; his home is in the outbuildings around the lord's courtyard. The lord can, if he choose, sell him and all his family.

If the slave marries and begets a numerous progeny, a time will

---

[1] Alexander, Presidential Address, DA LXIV, 1932, p. 98.   [2] PND, p. 304.

come when the outbuildings will be overcrowded and there will be, from the lord's point of view, too many mouths to feed. It will then be convenient to allow the slave a measure of economic independence. As a first step, he will be granted a supply of timber from the lord's wood to build himself a cottage. The cottage may be erected in some corner of the demesne, as was Briscott, near Tavistock, originally Beorhtwine's *cote*.[1] In that case, the cottager will probably spend most of his time working on the lord's demesne, receiving food or perhaps wages in return, and when not so engaged will be tilling his garden-plot. Or he may work for the lord one day a week throughout the year if required, and three days at harvest; for the rest of the time hiring himself out to his more prosperous neighbours. Or again, the lord may grant him a small holding, perhaps in severalty, perhaps in the form of strips in the common field, on condition that he will lend a hand on the demesne when summoned. The author of the *Rectitudines Singularum Personarum*, writing a generation or so before the Norman Conquest, is of opinion that he ought to have at least five acres to cultivate on his own account. His livelihood is scanty, but he is no longer a *theow*, a slave. Being now a householder, he pays his hearth-penny to the Church "as every freeman should". In the eyes of the Church, indeed, he is now indistinguishable from the younger son of a poor freeman, who may also be a *kotsetla*, earning his living in the same way; but the former *theow* is more properly styled a freedman, or—if we wish to emphasize the remnants of servility that still cling to him—a serf. Place-names ending in *-cote* or *-cott* occur all over Devonshire; they are particularly numerous in the manor of Werrington. As a rule they are linked with a *kotsetla*'s personal name, and many of them presumably began as small holdings occupied by members of this agrarian lower class.[2]

The *servus casatus*, or 'hutted slave', as he was called on the

---

[1] PND, p. 221.

[2] A late instance may be quoted from a Werrington court roll. In 1366 a serf of the manor, Roger Knyght, asked the court to adjudicate upon his right to a holding called Knyghtyscote (now Nescott). But the Old English *cotlif* meant a manor; and this sense of *-cote* also occurs in place-names. Some two dozen *-cotes* figure as manors in the Devonshire Domesday, four of them (Dodecota, Godevacota, Wadelescota, Wolestanecota) being named after their owners in 1066.

D

other side of the English Channel, is not the only type of freed-man. Where there is much land waiting to be cleared, it may suit the lord as well or better to plant out his former *theow* on a hold-ing large enough to make him self-supporting. This is done by granting him the use of fifteen acres or so of ploughland, with a cottage, and enough livestock and seedcorn to begin farming on his own account. Such a tenant farmer will be known as a *gebur*, or boor. Though now responsible for his own maintenance, he is still closely bound to his lord's service. He may have to work one or more days a week on the lord's demesne, and even more at har-vest. Apart from this, the degree of freedom he enjoys will vary from place to place. In general, he is still a being without rights. He must not quit the manor, must not marry without leave; his plot of land is held at the will of the lord; in his chattels he has only the usufruct.[1] His livelihood is at the best precarious. A full plough-team is beyond his reach. He may have to put his single ox, or pair of oxen, under one yoke with those of his fellow boors. In the midlands it will be natural for his ploughland to lie open in the form of strips, intermixed with those of his neighbours in the two or three large common fields adjoining the village; but amid the combes of Devon small groups of *geburas* will be more likely perhaps to cluster together in hamlets, and there to prac-tise co-operative ploughing both on the in-ground strips belong-ing to the hamlet and also on the outfield. In support of this con-jecture we can point to such place-names as Bowerland, Burraton, Bourton, meaning lands or farms cultivated by *geburas*.[2] Three fields in the parish of Halberton, called Hither Burland, Yonder Burland, and Great Burland, are shown on the tithe map as be-longing to a farm called East Manley; and Manley, we are told, signifies a communal woodland clearing.[3] Their combined area is roughly seventeen acres; and they adjoin a group of fields which have self-evidently been enclosed from arable strips. To find such names on the map is to catch a glimpse of agrarian history in the making. We shall see that the *gebur* is not unrepresented on the map of Tavistock.

[1] Maitland, *Domesday Book and Beyond*, pp. 37, 38.
[2] PND p. 246. Cf. Davenport, *Economic Development of a Norfolk Manor*, pp. 13–15, on the East Anglian grouping of the servile tenants into villages, while the freemen occupied scattered farms.
[3] PND p. 549.

When the *gebur* died, his land and chattels all reverted to the lord. The free peasant who farmed land of his own was called a *geneat* or *ceorl*. In Devonshire he was not, like some East Anglian freemen, at liberty to choose his own lord; but there was nothing servile in his tenure or status. Often his farmstead was an enclosed *-tun*, *-ham*, or *-combe*. He occupied this in severalty, and for tillage used his own plough-oxen. If these were insufficient, he might hire an ox or two from the lord of the manor, or bargain for the assistance of a neighbour's team. Quite a number of Devon farms, however, included no arable. In such cases the peasant lived by stockraising and dairy-farming. His livestock grazed upon the enclosed pasture of the farm or on the open downland of the manor, and in summer might be sent up to graze on Dartmoor. He paid his lord a rent, most probably in kind, and might be asked to put in a couple of days' work annually on the lord's demesne by way of recognition for the use of the common pasture.

The formula by which these peasants were rated to the land-tax deserves notice here, as being a local peculiarity, and one dating perhaps from the dawn of English life in Devon. In the midlands the common unit of assessment was a virgate, or quarter-hide; in Devon it was a ferling, or' quarter-virgate. On the standard reckoning of a hundred and twenty acres to a hide, the ferling should have been seven and a half acres; but these are fiscal units, not areal measurements, and in point of fact the Devon ferling might represent anything from fifteen to thirty-two acres.[1] The assessment was laid primarily on the arable; meadow, wood, and pasture as a rule were left out of the reckoning. Hence the statement: X holds a ferling of land at Y, tells us nothing about the lay-out of the farm. Yet this, with details of the rent and service owed by X to the lord, is all the information given in manorial surveys. Seldom indeed is the record so explicit as when Ramsham in Tavistock is described as consisting, *circa* 1315, of forty acres of arable, sixty of pasture, ten of meadow, and six of wood.[2] With

---

[1] It was 16 acres at Ottery St Mary in 1381–2 (DA LXVI, 1934, p. 219); 30 at Paignton in 1567 (*ibid.*, LXIV, 1932, p. 247); and 32 at Churston Ferrers in 1198 (*Devon Feet of Fines*, no. 22). In 1256 the carucate or ploughland was equated at Ottery St Mary with 8 ferlings, i.e., 128 acres (*ibid.*, no. 558), not the 4 ferlings or 64 acres which Reichel gives as the Devonshire standard (VCH *Devon*, I, p. 386).

[2] Tavistock Abbey White Book, fo. xv.

a total extent of a hundred and sixteen acres, this riverside farm was assessed at two ferlings. At about the same date two ferlings at Ogbear, in the same parish, consisted of thirty acres of arable land with one acre of meadow;[1] and one ferling at Blackmoorham, *circa* 1275, of 14 acres 3 roods 8 poles with some unmeasured land adjoining.[2] The system clearly rested on the assumption that a peasant family could subsist upon fifteen or sixteen arable acres, with an indeterminate appendage of pasture, wood, and meadow. The same assumption held good in other parts of England; but in Middlesex, for example, a fifteen-acre holding would be assessed at half a virgate, so that when the land-tax stood at six shillings on the hide, its occupant paid ninepence, while the Devonshire peasant, being charged at the ferling rate, paid only half as much for a holding of the same nominal extent, with the added advantage of a larger customary acre. The reasons for this "beneficial hidation", as it has been called, remain obscure. An out-of-date assessment, which has failed to keep pace with expanding cultivation, is perhaps the most plausible hypothesis.[3]

Tavistock, which as the seat of the abbey claims particular attention, included within its boundaries all the characteristic features of the agrarian landscape. Down to the last quarter of the nineteenth century it consisted of some 11,600 statute acres, with an outlying portion of roughly eleven hundred acres at Cudlipptown.[4] The greater part of the area lay between the Tamar and the Tavy. Four minor streams, the Burn, the Wallabrook, the Fishlake, and the Lumburn, break up the intermediate surface with valleys running parallel from north to south. At its northern boundary the parish faded out into the great waste of Heathfield. Its territory was divided between arable, pasture, moor, and woodland in about the average proportions. Its topography and nomenclature will be studied here in some detail, for they illustrate a pattern of rural settlement which may fairly be regarded as typical of Devon as a whole.

Tavistock is the *stoc* of Petertavy and Marytavy, as Calstock is the *stoc* of Callington and Plymstock the *stoc* of Plympton. It used

---

[1] p. 46 below.   [2] W. D Bdle 3, no. 1.
[3] Cf. Maitland, *op. cit.*, p. 450.
[4] Cudlipptown was transferred to Petertavy in 1885. Ten years later the ancient parish was divided into the two civil parishes of Tavistock and Tavistock Hamlets.

to be thought that a *stoc* was a fortified outpost, a pioneer settlement guarded by a stockade; but recent scholarship has proved that it was nothing of the sort. It was an offshoot or dependency, which might, as in this case, be some miles distant from the mother-settlement. Furthermore, *stocs* are low-lying places, not as a rule more than four hundred feet above sea-level, and almost always near water. From the association of the name with so many places where there are rich water-meadows, it has been inferred that *stocs* originally were outlying pastures to which the herdsmen of the mother-villages drove their cows for summer grazing.[1]

At present the main road from Plymouth to Okehampton (A 386) runs through Tavistock, but the prehistoric trackway with which its course is nearly everywhere identical by-passed the site of the town, crossing the Walkham at Horrabridge and the Tavy at Harford Bridge. If it continued beyond Harford Bridge, it would reach the central corridor of Devon at Okehampton. Down to the eighteenth century this was one of the usual routes followed by travellers from Plymouth to Exeter.[2] It would naturally lead the earliest settlers to Marytavy and Petertavy. Tavistock then lay on a branch track, which ran from Harford Bridge through the midst of the Trendle and the site of the future borough to the lowest fordable point on the Tamar, just above New Bridge, after which it merged at Callington into one of the main roads through Cornwall. Viewed in relation to this primitive road-system, the siting of Tavistock confirms the inference already drawn from place-names, that it is not a scene of primary settlement.

After a while the *stoc* beside the Tavy was permanently occupied by a few settlers and established as an independent hamlet. Such is the normal mode of settlement throughout the highland zone: a periodical swarming from old hamlets into new.[3] On chalk and limestone soils the scarcity of water keeps people together in compact villages; but Devonshire, with its high rainfall and innumerable springs, has been from a very early date a region of dispersed settlement. With the growth of population the daughter hamlet in turn gives birth to new hamlets and isolated

[1] Ekwall, *Studies on English Place-Names*, pp. 17 sqq.
[2] Chope, *Early Tours in Devon and Cornwall*, pp. 103, 271.
[3] Vinogradoff, *The Growth of the Manor*, p. 146.

farmsteads, as more and more of the adjoining country is developed.

The future borough of Tavistock included within its boundaries just that extent of arable, woodland, and meadow on which the original hamlet-dwellers may be supposed to have subsisted. Fuel and building materials lay close at hand in the woods that fringed the surrounding hills and vales on the north and northeast, woods now remembered only by their names: Parkwood, Old Wooda, Waddon. The flat meadow-ground beside the Tavy would feed their dairy-stock, while the sheep grazed upon Inswell Down. And corn would ripen on the southward-facing slopes between the modern Launceston and Glanville Roads.

Of the settlement that went on during the next two hundred years we may safely guess that it consisted partly in enclosure from the upland wastes and partly in the reduction of the wooded area. The steep sides of the valleys have always been thickly clad with timber, and there is evidence that this formerly extended much further than it does now. The name Woodovis ("at the *efese*, or border, of the wood") testifies to a wide clearance in the western half of the parish, extending over the parish boundary to Woodley in Lamerton. Names ending in -*bearu* (Ogbear, Crebor, Billingsbear) and in -*leah* (Nutley, Rumonsleigh) record other woodland clearings. Intakes from heath and moor are denoted by names based on the suffix -*worthy*. Kilworthy and Gulworthy remain upon the map to-day; Hasworthy is found in early documents; and to these we should perhaps add Emsory, which occurs as a field-name near Rumonsleigh.[1] The -*hams*, or farms based on the flat ground in the bends of the rivers (Morwellham and Impham on the Tamar; Whitham, Ramsham, and Blackmoorham on the Tavy) represent another, and possibly later, phase of occupation.

All three of the recorded -*worthy* names in Tavistock, and seventy-two per cent. of those in Devon as a whole, are compounded with personal adjuncts. Clearly they denote farms occupied in severalty, many of them perhaps named after the pioneer who first enclosed them from the waste. A similar personal association is found in about half the Devon names ending in -*tun*. This suffix, and -*town*, its modern variant, were used for centuries as

---

[1] For the dialectal pronunciation of -*worthy* as -*ery*, cf. PND p. 80.

synonymous with 'farm'; thus, in Devonshire a farmyard was, till lately, "the town-place".

The boundaries of the manor must have been fixed at latest by 981, when the territory they circumscribed was made over to the newly founded abbey. At certain points their course appears to have been dictated by respect for the bounds of pre-existing farms. A line was drawn across the hog's-back between the Tamar and the Tavy at a point where the two streams are little more than a mile apart. This formed the southern boundary. On the west the Tamar and on the east the Burn and the Tavy provided natural frontiers, broken once at Langsford, the *landscore-* or boundary-*ford*.[1] Here the manor reached out towards Dartmoor to include five settlements: Radge, Nutley, Kingford, Taviton, and Whitham, all in Roborough hundred and all situated on the fringe of the moor. Several of them were venville tenements: that is, their occupiers, in return for a small annual payment, enjoyed the immemorial right of depasturing their sheep, cattle, and horses anywhere on the moor, and of taking therefrom peat for fuel, stone for building, and heath for thatching.[2] The northern boundary was more complicated. Its direction strongly suggests that Ottery and Chaddlehanger, two settlements in the adjoining parish of Lamerton, were already in existence in the third quarter of the tenth century. Beginning at a rivulet which flows into the Tamar opposite Latchley, it went up to Ottery Down and past Ogbear to the Lumburn, followed that river and one of its tributaries upstream until it reached the grounds of Chaddlehanger, then turned eastward to the Wallabrook, which it followed up to its source on Heathfield; after which it again ran eastward till it joined the Burn.

The area thus bounded was approximately eighteen square miles. We may picture it as dotted with tiny hamlets in each of which three or four households struggled for a bare subsistence, while here and there a more substantial peasant worked his en-

[1] Now Harford Bridge. The first element in this name is not *hart* (PND p. 201), but *har*, meaning boundary (*Chief Elements used in English Place-Names*, p. 33). Langsford survives as the name of a farm near by.

[2] Radge, Nutley, and Taviton appear to have been venville tenements, as also were Cudlipp and Twist in the detached portion of the manor. Venville = *fines villarum*; see *Publications of the Dartmoor Preservation Association*, I, pp. xxiv, 40, 75.

closed holding. The hog's-back in the south of the manor was predestined to supply common pasture for the *ham*-farms down on the river-banks, and occasionally to be tilled as outfield. In the west, the broad expanse of Blanchdown concealed its mineral El Dorado beneath a surface that defied cultivation. The difficult country between the Burn and the Wallabrook was probably already occupied by Winemær's *tun*, the modern Wilminstone. It was the central portion, lying between the Lumburn and the Wallabrook, and including Tavistock itself, that invited exploitation as manorial demesne.

From the free peasants the abbot could demand those food-rents or other dues which heretofore they had rendered to the king's high-reeve. The land outside their occupation could be cultivated by his slaves, or otherwise disposed of as he thought fit. By 1066 the assessment of the manor for purposes of land-tax was divided into three portions, one-seventh being laid upon the abbot's demesne, three-sevenths on the peasant holdings, and the remainder on lands distributed among four thegns. The thegn-lands are not named in Domesday Book, but six of them can be identified from later documents as Crebor, Ogbear, Hasworthy, Whitham, Taviton, and Nutley.[1] It will be observed that these names represent all the main types of settlement. Furthermore, with the exception of Crebor, all the thegn-lands were situated on the outskirts of the manor. So also were the two holdings, Cudlipp and Roborough, which abbot Wymund (*c.* 1091–1102) settled upon his brother as a supernumerary knight's fee. The former, now Cudlipptown, was an outlying property high up on the edge of Dartmoor, while Roborough appears to have been an older name for Morwell, near the Tamar.[2] The peculiar circumstances of this grant exposed Wymund to the charge of jobbery, but in devoting lands on the perimeter to the endowment of a military vassal he was true to the example of his predecessors.

In the eyes of the abbot and his brother the value of Morwell lay not so much in its agricultural possibilities, for very little of the land was suitable for tillage, but in its pastures and woods, and most of all perhaps in its riparian rights. The Tamar salmon fishery has always been profitable; and as the river is navigable

[1] See above, pp. 13, 14.   [2] DA LXXVII, 1945, p. 158.

up to this point, Morwellham served from the twelfth century on-wards as the port of Tavistock.

Of the settlements at Nutley and Crebor something will be said in the next chapter. Taviton was a submanor on the left bank of the Tavy.[1] In 1086, if its identification with Ermenald's holding is correct, it comprised enough arable for a full plough-team, with pasture for seven cows and grazing on the down for forty sheep. Its dependent population was not enumerated in the Domesday survey, but they could muster another full team of their own. Their hamlet was situated in a little combe between Taviton and Whitchurch Down, called Dunscombe; it is repre-sented to-day by a single farm which has usurped the name of Taviton. Since its inhabitants appear in records of the fourteenth century as owing servile dues, their ancestors in the eleventh were probably *geburas*.[2]

Hasworthy, like Kilworthy on the opposite bank of the Walla-brook, is an intake from the waste of Heathfield. Its name, Hæfer's *worthy*, to-day survives only as a field-name, pro-nounced Azzuries and spelt Azores. As Hæfer is a nickname mean-ing goat, we may perhaps infer that it was not regarded as a promising site, bounded as it was by Heathfield on the north, and on the south by the equally rough ground called Mana Butts. In course of time its occupants pushed the cultivated area eastward down the 'green *denu*' or valley of the Burn, thus establishing 'Grendon' as a distinct hamlet. The lord of Ogbear, Hasworthy, and Grendon drew a rent of seven shillings from the lord of Wringworthy and Warne, in Marytavy parish, who drove his mill with water from the Burn; but in 1283 this was relinquished, and the Grendon tenants received in exchange a grant of com-mon pasture on the waste of Blackdown.[3] When Hasworthy and Grendon, like the other thegn-lands, were recovered by the abbey, the rustics there held their tenements as fractions of knight's fees, subject to payment of an annual rent, and two boon-

---

[1] Its hall or barton stood near the spot where the road to Nutley branches off from the main road to Moretonhampstead.

[2] They are called *villani* in the Exon Domesday, but this word is sometimes used vaguely and generically on manors where there are only bordars, as at Colrige and Radecliva (DB IV, pp. 327, 384), or only bordars and slaves, as at Hax, Chentesbera, Lovenetorna, and elsewhere (*ibid.*, pp. 273, 281, 299).

[3] Extent of Hurdwick, 1416, m. 11.

works each at Hurdwick in return for pasture upon Heathfield.

Before its enclosure from the waste, Hasworthy may have been tilled as outfield from Wilminstone, which appears to have been the original and at first the only settlement between the Burn and the Wallabrook. The arable of Wilminstone lay above and round the *tun*. The pasture would have been limited by the enclosure of Hasworthy to twenty acres or so on Mana Butts had not the occupant retained a right of way up to Heathfield. For meadow there was the *ham* beside the Tavy. At some time in the twelfth century Wilminstone got into the hands of a baronial family, from whose representative, Robert de Veteri Ponte, the abbey eventually recovered it at a cost of ten marks.[1] Subsequently it was divided into two hamlets and occupied by servile tenants of the abbey who paid tallage and hatch-silver, with a halfpenny each at All Saints' for the communal meadow on the river bank. These hamlets became important enough to justify the building of a watermill at Indescombe beside the Wallabrook.

One other settlement is known to have been granted out as thegn-land before 1066. Ogbear derives its name from the oakwood that covered the steep side of a precipice on the west bank of the Lumburn. Below Ogbear-cliff a group of meadows and fields called Ogbear-ham sloped downwards to the Stenydich, a tributary stream which here forms the parish boundary; and above the cliff lay the comparatively level expanse of Ogbear-down. As a whole the area comprised about a hundred and fifty acres. Its arable lay partly in the valley, partly on the down; and its character is brought out very clearly in a charter whereby Richard de Ocbear conveyed to Walter his son a close, a curtilage, and two ferlings of land in Ogbear. This document bears no date, but the names of the witnesses date it *circa* 1302.[2] The two ferlings are described as consisting of: four acres between Ogbear and the Lumburn; ten acres lying in the furlong between Tor and Ogbear, and extending to the cross on the west of the township; eleven acres in Yerkysburghe furlong; two and a half acres in Broken-Cross furlong; two and a half acres of sanded land west of Broken-Cross furlong; and one acre of meadow.

Here we have, unmistakably, the language of open-field cultivation. To-day the Great Field of Braunton is the only arable

[1] Dugdale, II, p. 499.   [2] W. D Bdle 41, no. 2.

common field left in Devonshire; but notwithstanding frequent statements to the contrary, it is now known that such fields once existed in every part of the county. A single parish might include a compact village surrounded by arable strips in open field; hamlets with similar field systems of their own in miniature; and isolated farmsteads, the occupants of which raised some of the corn they needed on their in-grounds and the rest by outfield tillage.[1]

The portion of the manor reserved for exploitation as manorial demesne dwindled progressively throughout the period of written record. In the sixteenth century it was bounded on the east by the Fishlake and on the south by the Lamerton road; but originally it must have included nearly all the territory lying between the Lumburn and the Wallabrook. For proof that the Wallabrook once formed the eastern boundary we have, besides documentary evidence, the name Grammerby, which has nothing to do with any *grey mere*, as has been suggested: it is *gemære-byge*, or boundary curve.[2] In the south of this area, near the junction of the Lumburn and the Tavy, is Crowndale, which as late as 1313 was described as having formerly been demesne land of the abbey.[3] The name Lumburn, or 'loam stream', proclaims the fertility of the adjacent soil, and this southern portion of the original demesne was in fact the area most suitable for tillage, though Milemead, Stilesweek, and Parswell, three ancient freeholds lying close to the river, may originally have been stock-farms. It is within the broad expanse of gently undulating downland that stretches from the left bank of the Lumburn to Tavistock and the Lamerton road that we must locate most if not all of the five ploughlands cultivated by the abbey at the time of the Domesday inquest. Above the Lamerton road lay some eight hundred acres of higher and less fertile ground, stretching up to the northern limit of the manor, and there shading off into the great waste of Heathfield. In the centre of this upland stood the abbot's *heordewic*, or sheep-farm, destined later to give its name to all that was left of the

---

[1] Finberg, 'The Open Field in Devonshire', *Antiquity*, XXIII, 1949, pp. 180 sqq.

[2] Cf. the "white stone called Gremure" mentioned in W. D Bdle 39, no. 5, as one of the bounds of Morwellham, and the "great stone called Graymare" which in 1613 marked the parish boundary of Cardinham (Doble, *History of the Church and Parish of S. Meubred, Cardynham*, p. 13).

[3] W. D Bdle 8, no. 11.

original manor after its partition between abbot, knights, and burgesses.

It is possible that in early days the abbot's ploughlands lay in open strips, intermixed with those of his tenants, as did those belonging to the lord of Braunton Gorges in 1324 and indeed much later.[1] There is every reason to believe that his ploughs were driven by slaves. When he began to emancipate the slaves, he may have established some of them as *kotsetlan* at Tavistock itself, or in lonely corners of the demesne, like that Beorhtwine who, as we have already noted, gave his name to Briscott, and who was probably employed as a shepherd, since his cottage lies between the *heordewic* and the common pasture of Heathfield. Beorhtwine, however, may have been a free-born labourer, not a serf. We are on surer ground with those former slaves who were settled in hamlets, each with his own allotment of arable strips. Wilminstone, as we have seen, was eventually occupied by servile tenants; but Wilminstone lay outside the demesne, and it is natural to suppose that the demesne was used up first. Evidence that it was so is not lacking. Crowndale, in the far south of the original demesne, was a hamlet important enough in the thirteenth century to have its own corn-mill; and the servile origin of its inhabitants may be inferred from the fact that they paid tallage and hatch-silver. The modern Downhouse, about a mile north of Crowndale, represents the "land of la Doune", described in 1288 as lately held in villeinage.[2] But the heart and centre of all this bondland was Bowrish: that is, *bur-hiwisc*, the *hiwisc* or plantation on which the abbot settled those of his former slaves whom he was minded to establish not as *kotsetlan*, or farm-labourers, but as *geburas*, tenant farmers. It was this step which brought about the first great contraction of the demesne, making the Lamerton road its effective southern boundary. Although many slaves had been emancipated before the Norman Conquest, it is probable that this particular stage was not reached until after 1086, for at that date the abbot still had five ploughs at work; in later records he never has more than three. He could hand over part of his arable to *geburas* without much real loss, for as slaves they had themselves consumed most of the food grown on it by their own toil. If compensation were needed, it could be had by

[1] *Antiquity*, XXIII, 1949, p. 181.   [2] W. D Bdle 53, no. 27.

using their services to bring fresh ground under cultivation, on the far side of the Lumburn. This was in fact done; and the result was Newton: emphatically the new *tun*.[1]

After the Bowrish area had been lopped off, the residuary portion of the abbot's demesne came to be known as Hurdwick Barton. There is a sense in which these two names might be held to exclude each other, for a *heordewic* is a sheep-farm, whereas *beretun* signifies a granary. In Devonshire usage, however, barton represents not only *beretun*, but also *burhtun*, an enclosed manor farm. The latter is the original of the place-name Burton, so common in other counties, but in Devon quite unknown. How barton and its Latin equivalent *bertona* acquired this double meaning is a problem that will remain unsolved until many more examples of its early use have been collected and elucidated by their context. So far as can be seen at present, the *beretun* sense predominated in Devon until the end of the thirteenth century. The process of consolidation was then gathering speed. Many lords were quitting the open fields and, like the abbot of Tavistock, concentrating their ploughland round a manorial establishment which in some cases had been designed for the storage of grain, but in others, as at Hurdwick, had originally been a pastoral centre. In later centuries the *burhtun* sense is uppermost. All over the county 'barton' comes to signify a home-farm standing apart from the peasant holdings and occupied by the lord of the manor or by a prosperous yeoman who is graduating into the ranks of gentry. It may be that it first acquired this meaning through the deliberate withdrawal of the magnates into ring-fenced manor farms.[2]

There is evidence in plenty for the intermixture of arable holdings before the abbot withdrew to Hurdwick, and even later. Several deeds executed between 1310 and 1318 speak of acres and half-acres lying dispersedly near Pixon. In 1299 William de Bourhywis conveyed to the abbot and convent a selion on "La Doune"; and not long afterwards David Matheu, a burgess of

---

[1] Newton had its own mill by *c.* 1245 (W. D Bdle 8, no. 1). In 1309 David de Bourywysse assigned to the *salsarius* of the monastery a rent of 6d. from "a piece of land in Bourywysse" described as lying upon Kylmanstor Down, which is just above Newton (Bdle 8, no. 4). This shows that Bowrish now included land on both sides of the Lumburn.

[2] DCNQ XXIII, 1949, pp. 273–7, 326, 363.

Tavistock, acquired from the same William three dispersed parcels of arable with a meadow in Bowrish. In 1309 a piece of land in Newton is described as bounded on one side by "the land of all the men of Niweton", evidently a common field. Two years later the almoner of Tavistock purchased from David de Bourhywys a piece of land in Newton comprising several parcels held by bond tenants of the abbey who received in exchange land of equivalent value elsewhere in Bowrish. To augment this acquisition, the abbot made over 2 acres 1 rood west of Artiscombe; and the almoner then had a new ditch made dividing his furlongs from those belonging to the freeholder of Woodovis.[1]

In this transaction and its sequel we can discern the process of enclosure already at work. It begins with a consolidation of holdings, brought about by purchase and exchange. Then a trench is dug to mark the limits of the holder's land, and the soil removed from it is thrown up into a mound on the inner side of the ditch. (A lease of Furze Close at Woodovis in 1465 specifies that the ditch shall be four feet wide and four feet deep;[2] and the same dimensions are given at Leigh in 1398.) The mound is planted with a quickset hedge, and grows in course of time by the addition of soil thrown up whenever the ditch is cleared. No feature of the Devon landscape is more characteristic than these vast banks, crowned with oak, ash, hazel, or other coppice wood growing to a height of twenty feet or more and forming an impenetrable screen. Wasteful as they are of space and soil, they have the merit of permanence, and they provide cattle with the shelter that is badly needed in so boisterous a climate. Marshall suggests that coppice fences may have been designed at first to make good the loss of fuel attendant upon forest clearance. He adds: "Many farms have no other woodland, nor supply of fuel, than what their fences furnish; yet are amply supplied with this; besides, perhaps, an overplus of poles, cord wood, faggots, and the bark of oak, for sale."[3]

The space thus enclosed was locally termed a *park*. In size it might be anything from an acre or two upwards. Parks of twenty-five, thirty-four, and forty acres are by no means un-

---

[1] W. D Bdle 23, nos. 2–5; Bdle 8, nos. 3 and 7; Bdle 21, no. 2; Bdle 21, no. 6; Bdle 30, no. 3.

[2] *Ibid.*, Bdle 53, no. 160.   [3] Marshall, *op. cit.*, I, p. 66.

common,[1] but there is a tendency to divide them into smaller units. Thus a lease of two closes at Bowrish, one of twelve, the other of twenty acres, dated 1491, is endorsed with a note that each of them has since been divided into three; and as six fields they remain to this day.[2] Similarly, a close described in 1416 as containing one ferling and called Undertorland *alias* Betelonde, appears in a later rental as three fields, Lower, Middle, and Higher Down Parks, *alias* Beatland.[3] Division and subdivision would provide additional shelter for cattle and a larger crop of timber. Notwithstanding the high cost of raising hedge-banks,.it was carried on until many parks consisted only of a single acre. On the other hand, a number of enclosures, particularly on the edge of moorland, were minute from the beginning; so that where documents are lacking it is not easy to determine whether a close of one acre has been formed by piecemeal intake from the waste or by division of an old enclosure.[4]

In 1306 Robert Davy, acting on behalf of the abbot and convent, bought up several parcels of land in Ogbear-ham, "both enclosed and unenclosed".[5] Another document of the same period mentions "all the parks of Ogbear situated between Ogbear and Ottery".[6] The 1387 Extent of Hurdwick refers to eight "parcels" of land in Bowrish and Downhouse, occupied by as many tenants; but over "parcel" a later hand has written "close" in each case. After the first quarter of the fourteenth century we hear no more of selions and furlongs in the vicinity of Tavistock; and though in some parishes the open field survived for another century or two, by 1549 the arable lands of Devon were reported to be among the most completely enclosed in England.[7]

This transformation, begun in the thirteenth century, or even

[1] Ogbear-park, 25 acres (1483); North-park in Foghanger, Milton Abbot, 34 acres (1415); Hedwyll-park, Ottery, 40 acres (1516).
[2] White Book, fo. xvii; W. D Bdle 53, no. 11.
[3] Extent of Hurdwick, 1416, m. 6; Hurdwick Rental, 1768. Here again the threefold division has been permanent. The fields in question are just south of Honeytor.
[4] In his valuable paper on the reclamation of the waste in Devon, Dr W. G. Hoskins has taken account only of the former process (*Economic History Review*, XIII, 1943, p. 87).
[5] "... *tam infra clausur' quam extra*," W. D Bdle 41, no. 5.   [6] *Ibid.*, no. 17.
[7] *Discourse of the Commonweal*, quoted by W. E. Tate in DCNQ XXII, 1942, p. 6.

earlier, was encouraged by the spectacle of so many *tuns* and *hams* which had been enclosed from the beginning. Lords of manors could see all about them proof that enclosure raised the value of agricultural land. The movement was further hastened by the Black Death, which is known to have fallen upon Devonshire with catastrophic effect.[1] Whether as a result of the plague, or for some other reason, two at least of the Tavistock hamlets ceased to exist as such in the middle of the fourteenth century. In 1336 Crowndale had comprised seven holdings. By 1396 it was reduced to one, and its cornmill lay derelict until abbot Mey rebuilt it as a fulling mill. Dunscombe, which at the earlier date had consisted of five and a half ferlings divided between three tenants, was by 1387 combined with Taviton in one tenure. With this decay of the older nuclei, consolidation went on apace. In 1409 the arable at Ogbear, largely enclosed but still lying dispersedly, was held by three tenants. By 1486 it was equally divided between two. The expansion of the cloth trade in the fifteenth century increased the demand for wool, and further encouraged a process which, as Hooker noted, enabled the sheep to change their pasture frequently, and to "feede styll as it were upon a new springnynge grasse".

No doubt some arable was then converted into pasture; but the enclosure of the arable must be distinguished from the enclosure of the downs and hilltop wastes. Parts of these had been colonized and occupied in severalty well before the close of the thirteenth century, such occupation, as we have seen, being frequently denoted by names ending in -*worthy*; but stretches of waste on Blanchdown, Luscombe Down, Morwell Down, Mana Butts, and Heathfield, comprising some fifteen hundred acres altogether, or not quite one-seventh of the whole parish, remained unenclosed until the nineteenth century.

In the abbot's hundred court the parish of Tavistock was represented by seven tithings: Hasworthy, Grendon, Kilworthy, Wilminstone, Hurdwick, Newton with Gulworthy, and Woodovis. Taviton also was a tithing, but it lay in Roborough hundred; and Morwell was policed by its own manor court. This organization presupposes a well-peopled countryside, and a population more evenly distributed than it is now. To-day Milemead is in

[1] Lewis, *The Stannaries*, pp. 40, 141, 156; *Reg. Grandisson*, III, pp. lxv–lxx.

ruins; Pixon and Stilesweek are mere barns; a cow-shed alone remains at Blackmoorham. For centuries each of these farms housed and supported a whole family. Absorbed now into larger units, they still testify, if only by their names, to the thoroughness of earlier settlement. In all the eighteen square miles of the ancient parish there are only three farm-names recorded for the first time after 1320. All the others were in use before that date.[1]

The settlement of Tavistock has been illustrated here by detailed reference to its topography, its place-names, and the extant charters. In one respect, however, Tavistock was not a typical west-Devon parish. Its development was no doubt actively promoted by its monastic lords. As the seat of an important abbey, a centre of hospitality much visited by travellers, and ruled by an abbot who was in touch with the heads of similar communities elsewhere, Tavistock would be more abreast of the times than most Devon manors. Already in 1086 there was a cornmill in the abbey precinct, serving the domestic needs of the house; and since fewer than a hundred such mills are enumerated in all Devon, as against three hundred and fifty-one in Somerset, it seems likely that the water-mill was a technical improvement brought in from the east: one which, over most of Devonshire, had not yet ousted the old-fashioned hand-quern.[2] Again, a resident lord abbot would make for centralized control. Numbers of petty thegns were to be found in the vicinity, each of them so far independent that, in the Domesday phrase, "he could go with his land to any lord he chose." The Tavistock thegns enjoyed no such freedom; "they could not be separated from the church."[3]

These are factors which must certainly not be overlooked. Nevertheless the picture that emerges was probably reproduced, with local variations, in many another Devon parish. If we have interpreted the evidence correctly, its main features were: an original infiltration of pioneers directed by the king's reeves; the cultivation of the more immediately fertile tracts for the king or the king's grantees by slave labour recruited from British captives, English criminals, and ruined freemen; the gradual coloni-

---

[1] Buctor, a name which in recent times has been transferred to Crebor, is first recorded, as Bokatorre, in 1336; Artiscombe in 1409; and Crease, as Creyspedoune, in 1352.
[2] M. Hodgen, 'Domesday Water Mills', *Antiquity*, XIII, 1939, pp. 261 sqq.
[3] DB IV, p. 163.

E

zation of the valleys by peasants holding in severalty, who paid certain dues to the king or the lord of the manor and eked out the produce of their *hams* and *tuns* by outfield tillage; the establishment, usually in forest clearings, of new hamlets peopled for the most part by serfs, with some addition of free-born but poverty-stricken labourers; the piecemeal enclosure of the arable; and the transformation of the last remaining slaves into bond tenants. The imprint of this process on the landscape is to be seen negatively in the reduction of the wooded area, positively in the deep lanes overshadowed by enormous hedge-banks, in the minute enclosures pushed up from the foothills to the edges of the upland wastes, and in hundreds of manor-houses, farmsteads, and parish churches. By the early fourteenth century the main lines of settlement were complete. Much remained to be done, but it would be done within the existing framework, by gradual extension of a pattern already firmly drawn.

CHAPTER III

THE SOCIAL STRUCTURE

FROM Domesday Book, which had so much to tell us about the territorial possessions of the abbey on the eve and morrow of the Norman Conquest, we also gain the earliest direct information about rural society on the Tavistock estates. Unfortunately that information is expressed in somewhat cryptic terms. The language of Domesday Book is not the language of the Old English laws and charters, nor is it that of the later court rolls and manorial extents. It is a language peculiar to king William's great inquest; and no one key will unlock all its meanings. To interpret the Domesday of Tavistock, therefore, it will be necessary to examine it against a wider context. We shall have to ask what the record has to say of Devonshire at large; how its data can be reconciled with Devonshire topography and place-names; how it fits in with what we know from other sources about rural society in the Old English period; and what retrospective light is thrown upon it by later documents.

The first thing that strikes us in the Domesday record is that the thegns as a class have almost disappeared. It was a class which had embraced men of the most diverse economic standing, from the king's thegn, lord of many villages, to the petty squire who might be little if at all better off than some of his peasant neighbours. On the eve of the Norman Conquest these petty thegns were much in evidence in the vicinity of Tavistock. Two of them shared the small manor of Ottery in Lamerton; another owned Warne and Burntown in Marytavy; and four of them were settled within the manor of Tavistock itself on land which they were not at liberty to sell. They probably held it on lease from the abbot, paying but a trifling rent, the condition of their tenure being that they must perform the military service due from his land in time of war, and ride with him as his bodyguard when he visited his far-off manors. There is some reason to believe that by this time the rural thegns had taken the ordinary business of the hundred courts into their own hands, in much the same way as those greater men, the king's thegns, are known to have engrossed the business of the shire courts.[1]

The impact of the Norman Conquest upon the rural aristocracy was nothing short of disastrous. Of the introduction of knight service on the Tavistock estates, and the endowment of the abbot's French knights with former thegn-lands, enough was said in the first chapter. All over Devonshire the process was repeated. Two or three king's thegns managed somehow to weather the storm, but fewer than twenty of the lesser men escaped. By the date of the inquest all the other lordships of Devon had passed into foreign hands.

The agricultural population is enumerated under five main categories. Two of these, the *liberi homines* and the *sochemanni*, will not concern us here. Between thirteen and fourteen thousand *liberi homines* are to be found in Norfolk, Suffolk, and Essex; the remainder, fewer than two hundred altogether, are scattered over eleven other counties, none south of the Bristol Channel. The sokemen, or 'men subject to the jurisdiction of a lord', are most numerous in Lincolnshire and East Anglia. They are not found in any western county. It is clear from his name that the *liber homo* is in some specially emphatic sense a Free Man; and that the sokeman is so far free that one great species of freehold tenure, and that not the least coveted, will come to be known as 'socage'. But the Devonshire Domesday knows no peasant of higher rank than the *villanus*; and in many parts of England the *villanus* is already so little free that 'villein' will soon come to be synonymous with 'serf'. This is one of the great pitfalls of Domesday terminology, and we must be on our guard against it. For there are "free *villani*", even in Norfolk;[2] and that being so, we cannot take it for granted that the entire rural population of Devon is sunk in thraldom, simply because it is not labelled 'free'.[3]

---

[1] In one passage of the Exon Domesday the doomsmen of the local court are referred to as "the men of the hundred" (DB IV, p. 277); in another as "the thegns" (*ibid.*, p. 117).

[2] Vinogradoff, *English Society in the Eleventh Century*, p. 317.

[3] In 1279 the tenants of Tawstock (not Tavistock, as Vinogradoff supposed) sought the protection of the courts against their lord. Their plea was rejected by a bench of eight judges, headed by the Chief Justice Hengham, on the ground that the Domesday account of Tawstock did not mention

In the last chapter we classified the tillers of the soil into three categories: the freeman, the freedman, and the slave. But it is well to bear in mind that the distinction between the two first-named is one on which Old English law and custom were not careful to insist. One eminent scholar has suggested that it was deliberately blurred far back in the dawn of English history, perhaps even before the Anglo-Saxons invaded Britain.[1] Whether or not that was the case, there are certainly passages in the Old English laws where the term *ceorl* embraces not only the freeman cultivating his inherited land, but also the *gebur* who has been planted on a holding by his lord.[2] Further, on the eve of the Norman Conquest we find peasants called *ceorls* owing their lord services which both in quantity and kind point to servile antecedents.[3] We also find the *Rectitudines* putting the *gebur* and *kotsetla* on a level with the freeman, apparently for no other reason than that, being householders, they pay Church dues from which the slave is exempt. *Ceorl*, then, it seems, is a term used to denote both a genus and a species: a genus including several degrees of subordinate peasant, such as the *gebur* and the *kotsetla*, and a species in which a measure of subordination is linked with free birth and the ownership of heritable property: the *ceorl* proper. This makes for confusion, and unfortunately in Domesday Book we find a similar double use of the term *villanus*, which is the Latin equivalent of *ceorl*. It is not unusual to read that the *villani* of a manor have so much land and so many teams, and then to find that the only peasants on that manor are *bordarii*. This is the generic use; the specific, which is found in the majority of entries, divides the rural population into three main groups, *villani*, *bordarii*, and *servi*.

---

sokemen but only *villani* and slaves. As Vinogradoff observes: "There does not seem to be any possible doubt that Hengham and his companions were entirely wrong" in their construction of the record (*Villainage in England*, p. 119; cf. *The Growth of the Manor*, p. 378).

[1] Chadwick, *Studies on Anglo-Saxon Institutions*, pp. 400–11.

[2] *Ibid.*, pp. 86, 87.

[3] Stenton, *Anglo-Saxon England*, p. 469. The record does not say whether or not their holdings will revert to the lord when they die. On this ground Professor Stenton holds that they were "in origin unquestionably free". But can the argument from silence be safely pressed so far? Vinogradoff supports the view stated in the text, that heavy services are normally an indication of servile origin (*English Society in the Eleventh Century*, p. 466).

The distribution of these groups on the Tavistock estates in 1086, as recorded in the Exon Domesday, is shown in the following table.

TABLE I

A. DEMESNE MANORS

	Villani	Bordarii	Servi	Others
Tavistock	17	20	12	
Milton Abbot	14	12	12	
Leigh, with Liddaton	4	5	3	
Hatherleigh	26	0	6	6 *cosceti*
Abbotsham	21	6	4	
Worthygate	6	5	1	
Burrington	15	11	4	4 *buri* and 4 *porcarii*
Denbury	4	5	2	
Plymstock	4	9	5	
	111	73	49	14
Askerswell	7	17	4	2 *gablatores*
Poorton	5	3	0	
TOTALS	123	93	53	16

B. KNIGHTS' FEES

	Villani	Bordarii	Servi	Others
Tavistock				
Ermenald	?	?	?	
Ralph	1	0	0	3 *cosceti*
Hugo	1	6	2	
Robert	3	6	2	
R. de Tilio	1	4	0	
Geoffrey	0	1	0	
Liddaton	5	2	3	

TABLE I: B. KNIGHTS' FEES *(cont.)*

	Villani	Bordarii	Servi	Others
Hatherleigh				
Nigel	0	0	1	5 *cosceti*
Walter	7	2	1	
Geoffrey	4	0	1	
Ralph	1	4	0	
Thornbury	10	6	3	
Burrington				
Geoffrey	3	3	0	
Romansleigh				
Nigel	7	6	4	
Robert	3	4	3	
Houndtor	2	4	2	
Coffinswell	10	12	4	
Sheviock	6	17	4	
Antony	12	15	4	
Rame	4	15	4	
Trewornan	9	0	2	
Penharget	6	0	0	
Tolcarne	0	2	0	
TOTALS	95	109	40	8

C. OTHERS

	Villani	Bordarii	Servi	Others
Burrington				
William Capra	3	1	0	
Raddon	1	0	1	
TOTALS	4	1	1	

Villani	222
Bordarii	203
Servi	94
Cosceti	14
Others	10

543 + Ermenald's tenants.

In seeking to interpret this information, we shall do well to begin with the lowest class of all. There is no ambiguity in the position of the Domesday *servus*: he is a slave, the *theow* of the Old
English laws.[1] He can be bought or sold, and a passage in the Sussex Domesday implies that such transactions will normally take
place in the open market, at an average price of twenty shillings,
or eight times the value of an ox.[2] There is only one manor in
Devon where slaves appear unambiguously as owning land and
ploughs; and the case is so exceptional as to suggest a mistake in
the wording of the record.[3] Nearly always they are mentioned in
connection with the lord's plough-teams. It seems clear that agricultural work on the demesne is their usual occupation, and that
rarely if ever have they any holdings of their own.[4] There are over
five thousand of them in Devonshire, where they form twenty-six
per cent. of the enumerated population.[5] In the midland counties
the proportion is much less, and in York, Lincoln, Rutland, and
Huntingdon there are no slaves at all. Elsewhere we find indica-

[1] Maitland, *op. cit.*, p. 27; Stenton, *op. cit.*, p. 469.

[2] Chadwick, *op. cit.*, p. 2; Maitland, *op. cit.*, p. 33.

[3] The scribes of the Exchequer seem to have thought so in other cases.
Thus, at Gildescota the Exon Domesday is so worded as to suggest that two
slaves owned plough-oxen, but the Exchequer version does not support this
interpretation: it gives both slaves and oxen to the lord, leaving the *villani*
with a team apart (DB IV, p. 391; I, p. 113 *b*). Again, at Bolewis, where two
villani and two slaves are said to hold a ferling of land between them, the
Exchequer significantly turns the slaves into *bordarii* (IV, p. 316; I, p. 114 *a*).
At Bochelanda Drogo has one ferling and one team in demesne, "and a
slave dwells on the other ferling," apparently the sole inhabitant of the
manor; but the Exchequer Domesday reveals the presence of another slave,
and also of a *villanus* who is probably the real owner of the team (IV, p. 120;
I, p. 102 *d*). At Buckfast "the abbot has ten slaves who have two ploughs";
we are not told whether the ploughs are for use on any but the abbot's land.
There remains the one instance mentioned in the text. This is at Bosleia,
where the lord has one and a half teams in demesne, and the *villani* have one
team and the rest of the land, but the recorded population consists entirely
of *servi*. One cannot help suspecting that here again a *villanus* or two have
been omitted from the record.

[4] Vinogradoff, *op. cit.*, p. 463. Maitland holds that the south-western *servi*
are "too many to be menials"; but the average seems to be about five to a
manor. Ballard points out that the Domesday of Middlesex, which goes into
detail on the size of the tenants' holdings, nowhere assigns any land to a slave
(*The Domesday Inquest*, p. 151).

[5] There is a wide discrepancy between Burnard's figures, which are
adopted here, and Ellis's. See DA XXXIX, 1907, p. 202; Ellis, *General Introduction to Domesday*, II, pp. 435, 436. Burnard's figures are:

tions that the process of emancipation has been accelerated since the coming of the Normans. At Hayles in Gloucestershire there were formerly a dozen slaves, but the new lord has "made them free", thereby casting off the burden of their maintenance. Maitland calls attention to the decrease in the number of *servi* and increase of *bordarii* in Essex during the twenty years preceding Domesday. He justly infers that "there has been a considerable change in rural economy."[1] By 1086, as we can see from Domesday Book, this transition from slavery to serfdom is already complete in some counties; in others it is still in progress. Devonshire, as usual, is in no hurry to overtake the rest of England. Yet even in Devon there are something like a hundred manors without any slaves. Their presence or absence is quite unrelated to the size of the demesne.[2] On the great manor of Otterton the abbot of Mont St Michel has six ploughs, but no slaves to drive them. On the nine demesne manors of Tavistock the number of slaves is below the county average, being twenty per cent. of the enumerated population. At Tavistock itself the abbot has twelve slaves to five ploughs, and the proportion on the other manors is much the same.

The lord who has no slaves to do his ploughing must depend either upon wage-labour or upon the week-work of servile tenants. These, as we saw in the last chapter, may be either *kotsetlan*, cottagers, or *geburas*, tenant-farmers, both free in the eyes of the Church, but still bound to their lord by many servile obligations. The Domesday name for the *kotsetla* is *bordarius*. Now and then the record condescends to use the vernacular, and speaks of *cosceti*, putting them in the middle rank normally occupied by the *bordarii*.[3] That these are alternative names for the same type

---

	villani	8508 (43·38 per cent.)
	bordarii	4667 (23·80 per cent.)
	servi	5178 (26·40 per cent.)
Ellis gives:	*villani*	8070 (46·86 per cent.)
	bordarii	4936 (28·31 per cent.)
	servi	3295 (18·89 per cent.)

[1] *Domesday Book and Beyond*, p. 35; cf. Vinogradoff, *op. cit.*, p. 468.

[2] Clapham appears to suggest such a relationship, when he speaks of a lord having "demesne enough to employ slave ploughmen" (*Concise Economic History of Britain*, p. 71).

[3] So at Sladona, Coritona, Surintona, Melefort, Sutecoma, Hadreleia, Kari, Sidreham, and Mora (DB IV, pp. 111, 112, 164, 295).

of cottager is shown by the fact that we never find them both together in one entry. 'Bordar' is a term introduced from Normandy to denote a cottager: one who, unlike the slave, is established under a roof of his own. A passage in the Herefordshire Domesday informs us that the bordars at Ewyas worked one day a week on their lord's demesne.[1] Such week-work is one of the recognized characteristics of servile tenure. Bordars appear but seldom under that name in later documents; but in 1260 there were five at Otterton, who were bound to do any work demanded of them on all Mondays, Wednesdays, and Fridays throughout the year; and in proof of their servile status they paid tallage at Martinmas.[2]

On some manors we come across an inferior type of cottager styled a *cotarius*. He is always named after the bordars, and so unimportant is he that twice at least the Exchequer Domesday ignores his very existence.[3] Judging from the Middlesex Domesday, the *cotarii* as a rule hold less than five acres: sometimes only a garden plot, sometimes not even that. It is possible that they are free-born labourers, younger sons of the *villani*, who earn their living as handicraftsmen or farm-workers. Later evidence, as well as intrinsic probability, suggests the existence of such a class; and if its members are not *cotarii* they must be sought among the bordars or the less prosperous of the *villani*.

For the moment we may pass over the more substantial type of serf, the *gebur*, and consider the freemen, or peasants who though acknowledging a lord are not his property nor his tenants-at-will, and do not owe him week-work. If such peasants existed in the Devon of 1086, they must have been set down as *villani*, for the Exon Domesday recognizes no higher class. It is under this heading that we must also look for such thegns as may have lost their status through the Norman Conquest but continued to occupy their former lands. Nutley, a Tavistock hamlet situated on the fringe of the moor, provides a possible case in point. In 1066 it was held by one of the abbot's thegns; twenty years later it is held by the French knight Ralph, who keeps no oxen there, nor any livestock, and in fact has no demesne land. Its population con-

---

[1] Vinogradoff, *op. cit.*, p. 456.

[2] Oliver, p. 256. For bordars owing week-work on the lands of the Templars, see Vinogradoff, *Villainage in England*, p. 149 *n*.

[3] At Axminster and Brixham (DB i, pp. 100 *b*, 109 *a*; iv, pp. 75, 299).

sists of one *villanus* and three cottagers, with four plough-oxen between them. It may well be that this *villanus* is the former thegn, compelled perhaps to pay a higher rent, but still not reduced to absolute servitude. A parallel case is recorded at Witheridge, where "there still remain" (*adhuc manent*) on former thegnland three *villani* paying five shillings a year to the lord of the manor.[1] We read of one *villanus* who holds an entire manor "in demesne",[2] and of others who are so far independent that they can take over the manor under contract with their lord and run it for their own profit.[3] The Devonshire Domesday speaks very frequently of *villani* whose obligation to the lord consists only or chiefly in the payment of a money rent, and it does not distinguish them from the other tenants by a special name. At Askerswell in Dorset the abbot of Tavistock has two *gablatores* or *censores* who pay him fifteen shillings a year; but these terms are not found in Devon. Rents vary in amount from half a crown to ten shillings.[4] In the valley of the Otter there is one *villanus* whose rent is shared between two Norman lords, each of whom is accordingly said to have a "demi-villein".[5]

If we look somewhat ahead, we shall find no lack of freemen on the Tavistock estates. At the spot where the road from Tavistock to Lamerton was formerly crossed by the old highway from Morwellham to Brentor there stood, in the twelfth century, a milestone, or *mil-(ge)met*. This gave its name to an adjacent group of fields and meadows, to a farmhouse in the midst of them, now desolate and overgrown with nettles, and also to a family which long made its home there. Bartholomew "de Millimet" attests a charter in the time of abbot Herbert, that is, about 1186; and his descendants held their ground there for the best part of three hundred years. In surveys drawn up for the abbey they are said to hold Milemead "by ancient tenure". They had received no charter from the abbot, and needed none, for the whole countryside would swear that they had been there from time immemorial. They owed the abbot certain dues: a 'relief' of 12s. 6d. when one Milemead inherited from another; a yearly rent of 5s. 6d. pay-

---

[1] DB IV, p. 88.   [2] Madescama, *ibid.*, IV, p. 376.
[3] Herstanahaia, *ibid.*, IV, p. 371.
[4] Assacota, Haletrou, 2s. 6d.; Lacoma, 3s.; Haiserstona, 3s. 4d.; Stanehus, 5s.; Colum, 10s. (*ibid.*, IV, pp. 388, 393, 316, 169; I, pp. 113 c, 117 c).
[5] *Ibid.*, IV, pp. 321, 378.

able on St Rumon's Day; a penny a year for Sheriff's Aid; attendance at the three-weekly manor court; and two boonworks annually, a ploughing and a reaping. Milemead was one of several ancient freeholds near Tavistock. The Colmestor family, who took their name from a promontory a mile lower down the valley, were people of the same class: one of them, in 1426, is styled a "frankelyn".[1] They paid two shillings at Michaelmas, and the same 'relief' as the Milemeads; and they owed suit of court on the two law-days. At Werrington the freemen who constituted the jury of the manor court acted as a standing committee of the tenants. On the Michaelmas law-day, having completed their year of office, they elected two other freemen, who then co-opted ten more to act with them for the ensuing twelvemonth. It would seem that this practice was normal throughout Devon, for it is quite usual to find, on the thirteenth-century Assize Rolls, the letter *e*, for *electores*, placed against two names in each jury-list.[2]

It is difficult to believe that the Devon of 1086 knew no peasant intermediate in status between the freedman and the lord. There were free *villani* in other counties at that date: can we suppose the franklins of Devon to be all of later origin? If not, we must conclude that the ancestors of the Milemeads and Colmestors are described as *villani* in the Exon Domesday. This conclusion is not in the least repugnant to the findings of Domesday scholars.[3] Nor is there a single entry in the record which obliges us to think of the Devonshire *villanus* as a serf. We do indeed find manors where he appears to be doing all the work of the demesne,

[1] W. D Bdle 39, no. 9.

[2] Werrington court roll, 25 October 1365: "xij elexerunt Nicholaum Bate et Nicholaum Yunge ad elegendos ad se x, ut ex illis fieri possint xij secundum consuetudinem manerii per annum. Qui elexerunt ad se . . ." Ten names follow, the bearers of which are then sworn in; "et remanent per totum annum." The custom was abandoned at some date between 1396 and 1462.

[3] "Some of the general customs applied to the villein class disclose in its midst a considerable element reckoned to be free" (Vinogradoff, *English Society in the Eleventh Century*, p. 453). "In many villages in which Domesday Book mentions no peasant of higher rank than a *villanus*, medieval records reveal the existence of freeholders whose titles, to all appearance, were very ancient. In some cases there is good early evidence that a group of Domesday *villani* included men whom the *Rectitudines* would have described as *geneatas*" (Stenton, *op. cit.*, p. 471).

but there is nothing to show that he does it as a matter of servile obligation; he may equally well be a poor franklin taking the lord's pay for services rendered without thereby forfeiting his birthright as a freeman.[1]

In what category, then, are we to look for the *geburas?* There is one manor where they appear under their vernacular name. This is at Burrington, where the abbot of Tavistock has fifteen *villani*, eleven *bordarii*, four *servi*, and four *buri*. Two passages in the Hampshire Domesday inform us that *buri* is a synonym for *coliberti*, an unquestionably servile designation.[2] There are twenty-five *coliberti* at Werrington, and they appear on one other Devon manor; but *coliberti* and *buri* combined are fewer than forty in this county and fewer than a thousand in the whole of England.[3] It may be that they are particularized because they have only recently emerged from landless slavery. The *gebur*, however, was one of the most familiar figures in Old English society. The further back we go into English history, the more numerous the slaves appear; in the seventh century even the *ceorls* had been slave-owners.[4] But the tide of emancipation, as we have seen, was flowing strongly by the time king William ordered his great inquest. It is in every way probable that quite a number of slave-born or slave-descended peasants, occupying their land at the will of the lord and owing him week-work, are included among the upper ranks of the peasantry in Domesday Book.

If, however, the *villani* of Devonshire were in the main a free class, we shall have to seek the *geburas* chiefly or exclusively among the bordars, and to regard the latter as being in the main a servile class. We must also hold, as a corollary, that peasants of the most diverse economic standing are to be found in each. It must be confessed that the whole weight of received opinion is against this view. With impressive unanimity our leading authorities insist that the difference between *villanus* and *bordarius* is not legal but economic; the bordar is "economically inferior" to the

---

[1] At Brai, Holna, Biuda, Wellecoma, and Wiuleswilla there are demesne oxen, but no slaves or bordars to drive them; only, it seems, *villani*, who also have plough-teams of their own (DB IV, pp. 119, 285, 365, 380, 385).

[2] Vinogradoff, *op. cit.*, p. 468.

[3] Clistona, Devon, has a group of seven *coliberti* (DB IV, p. 87). Cf. Ballard. *op. cit.*, p. 155.

[4] Chadwick, *op. cit.*, p. 127; Clapham, *op. cit.*, p. 42.

villanus.[1] Nevertheless, there is a point at which the economic distinction converges with the legal. The slave who can be put up for sale, and the serf who can be tasked and taxed at will, are assets in quite another sense than the freeman who pays his rent and does a boonwork or two annually. In any careful valuation of a lord's property we should expect to find them kept apart. Moreover, the economic inferiority of the *bordarius* is by no means universally apparent. Mr Lennard has examined the entries relating to some 10,733 *villani* spread over thirty-two counties. He finds that the average number of plough-beasts works out at 2·9 to a *villanus*. For Devonshire the average is 3·0. Of 512 *villani* whose teams are unmistakably enumerated in the Devonshire Domesday, 66·1 per cent. possessed three oxen or more.[2] Nevertheless, it is easy enough to find *villani* with one ox or none.[3] Let us admit that this is not in itself conclusive evidence of poverty; a man who can support himself by pastoral husbandry may well dispense with plough-beasts. But this applies to the bordar as well. Let us also admit that the bordar, whose very name indicates a cottager with few resources in stock or land, is usually a poor man; even so there are exceptions. If we look at those manors where there are no slaves and no *villani*, we shall find bordars owning one or two oxen each.[4] If we extend the search to manors where there are slaves as well as bordars, and proceed to rule out the slaves, we shall find bordars with two, three, four, or even six beasts.[5] And when we are told that six *villani* and five bordars have sixteen oxen between them, what justification have we for assuming that one group has fewer than the other? While the record of many manors is so worded as to imply that the oxen

---

[1] Stenton, *op. cit.*, p. 470; Clapham, *op. cit.*, p. 72 (the *bordarii* are "the smaller men").

[2] *Economic Journal*, LVI, 1946, pp. 244 sqq.

[3] I have counted fifteen manors where the *villani* have no oxen at all; two where the average works out at a fraction of an ox; six where the average is one each; and sixteen where it is a fraction between one and two. Where there are both *villani* and *bordarii* it is impossible to strike an average for one class or the other; and where six *villani*, for example, are said to have three teams, we cannot assume that each man has four oxen: they may be quite unevenly distributed. On the validity of the equation 8 oxen = 1 team, see EHR LXV, 1951, pp. 67 sqq.

[4] As at Alwinestona, Colrige, and Bremelcoma (DB IV, pp. 301, 327, 421).

[5] Bera, Bicatona (2 oxen); Cridia (3·75); Bochelanda, Doneuoldehamma, Beneadona (4); Denesburga (6), *ibid.*, pp. 344, 421; 319; 122, 196, 290; 446.

all belong to the lord, or some to the lord and some to the *villani*, there are entries which suggest that this formula conceals the true state of affairs. At Webbery, for instance, the lessee of the manor, according to the Exon Domesday, has a virgate and a half and one plough-team in demesne; he has also four bordars, who are not credited with any oxen. But the Exchequer version omits all reference to the demesne; it merely says "four bordars there have one plough-team."[1] Evidently these four are tilling the soil on their own account, with oxen that 'belong' to them; their holdings are rated collectively at half a virgate. But they and their oxen are all "in demesne" because the lord has a right to their services, a right limited only by the custom of the manor. At Torilanda "Roger and his men" have one full team, the "men" being three bordars, with a slave added.[2] At Beneadona the lessee has two bordars, "and with them one plough"; in other words, these rustics, with eight oxen between them, can be called upon to plough for the lord.[3] A last example may be quoted from Tavistock. Geoffrey, one of the abbot's knights, "has one ferling of land, and he has there one plough, and one bordar, and six head of cattle, and thirty sheep."[4] Is this bordar a solitary hind, a farm-labourer with no arable of his own? He may be so, but in the light of the examples just quoted we cannot rule out the possibility that oxen and ploughland are both 'his', and that Geoffrey, while reserving his legal right to evict the man and confiscate his chattels, in practice contents himself with making him pay a rent.

On manor after manor there must have been poverty-stricken bordars living side by side with *villani* not a whit more prosperous. Yet the record puts them firmly into different classes. "Here are six *villani* and four bordars." By what criterion then are they distinguished? When the economic test breaks down so frequently, what other test can be applied but that of legal status? Its application would present little difficulty; as Clapham remarks, "there would always be the oldest free inhabitant of the village who remembered very well, or had been told by his grandmother,

---

[1] DB IV, p. 433 (Wibeberia); I, p. 117 *b* (Wiberie). [2] DB IV, p. 315.
[3] *Ibid.*, p. 290. Similar entries occur in the Cornish Domesday. At Trehauoc there is one team "between" two bordars and their lord. At Aisseton, where four bordars account for half a virgate, and the lord for as much again, lord and bordars share three oxen (DB IV, pp. 237, 238).
[4] *Ibid.*, p. 163.

that the ancestors of John Attewood, the shabby fellow whose hut was where his name tells, had been *servi.*"[1]

It would be rash to decide so difficult a question on evidence from one county alone, even if that evidence were clearer and more abundant than it is. We must content ourselves with pointing out that poor as the bordar very often was, many a *villanus* was no better off. If the Devonshire Domesday does not refute, neither does it confirm the notion that economic inferiority was the essential mark of the bordar. It permits us to hold, as at least a tenable hypothesis, that in this county the three main Domesday classes do roughly correspond with the Old English freemen, freedmen-serfs, and slaves.

Let us now turn from Domesday Book to later records, in order to learn what changes took place in the condition of the three classes during the next two hundred years.

If we are right in believing that the predecessors of the franklin class, the ancestors of the Milemeads and Colmestors, figure among the *villani* of the Tavistock Domesday, we must conclude that neither in status nor in tenure were they appreciably shaken by the Norman Conquest. But besides the ancient freeholds there were others which originated in grants made by the abbot, sometimes in fulfilment of a special bargain. Thus at Kilworthy a certain tenure, rated at three and a half ferlings, is held on conditions which, as to relief, boonworks, and Sheriff's Aid, closely resemble the tenure of Milemead, and as to suit of court, that of Colmestor. The tenant, however, is under the additional obligation of carrying the lord abbot's writ to Askerswell in Dorset whenever called upon to do so.[2] We may think this no light journey: the best part of a hundred miles each way; and what miles! But after all, the knight of Askerswell will not need to be summoned very frequently. And then the messenger from Kilworthy pays no rent at all. Kilworthy lies at the north-eastern corner of the demesne, and near the edge of Heathfield. Plainly it was a 'newtake' from that great waste, brought into cultivation by some enterprising countryman with the approval of the abbot, who allowed him to carve out for himself a freehold on these honourable terms.

[1] *Op. cit.*, p. 94.   [2] Extent of Hurdwick, 1387.

Another method of creating freeholds was to grant out small plots of ground as fractions of knights' fees. How small the plots might be is shown by an example that occurred during the abbacy of Baldwin: that is, between 1174 and 1184. This abbot made a bargain with Henry Daunay, lord of Sheviock, to whom he gave up two Cornish acres at Trewrickle in exchange for the half-virgate in Tavistock which that knight inherited from Ermenald, his Domesday ancestor.[1] The half-virgate has been identified with Taviton. Having this fief now at his disposal, the abbot decided to grant it out again, acre by acre. In the event the plan was not carried out, for only one acre near St Margaret's chapel was dealt with in this fashion;[2] but the humble burgess to whom that acre was granted held it under the same feudal obligations as the mail-clad Daunays who preceded him. Of course he did not go to the wars. The knights themselves by this time stayed at home as often as not, discharging their obligations by paying scutage and so providing the Crown with money to hire soldiers. A fraction of that scutage would henceforth be paid by the acre-tenant. In other details his tenure closely resembled that of the ancient freeholders. Similar grants were made very frequently, not indeed at Taviton, but elsewhere on the Tavistock estates, during the next hundred years.

The freeholders, whether they held by ancient tenure, or in socage, or by knight service, were a dignified element in rural society. Their pre-eminence was respected even when they rendered labour service; thus, at harvest, they did not themselves reap the lord's corn, but stood, wand in hand, directing the labours of the humbler tenants.[3] All over Devonshire they were to be found in appreciable numbers. The extensive manor of Hartland, in the north-west of the county, was found in 1301 to include no fewer than eighty-seven free tenants.[4] In East Teignmouth all but twenty-three and a half acres was freehold land.[5] We have seen that on the manors of Tavistock Abbey the free peasants constituted a far from negligible force.

[1] ETC XLI.   [2] Extent of Hurdwick, 1416, m. 16.
[3] So the free tenants of two ferlings at Woodovis and two at Buctor (Extent of Hurdwick, 1387).
[4] Chope, 'The Early History of the Manor of Hartland', DA XXXIV, 1902, p. 430.
[5] Ex inf. Dr W. G. Hoskins.

F

It is necessary to insist upon the point in face of the prevalent belief that by the thirteenth century, if not earlier, the bulk of the rural population had been degraded into serfdom. This is not in itself unlikely. A succession of bad harvests, a cattle-plague, a heavy tax, would spell ruin for small farmers whose livelihood was wrung from fifteen or twenty acres of indifferent soil. If, in addition, the lord was grasping, there were lawyers in plenty to abet him with a remorseless application of feudal principles. A widespread depression of the peasantry on the morrow of the Norman Conquest is well established.[1] The evidence for it is however drawn chiefly from the midlands and southern England. It is well known that serfdom never took root in Kent. In East Anglia the descendants of the Domesday sokemen maintained their free status;[2] so too in Lincolnshire and many villages of Leicestershire. Turning back to the south-west, we have to note several factors which told in favour of the poor rustic who found himself upon the brink of servitude.

In the first place, Devon at this period contained vast tracts of undeveloped land. Apart from the great moors, which have always defied cultivation, there were large patches of heath, fen, and woodland all over the county waiting to be tackled by stout-hearted pioneers. The government, which on any rational view of public policy might have been expected to promote such enterprise, instead subjected it to the rigour of the forest laws. Under this code essarts, or newtakes from the waste, were punishable as trespasses upon the king's demesne. In 1188 a number of small fines, amounting altogether to £10 9s., were imposed upon various Devon townships for such essarts.[3] Finally, in 1204, the county subscribed five thousand marks to purchase from king John a charter of disforestation.[4] This charter, issued on the 18th of May 1204 and deposited for safe keeping in Tavistock Abbey,[5] freed the whole of Devonshire from forest law, with the two exceptions of Dartmoor and Exmoor. The way was now open for extensive clearance and enclosure; and thousands of Devon place-names bear witness to the intensity with which the work

---

[1] Maitland, *op. cit.*, pp. 61 sqq.
[2] Douglas, *The Social Structure of Medieval East Anglia*, 1927, p. 129.
[3] PRS XXXVIII, p. 169; cf. *ibid.*, XVI, p. 29, and XXII, p. 62.
[4] *Ibid.*, LVI (N.S. XVIII), p. 85.   [5] *Reg. Stapeldon*, p. 139.

was pressed on. One case in point has already been quoted: the enclosure from the waste at Kilworthy. There was room for innumerable similar bargains between lord and tenant, in nearly every instance leading to the creation of a new freehold tenement on what had hitherto been virgin soil.

Another mainstay of freedom was provided by the ancient mining industry of the south-west. The second half of the twelfth century saw a rapid and considerable expansion of the Dartmoor tin trade, which was fostered by the central government and regulated by the so-called 'assize of mines'. The details of this code have not been preserved, but it may well have anticipated the provisions of the charter issued by king John in 1201, in extending to all working tinners throughout Devon and Cornwall the privileges of tenants on royal demesne. Under John's charter, any serf who managed to stake out a tin-claim was assured of protection by the royal courts. The Cornish landowners protested; and in 1215, amid the turmoil which preceded Magna Carta, they prevailed upon the Crown to declare that they should not lose, by reason of the stannaries, any dues or services they were accustomed to have from their tenants and serfs.[1] If any such concession was made to the neighbouring county, it was speedily revoked, for in 1222 the sheriff was ordered to put the stannary of Devon into the same condition as before the barons' war. In 1251 a royal mandate forbade Devon landowners to exact from the Dartmoor tinners other dues and services than those which had been customary, or to molest them in their ancient liberties;[2] and six months later the stannary charter of 1201 was solemnly confirmed.[3] The profits accruing from the mines to the Exchequer had brought about a virtual alliance between the Crown and the working tinners: an alliance which offered to the humblest countryman the chance of becoming, or remaining, his own master.

A slightly imperfect copy has been preserved of a letter written by archbishop Theobald to Walter, abbot of Tavistock (c. 1155– c. 1168), from which it appears that certain labour services due from the tenants had been remitted by Walter's predecessor.[4] The lord of a manor situated, like Tavistock, at the very edge of

---

[1] *Rotuli Chartarum*, p. 206.   [2] CPR 1247–58, p. 111.
[3] *Cal. Charter Rolls*, 1226–57, p. 380.
[4] ETC xviii; cf. DA lxxv, 1943, p. 250.

the mining region, was exposed to the full blast of stannary privilege; and the wisest course open to him was to meet the situation with a good grace. One way of doing so was to set up a borough. For *borough*, in the twelfth century, meant a place in which the tenements were held by burgage tenure; and burgage tenure was a species of freehold. Not only was the burgess at liberty to sell, bequeath, assign, or underlet his tenement without interference from the lord; he was also completely exempt from the personal incidents of serfdom. As a free suitor of the borough court, he paid few or no seignorial dues except a small burgage rent, and perhaps a 'relief' when the property changed hands. Occasionally, it is true, a lord, when introducing burgage tenure, might expressly deny borough privileges to his serfs, as the earl of Devon did at Plympton;[1] or he might keep in being some form of manorial service. This the abbot did at Tavistock, but the services he retained were not incompatible with free status. There is reason to believe that Tavistock, at the date of its transition from a rural township to a borough town, was inhabited by some eighteen cottagers. Whatever manorial services they had rendered in the past were now waived by the abbot, except in two particulars. One or other of these original burgage holders must go to Plymstock with a message to the reeve there whenever a fresh supply of corn was needed to replenish the abbot's granary. Secondly, they and their successors must provide a bodyguard whenever a dead monk lay in the abbey church at night awaiting burial.[2]

One of our leading authorities on English boroughs considers it possible that in some cases burgage tenure, or features of that tenure, may have been introduced into a rural market-centre without any formal act by the lord.[3] So far as Tavistock is concerned, that possibility may be ruled out. The formal partition of the Domesday manor into a borough of Tavistock and a rural manor of Hurdwick, and the brisk traffic in burgage property that went on at the close of the twelfth century, leave no room for doubt that the abbot had set up his borough with the avowed intention of developing the place on urban lines. It is less certain

[1] Ballard, *British Borough Charters*, 1216–1307, p. 141.
[2] Finberg, 'The Borough of Tavistock', DA LXXIX, 1947, pp. 129 sqq.
[3] Tait, introduction to *British Borough Charters*, 1216–1307, p. li.

that any such design was entertained at Hatherleigh and Denbury, two villages on which the abbots of Tavistock at unknown dates conferred the name of boroughs with a modest allowance of borough liberties. Still less can we be sure of the innumerable petty boroughs, so called, which are to be found in every corner of Devon. These village boroughs are a local phenomenon, and apparently *sui generis*. No complete list of them has ever been drawn up. In most cases their history is impenetrably obscure, a chance mention in a lawsuit, a reference to "burgesses" in a manorial survey, being often the sole indication that some tiny hamlet claimed to be marked off in this way from its neighbours. Whatever the circumstances of their origin, it is difficult to believe that their founders were inspired by any thought of urban development. Only the most wildly optimistic of landowners could have cherished any serious hope that a genuine urban community would grow up and flourish at Rackenford or Harton. In default of an alternative explanation we are free to surmise that some of these places owed their burgality, such as it was—and it was never much—in the first instance to the self-assertion of local peasants who deliberately sought this means of emphasizing their free status.

The situation may perhaps be conceived somewhat as follows. It is a fundamental maxim of feudal society that all land is held conditionally upon some form of service; and the lawyers are beginning to treat this as a criterion: in other words, they insist on deducing a man's personal status from the kind of service that he renders to his lord. Now many a free-born cottager has perhaps undertaken extra work on the lord's home-farm in return for the lord's help during a time of economic stress. He has done so without any thought of surrendering his legal status as a freeman; but now, thanks to the new doctrine, he finds himself in danger of being taken for a serf. In this situation he grasps eagerly at any label that will serve to mark him off emphatically from the servile class. One such label is provided when a man is said to hold in free socage. But socage, as Maitland has remarked, is "the great residuary tenure": one holds in socage if one does *not* hold by knight service or serjeanty or frankalmoign. For that very reason it is perhaps the last of these categories to win legal recognition.[1]

---

[1] Pollock and Maitland, *History of English Law*, I, p. 294. The earliest

But there is one species of freehold which has nothing new about it, and that is burgage tenure. Boroughs there have been long before the Conquest, places with courts of their own, places of which the inhabitants are decidedly not serfs.[1] Hence the thatcher and the blacksmith whose native village has somehow or other managed to set up a local market, thus becoming, in the language of Old English law, a *port*, or place of trade, will make the most of this fact: they will begin to call their reeve a *port-reeve*, and themselves *port-men*. In the Latin of the courts, both reeve and port-reeve are *prepositi*; but the Latin for *port-man* is *burgensis*. Once this fashion of speaking becomes habitual, a village 'borough' has been born. Perhaps a separate borough court will follow; or two juries will be sworn in at the manor court, one empanelled from the rural tenants, the other from the so-called burgesses. That will depend upon the lord, who, after all, stands to lose nothing, or very little, by the new arrangement. A prior of Otterton might declare that freemen were the worst of all plagues in a manor; but not every lord agreed with him.[2]

Enfranchisement by way of burgage tenure seems to be implied by more than one entry in the Domesday of Devon. We read, for instance, that Barnstaple has forty burgesses within the borough and nine outside it. At Lydford the same phenomenon recurs: the numbers are respectively twenty-eight and forty-one.[3] Three of the forty-one can be identified as inhabitants of Fernworthy, eight miles away on the other side of Dartmoor. They are not outsiders, paying scot and lot for the privilege of trading within the town, but actual burgesses whose tenements are reputed to be territorially part of the borough.[4] Barnstaple and Lydford are royal boroughs; but Totnes, which now belongs to Judhel, also has its extra-burghal burgesses, and here we are expressly told that they are peasants, farmers, land-workers.[5] Yet they all hold by payment of a money rent, which is a recognized mark of bur-

---

date given in the *Medieval Latin Word-list* for *socagium* as denoting a form of tenure is 1173.

[1] Tait regards the fully free status of the pre-Conquest burgess as "clearly established by the evidence of Domesday" (*The Medieval English Borough*, p. 82).

[2] Oliver, p. 255.   [3] DB IV, p. 80.

[4] *Publications of the Dartmoor Preservation Association*, I, pp. 65, 91.

[5] DB IV, p. 313.

gage tenure. As for the solitary burgess whom we come across at Lupridge, a hamlet in North Huish, we had better leave him out of the argument; he may be a mere slip of the pen.[1]

The countryman who could not stake out for himself a freehold on undeveloped land, or claim stannary privilege, or attach himself to a borough, real or nominal, might yet become a tenant by knight service on a small scale. The creation of freeholds in the form of subdivided knights' fees has already been mentioned.[2] Here it remains to add that where the lord was a great baron, under obligation to provide not one or two, but ten, fifteen, or twenty knights; where, moreover, he had sought to insure against possible defaults on their part by endowing one or more supernumerary knights, there would be ample room for subdivision. The system of compounding for actual service in the field by payment of shield-money, or scutage, and the attempt of the Exchequer under Henry II to exact scutage from the supernumerary as well as from the original knights' fees, must have given a great impetus to this process. Hence in course of time a baron like the abbot of Tavistock is found receiving homage and fealty not only from territorial magnates like the Daunays, but from scores of peasants holding each a few acres by the selfsame feudal tenure.

Thus, in the shifting landscape of tenurial relationships, there were several ways in which the agrarian middle class could secure its foothold. Perhaps it was never threatened to the same extent in the south-west as in some parts of England. We may here recall the very low rate at which land in Devonshire was taxed.[3] In many counties the *villanus*, borne down as much by pressure of taxation as by any other single factor,[4] might and did become the typical serf. In regions more favourably assessed, one main cause of degradation was removed. Against the others, there were remedies, as we have seen. Hence, in Devonshire, while individuals might rise or sink, there seems to have been no general depression of the free peasantry.

On the other hand, when we turn to the admittedly servile

[1] DB IV, p. 370.
[2] Cf. also CPR 1317–21, p. 580, for the militarization of a servile tenure in the episcopal manor of Bishop's Tawton.
[3] Above, p. 40.
[4] Maitland, *op. cit.*, p. 323; Ballard, *op. cit.*, p. 149; Stenton, *op. cit.*, p. 464.

class, we do find their condition notably altered. All over Devonshire the great-grandson of the Domesday *servus* is settled on land
which he cultivates for his own profit. Whether he is better fed
and better clad we cannot say; emancipation often leads to hard-
ship, while slavery has comforts of its own. At any rate, he now
fends for himself. This change for better or worse is expressed
by a new legal designation: he is no longer *servus*, but *nativus*, no
longer slave, but bondman, villein, serf.

We have already seen that the process of emancipation had begun long before the Norman Conquest, and that by 1086 it was
being pushed rapidly forward over a great part of England. In the
more conservative, and possibly more easy-going, south-west it
took longer; but now at last, by the end of the twelfth century,
this great social revolution was complete.

Momentous as the change unquestionably was, it is an exag-
geration to say that the slaves, as a class, disappeared. The
Church had recommended manumission as a pious act; and
sometimes, in the Old English period, a dying magnate would
enfranchise a batch of slaves for the good of his own soul. No
such consideration has moved the hard-headed Normans who
are now in charge. The slave, an asset while he works, becomes a
liability when he is old, or sick, or the father of young children,
or simply one of too numerous a band; and the slave-owners
have been limiting their liability. In so doing they have played
with some success the game proverbially known as trying to have
it both ways. They have got rid of a tiresome duty while reserving
practically all their rights. By planting their slaves upon the land,
they have cast off the burden of their maintenance, but they still
keep them in a state of utter personal subjection. The *nativus* is as
unfree as any man can be who earns his own living.

For details of his unfreedom we turn to later records. Remem-
bering the conservative outlook of the region with which we are
dealing, we may be sure that most, if not all, of the servile burdens
we find the *nativus* bearing in the fourteenth century will have
pressed with at least equal weight upon his forefathers in the
twelfth and thirteenth.

A slave can own no property; hence, all that a serf has belongs
to his lord. If a Werrington *nativus* died without heirs, the abbot
took all his chattels. More often he left a son or brother who could

step into his tenement; in such cases the abbot contented himself with a third of his movables, or with a money payment of equivalent value, according to a valuation made by the freemen jurors of the manor court.

The serf is himself a piece of property, and can be bought and sold like any slave. It is true that there is less inducement to get rid of him now that he supports himself; true also that in 1102 the Council of Westminster, under the presidency of St Anselm, laid the ban of the Church upon that "nefarious traffic", the sale of human livestock. I have found no record of such transactions on the Tavistock manors, though elsewhere, at the end of the twelfth century, and even later, serfs were still occasionally bought and sold with the cognizance and under the authority of the civil courts.[1]

Being himself a piece of property, the *nativus* must not quit the manor without leave; if he does so, his nearest relative is fined. This rule applies also to female serfs, as in 1366 when Joan Mayor leaves Werrington, taking her scanty goods and chattels with her, to become a housemaid at Bradstone parsonage.

In the old days, if the slave was allowed to beget children, the lord's overhead expenses might easily mount up at an alarming rate. To protect himself against the multiplication of dependent and unprofitable mouths, the slave-owner assumed the right to veto servile marriages, and to punish any slave who begot children out of wedlock. It is true that marriage was a sacrament, and as such could not lightly be withheld from any man. The English Pope Adrian IV decreed that servile marriages ought not to be prohibited, and that even when contracted against the will of the lord, they must be upheld by the Church courts.[2] But if the lords were thus inhibited from using their right of veto in order to keep down the servile birth-rate, they still could and did exploit it as a source of revenue. Marriages between the abbot's serfs at Werrington were subject to a duty of 1s. 3d.[3] This was doubled if

---

[1] See the instances quoted by Poole, *Obligations of Society in the XII and XIII Centuries*, p. 14.

[2] Decret. Greg. iv, tit. ix, cap. 1.

[3] On the St Albans manors the amount varied between sixpence and four shillings (Levett, *Studies in Manorial History*, pp. 237–9). At Crawley, Hants, it might be as much as 6s. 8d. (in 1233) or ten shillings (in 1211), though it is said to have been "out of the ordinary" (Gras, *Economic*

a woman of the servile class married outside the manor, while if she brought forth a child, being herself unmarried, the *layrwyta*, or fine for incontinence, was 5s. 0½d. In 1384 Isabella Lovya comes into court and purchases her freedom with a fine of ten shillings; but the steward's regard for female modesty does not deter him from proclaiming in full court that if she turns out to have been with child at the time of this transaction, the customary *layrwyta* will still be due.

As the rightful owner of all his serf's belongings, the lord could tax him at will. It may however be doubted if the serf's liability under this head was ever as unlimited as it sounds. At Werrington the 'aid' collected from the *nativi* by the two beadles of the manor at All Saints' and Holy Cross Day amounted in 1298 to twenty-three marks (£15 6s. 8d.). At Hurdwick 'tallage' was collected annually at All Saints'. In 1332 it brought in £3 0s. 4½d. By 1347 it had risen to £10 9s. 7d., but the 'extent' of 1387 shows a fall to £1 15s. 5½d. From the same document it appears that while the incidence was mainly upon the customary tenants, some few tenants in socage and leaseholders also paid; and that the normal rate of assessment was tenpence halfpenny per ferling. This presents an interesting contrast with the method pursued on the estates of Gloucester Abbey, where the tenant paid according to the number of his cattle.[1]

On the other Tavistock manors there is no mention of tallage or aids; but an attempt by the abbot in 1258 to impose a tax of this nature upon his burgesses of Tavistock led to the only recorded clash between the borough and its lord. At that time the abbey was undergoing a financial crisis. In November 1257 royal letters-patent were directed to all its tenants, informing them that the monastery was in debt, and requesting them to help the new abbot, Henry de Northampton, with a voluntary subsidy. The response to this appeal was presumably insufficient,

---

and Social History of an English Village, pp. 195, 197, 209). Perhaps the tendency was for it to disappear at an early date. The latest instance noted at Werrington occurred in 1366.

[1] Vinogradoff, *Villainage in England*, p. 293. At Wistowe, Hunts, a Ramsey manor, tallage was levied at the rate of tenpence per virgate (Neilson, *Economic Conditions on the Manors of Ramsey Abbey*, p. 71). The prior of Otterton held that tallage was essentially a poll-tax, and that to convert it into a rent-charge on the tenant's land was highly prejudicial to the lord's interest (Oliver, p. 256).

for the abbot shortly afterwards laid a tallage of ten marks
(£6 13s. 4d.) upon the borough. During the vacancy preceding
his election, the prior and convent had purchased the right to
act as custodians of the abbey. This entitled them to keep for
their own use the revenues that would otherwise have accrued
to the king during voidance, including "tallages of their men".
As the king still claimed and exercised the right to tallage boroughs on his own lands, abbot Henry maintained that the grant
of custody had put his convent in the same position as the king so
far as this right was concerned. When the burgesses of Tavistock
refused to pay, he called in the sheriff to distrain upon them. An
appeal to the king followed. On the 18th of June 1258, the sheriff
was forbidden by royal mandate either to distrain for the aforesaid tallage himself, or to let the abbot do so. It was explained that
the king had not intended the grant of custody to reduce any tenant of the abbey to servitude.[1]

When a servile holding fell vacant, a new tenant was elected by
the jury of the manor court. He then did fealty to the lord, and
paid a trifling sum by way of 'recognition'. He was not at liberty
to sub-let. If he died leaving an heir, the heir could normally suc-
ceed on paying a relief of 12s. 6d. But the succession to any tenement, bond or free, was liable to be upset by a mixed marriage.
In 1394 the House of Commons pointed out that if a free-born
heiress married a serf, her children would be serfs too, and if
the manor belonged to a monastic house, the lord would thus
acquire a title to her property without any special licence from
the Crown, notwithstanding the Statute of Mortmain. The Commons asked that a remedy might be ordained, but the Crown declined to alter the existing legislation.[2] There is a case in point in
an extent of Morwell drawn up twenty years later. A house and
some enclosed land at Gulworthy are said to have escheated to
the lord by the death of Walter Page, "because the same Walter
was the lord's *nativus*, and had the land aforesaid with the house
to him and his heirs in fee simple in right of Matilda Hunte his
wife; of which said Matilda Hunte by the same Walter was be-

[1] CPR 1247–58, pp. 313, 560; CCR 1256–59, p. 313.
[2] *Rotuli Parliamentorum*, III, p. 319. Bennett (*Life on the English Manor*,
p. 245) quotes this passage as evidence that the monasteries "caused their
serfs to marry free women with inheritances"!

gotten Alice Page, who is the lord's serf. Therefore the said land came to the lord."

An interesting entry in a Werrington court roll of 1368 shows that the same disability might operate in the reverse direction. John Davy pays 3s. 4d. to have inquiry made concerning his claim to a bond tenement in Cullacott. The verdict of the jury is that if either of his parents had been a serf he might have had a good claim, but that as he is of free descent on both sides he is disqualified.

The occupation of a bond tenement carried with it the obligation to serve the recognized manorial offices of tithingman, woodward, beadle, slaughterer, and reeve. The woodward reported trespasses in the lord's woods; the slaughterer accounted for losses of cattle through murrain or other causes. The beadle collected rents and fines. At Hurdwick he was allowed two shillings off his rent, and two quarters of oats. At Werrington there were two beadles, each of whom was allowed a shilling off his rent. Like the tithingmen and the reeve, they were theoretically chosen by "the whole homage": in practice, the appointment rested with the jury and the steward. The tithingmen were a sort of rural police-force. Curiously enough, this is the only manorial office to which a woman was ever nominated; when this happened, she was of course allowed to put a male deputy in her place.

The reeve, who bore the heaviest burden of responsibility for supervising the manorial routine and for seeing that the lord's dues were collected, was exempted from paying rent and from performing labour services during his term of office. At Werrington he was also entitled to the produce of a day's cheese-making. He was elected by the jury acting on behalf of the whole homage. The Werrington jury put forward three names: two of the nominees then paid a fine to be released, and the third was sworn in. At Plymstock only two candidates were presented.

In addition to his liability for service as a manorial officer, the tenant of bond-land owed a variety of 'works' or labour services. These were not, as they are often said to have been, the essential characteristic of serfdom, for they were owed by freemen also. We saw just now that tenants in free socage, and tenants of ancient freeholds like Milemead, owed the abbot a boonwork or two annually, while burgesses, or at least the occupants of the eighteen original burgages at Tavistock, might have to ride abroad on the lord's errands. The essence of villeinage is not labour service, but subjection to the will of the lord.

Of one most burdensome form of service, namely week-work, there is no trace on the Tavistock estates. Compulsory ploughing-works were performed at Werrington during the thirteenth century. On manors belonging to the see of Winchester, land ploughed compulsorily was called need-earth, in contrast with the boon-earth which was ploughed nominally by request; and it was priced at rates varying from sixpence halfpenny to ninepence an acre.[1] The same term, need-earth, was used at Werrington, where however the rate was only twopence. It appears that the obligation was confined to eighty customary tenants, the number of those who owed boonwork being a hundred and fifteen.

One day's ploughing boonwork was exacted at Hurdwick, Ottery, Werrington, Burrington, and Denbury; two days' at Leigh and Milton Abbot. On all these manors a day's ploughing was priced twopence, except at Denbury, where the price was threepence. At Hurdwick, and possibly elsewhere, the tenant was expected to bring with him a *fugator*. This assistant, in some documents called *stimulator*, was the lad who applied the ox-goad and encouraged the plough-team with a peculiar kind of chant. Marshall, who found the traditional method still being employed in the last decade of the eighteenth century, says that "the plow boy chants the counter tenor with unabated ardour through the day, the plowman throwing in, at intervals, his hoarser notes;" and he adds that he had never seen ploughing so cheerfully performed anywhere as in Devonshire.[2]

Harrowing was another recognized form of boonwork. At Hurdwick, in 1332, six tenants harrowed ten and a half acres of oatland. This work was priced twopence a day at Leigh and Werrington, a halfpenny at Burrington. The Hurdwick figures imply that each man accounted for one and three-quarters, whereas at Werrington the tenant was expected to harrow two acres.

The mowing of the lord's meadow, as a form of labour service,

[1] Levett, *The Black Death on the Estates of the See of Winchester*, p. 63.
[2] Marshall, *op. cit.*, I, p. 116.

is not found on the Tavistock estates except at Werrington, where each customary tenant was expected to mow half an acre and sixteen perches, or to pay a penny if the work was not required.

At Denbury there were eight customary tenants who owed five days' work in harvest, and six owing three days'. Both groups paid a penny for each day when they did not work. On the other manors, harvest-work was classified into the two main divisions, reaping and carrying, and further subdivided by crop and mode of carriage. For the reaping of the oat-crop, one day was allowed at Hurdwick, three days at Milton Abbot, and four at Leigh and Burrington. The Werrington *nativus* was required to reap two acres; if he did not, he paid fourpence halfpenny or gave three geese to the lord. For the hard-corn reaping two days were exacted at Milton, and priced twopence each, a halfpenny more than at Hurdwick, where only one day was demanded. The same boonwork was priced a penny at Ottery, a halfpenny at Burrington, and *nil* at Werrington, where the abbot reserved the right to demand it from all his tenants, free and customary, and gave no exemption if he required the work but took no payment if he did not.

The tenant of bond-land at Milton Abbot carried the lord's corn from harvest-field to grange, using his cart if he had one, his packhorse if not. Carts were taken for granted at Werrington, packhorses at Hurdwick. On these manors, and also at Leigh and Ottery, one day's carriage was required at harvest, or the tenant paid twopence in lieu of service.

At intervals throughout the year supplies of grain were brought to the abbey by customary tenants of the distant manors. Since the monks could not consume the produce of each manor on the spot, this form of carriage service must have been one of the most vital elements of their economy. At Werrington and Plymstock it was maintained to the very end. Packhorses were employed, and each Werrington *nativus* was liable for three "small works" of this kind, valued at a penny each.

The provisioning of the abbey kitchen and of the Tavistock market required transport not only from the various demesnes but also from external sources of supply. The Werrington serf might be sent once a year to any place within the bounds of Devon and Cornwall. In 1386 ten customary tenants of that manor fetched salted fish from St Michael's Mount, Probus, and Bodinnick; and in 1396 a similar expedition was made to Marhamchurch. The payment in lieu of this service was fourpence. At Plymstock the accounts rarely mention any other form of labour service, but show the tenants performing a great variety of errands. They brought fresh and salted fish, corn, salt, wine, and cider to Tavistock from Plymouth, Stonehouse, Oreston, Stoke Damerel, and Newton Ferrers, besides carting stone, lime, and timber within the manor when the court-house was under repair.

Lastly, there was a miscellaneous group of services, such as cleaning out the mill-leat, weeding the lord's cornfields, and paring off the sward in preparation for tillage. These three works at Burrington were priced a halfpenny each. At Hurdwick and Milton Abbot some of the tenants paid a rent of a penny called hatch-silver, which in all probability represents a commuted liability to repair the Tamar salmon-traps.

The longest list of services is found at Werrington, where the serf's total liability was assessed, for purposes of commutation, at 1s. 8½d. At Hurdwick the corresponding figure was sevenpence halfpenny.[1] It is well to remember that each list states a maximum which in practice would seldom be demanded.[2] Hence we find it stated in an extent of Leigh (1411) that "it is at the lord's choice to take the works in service or in money." The true state of the case is brought out in the earliest extant Werrington account (1298), where the payments made to the lord for works are entered under the title *Residuum Operum*. Evidently they had been paid in lieu of services not demanded by the husbandry of that particular year. Such temporary commutation, in later years always styled *Vendicio Operum*, was in all probability as old as the system of labour services itself.[3]

---

[1] The corresponding figure on the episcopal manor of Crawley, Hants, was 6s. 8d. (Gras, *op. cit.*, p. 271). At Watlington, Oxon, it was eight shillings (*Rot. Hund.* II, 815a).

[2] Kosminsky, 'The Hundred Rolls of 1279–80 as a source for English Agrarian History', *Economic History Review*, III, 1931, p. 41. Hence it may well be misleading to say that the peasant "was expected" or "was required" to do such and such works (cf. Stenton, *op. cit.*, p. 467) when all that we have is a formal statement of his total liability. Cf. also Bennett, *op. cit.*, p. 106: "Many more works were often owed than were in fact ever demanded."

[3] Vinogradoff (*Villainage*, pp. 306, 307) remarks that labour services were

What the records do not tell us is why the same day's work was valued differently on different manors, and how it was settled that a particular tenant in a given year should work or pay. Nor do we know if the abbots of Tavistock at any time relied for the cultivation of their demesne land solely upon the labour service of their tenants. Between the slave-labour of Domesday and the wage-labour of the fourteenth-century accounts, was there an intermediate period, during which no regular paid staff was kept at work? On the whole it seems unlikely. But let it be repeated that on these estates labour services were only one element of serfdom, and that not the most conspicuous or burdensome.

For Vinogradoff, 'serf' and 'slave' are synonyms.[1] This eminent scholar of the last generation, whose treatment of the subject still powerfully influences current opinion, dwelt much upon the downward trend, the descent of freemen into economic and legal servitude. He did so because in his opinion it had been insufficiently emphasized by previous writers.[2] At the same time he agreed, somewhat grudgingly, that "we have to make room for" the descendants of the *geburas* by the side of the downfallen *ceorls* whom he regarded as a main constituent of the unfree class.[3] This degradation of the peasantry has been a favourite theme with our historians ever since. There are reputable writers who treat of post-Conquest serfdom as "a consequence of the introduction and development of the manorial system" without so much as mentioning that there had ever been slaves in England.[4]

---

not solely dictated by the needs of demesne husbandry: they were also a percentage levied on the tenant's profits. Nevertheless he pictures exemption from actual service as a gradual progressive movement, varied by occasional retrogression. But unless we postulate an original golden age, there can never have been a time when the available services did not sometimes outrun the demand. Every well-organized estate would aim at providing a margin over current needs.

[1] *English Society in the Eleventh Century*, p. 463 and *passim*. By habitually using 'serf' to render the Domesday *servus*, the Victoria County Histories have made confusion worse confounded.

[2] *Ibid.*, p. 460.   [3] *Ibid.*, p. 467.

[4] Bennett, *op. cit.*, p. 99. There is a passing reference to the slaves of Domesday on p. 182, quoted from Ashley. Poole (*op. cit.*, p. 13) lays all the blame upon the lawyers, who, he says, "were ultimately successful in degrading most of the peasants into a condition of serfdom"; but in a footnote he limits this generalization to the midland and southern counties. Clapham, on the other hand, fully recognizes the connection between serfdom and antecedent slavery (*op. cit.*, pp. 50, 102).

Yet slavery was an institution deeply rooted in Old English life. Some fifty years before the Norman Conquest bishop Ælfwold of Crediton directed that after his death all the slaves he had purchased, and all those others on the episcopal estates who had been enslaved as a penalty for crime, should be set free.[1] We have seen that there were still thousands of slaves in the Devon of 1086. When the curtain goes up again, their place has been taken by *nativi* whose disabilities all explain themselves quite naturally as legacies from a servile and landless past. That the ranks of the *nativi* opened to admit a certain number of peasants driven by economic stress to surrender their inherited free status is not to be denied. But the persistent conservatism of this remote shire; its late colonization, so pregnant with opportunities for carving freeholds out of the waste; its privileged assessment; the diffusion of burgage tenure over scores of rural centres; and the pressure of stannary custom from the twelfth century onwards, all helped to arrest any tendency there may have been to multiply the unfree at the expense of the free population.

If the history of Tavistock Abbey as an agrarian organism is divided into two approximately equal halves, the transition from landless slavery to serfdom stands out as a process distinctive of the first half. The passage from bond tenure to leasehold is correspondingly distinctive of the second. It will be dealt with in a later chapter; but first, something must be said of agriculture and the husbandry of the demesne.

[1] *Crawford Charters*, p. 126. Bloch points out that during the eleventh century slaves were much more numerous in England than on the continent (*Cambridge Economic History of Europe*, I, p. 258). He might have added that they were far more numerous in Devon than in any other English county. The peculiar value and interest of Devonshire as a field of historical study lies precisely in this fact that it has so often preserved ancient usages long after they have been abandoned elsewhere.

G

CHAPTER IV

ARABLE HUSBANDRY

IN 1086 the abbot and convent had twenty-two plough-teams at work on their Devonshire lands. The distribution of those teams, and of the other demesne livestock, is shown in the following table. Particulars of the Werrington stock are subjoined, for although the manor was already in the king's hands by the time the record was drawn up, the figures probably give a trustworthy picture of the demesne as it stood when abbot Geoffrey was evicted.

TABLE II

	Plough-Teams	Bulls, Cows, etc.	Sheep	Goats	Swine
Tavistock	5	26	200	30	12
Milton Abbot	5	22	170	30	12
Leigh, with Liddaton	1	4	30	—	—
Hatherleigh	3	15	44	24	4
Abbotsham	2	6	118	—	4
Worthygate	1	—	20	6	—
Burrington	3	8	46	28	6
Denbury	1	4	70	15	—
Plymstock	1	4	70	34	—
	22	89	768	167	38
Werrington	6	25	150	—	20
	28	114	918	167	58

These figures present no anomalies. At first sight, perhaps, it may appear strange that tillage was not practised on a more extensive scale at Denbury and Plymstock, both of which manors lie within the highly fertile region of the South Hams. Plymstock, indeed, with its limestone soil, sheltered on the north by the high ground between Saltram and Plympton, and on the south by the ridge that runs inland from Staddon Heights, for centuries grew excellent wheat-crops. But here the manor was not co-extensive with the parish. It comprised little more than nine hundred acres, of which Pomphlett Barton, the demesne farm, accounted for 132 acres 0 roods 27 poles. When thirty acres have been deducted for pasture, and half an acre for meadow, in accordance with the Domesday measurements, the arable area of the demesne is brought down to something well within the capacity of a single plough-team. Denbury too was a small manor. No document that I have seen gives any clue to the situation and extent of its barton land, but a reeve's account dated 1393 refers to wheat as being sown "in divers furlongs (culturis) in the combes", while barley was cultivated "on the lord's land at Hewelegh", and oats "in divers furlongs" elsewhere on the demesne. The abbot's tillage thus appears to have been inconveniently scattered, perhaps because the limestone here is frequently interrupted by patches of igneous rock.

Three of the other manors in the list provide no further data for agrarian history. Worthygate appears to have been sold before the close of the thirteenth century.[1] Abbotsham and Hatherleigh were not granted with Tavistock to Lord Russell after the Dissolution, and consequently few of their records are now in the hands of his descendants. The history of the demesne at Hatherleigh would have been particularly interesting, for this was an extensive manor, lying at the western termination of the famous 'red earth', and including patches of the warm loam associated with the New Red sandstone, as well as large tracts of comparatively unprofitable heath and moorland.[2]

---

[1] Reichel, The Hundreds of Devon, p. 578.
[2] The manor of Hatherleigh included what are now the parishes of Hatherleigh and Jacobstowe; it also extended into Monk Okehampton. A number of freeholds: Pulworthy, Fishleigh, Great Velliford, Seldon, Broomford, Langabear, Marshford, Hannaborough, Kerswell, and Passaford, formed a ring round the church-town and Hatherleigh Moor. On the northern edge of the Moor, about half a mile east of the church-town, is Youlaberry, that is, 'the old burh'; and since burh often signifies 'manorial centre', this name may indicate the site of the original barton. With the church-town and the Moor, it is now within the borough. We know that the abbot had three ploughs at work in 1086, but once he had founded the borough and given the Moor to his burgesses there was little space left for

Burrington is situated in the relatively fertile area between the Torridge and the Taw, and its best land is to be found on the gravel subsoil of the Taw valley. The soil of Werrington and North Petherwin is a grey loam, acid, cold, and stony, on a sub-soil of white and yellow clays. All over north-west Devon soil of this character is developed on the so-called Culm Measures of the carboniferous age. Where this is mingled with decomposed drift from the trappean rocks, as it is in the vicinity of Tavistock, its fertility is much increased. Milton Abbot, which lies partly on chert, partly on shale and grit, has always been noted for its pockets of rich grassland. Tavistock is highly complex in its geology. Heathfield, the great waste on the north of the ancient parish, is part of the shale and grit area. Blanchdown and Mor-well lie on the metamorphic aureole which extends across the Tamar from the granite of Hingston Down. The centre of the parish lies on slate, variegated with streaks of elvan. To the east lies the huge granite mass of Dartmoor.

In general it must be said of the abbey demesnes that they included no extensive areas of first-rate land. They shared in that deficiency of phosphate which is characteristic of Devon as a whole. The clays were not intractable, but there was a great deal of shallow and stony soil which required generous manuring to make it agriculturally productive.

The earliest extant Hurdwick account shows two horses being shod in summertime "for dunging"; and elsewhere there are references to the "muck-stall" and to carts "commonly called dung-butts". That farmyard manure should have been in regular use is only what one would expect. But there were also two artificial methods of securing increased fertility: methods which have been employed in the south-western counties from time

---

any demesne arable. In 1269, when he kept sheep, cows, and oxen at Hather-leigh in appreciable numbers, the only corn of which we hear is tithe-corn (*Cal. Miscellaneous Inquisitions*, I, p. 130). Abbot Mey complained in 1412 that a band of rioters two dozen strong came to Hatherleigh, broke his closes, levelled the hedges, assaulted his servants, carried off his corn in sheaves, besieged a plot of his called Monkleigh (in Monk Okehampton), and pre-vented his servants from entering or leaving it (CPR 1408–13, p. 433). Here again the corn may have been tithe-corn; but the other terms of the com-plaint suggest an enclosure riot. At the date when it occurred, some barton land, with a meadow called Langabear-mead, was leased out at a rent of £4 9s. 4d. a year.

immemorial, although, as we shall see, they involved no small expense.

About the middle of the thirteenth century Richard, earl of Cornwall and king of the Romans, issued a charter permitting all the inhabitants of Cornwall to take sea-sand without payment for the purpose of increasing the fertility of their lands. This grant was confirmed by Henry III in 1261.[1] The privilege did not extend to Devonshire; and some nine years later John de Beaupré, steward of Trematon, a castle belonging to the earl-king, set up a ferry at Saltash and proceeded to levy tolls upon the navigation of the Tamar. Among other charges he imposed one of twelve pence a year upon every barge engaged in the transport of sand. Complaint was made of this exaction, during the great inquest of 1275, by the burgesses as well as by the hundred-jurors of Tavistock and Plympton, town and country showing themselves united in resenting what was evidently felt as a wrong done to the whole community.[2]

In 1332 wheat and oats were sown at Hurdwick on two acres and 1 acre 1 rood respectively of sanded land. The livestock account for Werrington in 1350 states that no foals were born that year "by reason of great toil in fetching sand". By 1386 expenditure on sand (custus sabuli) is a regularly recurring item in the Werrington accounts, and in the same year it makes its appearance in those of Ottery. After 1396 it is frequently the subject of a special clause in Hurdwick leases.[3]

There is naturally much variation in the qualities of sand, that from some parts of the coast being almost worthless. Bude sand was highly esteemed, and is continually in demand at the present day. It is composed chiefly of pulverized shells and corals, with occasional admixture of sea-weed; and it is rich in calcium carbonate.[4] A typical eighteenth-century lease quoted by Marshall speaks of one hundred and twenty seams, or horse-loads, of sea-

---

[1] Cal. Charter Rolls, 1257–1300, p. 36.   [2] Rot. Hund., I, pp. 76, 81.

[3] Here, and throughout this book, whenever reference is made to a year of account, the year is that in which the account was drawn up: e.g., 1452 means the twelve months ending at Michaelmas 1452. In The History of Agriculture and Prices in England Thorold Rogers calls this 1451 (op. cit., I, p. xii).

[4] Samples have revealed as much as fifty per cent. This makes it a very inexpensive liming to-day, when lime used in any form as a dressing for agricultural land is subsidized by the State.

sand as equivalent to a hundred bushels of lime: a proportion of roughly five to one.[1]

The distance from Werrington to the inexhaustible supply at Widemouth, on the shore of Bude Bay, is about fourteen miles. Year by year a train of six or seven packhorses went to and fro between the abbot's demesne and Widemouth Sand, a payment of three halfpence for each horse being made to the lord of Woolston—or, as he is called in the accounts, the lord of Widemouth—for way-leave across his manor. In 1386 three packhorses were purchased expressly for this journey at a cost of 19s. 11d., and a sandman was employed for twenty-four weeks during the summer at a weekly wage of sevenpence. This wagerate remained constant for the next hundred years; but from 1394 onwards two yards of linen were purchased for eightpence to provide the sandman with a smock (*camisia*). In 1477 the bailiff agreed to pay an extra five shillings for hire of the sandman's mare. This payment was also to cover the cost of providing twenty loads of sand. It soon established itself as a regular feature of the account: so much so that by 1499 the clerk is terming it an "ancient custom".

The quantities used are not stated in the accounts before 1413 nor after 1481. Between those dates they were as shown in the following table, reckoning two and a half hundredweight to the seam.

TABLE III

Year	seams	tons	cwt	Year	seams	tons	cwt
1413	85	10	12	1461	87	10	17
1452	64	8	0	1471	20	2	10
1454	40	5	0	1477	20	2	10
1459	100	12	10	1481	80	10	0

A comparison of these figures with Table VI (p. 101) fails to disclose any constant ratio between the acreage under cultivation and the quantity of sand applied.

For the manors near Tavistock sand was brought from the south coast and shipped up the Tamar to Morwellham, whence it

[1] Marshall, *op. cit.*, I, p. 81.

was carried overland on packhorses. While the cost of Bude sand remained constant between 1413 and 1481 at 1s. 2d. for twenty horseloads, the Hurdwick accounts testify to fluctuations of price. The average figure, 6s. 8d. a barge-load, when compared with the Werrington rate, suggests a normal load of some fourteen and a quarter tons.

TABLE IV

Year	Loads	Price per load	Year	Loads	Price per load
1427	4	8s. 0d.	1491	2	8s. 0d.
1450	2	6s. 8d.	1492	2	7s. 6d.
1454	2	7s. 0d.	1497	2	7s. 6d.
1458	2	6s. 0d.	1498	?	4s. 2d.
1460	1	6s. 8d.	1502	2	6s. 8d.
1463	1	11s. 0d.	1504	2	6s. 8d.
1464	3	8s. 11d.	1505	0	—
1466	3	6s. 8d.	1508	3	6s. 8d.
1470	3	6s. 0d.	1509	2	6s. 8d.
1471	3	6s. 0d.	1513	3	6s. 8d.
1473	1	6s. 8d.	1514	3	6s. 8d.
1475	1	6s. 8d.	1517	2	6s. 8d.
1480	1	6s. 0d.	1522	2	7s. 2d.
1482	1	6s. 0d.	1524	2	6s. 8d.
1489	1½[1]	12s. 6d.	1537	3	7s. 0d.
1490	1	8s. 2d.	1538	3	7s. 2d.

It will be noticed that exceptionally high prices ruled in 1463–4 owing to the disturbances that followed the accession of Edward IV, and again in 1489–97, the period of the Breton war and Perkin Warbeck's invasions.

The other distinctive method employed to prepare the ground for corn-crops was beat-burning. In the seventeenth century, when knowledge of it spread to other counties, this practice became known as Denshiring, or Devonshiring. It consisted in paring off the sward of waste ground or land which had gone back to grass, and burning it. The tangled mass of grasses and weeds, locally termed the *spine*, was lifted with a mattock or beat-axe.

[1] One barge and one boat-load.

Alternatively it could be turned over by the plough. After an interval during which it remained on the ground to dry, it was pulled to pieces with harrows until the loose earth was disengaged from the roots. The fragments of turf, in this state called *beat*, were raked into heaps, or *beat-burrows*; a handful of rough straw was thrust into each heap; and a lighted torch, made of unthreshed straw, was applied to the loose ends of the wisps, thus setting fire to the whole. When the heaps were quite consumed, the ashes were spread over the surface of the field.

Beat-burning is a practice of unknown antiquity. In the Tavistock records it can be traced back to 1246, when Robert Champeaux, lord of the manor of Leigh in Milton Abbot, granted a fifteen-year lease of his demesne to abbot Alan of Tavistock, and inserted a proviso limiting the area of beat-burning to that for which the lessee could provide manure.[1]

The evidence of field-names proves that beat-burning was frequently employed to bring marginal land into cultivation. Three fields on the edge of Blanchdown were called Beatland, and a group near Heathfield appear on the estate maps as Higher, Middle, Lower Beatland, and Three-Cornered Beatland. But the process also had its place in the routine of cultivation. There are two fields called Bate-parks in the former barton land of Taviton, and a field of twenty-seven acres, also called Bate-park, near Hurdwick. The occurrence of such names on the in-grounds of established farms implies that beat was regularly burnt to prepare ley ground for seeding.

The expenditure on beat-burning in any given year (*custus baticii*), as recorded in the accounts, is for piecework only. If the regular staff of the demesne did any of the work, the cost of such *auxilium famulorum* would be covered by their wages. Table V gives the piecework costs per customary acre. The cost of paring shown here is for hand-labour. At Burrington the task of "paring the lord's beat" was one of the recognized boonworks owed by the tenants. It was commuted at the rate of a penny a boonwork; and it is enumerated separately from the ploughing service, which was commuted at the usual twopenny rate. Moreover, the word used, *hoare*, implies a manual operation. The use of the mattock

---

[1] "Non liceat prefatis abbati et conventui plus in Bateyceum comburere de dicta terra de Legh quam possint compostare" (W. D Bdle 38, no. 5).

TABLE V

Year	Manor	Paring	Burning	Scattering
1298	Werrington			1½d.
1332	Hurdwick	1s.	6d.	2½d.
1335	Ottery	1s.	6d.	2½d.
1336	,,	1s.	6d.	3d.
1337	,,	1s.	6d.	
1338	,,			2½d.
1342	,,	1s.	6d.	3d.
1343	,,			2½d.
1344	,,			2½d.
1347	Hurdwick	11d.	6d.	3d.
1358	Burrington		8d.	4d.
1382	Week	1s. 4d.		4d.
1386	Werrington		5d.	4d.
1396	Ottery	1s.	1s. 8½d.[1]	6d.
1398	Leigh	1s. 2d.	1s. 1d.	6d.
1398	Werrington	1s. 4d.	1s. 4d.	5d.
1398	Hurdwick		1s. 2d.	5d.
1412	,,		1s.	6d.
1414	,,		11½d.	5d.
1416	,,		10d.	5½d.

or other hand-tool (*cum marrys*) is even more clearly indicated at Ottery in 1396 and at Werrington in 1398. But the operation was quite as frequently performed by ploughing. In that case it might sometimes be carried out by customary tenants for their boonworks. This seems to have been the case at Werrington in 1386, when 1s. 10d. was paid for scattering five and a half acres of beat, but nothing at all for paring it, that part of the work being accounted for by the eleven "customers" who ploughed on the demesne. The Hurdwick account for 1414 leaves no room for doubt upon the point, for it expressly states that twelve tenants, with their own ox-teams and drivers, ploughed six acres of beatland for rye by special request of the bailiff. It is clear that half an acre was the normal day's work.

The average area burnt in any one year was nine acres; and the

---

[1] Four acres burnt for 6s. 10d.; but evidently some abnormal factor was at work, for the actual rate per acre is left blank in the account.

maximum was twenty-one acres, burnt at Hurdwick in 1347. On the question whether the practice was or was not beneficial, opinions have differed. Marshall, while noting that "men who farm in closets seem desirous to extinguish the practice," puts it on record that the wheat crops of the Tavistock district, "notwithstanding the accumulated foulness of the soil . . . are, in general, beautifully clean . . . a circumstance, perhaps, which would be difficult to account for in any other way than in the check which the weeds receive from the burning."[1] This negative or sterilizing effect, however, could be overdone. Hence in some leases beat-burning was forbidden altogether. For example, in 1289 it is provided that the tenant of Parswell shall not burn any land "except la Clyveland";[2] and in 1447 a tenant at Bowrish is forbidden to burn any part of an eight-acre close on pain of forfeiting his lease.[3]

The lease of 1246, already quoted, is evidence of early recognition that burning might damage the soil, and that the fertilizing power inherent in the ashes of vegetable matter needed reinforcement by some other form of manure. At the close of the fourteenth century the abbey regularly insisted that leaseholders should give a dressing of sea-sand to any portion of their holdings they might choose to burn. By 1416 lessees were being allowed a choice between sea-sand and dung. When Simon Drake, reputed ancestor of Sir Francis the great seaman, took a lease of Crowndale in 1481, the abbot and convent inserted what was now the standard clause: if he wishes to burn any portion of the land, then he must apply sand or dung thereto in sufficient quantity.[4] Another lease adds "in the same year"; and in 1487 the clause is rounded off with an allusion to the established practice of the countryside.[5]

William of Malmesbury, who visited Devonshire in the first or second decade of the twelfth century, says nothing of manures; according to him, the soil was naturally so thin and poor as to be

---

[1] Marshall, op. cit., i, p. 148. [2] W. D Bdle 43, no. 1.
[3] Tavistock Abbey White Book, fo. xvii. [4] W. D Bdle 53, no. 25.
[5] ". . . secundum usum et modum patrie", ibid., no. 124. In 1668 it was reported that beatland was usually dressed with fifty or sixty sacks of sea-sand to the acre, the sacks containing eighteen gallons apiece (R. Lennard, 'English Agriculture under Charles II', Economic History Review, IV, 1932, pp. 33, 35).

hardly capable of bearing a satisfactory crop of oats.[1] It seems unlikely that this was true of the district round Exeter, and contemporary evidence proves that other cereals were being cultivated west of Dartmoor. A charter issued by queen Matilda between 1100 and 1107 specifies the dues paid from Ottery to the hundred of Lifton, as twenty-two pence and one 'amber', or about four bushels, of rye.[2] Nevertheless oats are certainly the crop best suited to so damp a climate, and the Tavistock records show three distinct varieties in cultivation at different periods.

In the first place, there was the naked oat, *avena nuda*, so called by modern botanists because its husks do not adhere to the grain but leave it bare. The grain is small and yellow; there is no bran; and the straw is said to be excellent for thatching. Its vernacular name is pill-corn. This oat, which flourishes in the coarsest soils, is not now cultivated in Great Britain, but there are place-names in Staffordshire and Yorkshire which testify that it was grown there in the twelfth century; and at that time it may well have been the standard oat-crop of the south-west. Pill-corn continued to be grown in Cornwall down to the last century, being sown in February at the rate of some two and a half bushels to the acre.[3] It appears, under the vernacular name, in the Werrington accounts from 1386 to 1459, and in those of Plymstock from 1392 to 1481, as grown by the tenants and brought by them to be ground at the abbot's mills. At Werrington it was sold at prices ranging from sixpence to ninepence a bushel, usually a penny a bushel cheaper than rye. At Plymstock, on the other hand, it nearly always fetched a higher price. Possibly the limestone soil there produced a heavier grain. Only once, in 1480, did the price fall below one shilling; in 1431 and the following year it had been as high as 1s. 8d.[4]

---

[1] *Gesta Pontificum*, p. 201; *Gesta Regum*, p. 148. Cf. Richard of Devizes: "Exonia eodem farre reficit homines et jumenta" (*Chronicles of the Reigns of Stephen, etc.*, ed. Howlett, III, p. 437).

[2] ETC III. There are references to hundred dues, paid partly in cash, partly in kind, in the Exon Domesday (DB IV, p. 78). Rye, in Matilda's charter, is *segle*. For the metamorphosis of this word into the *siligo* of later documents, cf. Ashley, *The Bread of our Forefathers*, pp. 67 sqq.

[3] Ekwall, *Studies on English Place-Names*, p. 105; DCNQ XXII, 1944, p. 199; Hector, *Introduction to the Botany of Field Crops*, I, p. 54 (*Avena strigosa*, proles *nuda*).

[4] For details of consumption and prices, see Table XVII, p. 128.

Down to 1332 only one kind of oat appears to have been grown on the abbot's demesnes. In the earliest accounts it is called simply *avena*. Certain recurrent entries, such as the customary gift to the beadle, identify it with the oat referred to in later accounts as *avena minuta*. It was sown at the rate of two bushels to the acre, or slightly less, and sold at much the same price as pill-corn, with which it was almost certainly identical. It served for rearing calves and foals; and its meal was used for porridge.

In 1332 the reeve of Hurdwick spent 2s. 4d. in purchasing—from what source is not stated—a quarter of "large" oats. These he caused to be sown on 1 acre 1 rood of soil which had been previously dressed with sea-sand. Apparently it was an experiment, and a successful one, for *avena grossa* was forthwith taken into regular cultivation here and on the other manors. It was the introduction of this new oat which caused the original variety to be distinguished as *minuta*.[1] The rate of sowing was reduced in 1342 to six bushels an acre; and for some years the surplus crop was all disposed of by sale at prices ranging from 2s. 3d. to three shillings a quarter.

By the close of the fourteenth century the cultivation of the large oat had so far improved that for some years a larger acreage was given up to it than to the small variety. At Werrington the rate of sowing was reduced in 1394 to four bushels an acre; at Hurdwick it was brought down more gradually. In 1412 the Hurdwick bailiff purchased four quarters of seed at North Hill; it was then, and in one or two subsequent years, described as *avena grossa et nigra*. This large black oat was fed to the lord's poultry and helped to fatten the boar that was served up every year for the Christmas feast. From 1460 onwards it was malted to provide ale for the harvesters.

Simultaneously with the adoption of the black oat, the rate of seeding for the smaller variety was increased to eight bushels an acre. In 1396 the two were blended at Ottery to form a mixed crop. The purpose of the mixture is disclosed in the account for Leigh two years later, when *avena mixta* was added, in the pro-

---

[1] *Avena grossa* was already in cultivation on some Devon manors. The bailiff's accounts of the earldom show that in 1287 both large and small oats were being sown at Exminster, Tiverton, Topsham, Barton, and Honiton (PRO Ministers' Accounts, S.C. 6, Bdle 827, no. 39).

portion of one third, "to improve the seed" of the *minuta*. In 1412 and 1416 *avena mixta* was sown at Hurdwick as a distinct crop at the rate of six bushels to the acre. The practice of mixing is recorded in the accounts of this manor from 1398 to 1416. Its effect was to bring about the gradual disappearance of the original small oat. After 1420 the black *avena grossa* formed the sole oat-crop on the Werrington demesne. At Hurdwick it was passed through a sieve, and the residue, called tail-oats, was sown as a distinct crop, to which the name *avena minuta* was thenceforth applied. Sometimes, as in 1435, the whole sowing was made from tail-oats; in other years these were added in the proportion of a quarter or a fifth to the seed reserved from last year's crop, which, from 1450 onwards, was sown at the reduced rate of four bushels to the acre. It was used chiefly for horse-fodder and for making porridge in Lent.

Pill-corn continued to be grown by the tenants at Werrington and Plymstock, and probably elsewhere. It appears under the heading "Receipts from Mill", and disappears from the accounts as soon as the mill is let out on lease. Its market value remained steady, and far higher than that of the new small oat which had ousted it from the demesnes. Thus, in 1480, when pill-corn was sold at Plymstock for 6s. 10d. a quarter, the small oat at Hurdwick fetched only 1s. 10d.

In 1332 the reeve of Hurdwick sold for 2s. 8d. four bushels of barley which he described as "lacking in grain". This was the year of the experiment with *avena grossa*; and it would seem that barley too was being tried as an experimental crop, but with less encouraging results. In the spring of the same year an acre and a half were sown with twelve bushels of seed. The result was a complete failure: in the words of the account, "nullus fructus proveniebat." Nevertheless three years later barley was sown at Ottery, a manor which for agricultural purposes included parcels of land at Newton and Ogbear in Tavistock. The seed had been purchased at a cost of fivepence the bushel, and 2 quarters 5 bushels were sown at six bushels to the acre. This produced a yield of seven quarters, including two bushels of chaff. For half a dozen years longer barley was grown on this manor; then it seems to have been given up. It was being sown at Denbury in 1393, at four bushels to the acre, but makes no further appearance in the

Tavistock records except that it was grown by some of the tenants at Plymstock and brought by them to be ground at Pomphlett mill.[1]

It has already been shown that rye was cultivated at Ottery in the first decade of the twelfth century. The surviving account rolls testify that it was grown at Werrington, Hurdwick, Newton, Ottery, Week, Milton, Leigh, and Burrington. After 1415 rye ceased to be grown at Werrington; but down to the Dissolution some twenty acres at Hurdwick were given up to this crop, of which a portion was regularly sold off at prices varying between fourpence a bushel in 1464 and 2s. 4d. in 1522. The 1524 account may be cited in illustration of its uses. At Michaelmas that year the bailiff accounted for 39 quarters 6 bushels as follows:

	qrs	bus.
Seed for 19 acres, at 2 bushels to the acre	4	6
To the farm labourers	4	6
Bread for the harvesters	2	0
To the servants during the lord's absence, 1 bushel a week for 29 weeks	3	5
Delivered to the lord abbot's lodging	8	4
Sold at 8d. per bushel	16	1
	39	6

Over the greater part of Devon rye went out of cultivation in the eighteenth century, and rye-bread vanished even from the tables of the poor. But in the period covered by these records wheaten bread, though regularly consumed in the abbey, was a luxury of which the humbler sort partook only on special occasions. Even within the abbey rye-bread kept its place to the very last. Each monk received for his weekly bread-ration four white 'meche' loaves and four black 'treyquarter' loaves, unless it was his turn to dispense hospitality, in which case he received seven of each.[2]

It was this 'treyquarter' loaf of rye-bread which was issued to the holders of the original burgages at Tavistock as food or

---

[1] In 1287 barley was cultivated on the demesnes of Plympton and Topsham, but not on those of Exminster, Tiverton, Hemyock, Barton, or Honiton (PRO Ministers' Accounts, S.C.6, Bdle 827, no. 39).

[2] W. D Bdle 84, no. 51.

recompense for their trouble when they were sent to call up supplies of wheat from Plymstock. In all probability wheat was
grown at Plymstock from the first. There are indications, which
however cannot be called decisive, that until the fourteenth century it played but a small part in the husbandry of the other
manors. None was sown at Werrington in 1298, and only four
bushels at Hurdwick in 1332. It makes no appearance in the
Ottery accounts before 1338; but four years later the reeve of that
manor was in a position to supply wheat seed to his brother reeves
of Hurdwick and Milton. The peak of cultivation was reached in
1454 at Werrington and 1458 at Hurdwick, when 29 acres 1
rood were sown with wheat at the former, and 42 acres 2 roods
at the latter. The rate of sowing, two bushels to the acre, never
varied except during the last two decades of the fourteenth century, when it was frequently increased at Ottery to two and a
half, three, and even three and a half bushels. In 1500, when the
bailiff of Werrington took a lease of the demesne, he agreed to pay
a rent of three pounds and to deliver annually, between Michaelmas and midsummer, thirty-two quarters of wheat, carriage
paid, at Tavistock, "according to the measure of the market
there". If the market price fell between Michaelmas and Lady
Day below one shilling a bushel, he paid the difference; if it rose
above that figure, the abbot and convent paid the excess. In 1529
the money rent was put up to eight pounds, and the wheat rent
brought down to twenty quarters "by Launceston measure".[1]
The year of highest price for this grain, as for rye, was 1522, when
a bushel fetched three shillings. In the other years covered by
the accounts the price ranged from eightpence to 1s. 8d. The
quantities delivered to the abbey for domestic consumption are
illustrated in the accounts for 1497.

	qrs	bus.
From Plymstock	79	5
Werrington	30	0
Hurdwick	29	2
Morwell	3	0
Leigh	5	4
	147	3

[1] W. D Bdle 73, nos. 112, 113.

At Christmas and Easter the farm labourers received an allowance of ale brewed from wheat-malt; this was called the prime brew (*braseum capitale*), in contrast with the common ale (*braseum cursale*) brewed from oats. After 1460 wheaten bread as well as rye was served up to the harvesters. Every year on Maundy Thursday the almoner distributed a quarter or two to the poor. Wheat-chaff was fed to the lord's pigeons, geese, and capons, and to the pigs in winter.

The late Sir William Ashley held "that the cultivation of rye was relatively more extensive the farther back we go in time; that during the Middle Ages rye was cultivated to some extent in almost all the arable districts, and that in some it preponderated over wheat."[1] So far as it goes, the Tavistock evidence is wholly in favour of these propositions.

Maslin, a mixture of wheat and rye, occurs once only, at Week in 1382, when a quarter was distributed among the labourers, and 12 quarters 6½ bushels were sold for £2 10s. 6½d. Vetches were grown on a small scale at Ottery in 1342–4. Peas find no place in the accounts except at Denbury in 1393, when they fetched one shilling a bushel; and beans only once, in 1413, when a bushel of seed costing eightpence was sown at Hurdwick.

The distribution of the staple crops, wheat, rye, and oats, on the two principal demesnes is shown in Tables VI and VII. Here the acre is of course the local customary acre. The accounts usually profess to give the acreage in terms of "measured land", and one Werrington account (1398) states that it was actually measured by the jury of the manor court. Later it was computed in more slipshod fashion, "by reckoning of seed". For the years marked with an asterisk the figures have been calculated from the quantities of seed-corn issued to the reeve, as declared in the granger's account. Such calculations can only be approximate, for the reeve might not sow all that was issued to him, or he might supplement it with seed purchased from elsewhere.

Concerning the routine of cultivation, the documents provide only scattered hints. Relating as they do solely to the abbot's barton lands, they throw no light upon the course of husbandry pursued by the tenants on the open fields or on the in-grounds of their farms. The agrarian landscape was diverse enough to

---

[1] Ashley, *op. cit.*, p. 132.

TABLE VI

WERRINGTON

Year	Wheat	Rye	Large Oats	Small Oats	Total Under Winter Corn	Total Under Oats	Grand Total
	a. r.	a. r.	a. r.	a. r.	a. r.	a. r.	a. r.
1298		22 2		106 0	22 2	106 0	128 2
1350	8 0	8 2	22 0	40 0	16 2	62 0	78 2
1356	12 1	14 2	28 0	31 0	26 3	59 0	85 3
*1383	19 0	1 2	13 0	23 2	20 2	36 2	57 0
1386	20 0	5 2	17 0	15 0	25 2	32 0	57 2
*1391	28 2	7 0	24 0	2 2	35 2	26 2	62 0
1394	24 2	6 2	?	?	31 0	36 0	67 0
1398	21 2	7 0	19 1	5 0	28 2	24 1	52 3
*1412	22 0	6 2	?	?	28 2	30 0	58 2
1413	20 0	5 0	24 2	1 2	25 0	26 0	51 0
1420	26 0		24 0		26 0	24 0	50 0
*1450	29 0		24 0		29 0	24 0	53 0
1452	25 0		26 0		25 0	26 0	51 0
1454	29 1		18 2		29 1	18 2	47 3
1459	24 2		17 2		24 2	17 2	42 0
*1460	25 0		20 0		25 0	20 0	45 0
1461	21 0		22 2		21 0	22 2	43 2
*1467	25 0		19 2		25 0	19 2	44 2
*1468	26 0		19 0		26 0	19 0	45 0
1470	24 0		21 3		24 0	21 3	45 3
1471	22 3		20 0		22 3	20 0	42 3
*1472	20 0		18 0		20 0	18 0	38 0
*1474	19 0		18 0		19 0	18 0	37 0
1477	20 0		14 2		20 0	14 2	34 2
*1480	20 0		16 2		20 0	16 2	36 2
1481	20 0		16 0		20 0	16 0	36 0
*1485	19 0		15 2		19 0	15 2	34 2
1486	18 0		14 0		18 0	14 0	32 0
1489	17 0		12 1		17 0	12 1	29 1
1490	16 0		14 1		16 0	14 1	30 1
1497	20 0		14 1		20 0	14 1	34 1
1498	20 0		14 1		20 0	14 1	34 1
1499	20 0		14 1		20 0	14 1	34 1

H

TABLE VII
HURDWICK

Year	Wheat	Rye	Large Oats	Small Oats	Total Under Winter Corn	Total Under Oats	Grand Total
	a. r.	a. r.	a. r.	a. r.	a. r.	a. r.	a. r.
1332	2 0	18 2	1 1	76 0	20 2	77 1	97 3
1347	?	18 0	?	?	?	50 0	?
1373	?	23 0	?	?	?	60 0	?
1398	8 2	33 2[1]	29 0[2]	60 2[3]	42 0[1]	89 3	131 3[4]
1412	22 0	31 3	35 0	44 0[5]	53 3	101 0	154 3
1413	20 0	40 0	69 0	32 0	60 0	101 0	161 0
1414	27 0	40 0	31 2[6]	41 0	67 0	72 2[6]	139 2[6]
1416	30 0	28 0	28 0	44 0[7]	58 0	80 0	138 0
1427	24 0	24 2	38 0	48 0	48 2	86 0	134 2
1433	7 0	12 0	40 0	9 2	19 0	49 2	68 2
1435	2 2	13 0	24 0	28 0	15 2	52 0	67 2
1441	0 2	10 2	0 0	24 0	11 0	24 0	35 0
1446	25 0	25 0	38 0	26 2	50 0	64 2	114 2
1450	23 0	24 3	35 0	37 0	47 3	72 0	119 3
1454	25 2	29 2	41 0	59 0	55 0	100 0	155 0
1458	42 2	28 0	61 0	72 0	70 2	133 0	203 2
1460	36 0	29 0	39 0	64 0	65 0	103 0	168 0
1463	38 0	22 0	44 0	15 0	60 0	59 0	119 0
1464	34 0	34 0	64 0	15 0	68 0	79 0	147 0
1466	21 0	24 0	25 0	20 1	45 0	45 1	90 1
1470	22 0	25 0	44 2	23 0	47 0	67 2	114 2
1471	26 0	29 0	50 0	28 0	55 0	78 0	133 0
1473	20 0	20 0	40 0	20 0	40 0	60 0	100 0
1475	16 0	20 0	40 0	16 0	36 0	56 0	92 0
1477	12 0	20 0	20 0	40 0	32 0	60 0	92 0
1480	12 0	20 0	40 0	24 0	32 0	64 0	96 0
1482	16 0	20 0	24 0	36 0	36 0	60 0	96 0
1489	14 0	22 0	17 1	54 2	36 0	71 3	107 3
1490	15 0	21 0	18 1	56 0	36 0	74 1	110 1
1491	16 0	24 2	22 0	48 0	40 2	70 0	110 2
1492	17 0	30 0	23 0	53 0	47 0	76 0	123 0

[1] and 36 p. [2] and 5 p.; "large and mixed" oats. [3] and 37 p.
[4] and 38 p. [5] 22 a. of mixed oats also sown. [6] and 33 p.
[7] 8 a. of mixed oats also sown.

TABLE VII: HURDWICK (*cont.*)

Year	Wheat	Rye	Large Oats	Small Oats	Total Under Winter Corn	Total Under Oats	Grand Total
	a. r.	a. r.	a. r.	a. r.	a. r.	a. r.	a. r.
1497	19 0	23 0	24 2	51 0	42 0	75 2	117 2
1498	16 2	20 3	24 2	55 0	37 1	79 2	116 3
1502	5 0	21 2	24 0	51 1	26 2	75 1	101 3
1504	17 0	29 0	28 2	56 0	46 0	84 2	130 2
1505	19 0	28 0	27 0	53 2	47 0	80 2	127 2
1508	20 0	20 2	32 2	40 1	40 2	72 3	113 1
1509	20 2	21 0	34 0	47 0	41 2	81 0	122 2
1513	22 0	19 0	30 2	48 0	41 0	78 2	119 2
1514	20 2	18 0	30 0	49 0	38 2	79 0	117 2
1516	21 0	18 2	31 0	48 2	39 2	79 2	119 0
1517	22 0	20 2	31 2	49 1	42 2	80 3	123 1
1522	20 2	18 2	30 1	46 0	39 0	76 1	115 1
1524	22 0	19 0	31 2	46 0	41 0	77 2	118 2
1533	20 0	20 0	34 0	42 0	40 0	76 0	116 0
1537	20 0	22 0	38 0	42 0	42 0	80 0	122 0
1538	20 0	18 0	36 0	46 0	38 0	82 0	120 0

accommodate more than one variety of practice. Where groups of husbandmen till intermingled strips in common, there can be little room for innovation; but in Devonshire, as we have seen, the open field had begun to disappear by the fourteenth century, and within their several enclosures both lord and tenants could be as unsystematic as they pleased.

The diversity of agricultural practice, and the difficulty of interpreting such information as the documents provide, may be illustrated from an extent drawn up in 1377 after the death of Hugh de Courtenay, earl of Devon. Fourteen of the earl's manors were described and valued, the demesne arable, pasture, wood, and meadow of each being separately enumerated; and a note was made not only of the arable acreage at its full extension, but also of the area actually tilled in 1377. The figures are set forth in Table VIII.[1] They could be read as indicating a two-course rotation in the first three manors, and a three-course in the next four; but

[1] PRO Inquisitions *post mortem*, C135, File 260 (3).

TABLE VIII

Manor	Total Arable Area	Acres Actually Tilled
Sampford Courtenay	80	40
Chawleigh	60	28
Kenn	145	60
Musbury	60	40
Hulham	30	20
Stedcombe	100	66
Colyton	105	60
Aylesbeare	107	30
Chulmleigh	100	38
Towsington	120	30
Exminster	120	106
Okehampton	100	30
Plympton	100	74
Tiverton	86	31

the others cannot be reduced to any common formula. Some of the manors may be suffering from the after-effects of the Black Death and later epidemics, a shortage of man-power causing a higher proportion of the land than usual to remain untilled. In some cases, again, the first figure may include a portion of outfield belonging to the demesne which in 1377 was awaiting its turn to be ploughed up.

In the seventeenth and eighteenth centuries convertible husbandry was the rule in Devon. A sequence of crops followed one another annually on the same ground, and was then begun again elsewhere, the first site remaining under grass for several years. In 1668 it was reported that a six-year course was generally practised, the usual sequence being: wheat, two crops of barley, oats, peas, and oats again.[1] Carew, who published his survey of the neighbouring shire in 1602, declares that as a rule the Cornish husbandman, after taking two crops of wheat and two of oats, was driven to leave the soil under grass for seven or eight years at least, and meanwhile "to make his breach elsewhere".[2]

[1] Samuel Colepresse: *A Georgicall Account of Devon and Cornwall*, p. 5 (MS. in Royal Society's Classified Papers, x, 3, no. 12).
[2] Carew, *Survey of Cornwall*, p. 63.

Except that a place must be found in it for rye, this scheme agrees very well with the indications given in the Tavistock records. There too we meet the same word as that used by Carew to denote land freshly broken up for cultivation. In provincial usage *breach, break,* and *breck* is frequently associated with the cultivation of the outfield. Thus in 1566 the arable holdings at Woodhuish were described as "lying at large in twoe commen feldes and *lez Breches*".[1] When we come across "four *breches* of wheatland and three of oat-land", as we do for example at Werrington in 1498, it is natural to suppose that the word is being used in this way to signify arable shifts tilled on the common pasture. As the area under wheat and oats that year was twenty and fourteen and a quarter acres respectively, the average size of these breaks may be taken as approximately five acres, or less if some of the crop was being raised on in-ground. To protect the growing corn the breaks would need to be surrounded with temporary fences. This may explain the frequent sums expended on "fencing in the lord's rye" or "making a fence around the wheat-park".

On the other hand, such names as Great and Little Brake, Higher and Lower Breaches, are often applied to fields which present no appearance of having been enclosed from common pasture, lying as they do quite near to ancient villages and in the midst of obvious in-grounds.[2] It may well be, therefore, that when the abbot "made his breach elsewhere", he did so not on the common pasture but within the permanent enclosures.[3] We have already noticed that the custom of outfield tillage varied from parish to parish. There is no parallel at Tavistock to the association of infield and outfield just noted at Woodhuish, or to the similar arrangement linking definite areas on Ramsdown with the holdings of the abbot's tenants in Milton. The riverside farms of Tavistock enjoyed only a right of pasture on the common, and even that right was subject to interruption if the abbot chose to till the common himself or to let off parts of it for cultivation by others. This custom stands in marked contrast with that of such

[1] DA XLIII, 1911, p. 282.   [2] As at Exminster and Kenton.
[3] Cf. the language of the by-law enacted at Cardington, Bedfordshire, in 1766, requiring all the tenants to mark off their holdings by grass balks. They are "to begin this Fallow, and then the next Breach, and then the last Field". This is simply a way of describing the third, second, and first fields of an open-field township (Orwin, *The Open Fields*, p. 47).

manors as Hemyock and Clayhidon, where it is noted that "the
Tenaunts may breake upp or eare any parte of the lordes'
waste to sowe any grayne in, payenge for every acre iiij*d*. as longe
as they shall sowe hit."[1]

To discover whether or how far outfield tillage entered into the
husbandry of the Tavistock demesnes is no easy matter. The surviving Plymstock accounts all belong to a time when the abbot
had ceased to cultivate the barton; those of the other manors, except Werrington and Hurdwick, are too few to answer this question; and the ancient outlines of the Werrington demesne have
been obliterated by conversion into park-land. But the topography of Hurdwick may even now be studied on the spot, with
the aid of a beautifully coloured map drawn in 1757 and still kept
in the Bedford Office. The names and acreage of all the ancient
fields are shown, and the total area of the barton land is stated, in
customary measure, as 672 acres 1 rood 27 poles. This agrees
closely enough with a survey drawn up in 1572, in which the same
field names occur but with acreages given in somewhat rounder
figures. From the total thus ascertained we have to deduct
approximately two hundred acres for the enclosures—Long-
stone, Muggleberry, Quarry-park, and Lillyford—which, as we
learn from the accounts, were rented by tenants-at-will or kept
in hand as pasture for the lord's cattle. Roads, farm buildings, and
hedges will use up at least twenty acres more. That leaves about
four hundred and fifty acres for possible cultivation; but since
the average under crops was only one hundred and eighteen acres,
and the fallow can rarely have taken much above fifty, it is clear
that the abbot had plenty of room for convertible husbandry without going outside his barton. There was no need to make temporary enclosures far out on the unrewarding soil of Heathfield.[2]

Maitland, writing of the Domesday period, supposes that tillage in Devon and Cornwall was "of that backward kind which
ploughs enormous tracts for a poor return".[3] But there is no proof
that it was so, even in the eleventh century. In the fourteenth it is

---

[1] DA XLIII, 1911, p. 290.

[2] In Vancouver's time the south-Devon farmer used about 20 per cent. of
his acreage as meadow and permanent pasture, and 33 per cent. for tillage;
the remainder lay under grass for three years or more, awaiting its turn to be
broken up (Vancouver, *op. cit.*, p. 159). Cf. Marshall, *op. cit.*, I, pp. 135, 136.

[3] Maitland, *op. cit.*, p. 425.

clear that so far from ploughing vast tracts, the monks of Tavistock ploughed only a fraction of the available soil, and by intensive manuring did their utmost to enhance its productivity. We shall find that judged by the standard of that age the returns were anything but poor.

There was probably no rule governing the length of time a piece of ground, after several years of cropping, was suffered to lie under grass. The method, or combination of methods, used in breaking it up for tillage may be illustrated from the accounts for 1398. We note, first, the contrast between the number of acres ploughed, as declared in the item "Cost of Ploughing", and the number sown.

	Acres ploughed	Acres sown
Hurdwick	185¾	131¾
Werrington	65¼	52¾
Leigh	60	49
Milton	49	43

The difference between the first and second figures represents the fallow, land ploughed during the year of account and left unsown until after the ensuing harvest. The fallowing might take place either in winter, that is, about Candlemas, or more commonly in May.[1] Little more than half the surface of the field would be stirred, and that only to a depth of three or four inches. Then the sheep might be folded on it to manure it with their dung and to eat down the remaining grass and weeds. There are constant references in the accounts to land thus ploughed "before the lord's fold".[2] Such land would naturally be far better manured than a fallow field of several hundred acres in the midlands, on which, under the two- or three-field system, the sheep were turned loose every second or third year. Alternatively, the field, after an interval, would be harrowed, and so much of the 'spine' as was not already rotted would be burnt; after which a dressing of sand or dung would be applied, and by October the ground would be ready for seed-ploughing. Of the fifty-four acres fallowed at

[1] Summer fallowing is expressly mentioned at Hurdwick in 1347. Cf. Vancouver, op. cit., p. 160.
[2] Cf. Vancouver, op. cit., pp. 160, 166; and for the sheepfold after wheat had been sown, pp. 148, 150, 151.

Hurdwick in the year under notice, thirty-eight were intended for burning and sixteen for dunging, but only half the beat, or to be exact 19 acres 1 rood 35 poles, had been actually burnt when the account for the year was closed.

Beat-burning was long esteemed a particularly suitable preparation for rye. Thus, of twenty-two and a half acres sown with this grain at Werrington in 1298, thirteen and a half were beatland and nine were *terra compostata*. A few examples may be given from other manors.

		Acres sown with rye		Beatland	*Terra compostata*
Hurdwick	1332	18½		14	4½
Ottery	1343	6½		5½	—
Week	1382	12¾	of which	4¾	8
Hurdwick	1398	33½		17	16½
Hurdwick	1412	31¾		10¾	21
Hurdwick	1413	40		6½	33½
Hurdwick	1414	40		6	33

It was also considered that while two and a half or three bushels of rye-seed were required for an acre of *terra compostata*, two bushels were enough on beatland. Rye uses less nitrogen than wheat; hence the loss of nitrogen attendant on beat-burning might not be detrimental, but the positive efficacy of the process, in liberating the mineral contents of the soil, would benefit wheat no less than rye. It is noticeable that the proportion of beatland grows less as the years pass, but whether because of rising costs or dwindling faith is not clear. After 1416 beat practically disappears from the accounts, and rye is sown at a uniform rate of two bushels to the acre. Sea-sand, as a dressing for wheat, continues in use to the last.[1]

Down to the middle of the fifteenth century, when reeves and bailiffs wished to speak of wheat and rye collectively, the term they used was not winter corn but hard corn (*durum bladum*). After 1470 the more usual term was clean corn (*purum bladum*).[2]

[1] From 1514 onwards it is always said to have been purchased *pro compostura terre frumenti*.

[2] Ashley, *op. cit.*, p. 30, is clearly wrong in supposing the conception of wheat and rye as hard corn to have been introduced from Denmark in the seventeenth century.

It is to be supposed that one or other of these grains, or some perhaps of each, was always sown on fallow ground, to be succeeded by oats, which in Cornwall were sometimes known as the farewell crop. But the tables give no clear picture. The area fallowed at Hurdwick in 1412, 48 acres 1 rood, does not correspond with any figure in the next year's account. We may fancy that the 31 acres 3 roods sown with rye in 1412 were identical with the 32 acres sown with small oats in the following year, and the 31 acres 2 roods 33 perches sown with large oats the year after; but no such exact correspondence is visible elsewhere in the statistics. By the middle of the fifteenth century the item "Cost of Ploughing" ceases to give trustworthy information concerning the acreage in fallow.[1]

Seed-ploughing for wheat began in October, and for rye early in November. In 1458 forty-two and a half acres of wheat and twenty-eight of rye were ploughed, sown, and harrowed in at Hurdwick by the demesne staff of two ploughmen and three drivers, with the aid of twenty-seven customary tenants who ploughed a day each for their boonworks, and three lads who were hired for four weeks at a weekly wage of tenpence. Meanwhile the produce of the year's harvest was being threshed and winnowed; it consisted of:

	qrs.	bus.			qrs.	bus.
Wheat	41	4		Large oats	80	0
Rye	73	5		Small oats	113	0
	115	1			193	0

Threshing was always done by piecework, and winnowing too as a rule, but this year all the grain was winnowed by one maid, who was employed for thirty-one weeks at threepence weekly. For oats the land was ploughed once, in February and March. This year it took six weeks or more to plough and sow one hundred and thirty-three acres. During the spring and summer months the growing corn was fenced in; fallowing was begun for next year's hard corn, with its attendant operations of beat-burning and sanding; and all the crops were weeded and hoed.[2] Finally, by the

[1] In 1458, for example, when 203½ acres were sown, only 28 are accounted for as an item in the ploughing costs.

[2] Marshall, *op. cit.*, I, p. 165, says: "The hoeing of field crops has not yet

first week in August, or thereabouts, it was time to begin cutting the wheat.

As the account for the year was closed at Michaelmas, before threshing had begun, the results of the harvest must be sought in the next year's account. For most of the abbot's manors, unfortunately, very few consecutive accounts have survived, but for Hurdwick they are extant in sufficient numbers to enable averages to be struck. It is unnecessary, in the case of this manor, to make any addition or deduction in respect of tithe, for as rectors of the parish the abbot and convent owned the tithes of their demesne, and consequently paid none, while the tithe-corn due to them from the parishioners was accounted for separately, not by the reeve of Hurdwick but by the monk-steward of the abbey.[1]

In the following tables the third column gives the *Exitus Grangie*, or quantity threshed during the year of account succeeding that in which the crop was sown. The fourth column gives the yield per quarter, obtained by dividing the second column into the third; and the fifth gives the acre yield, obtained by dividing the number of acres sown into the *Exitus*.

TABLE IX
YIELD OF HARD CORN

WHEAT				
Year of sowing	Seed qrs bus.	Yield qrs bus.	Yield per quarter	Yield per acre (bus.)
OTTERY				
1342	1 4	6 4	4·33	8·66
1343	1 0	5 1	5·12	10·25
HURDWICK				
1412	5 5	27 3	4·86	9·95
1413	5 5	22 7	4·08	9·20

been introduced"; and cf. Vancouver, *op. cit.*, p. 144. But the cost of "hoeing all the corn in summer" is regularly entered in these Tavistock accounts.

[1] During the thirteenth century the Hurdwick demesne had been tithed in order that the almoner might distribute a percentage to the poor, but in 1295 he exchanged this for the Ottery demesne tithes of corn and hay (W. D Bdle 42, no. 2).

TABLE IX: YIELD OF HARD CORN *(cont.)*

Year of sowing	Seed qrs	bus.	Yield qrs	bus.	Yield per quarter	Yield per acre (bus.)
1463	9	4	50	5	5·32	10·66
1470	5	4	21	1½	3·85	7·70
1489	3	4	17	4	5·00	10·00
1490	3	6	30	0	8·00	16·00
1491	4	0	24	0	6·00	12·00
1497	4	6	24	1	5·07	10·16
1504	4	3	27	4	6·28	12·94
1508	5	0	46	5	9·32	18·65
1513	5	4	36	6	6·68	13·36
1516	5	2	33	0	6·28	12·57
1537	5	0	23	1	4·62	9·25

WERRINGTON

1459	6	1¼	47	2	7·67	15·44
1471	5	5¼	33	5	5·94	11·82
1498	5	0	38	0	7·60	15·20

RYE

OTTERY

1335	6	2	47	6	7·64	19·10
1342	1	4	13	6	9·16	18·33
1343	1	5	10	3	6·30	12·76

HURDWICK

1412	9	1	109	4	12·00	27·58
1413	10	4½	126	6	12·07	25·35
1463	5	4	39	2½	7·14	14·29
1470	6	2	33	0	5·28	10·56
1489	5	4	54	4	9·90	19·81
1490	5	2	58	2	11·09	22·18
1491	6	1	41	0	6·69	13·38
1497	5	6	37	1	6·45	12·91
1504	7	2	49	0	6·75	13·51
1508	5	1	40	0	7·80	15·61
1513	4	6	42	0	8·84	17·68
1516	4	5	54	0	11·67	23·35
1537	5	4	30	0	5·45	10·90

TABLE X

YIELD OF OATS

LARGE OATS					
Year of sowing	Seed qrs	bus.	Yield qrs	bus.	Yield per quarter	Yield per acre (bus.)

OTTERY					
1335	20	0	80	4	4·02	30·66
1342	4	4	20	4	4·55	20·85
1343	3	0	16	4	5·50	33·00
HURDWICK					
1412	24	2	111	7	4·61	25·57
1413	43	1	72	0	1·66	8·35
1463	22	0	52	0	2·36	9·45
1470	22	2	42	4	1·91	7·76
1489	8	5	47	4	5·50	22·00
1490	9	1	54	0	5·91	23·67
1491	11	0	59	0	5·36	21·45
1497	12	2	62	0	5·06	20·24
1504	14	2	63	0	4·42	17·68
1508	16	2	76	4	4·70	18·83
1513	15	2	83	4	5·47	21·90
1516	15	4	81	0	5·22	20·90
1537	19	0	46	1	2·55	9·70
WERRINGTON					
1459	8	6	35	0	4·00	16·00
1471	10	0	40	0	4·00	16·00
1498	7	1	28	4	4·00	16·00

SMALL OATS					
OTTERY					
1335	67	0	230	7	3·44	26·38
1342	33	4	146	7	4·38	35·07
1343	28	4	97	3	3·42	27·33

TABLE X: YIELD OF OATS (*cont.*)

Year of sowing	Seed qrs bus.		Yield qrs bus.		Yield per quarter	Yield per acre (bus.)
			HURDWICK			
1412	41	5	231	0	5·55	42·00
1413	28	3	236	6	8·34	59·19
1463	7	4	94	0	12·53	50·13
1470	11	4	98	4	7·50	34·21
1489	27	2	119	4	4·38	17·53
1490	28	0	145	0	5·17	20·71
1491	24	0	115	0	4·79	19·16
1497	25	4	99	0	3·88	15·53
1504	28	0	102	0	3·64	14·57
1508	20	1	100	1	4·97	19·90
1513	24	0	104	0	4·34	17·33
1516	24	2	97	0	4·00	16·00
1537	21	0	108	6½	5·18	20·72

Lord Beveridge, who has worked through the accounts of eight manors in Somerset, Wilts, Hants, Oxfordshire, Berks, and Bucks, ranging in date from 1208 to 1453, calculates that the average yield of wheat on those manors was 9·36 bushels to the acre.[1] The Hurdwick average was 11·73. It must however be remembered that the acre in Devon was nearly one-fifth larger than the statute acre, and that the bushel at Tavistock may have been larger than the standard bushel, as it certainly was at Exeter and in Cornwall.[2] For purposes of comparison, therefore, it is safer to express the yield as a multiple of the grain sown. This will give what is usually called the yield per quarter, or, what comes to the same thing, the yield per bushel; and the validity of the result is unaffected by local peculiarities of weights and measures.

[1] *Economic History*, I, 1926–9, p. 158. It has been argued that this figure should be increased by one-ninth on account of tithe (*ibid.*, III, 1934–7, p. 183). If so, the true acre-yield was 10·4 bushels.

[2] See above, p. 30, and for Cornwall, Carew, *op. cit.*, p. 146. The accounts make it clear that 4 pecks = 1 bushel, and 8 bushels = 1 quarter, but they do not reveal how many gallons went to the peck.

The anonymous author of a thirteenth-century treatise on husbandry declares that "barley ought to yield to the eighth grain,
that is to say, a quarter sown should yield eight quarters; rye
should yield to the seventh grain; and wheat ought by right to
yield to the fifth grain, and oats to the fourth."[1] These, however,
were ideal figures, by no means universally attained in practice.
On the eight manors for which Lord Beveridge has compiled
statistics the mean yield per quarter of barley was 3·82, of wheat
3·89, and of oats 2·43.[2] On the carefully managed Kentish
estates of Canterbury Cathedral Priory, the wheat yield varied
between 3 and 3·5, and barley yields were seldom higher.[3] At
Hawstead, in Suffolk, the wheat yield rose to fourfold only in
good years.[4] At Forncett, in Norfolk, it was usually about five-
fold.[5] We turn to Cambridgeshire, the county which has been
described as our champion wheat-grower. There, at Oakington,
taking fifty-nine years of account between 1272 and 1409, we
find an average yield of 5·43 per quarter.[6]

At Hurdwick the average wheat yield was 5·79. It is true that
an average struck from only thirteen years may well give an un-
trustworthy picture; but much the same quantities of grain were
threshed in other years, when the acreage under wheat did not
greatly vary and the rate of seeding remained constant.[7] Moreover, the yield at Werrington, in the few years for which it can
be computed, was even higher; and on the much more favourable
soil of Plymstock it is unlikely to have been less.[8]

The cultivation of the other grains was equally successful. With
rye, the sevenfold yield postulated by the author of *Hosebonderie*
was exceeded by the average of 8·54 at Hurdwick, where the

[1] Walter of Henley's *Husbandry*, p. 71.   [2] *Economic History*, loc. cit.
[3] Smith, *Canterbury Cathedral Priory*, p. 135.
[4] Cullum, *History of Hawsted*, p. 187.   [5] Davenport, *op. cit.*, p. 30.
[6] Page, *The Estates of Crowland Abbey*, pp. 329, 330. At Grantchester in
the same county the wheat-yield was only 3·4 (*Economic History*, III, 1934–7,
p. 165).
[7] Cf. Table XI, p. 116.
[8] At Werrington it was the granger who accounted for the *exitus*. He
issued seed-corn to the reeve, who was responsible for sowing. Hence the
yields on this manor can only be computed when the reeve's account for one
year and the granger's for the next have both survived.
The exactly fourfold yield of oats here is curious, and prompts a suspicion: was the abbot being cheated? If so, the true yield must have been
still higher.

acre-yield was 17·47 bushels. The same writer's fourfold yield of oats may be contrasted on the one hand with that of 2·43 on the demesnes examined by Lord Beveridge, where the acre-yield was 10·56 bushels, and on the other with the Hurdwick averages of 4·21 for large oats and 5·71 for small oats, with acre-yields of 17·50 and 26·69 bushels respectively.

Thus, in a county which has never in modern times been accounted a pre-eminent corn-grower, the monks of Tavistock raised crops well up to the highest standards of their contemporaries. They possessed little first-rate soil, and their system of tillage would hardly commend itself to modern farmers. But the abuse of continuous cropping touched only a small proportion of their lands at any one time, and it was largely counteracted by repeated applications of sea-sand, dung, and ashes. This intensive and costly manuring enabled them to achieve results which by contemporary standards may fairly be called brilliant.

We may here recall an observation made by Oliver Cromwell. "I have been in all the counties of England," he is reported to have said, "and I think the husbandry of Devonshire the best."[1] There is no evidence that the agricultural practice of Devon underwent any fundamental change in the interval of a hundred years between the Dissolution and Cromwell's time. Hence the excellence ascribed to it in the seventeenth century must have been a legacy from the age of monastic landlords. It was not until the eighteenth century that through the obstinate conservatism of its farmers, and the injudicious use of beat-burning, the arable husbandry of Devon forfeited its old pre-eminence.

---

[1] Powell, *John Aubrey and his Friends*, p. 91, quoting Bodleian MS. Aubrey 2, fo. 83.

Tables XI–XVII
GRAIN STATISTICS

In the following tables the first column gives the year of the account from which the statistics are drawn. Thus "1332" means the twelve months ending at Michaelmas 1332.

The third column records the total quantity of grain of which account is rendered. Most of it represents the yield of the previous year's harvest, but in some years this is supplemented by seed-corn purchased from outside sources, and occasionally also by grain delivered from one of the other manors.

The fourth column gives the quantity used for seed on the demesne during the year of account.

The fifth gives the quantity consumed by the abbey and its dependents. This is a composite item, including grain delivered to the abbey for domestic consumption, with that given away in charity, and that supplied to officials and servants as part of their remuneration.

The seventh gives the quantity sold, and the eighth the price per quarter. Prices marked * are mean prices: those marked † refer to toll-corn.

Table XI
WHEAT

Year	Manor	In stock		Used for seed		Consumed		Sold		Price per qr
		qrs	bus.	qrs	bus.	qrs	bus.	qrs	bus.	
1332	Hurdwick	16	4½		4	16	0½			
1338	Ottery		7		7					
1342	,,	13	6	1	4	1	3	10	7	4s. 0d.
1343	,,	10	1	1	0	1	0	8	1	4s. 8d.
1344	,,	5	1		4		4	4	1	
1350	Werrington	2	0	2	0					
1356	,,	3	0½	3	0½					
1358	Burrington	13	1½	1	4	2	6½	8	7	6s. 8d.
1381	Ottery	16	3	3	6	2	7½	9	5½	7s. 4d.
1382	Week	11	1½	2	0	8	7		2½	7s. 4d.
1383	Werrington	15	2	4	6	10	0		4	6s. 8d.
1385	Week							7	4	5s. 8d.
1386	Ottery	9	3	2	2	1	2	5	7	7s. 4d.
,,	Werrington	32	0	5	4	25	4	1	0	6s. 0d.
1390	Ottery	19	7	4	5½	3	6	11	3½	6s. 0d.*
1391	Werrington	41	5	7	1	32	4	2	0	12s. 0d.
1392	Plymstock							1	6†	7s. 4d.*†
1393	Denbury	17	0	5	0		3	11	5	5s. 4d.
1394	Werrington			6	1					
1396	Ottery	12	5	3	4	2	2	6	7	6s. 2d.*

TABLE XI: WHEAT (*cont.*)

Year	Manor	In stock		Used for seed		Consumed		Sold		Price per qr	
		qrs	bus.	qrs	bus.	qrs	bus.	qrs	bus.		
1397	Plymstock							1	4†	6s.	2d.*†
1398	Hurdwick	12	0	2	1			9	7	7s.	8d.*
,,	Werrington	36	2	5	3	25	0	5	7	7s.	8d.*
1412	Hurdwick	52	3½	5	5	8	0	38	6½	6s.	0d.
,,	Werrington	49	4	5	4	18	1		7	8s.	0d.
1413	,,	33	1	4	5	28	0		3¾	6s.	8d.
,,	Hurdwick	28	7	5	5	18	5½	4	4½	6s.	8d.
1414	,,	37	4½	8	4½	16	0	13	0		
,,	Plymstock							3	1†	5s.	4d.*†
1416	Hurdwick	25	6	7	4	16	6	1	4	8s.	0d.
1420	Werrington			6	4						
1427	Hurdwick	27	0	6	0	16	0	5	0	6s.	8d.
1431	Plymstock							1	6½†	10s.	0d.*†
1432	,,							2	2†	7s.	8d.*†
1433	,,							2	3½†	10s.	0d.*†
,,	Hurdwick	8	2					6	4	9s.	4d.
1435	,,	4	0		6			3	2	6s.	8d.
1441	,,		1		1						
1442	Plymstock							4	5¾†	5s.	4d.*†
1446	Hurdwick	28	3½	7	0	20	5		6½	5s.	0d.*
1450	,,	31	3½	5	6	17	6½	7	7	9s.	4d.*
,,	Werrington	46	7	7	2¾	39	0				
1452	,,			6	1¾						
1454	,,	43	2½	7	2½	36	0			6s.	0d.
,,	Hurdwick	45	7	6	3	23	3	16	1		
1458	,,	41	4	10	5	15	1	15	6	8s.	0d.*
1459	Werrington			6	1¼						
1460	Hurdwick	77	6	9	1	52	0	16	5	7s.	4d.*
,,	Werrington	47	2	6	2	41	0				
1461	,,	37	0¾	5	2¼	31	2½		4	8s.	0d.
1463	Hurdwick	61	2	9	4	51	0		6	5s.	4d.
1464	,,	50	5	8	4	40	4½	1	3½	4s.	8d.
1466	,,	28	2	5	2	23	0				
1467	Werrington	47	4½	6	2¼	33	7	7	3¼		
1468	,,	44	2¼	6	4¼	37	6				
1470	Plymstock							2	6½†	8s.	5½d.*†
,,	Hurdwick	24	0	5	4	18	0		4	13s.	4d.

I

TABLE XI: WHEAT (*cont.*)

Year	Manor	In stock	Used for seed	Con-sumed	Sold	Price per qr
		qrs bus.	qrs bus.	qrs bus.	qrs bus.	
1470	Werrington		6 0			
1471	,,		5 5¼			
,,	Hurdwick	21 1½	6 4	8 0	6 5½	8s. 0d.
1472	Werrington	33 5	5 0½	27 0½	1 3¾	9s. 4d.
1473	Hurdwick	21 0	5 0	13 4	2 4	6s. 8d.
1474	Werrington	32 5½	4 2½	28 3		
1475	Plymstock				3 4½†	6s. 0d.
,,	Hurdwick	20 1	4 0	14 1	2 0	6s. 8d.
1477	Werrington		5 0			
,,	Plymstock				3 2½†	6s. 4d.*†
,,	Hurdwick	20 5	3 0	15 3	2 2	8s. 0d.
1480	Plymstock				2 5†	6s. 0d.*†
,,	Hurdwick	22 6	3 0	19 5	1	7s. 4d.
,,	Werrington	36 0	5 1	30 7		
1481	Plymstock				1 7¾†	6s. 8d.†
,,	Werrington		5 0			
1482	Hurdwick	26 4	4 0	19 2	3 2	8s. 0d.
1485	Werrington	36 2	4 5½	31 4½		
1486	,,		4 3¾			
1489	,,		4 2			
,,	Hurdwick	31 0	3 4	26 6½	5½	8s. 0d.
1490	,,	17 4	3 6	13 2	4	9s. 4d.
,,	Werrington		4 0			
1491	Hurdwick	30 0	4 0	26 0		
1492	,,	24 0	4 3	18 6	7	8s. 0d.
1497	,,	35 4	4 6	30 4	2	12s. 0d.
,,	Werrington		5 0			
,,	Morwell	11 3	1 1½	3 4	6 5½	12s. 0d.
,,	Leigh	8 0	1 4½	5 6	5½	10s. 8d.
1498	Hurdwick	24 1	4 1	19 4	4	10s. 8d.
,,	Werrington		7 1			
1499	,,	38 0	5 0	32 0	1 0	5s. 0d.
c.1500	Leigh	12 0	2 0½	8 2	1 5½	8s. 0d.
1502	Hurdwick	26 0	4 2	20 4	1 2	13s. 4d.
1504	,,	26 0	4 3	20 4	1 1	13s. 4d.
1505	,,	27 4	4 6	21 6	1 0	8s. 0d.
1508	,,	28 1	5 0	23 1		

TABLE XI: WHEAT (*cont.*)

Year	Manor	In stock		Used for seed		Con-sumed		Sold		Price per qr
		qrs	bus.	qrs	bus.	qrs	bus.	qrs	bus.	
1509	Hurdwick	46	5	5	1	40	6		6	6s. 8d.
1513	,,	25	6	5	4	20	1		1	
1514	,,	36	6	5	1	31	3		2	13s. 4d.
1516	,,	23	0	5	2	17	6			
1517	,,	33	0	5	4	26	0	1	4	12s. 0d.
1522	,,	32	5	5	1	27	3		1	24s. 0d.
1524	,,	25	6	5	4	20	1		1	9s. 4d.
1533	,,	20	2	5	0	15	2			
1537	,,	21	1	5	0	16	1			
1538	,,	23	1	5	0	18	1			

TABLE XII
WHEAT-CHAFF

Year	Manor	In stock		Consumed		Sold		Price per qr
		qrs	bus.	qrs	bus.	qrs	bus.	
1332	Hurdwick	1	4	1	4			
1342	Ottery	1	4			1	4	1s. 10d.
1343	,,	1	3		3	1	0	2s. 0d.
1344	,,	1	4		2	1	2	
1356	Werrington	1	0	1	0			
1358	Burrington	3	6½	1	4	2	2½	2s. 0d.
1381	Ottery	1	2	1	2			
1382	Week		4½		4½			
1383	Werrington	12	5	12	5			
1386	,,	10	6	10	6			
1390	Ottery	1	1		3		6	1s. 4d.
1391	Werrington	14	4	13	4	1	0	
1393	Denbury	11	6			11	6	4s. 0d.
1396	Ottery	2	2	2	2			
1398	Werrington	6	2	5	0	1	2	3s. 0d.
1412	,,	10	0	6	5	3	3	3s. 0d.*
,,	Hurdwick	16	4½	2	5	13	7½	3s. 0d.*
1413	,,	24	7	3	7	21	0	3s. 0d.*

TABLE XII: WHEAT-CHAFF (*cont.*)

Year	Manor	In stock	Con-sumed	Sold	Price per qr
		qrs bus.	qrs bus.	qrs bus.	
1413	Werrington	11 2	5 6	5 4	3s. 4d.
1414	Hurdwick	12 1	2 0	10 1	2s. 10d.*
1416	,,	11 4	4	11 0	3s. 0d.*
1427	,,	15 0	1 4	13 4	2s. 8d.
1435	,,	1 1		1 1	3s. 4d.
1446	,,	5 0	4 6	2	2s. 8d.
1450	,,	5 1	1 6	3 3	3s. 4d.
1450	Werrington	12 2	11 2	1 0	2s. 0d.
1454	,,	11 4	9 4	2 0	1s. 8d.
,,	Hurdwick	6 0	3 0	3 0	3s. 4d.
1458	,,	8 4		8 4	3s. 4d.
1460	,,	1½		1½	3s. 4d.
,,	Werrington	3 0	2 4	4	2s. 0d.
1461	,,	11 4	1 4	10 0	6s. 8d.
1466	Hurdwick	5		5	
1467	Werrington	7 3	7 3		
1468	,,	7 0	7 0		
1470	Hurdwick	1 0		1 0	4s. 0d.
1472	Werrington	11 5	11 5		
1473	Hurdwick	2		2	
1474	Werrington	8 3	8 3		
1475	Hurdwick	2 4		2 4	3s. 4d.
1477	,,	2		2	4s. 0d.
1480	Werrington	5 0	5 0		
1485	,,	1 0	1 0		
1499	,,	2 0	2 0		

TABLE XIII

RYE

Year	Manor	In stock	Used for seed	Con-sumed	Sold	Price per qr
		qrs bus.	qrs bus.	qrs bus.	qrs bus.	
1298	Werrington	21 0	4 5½	11 3	4 7½	12s. 0d.
1332	Hurdwick	16 0	4 6½	10 4	5½	6s. 8d.

TABLE XIII: RYE (cont.)

Year	Manor	In stock		Used for seed		Con-sumed		Sold		Price per qr
		qrs	bus.	qrs	bus.	qrs	bus.	qrs	bus.	
1335	Ottery	6	2	6	2					
1336	,,	47	6	4	7	37	4	5	3	3s. 8d.
1337	,,	1	4	1	2					
1338	,,	4	2	3	2	1	0			
1342	,,	14	0	1	4		3	12	1	4s. 0d.
1343	,,	13	6	1	5	4	0	8	1	4s. 0d.
1344	,,	10	3	2	3	4	3	3	5	
1347	Hurdwick							10	0	4s. 0d.
1350	Werrington			2	3				4½	
1356	,,			3	5					
1358	Burrington	14	1	2	1½	7	0	4	3½	5s. 4d.
1380	Ottery	8	6			6	6	2	0	5s. 4d.
1381	,,	51	0	4	3¼	3	3½	43	1¼	5s. 4d.
1382	Week	6	2½	4	1			2	1½	5s. 4d.
1383	Werrington	19	6		3	18	4		7	4s. 8d.
1385	Week							3	6	4s. 6½d.
1386	Ottery							10	3	4s. 8d.
,,	Werrington	13	4	1	2	2	3	9	7	4s. 8d.
1390	Ottery	18	1	3	4½	3	1	11	3½	4s. 8d.*
1391	Werrington	24	0	1	6	11	0	11	1½	10s. 0d.
1394	,,			1	5					
1396	Ottery	18	6½	2	1½		2	16	3	3s. 0d.
1398	Hurdwick	120	6	9	3½	9	3	101	7	5s. 8d.*
,,	Werrington	26	4	1	6	20	6	4	0	6s. 8d.
,,	Milton									5s. 0d.*
,,	Leigh									5s. 0d.*
1412	Werrington	10	5½	1	5½			9	0	5s. 4d.
,,	Hurdwick	108	0	9	1	14	0½	84	2½	4s. 4d.*
1413	,,	109	4	10	4½	18	0	80	7½	4s. 4d.*
,,	Werrington	20	2	1	2	6	3	12	5	5s. 4d.
1414	Hurdwick	126	6	10	5		4	104	3	4s. 0d.*
1416	,,	125	2	7	4			117	6	8s. 0d.*
1427	,,	83	7	6	1	13	6½	63	7½	5s. 8d.*
1433	,,	24	1	3	0	7	5	13	4	6s. 8d.
1435	,,	21	0	3	2	4	4	13	2	5s. 4d.
1441	,,	17	3	2	5	2	5	12	1	3s. 0d.
1446	,,	21	6	7	0	10	2	4	4	3s. 4d.

TABLE XIII: RYE (*cont.*)

Year	Manor	In stock		Used for seed		Con- sumed		Sold		Price
		qrs	bus.	qrs	bus.	qrs	bus.	qrs	bus.	per qr
1450	Hurdwick	39	5½	6	1½	13	7	19	5	3s. 4d.
1454	,,	52	0	7	3	12	0	32	5	4s. 0d.
1458	,,	73	5	7	0	13	1	53	4	6s. 0d.*
1460	,,	63	5	7	2	15	6	40	5	5s. 8d.*
1463	,,	33	3	5	4	16	0	11	7	3s. 4d.
1464	,,	39	2½	8	4	14	6	16	0½	2s. 8d.
1466	,,	32	4	6	0	12	6½	13	5½	4s. 0d.
1470	,,	26	0	6	2	15	0	4	6	8s. 0d.
1471	,,	33	0	7	2	10	0	15	6	
1473	,,	20	1	5	0	10	2	4	7	4s. 0d.
1475	,,	27	2	5	0	12	2	10	0	4s. 8d.
1477	,,	30	1	5	0	15	2	9	7	4s. 0d.
1480	,,	41	0	5	0	21	2	14	6	4s. 0d.
1482	,,	40	0	5	0	17	6	17	2	5s. 4d.
1489	,,	45	4	5	4	17	2	22	6	5s. 4d.
1490	,,	54	4	5	2	18	4	30	6	6s. 8d.
1491	,,	58	2	6	1	23	4½	28	4½	10s. 0d.
1492	,,	41	0	7	4	14	0	19	4	4s. 8d.
1497	,,	46	4	5	6	18	2	22	4	8s. 0d.
,,	Leigh	28	0	3	0	13	7	11	1	8s. 8d.
1498	Hurdwick	37	1	5	3	22	2¼	9	3¾	
c.1500	Leigh	33	0	3	1	20	0	9	5	5s. 4d.
1502	Hurdwick	42	2	5	4	22	2	14	4	8s. 0d.
1504	,,	52	0	7	2	22	4	22	2	9s. 4d.
1505	,,	49	0	7	0	23	2	18	6	4s. 8d.
1508	,,	49	4	5	1	27	3½	16	7½	9s. 4d.
1509	,,	40	0	5	2	27	0	7	6	4s. 8d.
1513	,,	41	0	4	6	19	0	17	2	8s. 0d.
1514	,,	42	0	4	4	23	6	13	6	9s. 4d.
1516	,,	53	0	4	5	38	4	9	7	13s. 4d.
1517	,,	54	0	5	1	34	0	14	7	8s. 8d.
1522	,,	41	0	4	5	31	0	5	3	18s. 8d.
1524	,,	39	6	4	6	18	7	16	1	5s. 4d.
1533	,,	36	4	5	0	27	1	4	3	
1537	,,	32	4¾	5	4	21	4	5	4¾	
1538	,,	30	0	4	4	23	0	2	4	7s. 8d.*

TABLE XIV
BARLEY

Year	Manor	In stock	Used for seed	Con- sumed	Sold	Price per qr
		qrs bus.	qrs bus.	qrs bus.	qrs bus.	
1332	Hurdwick	2 0	1 4		4	5s. 4d.
1335	Ottery	2 5	2 5			
1336	,,	9 1		5 4	2 6	3s. 0d.
1342	,,	2 0			2 0	2s. 8d.
1385	Week				2 0	2s. 8d.
1392	Plymstock				4 1†	4s. 6d.*†
1393	Denbury	13 0	3 5		9 3	3s. 8d.*
1397	Plymstock				2 0†	3s. 4d.*†
1414	,,				4 0†	3s. 0d.*†
1431	,,				2 4†	5s. 4d.*†
1432	,,				1 5$\frac{3}{4}$†	4s. 8d.†
1433	,,				2 5$\frac{1}{2}$†	5s. 8d.*†
1442	,,				2 1†	3s. 4d.†
1470	,,				3 7†	5s. 4d.*†
1475	,,				3 4$\frac{1}{2}$†	3s. 6d.†
1477	,,				2 2†	3s. 4$\frac{1}{2}$d.†
1480	,,				2 4†	2s. 9$\frac{1}{2}$d.*†
1481	,,				2 1$\frac{1}{2}$†	2s. 8d.†

TABLE XV
LARGE OATS

Year	Manor	In stock	Used for seed	Con- sumed	Sold	Price per qr
		qrs bus.	qrs bus.	qrs bus.	qrs bus.	
1332	Hurdwick	1 0	1 0			
1335	Ottery	20 0	20 0			
1336	,,	80 4	36 0	40 4	4 0	1s. 3d.
1342	,,	17 4	4 4		13 0	1s. 3d.
1343	,,	20 4	3 0		17 4	1s. 4d.
1344	,,	16 4	3 4		13 0	
1350	Werrington	22 2	16 4		5 6	
1356	,,		21 0			

TABLE XV: LARGE OATS (*cont.*)

Year	Manor	In stock		Used for seed		Consumed		Sold		Price per qr
		qrs	bus.	qrs	bus.	qrs	bus.	qrs	bus.	
1358	Burrington	7	2	1	2			6	0	1s. 2d.
1382	Week	40	4	19	6	1	7	18	7	2s. 8d.
1383	Werrington	26	1	10	1	2	0	14	0	2s. 6d.
1386	,,	41	0	13	0			28	0	2s. 3½d.*
1390	Ottery	53	7	23	4			30	3	2s. 8d.
1391	Werrington	60	0	19	0		2	40	6	3s. 0d.
1396	Ottery	8	4	8	4					2s. 6d.
1398	Hurdwick	182	6	21	6			161	0	2s. 9d.*
,,	Werrington	58	6	9	5		2	48	7	3s. 0d.
,,	Leigh							28	7	2s. 4d.
1412	Werrington	50	0	15	3	5	2	29	3	3s. 4d.
,,	Hurdwick	114	0	24	2	25	0	64	0	3s. 0d.
1413	,,	111	7	43	1	21	0	47	6	2s. 10d.*
,,	Werrington	61	4	12	2	11	1	38	1	3s. 0d.
1414	Hurdwick	72	0	33	0	30	0	9	0	2s. 4d.
1416	,,	102	0	18	0	7	4	76	4	3s. 0d.
1420	Werrington			12	0					
1427	Hurdwick	66	0	19	0	6	4	40	4	2s. 8d.
1433	,,	86	4	20	0	37	0	29	4	3s. 0d.
1435	,,	36	0	12	0	14	0	10	0	3s. 0d.
1446	,,	37	3	23	0	4	3	10	0	3s. 0d.
1450	,,	30	7½	20	0		4	10	3½	2s. 8d.*
,,	Werrington	47	5½	12	0	4	5½	29	0	2s. 8d.
1452	,,			13	1					
1454	,,	45	0¾	9	2	5	2¾	30	4	2s. 8d.
,,	Hurdwick	91	0	20	4	46	1	24	3	3s. 4d.
1458	,,	80	0	30	4	2	3	47	1	3s. 4d.
1459	Werrington			8	6					
1460	,,	35	0	10	1	2	7¾	21	2¼	3s. 8½d.
,,	Hurdwick	70	3	19	4	10	6½	40	0½	4s. 6d.*
1461	Werrington	40	6	11	2	4	4½	24	7½	2s. 6d.*
1463	Hurdwick	67	4	22	0	8	1	37	3	3s. 8d.
1464	,,	52	0	32	0	3	0	17	0	3s. 4d.
1466	,,	26	4	12	4			14	0	4s. 0d.
1467	Werrington	38	1	9	6	6	3	22	0	2s. 0d.
1468	,,	38	6½	9	5½	7	1	22	0	2s. 0d.
1470	Hurdwick	28	2	22	2	6	0			

TABLE XV: LARGE OATS (cont.)

Year	Manor	In stock		Used for seed		Con-sumed		Sold		Price per qr
		qrs.	bus.	qrs	bus.	qrs	bus.	qrs	bus.	
1470	Werrington			10	7					
1471	,,			10	0					
,,	Hurdwick	42	4	25	0	2	0	15	4	3s. 4d.
1472	Werrington	40	0	8	7	9	$2\frac{3}{4}$	21	$6\frac{1}{4}$	2s. 8d.
1473	Hurdwick	50	0	20	0	4	0	26	0	3s. 0d.
1474	Werrington	30	4	9	3	9	2	11	7	2s. 6d.
1475	Hurdwick	50	1	20	0	6	0	24	1	3s. 0d.
1477	Werrington			7	3					
,,	Hurdwick	40	4	10	0	6	0	24	4	3s. 0d.
1480	,,	45	5	20	0	6	4	19	1	3s. 0d.
,,	Werrington	32	0	8	2	9	3	14	3	2s. 0d.
1481	,,			8	0					
1482	Hurdwick	19	2	12	0	5	0	2	2	3s. 4d.
1485	Werrington	32	0	7	$6\frac{1}{2}$	12	$4\frac{1}{2}$	11	5	2s. 8d.
1486	,,			6	7					
1489	,,			6	1					
,,	Hurdwick	54	4	8	5	7	2	38	5	4s. 0d.
1490	,,	47	4	9	1	6	3	32	0	4s. 0d.
,,	Werrington			7	1					
1491	Hurdwick	54	0	11	0	7	6	35	2	4s. 4d.
1492	,,	59	0	11	4	7	0	40	3	
1497	,,	55	0	12	2	7	3	35	3	4s. 0d.
,,	Werrington	28	4	7	1	5	$1\frac{3}{4}$	16	$1\frac{1}{4}$	3s. 0d.
,,	Leigh	13	0	6	6	3	0	3	2	4s. 8d.
,,	Morwell	17	4	6	2	3	$6\frac{1}{2}$	7	$3\frac{1}{2}$	3s. 8d.
1498	Hurdwick	62	0	12	2	5	2	44	4	
1499	Werrington	28	4	7	0	5	2	16	2	3s. 4d.
c.1500	Leigh	18	0	5	0	4	4	8	4	5s. 0d.
1502	Hurdwick	69	0	12	2	8	1	48	5	4s. 2d.
1504	,,	62	0	14	2	6	1	41	5	4s. 6d.
1505	,,	63	0	13	4	8	0	41	4	4s. 4d.
1508	,,	59	$1\frac{1}{2}$	16	2	7	5	35	$2\frac{1}{2}$	4s. 8d.
1509	,,	76	4	17	0	6	4	53	0	4s. 0d.
1513	,,	80	4	15	2	8	4	56	6	4s. 8d.
1514	,,	83	4	15	0	8	0	60	4	4s. 8d.
1516	,,	64	4	15	4	8	2	40	6	5s. 4d.
1517	,,	81	0	15	6	9	6	55	4	5s. 0d.

TABLE XV: LARGE OATS (*cont.*)

Year	Manor	In stock		Used for seed		Con-sumed		Sold		Price per qr
		qrs	bus.	qrs	bus.	qrs	bus.	qrs	bus.	
1522	Hurdwick	58	0	15	1	8	0	34	7	6s. 8d.
1524	,,	79	4	15	6	7	0	56	6	4s. 0d.
1533	,,	57	0	17	0	5	0	35	0	
1537	,,	44	4	19	0	7	0	18	4	
1538	,,	46	1	18	0	6	0	22	1	5s. 4d.*

TABLE XVI
SMALL OATS

Year	Manor	In stock		Used for seed		Con-sumed		Sold		Price per qr
		qrs	bus.	qrs	bus.	qrs	bus.	qrs	bus.	
1298	Werrington	51	0	25	4	24	0	1	4	7s. 0d.
1332	Hurdwick	100	0	25	0	65	0	10	0	4s. 0d.
1335	Ottery	77	0	67	0	3	0	7	0	1s. 0d.
1336	,,	230	7	74	0	112	6	44	1	1s. 0d.
1337	,,	90	0	88	0	2	0			
1342	,,	90	0	33	4	1	0	55	4	1s. 0d.
1343	,,	146	7	36	4	8	0	102	3	11d.
1344	,,	97	3	22	4	14	2	60	5	
1350	Werrington			40	0					
1356	,,	47	0	31	0	15	4		4	1s. 0d.
1358	Burrington	51	5	20	2	8	4½	22	6½	1s. 2d.
1382	Week	13	2	1	0	11	0	1	2	1s. 4d.
1383	Werrington	68	0¼	23	4¼	43	0	1	4	1s. 8d.
1386	,,	38	4	20	4	14	0	4	0	1s. 4d.
1390	Ottery	51	2	24	0	5	5	21	5	1s. 10d.*
1391	Werrington	12	0	2	4			9	4	
1394	,,			19	3					
1398	,,	16	0	3	6	12	2			
,,	Milton	120	0	33	0	21	2	65	6	1s. 6d.
,,	Leigh	80	0	24	0	22	0	34	0	1s. 6d.
,,	Hurdwick	279	0	60	5½	118	6	99	4½	1s. 8d.*
1412	,,	135	2½	41	5	84	1½	9	4	1s. 8d.
1413	,,	231	0	28	3	111	4	91	1	1s. 6d.*

TABLE XVI: SMALL OATS (cont.)

Year	Manor	In stock		Used for seed		Con-sumed		Sold		Price per qr
		qrs	bus.	qrs	bus.	qrs	bus.	qrs	bus.	
1413	Werrington	11	1	1	2	9	7			
1414	Hurdwick	236	6	35	0	96	0	105	6	1s. 8d.*
1416	,,	181	0	38	0	97	0	46	0	1s. 8d.
1427	,,	209	1	30	0	140	0	39	0	1s. 8d.
1433	,,	90	0	6	0	61	0	23	0	1s. 8d.
1435	,,	87	0	14	0	57	1	15	7	1s. 8d.
1441	,,	39	0	15	0	19	5	4	3	1s. 8d.
1446	,,	78	3	16	4	58	5½	3	1½	1s. 4d.
1450	,,	125	2	18	4	67	0	39	6	1s. 8d.
1454	,,	111	4	29	0	33	4½	48	7½	2s. 0d.
1458	,,	113	0	36	0	57	0	20	0	2s. 0d.
1460	,,	111	6½	32	0	54	2	25	4½	2s. 0d.
1463	,,	107	4	7	4	94	1	5	7	2s. 0d.
1464	,,	94	0	7	4	72	4	14	0	2s. 0d.
1466	,,	103	2	10	2	71	6	21	2	2s. 0d.
1470	,,	122	0	11	4	93	2	17	2	2s. 0d.
1471	,,	98	4	14	0	73	1	11	3	2s. 0d.
1473	,,	89	2	10	0	59	7	19	3	2s. 0d.
1475	,,	78	0	8	0	57	7	12	1	2s. 0d.
1477	,,	124	4	20	0	66	1	38	3	1s. 10d.
1480	,,	106	1	12	0	65	7	28	2	1s. 10d.
1482	,,	102	1	18	0	59	3	24	6	2s. 4d.
1489	,,	113	4	27	2	70	7	15	3	2s. 4d.
1490	,,	119	4	28	0	80	2	11	2	2s. 4d.
1491	,,	145	0	24	0	94	3	26	5	2s. 4d.
1492	,,	115	0	26	4	73	1	15	3	2s. 4d.
1497	,,	109	0	25	4	72	5	10	7	2s. 6d.
,,	Leigh	86	0	18	4	28	6	38	6	2s. 8d.
1498	Hurdwick	99	0	27	4	61	6½	9	5½	
1502	,,	118	0	25	5	92	0		3	2s. 8d.
1504	,,	103	0	28	0	62	4	12	4	2s. 8d.
1505	,,	102	0	26	6	66	5½	8	4½	2s. 4d.
1508	,,	101	4	20	1	72	2	9	1	3s. 0d.
1509	,,	100	1	23	2	67	3	9	4	2s. 0d.
1513	,,	100	4	24	0	70	3½	6	0½	2s. 8d.
1514	,,	104	0	24	4	73	2	6	2	2s. 8d.
1516	,,	96	0	24	2	69	2	2	4	3s. 0d.

TABLE XVI: SMALL OATS (*cont.*)

Year	Manor	In stock	Used for seed	Con- sumed	Sold	Price per qr
		qrs bus.	qrs bus.	qrs bus.	qrs bus.	
1517	Hurdwick	97 0	24 5	66 1	6 2	2s. 8d.
1522	,,	81 0	23 0	57 2	6	3s. 8d.
1524	,,	98 0	23 0	59 7	15 1	3s. 0d.
1533	,,	112 3	21 0	56 7	34 1	
1537	,,	97 4	21 0	51 4	25 0	
1538	,,	108 6½	23 0	51 6½	34 0	4s. 11d.*

TABLE XVII
PILL-CORN

Year	Manor	Sold	Price per qr
		qrs bus.	
1386	Werrington	5 5¾†	4s. 8d.†
1392	Plymstock	3½†	8s. 0d.†
1394	Werrington	3 4½†	4s. 0d.†
1398	,,	2 4†	5s. 8d.*†
1413	,,	2 1½†	4s. 8d.†
1420	,,	1 2†	6s. 0d.†
1431	Plymstock	2½†	13s. 4d.†
1432	,,	1¾†	13s. 4d.†
1433	,,	3†	12s. 0d.†
1442	,,	5½†	12s. 8d.†
1452	Werrington	1 3†	5s. 0d.†
1454	,,	3½†	4s. 0d.†
1459	,,	1 4†	3s. 4d.†
1470	Plymstock	1 1¼†	8s. 4d.†
1475	,,	4½†	10s. 8d.†
1477	,,	4¼†	9s. 4d.†
1480	,,	2¼†	6s. 8d.†
1481	,,	4†	8s. 0d.†

CHAPTER V

PASTORAL HUSBANDRY

WHEN the particulars of livestock endorsed on the Tavistock account rolls of the fourteenth century are compared with those given in the Exon Domesday,[1] the chief difference between them is found to lie in the elaborate subdivisions of the later documents. Bovine stock, for example, is now particularized under no fewer than eight categories: oxen, bulls, cows, heifers, three-year-old steers (*bovetti*), two-year-old bullocks (*boviculi*), yearlings, and calves. Sheep are classified as wethers, rams, ewes, hoggasters or two-year-olds, and lambs. For swine there are four categories: boars, sows, hoggets, and porklings or sucking-pigs (*porcelli*). The list is completed by the *affri* or draught-horses with their foals, and the capons, geese, and peacocks that were fattened for the lord's table. One animal, the goat, which had been kept in great numbers all over Devon in 1086, has no place in these later records. Behind its disappearance lay some notable but unrecorded change in the technique of dairy farming.[2]

The tedium of the livestock inventories is frequently enlivened by glimpses of rural merry-making. Thus, in one year four calves, one bullock, two hoggets, three ewes, and seven wethers are slaughtered for the harvest festival at Hurdwick, besides the "feasting-wether" to which the farm labourers were entitled by ancient custom. An ox is killed for the servants when they begin to salt the winter meat at Martinmas. After the Easter and Michaelmas law-courts more stock is killed off to regale the tenants with a dinner. The Michaelmas goose is in evidence from the first, and often a lamb is stated to have been "given to St Antony". This gift remains as mysterious as the payment of a

---

[1] Above, p. 86.
[2] There were no goats on the bishop of Exeter's estates in 1328 (*Reg. Stapeldon*, pp. 571 sqq.). In 1338 the Hospitallers had pasture for 100 goats at Bodmiscombe, near Uffculme (*The Knights Hospitallers in England*, ed. Larking, p. 13).

penny "to St German's bells" which occurs as a dairy expense in
1332 and 1337.[1]

The comings and goings of the great are also reflected in these
inventories. On the 29th of March 1395 Elizabeth, daughter of
John of Gaunt and wife of John Holland, earl of Huntingdon,
had her infant son christened at Dartington, with the prior of
Plympton and abbot Cullyng of Tavistock standing godfathers.
The abbot gave a gold cup and stand shaped like a lily, and in the
cup ten pounds of gold, besides twenty shillings for the nurse. A
few months later the countess visited Tavistock, and in preparation for her entertainment four lambs were dispatched from
Ottery to the abbot's kitchen. Her husband, the future duke of
Exeter, had sided with Richard II against the Lords Appellant,
and her travels may have been undertaken with the object of
enlisting parliamentary support from the lords of the Devon
boroughs.[2] Her grandson, the last duke, received a gift of seven
oxen from abbot Dynyngton in 1459. In 1501 an entry concerning four sheep delivered to the abbot's lodging "against the coming of the lady Princess" reminds us that Catharine of Aragon
had just landed at Plymouth, a girl of fifteen making her first
acquaintance with the land that in after years was to show her
little kindness.

While the inventories are concerned mainly with stock reared
on the demesne, they also take account of heriots and strays. A
stray beast would be impounded in the lord's fold, which at
Hurdwick was a field near the barton, still known as Stray-park.
It could be reclaimed by its owner within twelve months on payment of sixpence; failing proof of ownership within that time, it
was adjudged to the lord at the next manor court. The heriot was
a form of death-duty, exacted from some tenants in cash, from
others in kind; and when paid in kind, it was usually the best
beast on the farm. Occasionally tithe-stock figures in the accounts,
as in 1490, when thirty-five tithe lambs from the parish of Tavistock were folded with the offspring of the lord's ewes.

The livestock fed on natural grasses, and on the thistles, heath,

---

[1] In the *Rituale Romanum* (Appendix, no. 65) St Antony is invoked on behalf of horses and animals in general. He was the patron of swineherds, and
the smallest pig in every litter was dedicated to him.
[2] DA LXIX, 1937, p. 251.

and bracken with which the pastures were heavily infested. Root crops and cultivated herbage still lay in the far future. For a number of manors in the neighbourhood of Tavistock, Heathfield provided common pasture. All landowners in Devon, except the inhabitants of Barnstaple and Totnes, had the right to depasture their cattle without payment upon the purlieus or outer fringe of Dartmoor, and upon the forest, or central portion of the moor, on payment of three halfpence per head a year for horned cattle, and twopence per head for horses and colts.[1] In the exercise of this right the abbot sent forty bullocks up to the moor in the summer of 1473, paying, however, only 4s. 8d. on this occasion. Seven years later all the Hurdwick farm horses, fourteen in number, and a hundred yearlings, were depastured on the forest.

In return for access to the common pastures, which were nearly always over-stocked, the lord exacted from his tenants a small payment or a boonwork. This was but one of several ways in which he profited by the demand for herbage. A tenant whose beasts were too few to be depastured on the moor, but too many for the grassland closes of his farm, might have them folded with the abbot's beasts on payment of a small sum, usually twopence a head. Sometimes, if he had done the abbot a service, the charge would be waived. Alternatively he might rent some of the demesne closes by the year. The Ottery account for 1342 shows pasture being sold in Head-Weir-park, Cholwell-park, Ogbear-park, parcels of Ogbear Down, and even the garden in front of the court-house; at the same time, various sums were collected for the agistment of a couple of oxen, two cows, and thirty-two lambs. At Hurdwick the pastures of Muggleberry, Lillyford, and Billingsbear, in the valley of the Fishlake, were let for six pounds in 1433, when the rents for these and other closes of demesne grassland amounted to no less than thirteen per cent. of the year's receipts. At Werrington the waste of Michelcroft Down, *alias* Werrington Down, was let for twelve shillings in the years before the Black Death. In 1350 this rent had sunk to 5s. 2d., but by 1386 it had reverted to the old figure, and from 1452 onwards it remained constant at twenty shillings. Throughout the fifteenth century agistment charges on this manor brought in sums varying between four shillings and ten shillings a year.

[1] *Publications of the Dartmoor Preservation Association*, I, p. xxv.

The tenants also paid for pannage, or the privilege of letting their swine roam through the lord's woods, there to feed on beechmast and acorns. This was usually arranged at the Michaelmas law-day or the ensuing bye-court. The charge was twopence a head. In 1413 the pannage of Parkwood, near Tavistock, amounted to nineteen shillings, and that of Grenoven wood, by the Tamar, to as much again, the rector of Sydenham Damerel being one of the contributors. At no time did the abbey keep large herds; indeed, swine hardly figure in the Hurdwick accounts until the fifteenth century. In 1538 there were three boars, one of which was roasted for the abbot's table at Christmas; half a dozen sows, one of which died of measles; and the same number of hoggets, five of which were eaten. Of the thirty-one *porcelli* farrowed during the year, thirteen were eaten and five sold for 10s. 8d.

In the seventeenth century horses were sometimes joined with oxen in a plough-team,[1] but it does not appear that the monks of Tavistock ever yoked their *affri* to the plough. They employed them constantly for harrowing, a pair to each harrow as a rule, and for every kind of transport. Farm carts were in more general use at this time than they are said to have been in the eighteenth century;[2] but carriage by packhorse was commoner still. The wooden pack-saddle was fitted on each side with a pair of downward-curving willow poles seven or eight feet long, joined by crossbars, and rising fifteen or more inches above the horse's back. Within and between these crooks, as they were called, the load of corn, hay, or straw was piled. For the carriage of building stone and other heavy articles, wooden panniers were slung to the pack-saddle.[3] Of small build as these animals were, seldom exceeding fourteen hands, they were hardy and could take their loads at a remarkably swift pace.

The heriot left by the tenant of a ferling at East Troswell, in the manor of Werrington, who died in 1366, was described in the court roll as a red bull. It is tempting to see in this animal a forerunner of the famous Devon breed, the 'Red Rubies of the West', pronounced by Marshall to be in many respects the most perfect

[1] *Economic History Review*, IV, 1932, p. 30.
[2] Marshall, I, p. 31.
[3] DA L, 1918, plates D and E.

breed of cattle in the island.[1] But the adjective of colour would
have been superfluous had other varieties been unknown; and
it is certain that no attempt was made at selective breeding, for
purchases of bulls were rare, and the selling price was generally
about half the price of oxen. The Devonshire cattle were valued
not so much as dairy stock as for their working qualities and for
their meat. When their working days were over, they were fattened, bled in the same way as calves were bled for veal, and
finally killed off. Bleeding was held to improve the colour of the
beef and to make it keep better.[2] This troublesome operation was
carried out at a cost varying from twopence to fivepence a year.[3]
The animals were subject to all the diseases which husbandmen
in those days comprehended under the word murrain; and it was
the duty of the *carnarius*, or slaughterer, elected each year at the
manor court, to certify whether or not the sickness was due to
want of proper care.

The monks of Tavistock carried on a brisk trade in oxen. Their
bailiffs attended fairs and markets at Callington, Launceston,
Holsworthy, and Crediton, where they made frequent purchases;
and a number of beasts were sold nearly every year. The following table shows the actual prices paid and received down to 1470,
and thereafter average prices.

TABLE XVIII
PRICES OF OXEN

Year	Manor	Purchase	Sale
1332	Hurdwick	11s., 8s.	7s. 9d.
1335	Ottery		7s. 7½d.
1344	,,		10s. 1d.
1381	,,	10s. 4½d.	9s., 6s.
1386	,,	11s. 1d.	8s. 10d.
,,	Werrington	10s. 7¼d.	
1390	Ottery	14s.	16s., 10s.
1393	Denbury		10s. 2d.

[1] Marshall, I, p. 239. [2] *Ibid.*, I, p. 247.
[3] e.g. Ottery, 1390, 3d.; Hurdwick, 1463, 5d.; Werrington, 1477, 1486,
2d.; Leigh, 1497, 2d.; Hurdwick, 1497, 4d.

K

TABLE XVIII: PRICES OF OXEN (*cont.*)

Year	Manor	Purchase	Sale
1394	Werrington		11s. 9d., 11s.
1396	Ottery	15s.	17s. 6d., 16s.
1398	Milton Abbot		10s. 6d.
,,	Leigh		9s.
,,	Hurdwick	17s., 15s. 6d., 15s. 4d. 14s. 11d., 12s.	14s. 2d., 13s. 4d., 13s. 2d., 12s. 10d. 8s.
,,	Werrington		14s.
1413	,,		10s.
1435	Hurdwick	12s.	
1446	,,	22s.	
1450	,,	12s. 6d.	
1452	Werrington		13s. 4d.
1458	Hurdwick	18s.	
1459	Werrington	10s.	10s.
1460	Hurdwick		20s., 17s.
1463	,,		13s. 4d.
1464	,,	14s.	20s., 12s.
1466	,,		16s., 14s.
1470	,,		15s.
,,	Werrington		12s. 6d.
1471	,,		10s.
1473	Hurdwick	22s.	
1475	,,	15s. 10d.	
1477	,,	12s. 5d.	
,,	Werrington		11s.
1480	Hurdwick	13s. 11d.	
1481	Werrington		11s., 9s. 6d.
1482	Hurdwick	17s.	
1489	,,	17s. 3d.	
,,	Werrington		13s. 1d.
1490	,,	15s. 9½d.	15s. 11d.
,,	Hurdwick	20s. 10d.	
1492	,,	16s. 2¾d.	
1497	,,	17s.	15s.
,,	Leigh	14s. 10½d.	16s. 6d.
1498	Hurdwick	16s. 1d.	
1500	Werrington	16s. 8d.	12s. 3d.
1502	Hurdwick	22s. 4d.	

TABLE XVIII: PRICES OF OXEN (*cont.*)

Year	Manor	Purchase	Sale
1504	Hurdwick	19s. 9d.	
1505	,,	19s. 9d.	
1513	,,	22s. 11d.	
1514	,,	22s. 5d.	
1516	,,	30s. 9d.	
1517	,,	29s. 2d.	
1522	,,	29s. 9d.	
1524	,,	23s. 6d.	
1537	,,	32s.	
1538	,,	34s. 11½d.	

At Hatherleigh the abbot's tenants paid a rent called cow-*gafol* (*gabula vaccarum*). This may have been a commuted render in kind, but more probably it was an agistment due payable for each cow depastured on the common.[1] In 1410 it brought in 11s. 2d. No such *gafol* is recorded on the other manors; and we shall see that cows' milk was not used on any great scale in the dairy.

The three most important dairies on the Tavistock estates were those at Hurdwick, Leigh, and Werrington. They were equipped with strainers, presses, wooden milking buckets, earthenware pans, and butter-crocks, also of earthenware, having a capacity of some forty pounds. Rennet, salt, and crash linen for cheese-cloths were purchased annually.[2]

Down to the last decade of the fourteenth century the *daya*, or

---

[1] Similar dues were paid on some of the Ramsey manors (Neilson, *op. cit.*, p. 57). Some of the bishop of Exeter's tenants at Ashburton paid ox-*gafol* (*Reg. Stapeldon*, p. 25).

[2] According to the Oxford English Dictionary, 'crash' in the sense of coarse linen cloth does not occur until the nineteenth century, and its origin is doubtful. In 1396 five feet of *craste* were entered in the Ottery account as costing 5d. A precentor's account of *c.* 1399 records the purchase of 4½ *Cress' panni linei* at 1s. 8d. per *cresse*, and the Hurdwick account for 1516 refers to *pannus lineus voc' Cresecloth*. The Oxford Dictionary discusses this word s.v. crest, and derives it from the Latin *crista* = tuft. It may however be questioned whether it is not identical with the modern English *crease*, itself a word of doubtful origin. If so, the examples quoted here would stand for 'crease-cloth' or 'creased cloth', a piece of which was apparently sometimes called a 'crease'.

chief dairywoman, appears to have had no other task but cheese-making. She was hired for the five months between Holy Cross Day (May 2) and Michaelmas, at a 'stipend' of 1s. 6d. for the whole season, plus a wage of twopence halfpenny a week. These were the Hurdwick rates; at Werrington the stipend was two shillings and the weekly wage threepence. But in 1394 a new arrangement was made, which brought her total earnings up to seventeen or eighteen shillings. She was now employed all the year round. At Hurdwick the weekly wage was increased to threepence and the stipend to five shillings. At Werrington a distinction was maintained between her summer and winter engagements. The former now began at Candlemas (February 2) and continued for thirty-four weeks, at threepence a week, with a stipend of three shillings. During the eighteen weeks of winter she was expected to look after the cows and calves, for which service she received the cash value of two bushels of toll-corn: that is, something between one shilling and 1s. 10d. according to the current price. She was now a general farm servant, to whom miscellaneous duties could be assigned in the poultry-yard and grange when she was not busy in the dairy. Thus, at Hurdwick, she winnowed half the oat-crop in 1398, and in 1416 twenty quarters of rye and twice that quantity of oats. Her descendants were still winnowing by means of a fan in the open air at the close of the eighteenth century, as Marshall noted with some indignation. "Farmers of every class (some few excepted) carry their corn into the field, on horseback, perhaps a quarter of a mile, from the barn, to the summit of some airy swell; where it is winnowed, *by women*! the mistress of the farm, perhaps, being exposed, in the severest weather, to the cutting winds of winter, in this slavish, and truly barbarous employment."[1]

A whole-time dairywoman was employed at Werrington to the last. In 1489 and the following year she was paid an extra 3s. 4d. as "reward for her good service", which brought her total pay up to 16s. 8d.; but in 1497 she reverted to a weekly wage-rate. She now received fourpence a week during the summer term, and a penny in winter, earning altogether 13s. 4d. in some years, and in others a shilling more. At Hurdwick, and also apparently at Leigh, the whole-time arrangement was given up after 1416, and

[1] Marshall, I, p. 184.

the dairywoman was engaged for terms varying from sixteen to twenty-one weeks, at fivepence a week. Her total earnings in this final period were never less than 13s. 4d. for the shortened period, and sometimes rose to 17s. 4d. By the custom of the dairy she was entitled to keep one cheese for her own use.

The dairywoman was usually assisted by a maid; sometimes, at Hurdwick, by more than one. It was exceptional for the dairy-maid to be employed all the year round. Terms of service varied from twelve to twenty-six weeks. The weekly wage rose at Werrington from twopence halfpenny to fourpence in 1481, and at Hurdwick from threepence to fourpence in 1446. During the last half-century of these accounts the dairymaid could always earn at least six shillings, and sometimes twice as much.

In 1298 the dairywoman at Werrington made the first cheese of the year on Wednesday the 23rd of April. Production was carried on without a break till Michaelmas, at the average rate of one cheese a day, Sundays included. In all, a hundred and sixty cheeses were manufactured in as many days.[1] As the price of cheese was eightpence per stone, and fourteen cheeses were sold for 4s. 8d., it appears that a single cheese weighed half a stone: that is, by the local standard, eight pounds. Whether the dairy pound in Devonshire weighed eighteen ounces then, as it did in Vancouver's time, is not revealed in these accounts. We may say, therefore, that the total production that year, being 1,280 lb., amounted to not less than eleven, and may have reached nearly thirteen, hundredweight. During the same period the dairy also made four stones of butter.

Cheeses varied from five to twelve pounds and more, the largest recorded being two of eighteen pounds each; but ten or eleven pounds was the most usual size. Vancouver thought the large customary butter-weight of Devonshire might be connected with the practice of heavily salting the butter.[2] Judging from the quantities of salt purchased for the dairy, it was the same in the fourteenth century. The average consumption seems to have been about one bushel of salt to some thirty-two stones of butter and cheese: a ratio of 1 to 6·4, where nowadays 1 to 47 would be nearer the mark. In justice to the men of those days

[1] Cf. Smith, *op. cit.*, p. 162 (manor of Ebony, Kent).
[2] Vancouver, p. 231.

we should bear in mind their habit of consuming salted meat, fish, and dairy produce; it helps to explain their oceanic thirst.

It will have been noticed that the Tavistock dairies were not equipped with churns. The absence of this utensil was characteristic of dairies in which cream was raised by scalding. When the milk had stood for some hours in a broad earthenware pan, it was placed over a slow fire, and there left until the cream rose to the surface. This, the clotted cream for which Devonshire has long been famous, required no churning; as soon as it had grown cold, it was removed into a wooden bowl and stirred with a wooden implement. The butter then separated far more freely, and coagulated sooner, than when churned from raw cream.[1]

It seems likely that scalded cream dates from a period before the churn came into general use. As an element in dairy technique it had much to recommend it. In the first place, the freshly made cream provided a ready substitute for butter. Hence there was no necessity to separate any butter at all for immediate consumption; and the butter required for cooking or storage could be separated with a reduced expenditure of manual toil. The appeal of Devonshire cream to the palate was thus reinforced by practical advantages.

Ewes were milked as well as cows, and indeed contributed the greater share of milk. A few examples will show the relative proportions.

Hurdwick	1332	48½	stones	7 cows and 69 ewes
Ottery	1337	45	of	8 ,, ,, 58 ,,
Hurdwick	1347	58	cheese	3 ,, ,, 80 ,,
Burrington	1358	11	from	12 ,, ,, 66 ,,

The comparative dairy value of cows and ewes was often debated by agricultural experts. According to the author of *Hosebonderie*, a cow should produce, between the 1st of May and Michaelmas, enough milk for ninety-eight pounds of cheese and fourteen pounds of butter, while a ewe should produce one gallon for every gallon and a half of cow's milk.[2] A statement in such terms implies that the cheese was made of skimmed milk. At Werrington, in the fourteenth century, the same proportion of seven to one was maintained between cheese and butter, but there and at

[1] Vancouver, p. 214.   [2] Walter of Henley's *Husbandry* etc., pp. 77, 79.

TABLES XIX AND XX

STATISTICS OF DAIRY PRODUCE

TABLE XIX

CHEESE

Year	Manor	Made		Con-sumed		Given away		Sold		Price per st.
		st.	lb.	st.	lb.	st.	lb.	st.	lb.	
1298	Werrington	80	0	4	8	18	0	15	0	8d.
1332	Hurdwick	48	8	26	0	3	0	19	8	,,
1334	Ottery	23	8	—		4	0	19	8	,,
1335	,,	29	8		12	3	8	25	4	,,
1336	,,	37	0	—		3	8	33	8	,,
1337	,,	45	0		5	3	0	41	6	,,
1347	Hurdwick	58	0	13	0	3	0	42	0	,,
1350	Werrington							50	4	5½d.
1356	,,							54	0	9d.
1358	Burrington	11	0							
1373	Hurdwick	59	0	10	0	11	0	38	0	?
1380	Ottery	22	0	—		6	0	17	0	9d.
1381	,,	30	8	—		12	8	18	0	6d.
1382	Week							37	8	7½d., 8d.
1386	Werrington	142	0	4	8	—		137	8	9d.
,,	Ottery	27	4	—		7	8	19	12	8d.
1390	,,	34	0	—		6	0	28	0	8½d.
1394	Werrington	74	8	4	8	1	8	68	8	8d.
1396	Ottery	46	0	—		2	0	44	0	,,
1398	Werrington	52	8	7	7	1	0	43	9	9d.
,,	Hurdwick	54	0	9	8	1	0	43	8	8d.
,,	Leigh							19	0	,,
1412	Hurdwick	90	0	17	7		15	71	10	,,
1413	,,									,,
,,	Werrington	69	0	6	4	2	8	60	4	,,
1414	Hurdwick	91	0					72	2	,,
1416	,,	112	0	10	6	21	11	79	15	,,
1427	,,	128	0					103	0	,,
1433	,,	30	0					18	8	
1435	,,	21	2					14	10	
1441	,,	56	0	10	0	2	0	44	0	8d.
1446	,,	48	0	12	0		12	35	4	,,

TABLE XIX: CHEESE (*cont.*)

Year	Manor	Made		Con-sumed		Given away		Sold		Price per st.
		st.	lb.	st.	lb.	st.	lb.	st.	lb.	
1450	Hurdwick	108	0	17	0	1	0	90	0	8d.
1452	Werrington	47	10	7	0	1	10	39	0	,,
1454	,,	47	5	10	10		11	36	0	,,
,,	Hurdwick	54	0	16	12	—		37	4	,,
1458	,,	63	0	17	0	1	0	45	0	,,
1459	Werrington	56	10	13	0	1	10	42	0	,,
1460	Hurdwick	57	8	18	0	10	0	29	8	,,
1461	Werrington	56	0	7	0	1	10	47	6	,,
1463	Hurdwick	50	0	20	0	5	0	25	0	,,
1464	,,	40	0	15	0	4	12	20	4	,,
1466	,,	85	0	17	8	1	0	66	8	,,
1470	,,	70	0	18	0	8	0	44	0	7d.
,,	Werrington	38	0	9	9	5	9	23	0	8d.
1471	,,	31	6	8	15	2	7	20	0	,,
,,	Hurdwick	65	0	17	0	8	0	40	0	7d.
1473	,,	70	0	15	0	9	0	46	0	6d.
1475	,,	76	0					50	0	,,
1477	,,	60	0	13	0	11	0	36	0	,,
,,	Werrington	41	3	12	9	8	10	20	0	,,
1480	Hurdwick	56	0	16	0	9	0	31	0	,,
1481	Werrington	37	0	12	0	9	0	16	0	,,
1482	Hurdwick	46	0	14	0	8	0	24	0	,,
1486	Werrington	29	8	10	0	6	8	13	0	,,
1489	,,	37	8	14	0	6	8	17	0	,,
,,	Hurdwick	73	0	16	0	18	0	39	0	,,
1490	,,	72	0	17	0	14	0	41	0	,,
,,	Werrington	34	0	15	0	5	0	14	0	,,
1491	Hurdwick	58	0	13	0	14	0	31	0	,,
1492	,,	71	0	16	0	9	0	46	0	,,
1497	,,	52	0	21	0	10	0	21	0	,,
,,	Leigh	36	0	16	0	9	0	11	0	8d.
,,	Werrington	37	2	12	12	6	0	18	6	6d.
1498	,,	29	8	10	8	7	0	12	0	,,
,,	Hurdwick	51	0	21	0	7	0	23	0	,,
1499	Werrington	24	0	10	8	7	4	6	4	,,
1502	Hurdwick	72	0	18	0	9	0	45	0	,,
1504	,,	70	0	21	0	9	0	40	0	,,

TABLE XIX: CHEESE (*cont.*)

Year	Manor	Made		Con-sumed		Given away		Sold		Price per st.
		st.	lb.	st.	lb.	st.	lb.	st.	lb.	
1505	Hurdwick	74	0	20	0	9	0	45	0	
1508	,,	88	0	20	0	12	0	54	0	7d.
1509	,,	83	0	16	0	12	0	55	0	,,
1513	,,	64	0	21	0	16	0	27	0	?
1514	,,	73	0	16	0	11	0	31	0	
1516	,,	64	0	19	0	14	0	31	0	7½d.
1517	,,	62	0	18	0	16	0	26	0	,,
1522	,,	63	0	20	0	16	0	27	0	9d.
1524	,,	81	0	20	0	14	0	47	0	8d.
1537	,,	52	0	20	0	14	0	18	0	,,
1538	,,	50	0	18	0	16	0	16	0	,,

TABLE XX
BUTTER

Year	Manor	Made		Con-sumed		Given away		Sold		Price per st.
		st.	lb.	st.	lb.	st.	lb.	st.	lb.	
1298	Werrington	4	0	—		4	0	—		—
1332	Hurdwick	3	8	3	8	—		—		—
1334	Ottery	2	0	—		—		2	0	1s. 4d.
1335	,,	4	0	—		—		4	0	,,
1336	,,	4	0	—		—		4	0	,,
1337	,,	4	0	—		—		4	0	,,
1347	Hurdwick	1	8	1	0	—			8	,,
1350	Werrington							7	8	1s. 0d.
1356	,,							10	0	,,
1358	Burrington	6	0							
1373	Hurdwick	7	0							
1380	Ottery	3	0	—		2	0	1	0	1s. 4d.
1381	,,	4	0	—		3	0	1	0	,,
1382	Week							5	0	,,
1386	Werrington	20	0	—		—		20	0	,,
,,	Ottery	2	6	—			12	1	10	,,
1390	,,	5	0	—		3	0	2	0	,,
1394	Werrington	9	3	—		—		9	3	,,

TABLE XX: BUTTER (*cont.*)

Year	Manor	Made		Consumed		Given away		Sold		Price per st.
		st.	lb.	st.	lb.	st.	lb.	st.	lb.	
1396	Ottery	5	8	—		1	8	4	0	1s. 4d.
1398	Werrington	7	6	—		—		7	6	,,
,,	Hurdwick	4	8	1	0	—		3	8	,,
,,	Leigh							2	8	,,
1412	Hurdwick	12	12	11		—		12	1	,,
1413	,,									,,
,,	Werrington	9	13	—			8	9	5	,,
1414	Hurdwick	5	8					4	0	,,
1416	,,	16	0					14	9	,,
1427	,,	14	8	1	0	—		13	8	,,
1433	,,	4	0	—		—		4	0	,,
1435	,,	4	8	—		—		4	8	,,
1441	,,	3	8	—		2	0	1	8	,,
1446	,,	3	8	—		—		3	8	,,
1450	,,	7	0	—		—		7	0	,,
1452	Werrington	5	5	—		—		5	5	,,
1454	,,	5	4	—		—		5	4	,,
,,	Hurdwick	7	3	7	0	—			3	,,
1458	,,	14	8	—		—		14	8	,,
1459	Werrington	5	0	—		—		5	0	,,
1460	Hurdwick	10	0	—		10	0	—		,,
1461	Werrington	5	4	—		—		5	4	,,
1463	Hurdwick	12	8	1	0	9	8	2	0	,,
1464	,,	8	0	12		5	8	1	12	,,
1466	,,	11	0	—		5	0	6	0	,,
1470	,,	9	0	—		8	0	1	0	2s. 0d.
,,	Werrington	5	8	—		1	4	2	12	1s. 4d.
1471	,,	4	0	—		1	8	2	8	,,
,,	Hurdwick	10	0	—		8	0	2	0	,,
1473	,,	9	0	—		3	0	6	0	,,
1475	,,	12	0	—		7	0	5	0	,,
1477	,,	10	8	—		6	0	4	8	,,
,,	Werrington	7	8	—		2	0	5	8	,,
1480	Hurdwick	11	0	—		6	0	5	0	1s. 6d.
1481	Werrington	7	8	—		2	0	5	8	1s. 4d.
1482	Hurdwick	10	0	—		6	8	3	8	1s. 6d.
1486	Werrington	8	12	—		2	12	6	0	1s. 4d.

TABLE XX: BUTTER (*cont.*)

Year	Manor	Made		Con-sumed		Given away		Sold		Price per st.
		st.	lb.	st.	lb.	st.	lb.	st.	lb.	
1489	Werrington	7	0	—		2	8	4	8	1s. 4d.
,,	Hurdwick	14	8	—		8	0	6	8	,,
1490	,,	14	0	—		5	0	9	0	,,
,,	Werrington	8	12	—		2	12	6	0	,,
1491	Hurdwick	13	8	—		7	0	6	8	,,
1492	,,	11	0	—		4	8	6	8	1s. 8d.
1497	,,	16	8	—		5	8	11	0	1s. 4d.
,,	Leigh	15	8	—		6	8	9	0	1s. 8d.
,,	Werrington	7	2	—		3	2	4	0	1s. 4d.
1498	,,	8	8	—		2	0	6	8	,,
,,	Hurdwick	16	8	—		4	8	12	0	,,
1499	Werrington	8	4	—		2	0	6	4	,,
1502	Hurdwick	20	8	—		6	0	14	8	1s. 5d.
1504	,,	25	0	—		6	8	18	8	,,
1505	,,	21	8	—		6	0	15	8	
1508	,,	23	0	1	0	6	0	16	0	1s. 6d.
1509	,,	24	8	—		6	8	18	0	1s. 8d.
1513	,,	20	8	—		7	0	13	8	,,
1514	,,	20	8	—		6	0	14	8	,,
1516	,,	18	0	—		6	0	12	0	,,
1517	,,	16	8	—		5	0	11	8	,,
1522	,,	20	0	—		3	8	16	8	2s. 0d.
1524	,,	19	8	—		4	0	15	8	,,
1537	,,	19	0	1	0	5	0	13	0	,,
1538	,,	15	8		8	5	0	10	0	,,

Hurdwick a cow was expected to yield only thirty-two pounds of cheese, with butter in proportion, and the ratio of cow to ewe was variously stated as three to one (Hurdwick 1347, Werrington 1386, 1394), four to one (Hurdwick 1332), and six to one (Hurdwick 1427). When we find Vancouver, in 1813, reckoning that a cow should yield 140 pounds of cheese and 206 pounds of butter, the progress made in four centuries of dairy farming becomes apparent.[1]

[1] Vancouver, *op. cit.*, p. 233. Of cheeses made from ewes' milk, Roquefort

Some of the butter made in these dairies was given to officials and farm labourers as part of their remuneration, but most of it was sold, the monks apparently preferring to eat butter purchased from some outside source.[1] With cheese the case was different, substantial quantities being delivered yearly to the abbey for domestic consumption; but here too manufacture was carried on chiefly for the market. The production and sale of cheese rose to its maximum at Hurdwick during the first thirty years of the fifteenth century, and at Werrington somewhat earlier. Throughout the period for which accounts are extant the market for dairy produce remained noticeably steady. Cheese was almost invariably sold at eightpence a stone down to 1466. It dropped to sixpence in 1473, and so remained until the turn of the century, after which it gradually rose again to eightpence. Butter went up from 1s. 4d. a stone, the ruling price throughout the century, to 1s. 8d. in 1509 and two shillings in 1522.

At the close of the thirteenth century the shepherd (*bercarius* or *pastor*) was paid threepence a week, with an additional 'stipend' of two shillings for the summer months which brought his total cash earnings up to fifteen shillings. The same rate was being paid in 1347, but the Black Death brought about a sharp increase. Nine years after the pestilence the weekly wage at Burrington was fourpence and the stipend 8s. 6d. This made a total of 25s. 10d., nearly equivalent to the flat rate of sixpence a week that was adopted shortly afterwards. The next rise took place in the last decade of the century. It was presaged by the 'reward' given to the shepherd at Denbury in 1393; in addition to his pay, he was allowed to use the lord's oxen for two days' ploughing on his own land. An interesting concession, for it shows that some at least of these wage-earners had independent sources of income. By 1398 the weekly rate had gone up to sevenpence at Werrington and eightpence at Hurdwick. Thenceforth it remained unaltered until the Dissolution.

---

is the best known at the present day. "Ewe's milk, when freshly drawn, has an appearance very similar to that of the cow, except that it often has a peculiar oiliness about it: it yields however a greater quantity of cream, and forms a very soft kind of butter" (Youatt, *Sheep*, p. 43).

[1] This was also the case at Farnham, Surrey (Robo, *Mediaeval Farnham*, pp. 113, 131).

The cost of repairs to the sheepfold is a frequent entry; so also is the purchase of tar and tallow, with which the sheep were smeared as a remedy for scab. Yet losses from one cause or another were very heavy. Sixteen of the Hurdwick ewes were driven off one year by thieves. In 1538 there died from 'murrain' twelve wethers, five ewes, three rams, twenty-four hoggasters, and fifty-eight lambs: in all, one seventh of the entire flock.

In 1086 the abbey possessed seven hundred and sixty-eight sheep, more than half of which were concentrated in the vicinity of Tavistock. This number does not include the flock of one hundred and fifty on the lately confiscated manor of Werrington, which would have brought the total up to nine hundred and eighteen. Particulars for the next two hundred years are lacking; but in 1297 the Werrington flock numbered one hundred and fifty-four, and the earliest extant Hurdwick account (1332) gives a figure, one hundred and eighty-five, which again is very close to that of the Domesday record. Passing to the close of the fourteenth century, we find sheep at Hurdwick, Werrington, and Leigh, to the number of eight hundred and one. Those at Denbury and Morwell, the two other manors where sheep were reared at this time, may be estimated at another four hundred all told, giving an approximate total of 1,200. This was in 1398. By 1497 Denbury had been leased out. The combined flocks of Werrington (167), Hurdwick (415), Leigh (249), and Morwell (243) in that year totalled 1074.

On some large estates the sheep-farming was managed intermanorially. During part of the year the flocks of several manors were depastured together on a central sheepwalk. They were all shorn together, and the wool of the whole estate was sold under a single contract. Responsibility for buying and selling was taken out of the hands of the manorial officials and entrusted to a stock-keeper who rendered his own separate account.[1] This intermanorial system was characteristic of regions having extensive pastures, and would therefore have been specially well suited to a group of manors on the fringe of Dartmoor. No trace of it, however, appears in the Tavistock accounts. Some slight interchange of stock took place at intervals, and the sale of wool may have been centrally managed, as it is known to have been on some

[1] Power, *The Wool Trade in English Medieval History*, p. 28.

other Devonshire estates; but each manor took care of its own sheep.[1]

The native sheep of Devon was a small-boned, flat-sided, coarsely woolled animal. When ewes are milked and the lambs are thereby stinted of their natural food, a diminutive growth and a coarse fleece are the inevitable consequences.[2] By the standard reckoning one hundred fleeces made a hundredweight. At Leigh, in 1398, when the current price was three shillings a quarter, one hundred and fifty-six fleeces were sold for eighteen shillings. This gives an average weight of not quite 1 lb. 1¼ oz. to the fleece. Thorold Rogers, from numerous accounts which he examined, struck an average of 1 lb. 7¾ oz.;[3] but at Crawley, in Hampshire, a manor which specialized in sheep-farming, the average was only two ounces higher than in Devon.[4] The lamb's fleece appears from the Tavistock accounts to have weighed about 5¼ oz.

In the Ottery account for 1396 the cost of shearing is entered as *nil*, "because the purchaser of the wool sheared them by agreement". More often the shearing was done by piecework, at the rate of a penny a score. As nothing is ever said of washing, it seems likely that the practice, noted by Marshall as prevalent throughout Cornwall and west Devon, of shearing wool "in the yolk", was already established in the fourteenth century. Unwashed wool weighed more, but fetched a lower price; and the additional cost of transport hardly counted so long as the wool was manufactured locally.[5]

During the thirteenth century the wool trade prospered exceedingly, but the monks of Tavistock took small advantage of the boom. Impoverished by a succession of troubles, and notably by the four vacancies that occurred in quick succession between 1257 and 1262, they had not the capital required for launching out into sheep-farming on the grand scale. A list of monastic houses which exported wool to Flanders about 1280 includes Ford Abbey, a Cistercian house in east Devon; and

---

[1] In 1347 Oliver de Dynham sold "all the wools he had of his own shearing in the county of Devon" to a syndicate of four local woolmongers (*Calendar of Inquisitions post mortem*, 1st series, XI, p. 302).

[2] Youatt, *op. cit.*, pp. 48, 251.   [3] Thorold Rogers, *op. cit.*, I, p. 395.

[4] Gras, *op. cit.*, pp. 41, 192, 302: in 1209, 489 fleeces = 3¼ weys = 591 lb. 8 oz., an average of 1 lb. 3·3 oz.; in 1410, 969 fleeces = 3 sacks 15 cloves = 1197 lb., an average of 1 lb. 3·7 oz.   [5] Marshall, I, p. 269.

Ford is named again in 1315, with three other Devon monasteries, Newenham, Buckfast, and Tor, as trading with the Florentine wool merchants; but Tavistock does not appear in either list.[1] Remoteness from Dartmouth, then the principal south Devon port, was another obstacle.[2] But Devonshire was not at this time a great wool-producer. In the list of counties rated to the subsidy of 1341 it takes the fifteenth place, being assessed at some eighty-three and a half tons (514 sacks), less than a quarter of the amount contributed by Norfolk, which heads the list with over two thousand woolsacks.[3]

From this time onwards the movement of prices can be studied in the Tavistock accounts. Sometimes the price varied from place to place, as in 1497, when five different prices are quoted from as many manors. Hurdwick wool seems always to have fetched the highest price, and Werrington the lowest. Woolfells, or unshorn sheepskins (*pelles lanute*) were almost invariably sold at a penny each. During the fourteenth century lambs' wool usually fetched a halfpenny a fleece. This price was doubled at Hurdwick in 1446 and at Werrington in 1461, after which it remained constant at a penny a fleece until the Dissolution.

TABLE XXI

SALES AND PRICES OF WOOL

Year	Manor	Fleeces sold	Price per cwt.	Lambs' fleeces sold	Woolfells sold
1298	Werrington	130		44	9
1332	Hurdwick	136		61	14
1335	Ottery	91		14	32

[1] Cunningham, *The Growth of English Industry and Commerce*, I, p. 626.

[2] In 1273 Gerard de Dertemuth was licensed to export 20 sacks of wool to any foreign country except Flanders (CPR 1272–81, p. 23). Wool was exported from Teignmouth in 1323 and from Exeter in 1347–8 (Gras, *The Early English Customs System*, pp. 252, 524, 525). Thus when the sheriff of Devon asserted that there were no considerable wool merchants in the county, the local wool being too coarse and poor to attract either foreign or native buyers, his report was not wholly consistent with the facts (EHR XXXI, 1916, p. 600; cf. Power, *op. cit.*, p. 23).

[3] Thorold Rogers, *op. cit.*, I, p. 110.

TABLE XXI: SALES AND PRICES OF WOOL (cont.)

Year	Manor	Fleeces sold	Price per cwt.	Lambs' fleeces sold	Woolfells sold
1336	Ottery	100		54	5
1337	,,	138	25s. 0d.	52	9
1350	Werrington				
1356	,,	208	17s. 0d.		29
1358	Burrington	167	8s. 4d.		
1373	Hurdwick	196		102	29
1381	Ottery	164	15s. 10d.	60	49
1382	Week			161	59
1386	Werrington	220	14s. 0d.	112	81
,,	Ottery	157	16s. 8d.	49	40
1390	,,	176	16s. 8d.	72	12
1394	Werrington	266	10s. 6d.	76	30
1396	Ottery	100	14s. 0d.	37	16
1398	Werrington	250	12s. 0d.	104	
,,	Leigh	156	12s. 0d.		13
,,	Hurdwick	250	14s. 0d.	95	61
1412	,,	337		84	12
1413	Werrington	212	17s. 7d.	61	26
1414	Hurdwick	318		52	33
1416	,,	295		63	22
1427	,,	350		102	10
1433	,,	300		128	111
1435	,,	303		84	68
1441	,,	150		84	
1446	,,	323	24s. 0d.	300	
1450	,,	174		132	36
1452	Werrington	216	12s. 2d.	22	65
1454	,,	157	10s. 4d.	54	63
,,	Hurdwick	151		260	120
1458	,,	464		118	48
1459	Werrington	202	13s. 4d.	80	32
1460	Hurdwick	450	21s. 0d.	84	
1461	Werrington	170	14s. 9d.	64	38
1463	Hurdwick	450	25s. 10¼d.	160	
1464	,,	511	26s. 8d.	140	
1466	,,	426	40s. 0d.	159	
1470	,,	300	36s. 8d.	95	
,,	Werrington	120	19s. 11d.	27	14

TABLE XXI: SALES AND PRICES OF WOOL (*cont.*)

Year	Manor	Fleeces sold	Price per cwt.	Lambs' fleeces sold	Woolfells sold
1471	Werrington	105	24s. 0d.	34	26
,,	Hurdwick	500	33s. 4d.	180	
1473	,,	616		144	46
1475	,,	455		156	41
1477	,,	427		53	68
,,	Werrington	100	23s. 4d.	14	38
1480	Hurdwick	413	26s. 8d.	150	
1481	Werrington	31	25s. 4d.	9	26
1482	Hurdwick	320	32s. 3d.	128	
1486	Werrington	114	17s. 0d.	41	
1489	,,	130	20s. 6d.	109	
,,	Hurdwick	395	20s. 0d.	127	
1490	,,	334	24s. 0d.	133	
,,	Werrington	113	24s. 2d.	72	32
1491	Hurdwick	330		96	
1492	,,	300	26s. 8d.	89	
1497	,,	350	28s. 4d.	84	
,,	Leigh	200	27s. 0d.	66	
,,	Morwell	100	26s. 8d.	101	
,,	Werrington	100	23s. 4d.	48	
1498	,,		23s. 4d.	36	
,,	Hurdwick	325	28s. 4d.	95	
1499	Werrington		24s. 4d.	52	
1502	Hurdwick	250	30s. 0d.	52	
1504	,,	200	28s. 4d.	30	
1505	,,	275	21s. 10d.	69	
1508	,,	300	28s. 4d.	100	
1509	,,	275	28s. 4d.	55	
1513	,,	250	30s. 0d.	96	
1514	,,	300	30s. 0d.	49	
1516	,,	350	31s. 5d.	120	
1517	,,	350	33s. 4d.	83	
1522	,,	425	28s. 0d.	101	
1524	,,	400	30s. 0d.	116	

NOTE. In the later accounts the woolfells (*pelles lanute*) are not enumerated separately from the sheepskins (*pelles nude*); they have therefore been omitted from this table.

L

As a rule, down to the middle of the fourteenth century, dairy sales predominated over sales of wool. Towards 1400 the latter drew nearly level, and occasionally even took the lead. During the first thirty years of the fifteenth century wool fetched a very high price;[1] but this was the period when dairy manufacture at Hurdwick rose to its maximum. After 1416, wethers vanish from the stock accounts for nearly thirty years: a clear indication of the emphasis laid on milk-production at this time. To the intensified demand for wool created by the progress of the local cloth industry the monks of Tavistock gave only an indirect response. Instead of enlarging their flocks, they let off the demesne pastures at a high rent. Not until 1446 did they take the pastures in hand again. Sales of wool then mounted steadily, rising to their maximum at Hurdwick in the seventies.

Meanwhile the manufacture of woollen cloths was undergoing a remarkable expansion. In the development of this local industry the abbey had its part to play, though not, as we shall see, a very active part.

One of the earliest references to south-western cloth occurs in the Pipe Roll for 1181, when a consignment of burels was dispatched from Cornwall to Winchester for the use of the king's almoner.[2] Burels were rough, hairy cloths, woven from just such coarse wool as was characteristic of the native sheep. At this time there was a trade in dyed cloths at Exeter, which was evidently of some consequence, for when certain restrictions were placed on it in John's reign, the burgesses paid ten marks to have them lifted.[3] Their by-laws forbade any stranger to manufacture cloth in the city.[4] Soon afterwards the fulling mill makes its first appearance in Devon, signifying that the industrial revolution of the thirteenth century was now in full swing.

Before the invention of the fulling mill, newly woven cloth was shrunk and felted by one of three primitive methods. The fuller might work it to and fro by hand, or beat it with clubs, or tread it underfoot in a water-trough, this last method being the one best suited to long and heavy cloths. In the fulling mill the

---

[1] Thorold Rogers, *op. cit.*, IV, p. 328.   [2] PRS XXX, p. 33.
[3] *Ibid.*, LIII (N.S. XV), p. 253.
[4] *Report on the Records of the City of Exeter* (Hist. MSS. Comm.), p. 387.

action of beating was performed by two wooden hammers, alternately raised and dropped on the cloth. They were moved by a revolving drum attached to the spindle of a water-wheel, the whole action being thus mechanized, with running water supplying the motive power. It is not known when or where these mills were invented, but in England they seem to have been first built in the latter half of the twelfth century. The introduction of the new technique effected a decisive change in the location of the cloth trade. Hitherto the industry had been centred chiefly in the towns and cities of the eastern lowlands, many of which had their guilds of weavers and fullers; but now it moved into the country and established itself wherever the streams were numerous and swift.[1]

In the south-western counties fullers were called tuckers, and their mills tucking mills.[2] The earliest reference to such a mill in Devonshire so far discovered occurs in the Assize Roll of 1238. There was then a fulling or tucking mill at Dunkeswell.[3] A few years later there is mention of similar mills at Honiton and Tiverton; and by the end of the thirteenth century they were to be found on nearly every stream in the peninsula. In 1309 the mayor and burgesses of Barnstaple declared that the cloths made in their district were of but little value; but almost simultaneously they entered into an agreement with the bishop of Exeter for the construction of fulling mills on either side of the water that divided his land from theirs.[4] Six years later the cloths of Devon and Cornwall are named with those of the eastern counties in letters patent appointing an aulnager of woollen and other cloths, whose duty it was to see that all cloth put on sale conformed to the requirements of the statutes.[5]

A number of the aulnage returns are extant, but it would be unprofitable to consult them for information respecting the growth and distribution of the trade, for in many cases they are known to

[1] Carus-Wilson, 'An Industrial Revolution of the Thirteenth Century' (*Economic History Review*, XI, 1941, pp. 39 sqq.).
[2] Strictly speaking, cloth was not *tucked* until it had been already fulled, and the surface dressed with teasels. Tucking was the final operation of stretching it on a rack.
[3] PRO Assize Rolls, J.I. 1, 174, m. 32.
[4] Chanter and Wainwright, *Barnstaple Records*, I, pp. 110, 115.
[5] CPR 1313–17, p. 344.

have been faked by the officials who drew them up.[1] More trustworthy indications are provided by the customs accounts. These
show that substantial quantities of grey and russet cloth were
being exported from Dartmouth, Exmouth, and Topsham during the Breton war of succession (1341–64).[2] It would seem that
the intercourse between the south-western peninsula and Brittany, always close, had been stimulated by Edward III's alliance
with the Breton dukes, and that a manufacture which until then
had been carried on mainly if not entirely for the home market
had now secured outlets abroad. Brittany was not the only
foreign market. In 1364 the commonalty of Plymouth, now a
flourishing port, obtained licence to export two thousand packs
of local cloth and two thousand dyed cloths to Gascony, Spain,
and elsewhere.[3]

An account dated Michaelmas 1396 shows the almoner of
Tavistock purchasing twenty-three and a half "dosyns" of white
and grey cloth, at 4s. 4d. a "dosyn", for the customary distribution to the poor on All Souls' Day. The dozens were so called
from their dimensions, being twelve yards long and one yard
wide; and the name covered several varieties of local cloth. The
original white, grey, and russet 'straits' of Devon and Cornwall
were rough, hairy cloths, but during the fifteenth century a new
manufacture of finely spun and woven kerseys was developed
alongside these older fabrics.[4] Exports rose, and from 1430 until

---

[1] Carus-Wilson, 'The Aulnage Accounts: A Criticism' (*Economic History
Review*, II, 1929, pp. 114 sqq.).

[2] Gras, *The Early English Customs System*, pp. 395–7, 429.

[3] CPR 1361–4, p. 496; cf. *ibid.*, p. 510, similar licence for Roger Plente of
Exeter, and p. 521, for Warin Bailly of Exeter; also CPR 1429–36, p. 351, a
shipment of cloth from Dartmouth to Lisbon.

[4] In this connection a mis-statement by Westcote, the seventeenth-century
topographer, is often quoted. According to Westcote, "one Anthony Bonvise,
an Italian, taught us the knowledge of making kersies and our women to spin
the distaff" in the time of Edward IV (*A View of Devonshire*, p. 59). Antonio
Bonvisi was a merchant banker and an intimate friend of Sir Thomas More.
He is said to have promoted the manufacture of fine cloth at Coggeshall in
Essex (*Tudor Economic Documents*, III, p. 186). Westcote seems to have been
misled by a loosely worded passage in Leake's *Treatise on the Cloth Industry*,
published in 1577, which reads as follows: "About the 20 of H. 8. [1528–9]
began the first spinning on the distaffe and making of Coxall Clothes, and
about the same tyme began Devonshire dossens, which nowe is a merveillous
greate commoditie. Theis Coxall Clothes weare first taught by one Bonuise,
an Italian" (*ibid.*, III, p. 211). It will be noticed that Leake does not explicitly

the middle of the century the trade prospered exceedingly.[1]
The older style of cloth-making was now restricted mainly to
the region between Plymouth and Okehampton. In 1464 an Act
of Parliament forbade the putting into cloth of any lambs' wool,
flocks, or cork, on pain of forfeiture. This regulation caused the
utmost dismay in Tavistock, and when the next parliament met a
petition against it was drawn up in the name of all the "inhabitants
and residents" of the hundreds of Lifton, Tavistock, and Roborough. The petitioners declared that they had been accustomed
time out of mind to put flocks into cloth made from the local wool,
and could not help doing so, "because of the gretnesse and
stobournesse of the same woole". The alternative would be to
give up the manufacture. To avert this calamity, they asked for a
new Act authorizing them to make all manner of woollen cloth,
and therein to put such quantity of flocks as might be needful and
profitable to the makers.[2] The petition was successful, and the
exemption thus secured for Tavistocks, as the local cloths were
thenceforth named, was continued in several later statutes.[3]

A Tavistock rental drawn up in 1388 refers to a tucking mill by
Parkwood, then leased out at a yearly rent of fourteen shillings.[4]
So far as can be ascertained, there was at that time no other mill
of the kind at Tavistock; nor is it clear how long this one had been
at work. But in the following century a number of old buildings
were adapted to the process of fulling, and new mills went up
apace, their multiplication bearing eloquent witness to the
growth of the local manufacture. Between 1400 and 1413 a tan-
mill at Taviton belonging to the precentor was converted into a
tucking mill,[5] and the Crowndale cornmill which had been lying
derelict ever since the depopulation of that hamlet by the Black
Death was rebuilt as a tucking mill by abbot Mey, at the same
time acquiring a new name, Shillamill (or "Shyndel-mylle"),
from the noise that echoed through the valley as its hammers

associate Bonvisi with the Devon manufacture; and his statement about
Devonshire dozens is in any case anachronistic.
  [1] Power and Postan, *English Trade in the Fifteenth Century*, pp. 337–9,
352–4.
  [2] *Rotuli Parliamentorum*, v, p. 621.
  [3] 7 Edward IV, c. 2; 6 Henry VIII, c. 9; 27 Henry VIII, c. 12; 5 and 6
Edward VI, c. 6.
  [4] W. D Bdle 84, no. 22.
  [5] Extent of Taviton, 1413, in Tavistock Abbey White Book, fo. xxx.

rose and fell.[1] In 1447 some land at Nether Wilminstone was let
on a forty-year lease to a tucker who engaged to build a mill there.[2]
In 1479 a mill at Parkwood belonging to the sacristan, which had
been used as a tan-mill for the last two hundred years, was leased
out on the same condition. Nine years later an edge-tool mill outside the abbey gate was similarly converted by the lessee, whose
successor in 1522 obtained leave to extend the premises by adding
a "tesyng myll". In 1493 there is mention of a tucking mill
recently built inside Parkwood gate, and three years later the
abbot and convent provided materials for the construction of
another on the same water-course.[3] By 1500 there were no fewer
than sixteen of these mills at work within a radius of two miles
from the abbey.[4]

There is no reason to suppose that the abbots ever tried to
maintain an exclusive hold over the construction and ownership
of tucking mills. Nor did they insist that all cloth made within
their jurisdiction should be fulled at their own mills. The
attempt to enforce a seignorial monopoly over fulling, parallel to
the ubiquitous monopoly of corn-grinding, had been made elsewhere, notably at St Albans in 1274, when it had provoked a
serious insurrection.[5] Had the cloth trade of Tavistock developed
in the thirteenth century, similar troubles might have arisen
there; but the fifteenth century was no time for pressing home
seignorial rights. The rebuilding of Shillamill is the one case in
which the abbot is known to have taken the initiative. As a rule he
confined himself to granting leases. A tucker wishing to build a
new mill would find the abbey ready enough to let him have a
forty-year lease of some convenient site, with a supply of timber
for construction and repairs. The rents were not exorbitant. That
of Lomehole mill remained constant at ten shillings from 1414 to
the Dissolution. In 1416 Walter Toker took a lease of some land
and buildings at Indescombe, paying twenty-seven shillings a

---

[1] Rental of lands belonging to the prior and convent (Table 2, B 2);
Hurdwick bailiff's account, 1412.
[2] White Book, fo. xxi.   [3] W. D Bdle 53, nos. 68, 73, 84, 76, 78.
[4] One at Lomehole and two at Indescombe, in the Wallabrook valley; six
in Parkwood; three at Taviton; two within the borough; Shillamill; Lower
Wilminstone. In 1474 there had been a fulling mill as well as a cornmill at
Newton (W. D Bdle 53, no. 88).
[5] *Economic History Review*, xi, 1941, pp. 51–4.

year. He was succeeded by Nicholas Toker; and in 1477, by which time the premises included two fulling mills, the lease was renewed to a third member of the family at twenty-eight shillings. In 1517 the reversion was sold to William Brune for two pounds, the new tenant agreeing to pay 33s. 4d. a year. This agreement took effect in 1538, and members of the Brune family were still holding the premises at that rent fifty years later.[1] Thus, while the abbey did its part in fostering the local trade, its rôle was that of a ground landlord taking his profit chiefly in the shape of premiums for the granting and renewal of leases. Such profits were in an altogether different category from those earned by the sale of corn, livestock, and dairy produce.

The cash receipts from pastoral husbandry were entered in the annual accounts under the two main headings *Exitus manerii* and *Vendicio stauri*. Under the first the reeve or bailiff accounted for sales of wool, fells, hides, cheese, and butter, and also for agistment dues and rents received for the demesne pastures. Under the second he entered sales of livestock. But very often a certain amount of selling took place after the account was drafted, and the proceeds from such last-minute transactions were entered summarily, without analysis, under the heading *Vendicio super compotum*. This item frequently covers nearly fifty per cent. of the gross receipts, but seldom is it made clear in what proportions it should be divided up and credited to grange, dairy, and stock-farm. To extract from these documents a full and correct account of sales is therefore an impossible task. Nor is it any easier to draw up a statement of net profit and loss. The expenses of cultivation are known, and could be set against the gross receipts; but we should also need to estimate the value, at current market prices, of the grain, meat, and dairy produce consumed in the abbey or given to the staff. We should also have to decide in what proportions the bailiff's wages ought to be charged against the two departments, arable and pastoral. Such accountancy demands a fuller knowledge of the facts than we possess.

On the other hand, it is possible for us, without indulging in guess-work, to assess the relative importance of the two departments. We can do so by giving the sum of the *exitus* and stock sales entered as such, and contrasting it with the sales of corn

[1] W. D Bdle 53, nos. 42, 44, 46, 48.

entered as *Vendicio bladi*. The *Vendicio super compotum* will have to be ignored, and the result will be an admittedly incomplete picture even of the gross cash returns. But taken together over the whole period, the two figures will illustrate at least the prevailing trend of husbandry on these demesnes.

TABLE XXII

Year	Manor	Receipts from pasture farming			Receipts from corn sales		
		£	s.	d.	£	s.	d.
1298	Werrington		12	5¾	3	8	6
1332	Hurdwick	1	17	1¼	5	9	11
1335	Ottery	3	3	1	1	10	4
1336	,,	2	4	8	4	18	7
1337	,,	4	9	1½			11
1342	,,	1	15	2	8	10	2
1343	,,	1	18	8	9	10	5½
1344	,,	2	10	4	6	3	6¾
1358	Burrington	3	15	9½	5	19	9¼
1381	Ottery	9	7	4	20	5	11¾
1382	Week	3	7	9½	6	10	10
1385¹	,,	1	18	4	6	17	2
1386	Ottery	6	7	8	9	9	0
,,	Werrington	4	11	6½	5	15	9
1390	Ottery	7	9	10½	12	4	0
1393	Denbury	3	16	0	7	10	7½
1396	Ottery	6	15	8	10	1	1½
1398	Hurdwick	11	10	0½	28	17	1½
,,	Werrington	12	3	11	11	2	4½
,,	Leigh	4	3	7½	9	1	6¾
,,	Milton	5	3	2	9	12	2
1412	Hurdwick	17	17	11	31	18	9¾
1413	Werrington	11	2	7½	10	3	7¾
,,	Hurdwick	11	9	9	32	8	10
1414	,,	9	10	0½	17	12	2½
1416	,,	13	11	1½	39	5	2
1427	,,	12	3	6	17	3	7
1433	,,	18	15	7	16	2	11
1435	,,	26	6	2	7	12	10½
1441	,,	6	16	0	2	3	8
1446	,,	14	5	1	2	8	11

¹ Half-year.

TABLE XXII (*cont.*)

Year	Manor	Receipts from pasture farming			Receipts from corn sales		
		£	s.	d.	£	s.	d.
1450	Hurdwick	24	4	3	16	1	0½
1454	Werrington	4	9	4	3	11	9
,,	Hurdwick	18	10	9	17	17	4
1458	,,	13	9	10	33	11	10
1460	,,	13	3	10	30	11	10¾
1461	Werrington	5	19	11	7	11	11
1463	Hurdwick	13	17	6	9	12	5¼
1464	,,	18	3	9	6	14	2½
1466	,,	16	18	6	8	4	6
1470	,,	16	4	6	4	3	2
1471	,,	13	16	6	11	5	11
1473	,,	21	11	9	7	13	5
1475	,,	17	11	7	8	4	11½
1477	,,	18	7	2	10	2	4¼
1480	,,	21	4	1	8	10	1
1482	,,	18	4	8	9	4	7
1489	,,	18	19	2	15	17	2½
1490	,,	17	6	0	18	7	3
1491	,,	11	11	6	25	0	6
1492	,,	18	14	9	15	2	2
1497	,,	16	5	6	17	11	8¼
,,	Morwell	2	8	10	5	7	6¼
,,	Leigh	9	17	6	11	2	5
1498	Hurdwick	16	4	11½	11	19	4¾
1499	Werrington	3	3	4½	2	19	2
c.1500	Leigh	8	15	4	7	6	0
1502	Hurdwick	15	13	3½	17	12	0¼
1504	,,	14	17	4½	22	0	3¾
1505	,,	15	2	2	14	16	3¾
1508	,,	20	9	11	17	10	3
1509	,,	19	9	7	18	5	4
1513	,,	16	14	7	21	0	8
1516	,,	21	7	7	17	16	6
1517	,,	20	4	11	22	1	1
1522	,,	25	2	0	16	18	7
1524	,,	18	10	9	17	19	6½
1537	,,	26	14	3	14	19	7
1538	,,	26	0	0	15	7	7

Nowadays Devon is regarded as pre-eminently a grassland county. The picture that emerges from this table is therefore hardly what one would expect. It is based on accounts ranging over nearly two and a half centuries, and representing nine different manors. There are sixty-nine of them; and in thirty-five the corn sales predominate. In the first twenty-seven of the series there are only four accounts in which pastoral sales take the lead. This brings us down to 1427. From 1433 to 1454 the pastoral receipts have the advantage, being swollen by the high rents paid for the demesne grassland. Such rents, however, indicate a change of emphasis in the husbandry of the tenants rather than in that of the demesne. For a few years corn leads again; then, in 1463, it falls back, not to recover until a quarter of a century has passed. In the final period, from 1490 to the Dissolution, the pendulum swings to and fro, but pasture on the whole predominates.

These findings accord well enough with the conclusion to which we came in the last chapter. The high level of agriculture attained on the Tavistock estates brought its reward in the shape of steady grain-sales. In the system of intensive manuring to which its excellence was due, the sheepfold played an important part. Here, as a matter of course, arable and pastoral husbandry were interlocked. During the fifteenth century the demands of an expanding cloth trade brought about a gradual intensification of pasture-farming, but equilibrium between the two branches of husbandry was never quite upset. Viewed in the light of this investigation, the agrarian economy of Tavistock reveals itself as combining the elements of sound farming into a remarkably well-balanced whole.

CHAPTER VI

FISHERIES

AN AMPLE supply of fish was requisite in an age when the Lenten fast was generally observed. To monks, especially, it was of vital consequence, for the original Benedictine rule, not officially modified in this respect until the thirteenth century, forbade them to eat meat. Hence, in the eyes of a monastic founder, no site could be more eligible than the bank of some teeming river. At Tavistock the abbey site was bounded by the Tavy, and additionally watered by the so-called Fishlake. This little stream, rising in a field near Hurdwick, flows along the Billingsbear valley, then down Lakeside and Market Street. Originally, when it reached the foot of the hill, it must have run straight across the west end of the present churchyard, and so out to the Tavy; but the builders of the abbey divided the outflow into three artificial channels. One of these was carried by two right-angle turns round to the main gateway and across the great courtyard to drive the abbey mill. The second flushed the drains that were laid beneath or alongside the western range of the monastic buildings, and the third supplied fresh water to the fish-pond: hence the name by which this rivulet came to be known.[1] William of Malmesbury, who pays a warm tribute to the amenities of Tavistock, refers with especial enthusiasm to its plentiful supply of timber, its abundant fishery, and its admirable sanitation.[2]

The salmon begin to go up the Tavy and the Tamar in the middle of February. Salmon peal and trout also frequent these waters. Early in the twelfth century Baldwin de Redvers, the future earl of Devon, gave the monks of Tavistock his tithe of all the fish caught at Buckland, a manor situated on the left bank of the Tavy, opposite the southernmost portion of Tavistock.[3] This donation may or may not have been renewed by Baldwin's heirs; but in 1278 the widow of the sixth earl founded a Cistercian abbey at Buckland, and made over to it all the rights pertaining to

[1] DCNQ xxii, 1946, p. 369.   [2] *Gesta Pontificum*, p. 202.   [3] ETC viii.

the lordship of that manor. It was not to be expected that the fishing rights would lie dormant in such hands: and within a couple of years the newcomers were at odds with the senior house on this account. The Tavistock woodward, entering Blackmoor-ham wood one day at a spot then called Ivy Oak, found the men of Buckland cutting down branches of oak, and endeavoured to prevent them by force, but after a brief scuffle had to quit the field with an arrow lodged in his right arm, leaving behind his bow, hatchet, and "a grey outer garment called a tabard". In the ensuing litigation it was established that the abbot of Buckland had a weir in the river Tavy, and was entitled to repair it with timber from the wood on the opposite bank.[1]

Remains of the Abbot's Weir can still be seen at a highly picturesque spot a few hundred yards below the confluence of the Tavy and the Walkham. It was in full working order at the close of the eighteenth century, and the description of it given by Marshall may be applied retrospectively to the period when it was first constructed. The weir consisted of "a strong dam or breastwork, ten or twelve feet high, thrown across the river". In the abbot's time this was always made of timber. Below it, on the Buckland side, was the salmon trap, a compartment twelve or fifteen feet square, with an entrance "outwardly large, but con-tracted inwardly, so as to elude or prevent the escape of the animal which has taken it. It is remarkable, however, with re-spect to salmon, that although the entrance is by no means so narrow as to prevent even the largest from returning, it is be-lieved that there is no instance of those which have once entered, quitting their confinement, though they may have remained in it several days. A circumstance, perhaps, which can only be accounted for, in the natural propensity or instinct, which directs them against the stream, and will not suffer them to give up any advantage which they may have gained; the ascent into the trap being an effort of difficulty: in this case perhaps too great." The trap was covered by a floor of planks, and was fitted with a hatch or sluice opposite the entrance. "This opening has two lifting floodgates: the one close, to shut out the water; the other a grate, to suffer the water to pass, and at the same time to prevent fish of any considerable size from escaping. When the trap is set, the

[1] PRO Assize Rolls, J.I. 1, 186, m. 18*b*; Oliver, p. 384 *n.*

close gate is drawn up, with an iron crow: thus suffering the water to pass through the house. On the contrary, to take the fish which have entered, the close gate is let down, and the trap is presently left in a manner dry."

Fishing nets were also employed. "The river, for near a mile below the weir, is broken into rapids and pools, some of them very deep. Seven or eight of these pools are adapted to the seine or draw net, which is drawn once or twice a day, by four men: with horses to carry the net, and the fish caught; and with dogs to convey the end of the rope across the water, where it is too deep or inconvenient to be forded."[1]

The men who routed the forester in Blackmoorham wood were tenants of the abbot of Buckland who were bound, as a condition of their tenure, to repair the salmon-hatch at Abbot's Weir. In an earlier chapter we have noted the payment of a rent called hatch-silver. This consisted of a penny due to the abbot of Tavistock from certain of his tenants in the manor of Hurdwick on All Saints' Day and in Milton Abbot at midsummer. Judging from the analogy of similar rents paid elsewhere, we are probably safe in taking this to represent a commutation of the same labour service on the Tavistock estates.

In the tenth century, when the abbot owned the Cornish manor of Stoke Climsland, he was in the fortunate position of controlling several miles of river bank on both sides of the Tamar. But Stoke Climsland passed into other hands before the Norman Conquest, and Calstock, which adjoined it on the south, formed part of the great Vautort fief, the so-called honour of Trematon. Towards the close of the twelfth century an agreement was concluded between Herbert, abbot of Tavistock, and Roger de Vautort. It appears from this document that Roger, as lord of Trematon and Calstock, had a salmon weir, built across the Tamar to within a couple of yards of the opposite bank; and that the abbot had one further upstream. The parties agreed to co-operate in preventing any enlargement of the channel between the Calstock weir and the Devonshire bank. The stretch of water between the two weirs was reserved to the abbot. For repairing the weirs each party might supply himself with timber from the other's woods: in Roger's case, without restriction; in the abbot's,

---

[1] Marshall, II, pp. 256 sqq.

with exception of oak, ash, and coppice-wood. Finally, Roger
agreed not to fish the pool immediately above his weir except
during a season of eleven weeks, from the 17th of February to
the 3rd of May.[1]

The Calstock weir was situated at the spot now called Weir
Head; and the site of the abbot's, which was variously known as
Gulworthy hatch or the Over-hatch, is now occupied by New
Bridge. Notwithstanding his agreement with the lord of Trematon, the abbot presently found it expedient to take a lease of the
Calstock hatches. In 1292 his fishing rights were assessed, for
purposes of taxation, at one pound.[2] Receipts are extant, dated
1305 and 1310, showing that he then paid, for "the fishery of
Kalystok", a yearly rent of eight pounds. By 1328 this had been
increased to ten pounds.[3] Nine years later the Black Prince was
created duke of Cornwall, and Calstock was one of the numerous
manors assigned to him for the support of the new dignity. During the troubled abbacies of Bonus (1327–33) and his successor
John de Courtenay (1334–49) the lease was allowed to pass into
other hands, and after the Black Death its annual value sank to
six pounds.[4]

In February 1352 orders were given by the Black Prince's
council to distrain the abbot and cause him to show by what title
he was taking great abundance of salmon at the Over-hatch,
"within the prince's manor of Calstock". According to the council, the whole river belonged to the prince as parcel of the honour
of Trematon. The abbot, in reply, produced a copy of Roger de
Vautort's charter, and the council, having studied this, gave
orders that the abbot should be left undisturbed.[5]

In the following year a prominent burgess of Tavistock, William Stacy, offered the duchy eight pounds a year for a seven-year
lease of the Calstock fishery. The offer was accepted; but shortly
afterwards the abbot came forward with a counter-proposal. He
intimated that he was prepared to pay the old rent of ten pounds.
Thereupon the prince's advisers cancelled Stacy's lease, awarded
him three pounds as compensation for his expenditure on the

[1] ETC xlviii.   [2] *Taxatio Ecclesiastica*, p. 153.   [3] W. D Bdle 77, nos. 1–3.
[4] *Register of Edward the Black Prince*, ii, p. 54. Cf. Lewis, *op. cit.*, p. 40,
on the effect of the plague upon the Prince's mining revenue.
[5] *Ibid.*, pp. 27, 31.

weir during the nine months of his tenancy, and on the 1st of October 1354 granted a perpetual lease of the fishery to the abbot and his successors for all time. This covered the entire stretch of water from Okeltor up to Gulworthy hatch. The lessee was authorized to draw nets along the Cornish bank, to dry fish there, to dig turves, and to carry out any repairs to the weir that might be necessary on the soil of Calstock.[1]

The rector of Calstock at this time was a churchman who combined in equal proportions a propensity towards litigation and a taste for salmon. In December 1350 he brought a suit against the abbot in the consistorial court of Exeter, claiming tithe of the fish caught at the Over-hatch. A number of his parishioners gave evidence in support of this improbable claim, but their testimony carried less than no weight, for it appeared that several of them had been convicted before the archdeacon or his deputy of offences ranging from simple adultery to incest, and with their partners in guilt had been publicly flogged round Calstock church. The case dragged on for sixteen months; at last judgement was given in favour of the abbot.[2] After an interval the parson launched a second attack from a new base. He complained to the council of the duchy that whereas his predecessors time out of mind had enjoyed the right to have four "settels"—probably some kind of wicker trap—affixed to the soil of their glebe-land beside the Tamar, for taking salmon and other fish, the abbot was now denying him this right. On inquiry it was found that the exercise of the right had been interrupted not by the abbot but by a previous leaseholder in 1346.[3]

From the documents which have been quoted it is evident that the weirs were normally of timber construction. In 1527 Gulworthy weir is described as consisting of a great number of oaks with all their boughs and branches interlocked; to these, boards were fastened with iron clamps, making the whole as "close as a wall". The dam had been considerably strengthened by abbot Banham, and his successor continued the work until it was nearly sixteen feet high. By so doing, he aroused great discontent on the Cornish bank. Many inhabitants of Stoke Climsland made no

[1] *Register*, II, pp. 54, 58, 71.
[2] W. Table 4 A, Drawer 2, Tavistock Addenda.
[3] *Register of the Black Prince*, II, pp. 74, 90.

secret of the fact that they had been accustomed to help themselves to salmon, lampreys, trout, and other fish, in quantities sufficient to pay their rents. They now complained that the fish could no longer pass upstream, that salmon fry, in time of spawning, perished on the gravel that collected round the base of the weir, and that fish bred higher up could not return once they had passed the weir on their way to the sea. The abbot, in reply, declared that the weir did not run from bank to bank, as was alleged, but left enough room for a boat to pass. In the spring of 1527 Sir Edward Pomeroy, John Gilbert, and two other royal commissioners held an inquiry at Tavistock, and decided that the complaints were unfounded. The malcontents, however, were not persuaded to let the matter drop. They were egged on by two gentlemen, William Harris of Radford, and John Kelly, squire of Kelly. On Whit Sunday afternoon these two caused proclamation to be made, with triple Oyez, in the churchyard of Stoke Climsland, appointing a rendezvous at Toker's blowing-mill. There, in the course of the evening, they were joined by about two hundred farmers, labourers, and youngsters out for mischief. At ten o'clock the whole concourse went up to light bonfires on Hingston Down, where they remained singing and shouting until one o'clock in the morning. They were now some three hundred strong. Finally Harris, on horseback, and brandishing a pistol which he fired off at intervals (but only "for his pleasure", and with paper pellets, it was later urged in his defence), led them to the grand assault upon the weir. Some of the rioters were armed with bows and arrows; others carried axes, hand-saws, and mattocks. They broke the iron bars and locks of the hatch, and set fire to it, and had begun to tear down the weir itself, when they saw a hundred and sixty men of Tavistock approaching, about half of them "well harnessed", with the abbot in person at their head. Thereupon, as one of the rioters afterwards declared, "every man was glad to make shift for himself and to go his way; and so, for fear of them, this deponent took little heed what was done there." On the following day Harris and Kelly met again at Launceston, where the Lord Chief Justice was holding the assizes; and the air grew thick with indictments and countercharges. The abbot sought redress from the court of Star Chamber; depositions were taken from a number of witnesses; and presently the ringleaders, including Harris, were ordered to give security for the payment of such fines as the court might think fit to impose.[1] In a last attempt to confuse the issue, the defendants preferred a complaint against the abbot in the court of Requests; with the result that on the 8th of July 1530 Sir John Fitzjames, Sir John Arundell, Sir William Courtenay, and Sir Piers Edgcumbe were commissioned to hold a fresh inquiry.[2] Their report has not come to light; but five years later Henry VIII gave orders for a general destruction of weirs, and on the 17th of November 1535 all those in Devon were reported to be down. Shortly afterwards the building of New Bridge was begun by Sir Piers Edgcumbe on the scene of these nocturnal excitements.[3]

Below Calstock weir there were a number of pools which the abbot from time to time sublet, reserving to himself a moiety of the fish netted there, and also certain annual rents, which in 1414 were detailed as follows:

Wympull Water[4]	8s.	Forde Lew	18d.
Wympull Lew	2s.	Gyade Lew	2s.
Guddegyrie	2s.	Stone Lew	12d.
Kyte Lew	2s.	Troddepoll	3s.
By Lew	12d.	At Stone	6d.
Barbygan	6d.	Okelator	20s.
Scobbe	6d.	Nunnepoole	23s. 6d.

These rents, amounting in all to £3 7s. 6d., were paid to the abbot as lord of Morwell, for the Devonshire bank from Calstock weir down to Morwellham lay within that manor.

At Tavistock, as at other monasteries, fish had by this time ceased to be the all-important article of diet. A custom had grown

[1] PRO Star Chamber Proceedings, St. Ch. 2, Bdle xxx, no. 115; Bdle xxii, no. 56.

[2] PRO Court of Requests, Req. 2, Bdle ix, nos. 52, 6.

[3] L. & P. Hen. VIII, ix, p. 279, §833; Chope, Early Tours in Devon and Cornwall, p. 8.

[4] The pool immediately below the far-famed Morwell Rocks is much favoured by congregations of salmon. Its name is a compound of two British words corresponding to the Welsh gwyn pwll, or 'white pool' (cf. PND, p. 579). Hence the name Whimple, now given to a farm on the Cornish bank, and formerly also to Morwell Rocks, which used to be called the Whimple or Umple Rocks.

M

up which authorized the use of a second dining-hall, adjoining the infirmary, and known as the misericord. Here the abbot and the greater part of the community might eat meat with a good appetite and conscience, leaving the refectory proper almost or quite deserted except on high festivals. The Tavistock misericord stands to this day, one of the completest remaining portions of the abbey. It is used, incongruously enough, as a Unitarian chapel; but apart from the insertion of a plaster ceiling, and the removal of a stone pulpit in the north wall from which a homily was read while the monks ate their dinner, it has undergone little alteration. Notwithstanding the alleviation of their rule, the Tavistock community always observed the Lenten abstinence and the usual fasts. A cellarer's account-book which has escaped destruction testifies to frequent purchases of cod, hake, bass, ling, herring, mackerel, and pilchards. Salmon too were purchased, the average price of a whole fish being 1s. 3d.[1] As the gross revenue from the Tamar fishery was stated in 1535 to be fifteen pounds, this points to a total catch of some two hundred and forty salmon, which is about half the number taken at the present day in the same water.[2]

---

[1] DCNQ xxiii, 1948, pp. 253 sqq.

[2] *Valor Ecclesiasticus*, ii, p. 381. The average weight of a Tamar salmon is a little over ten pounds, and the average catch of the season is just over 500. It is possible that the 1535 valuation refers only to the Calstock weir. If so, the fish taken at Gulworthy Hatch may have brought the total nearly up to the present figure.

CHAPTER VII

THE STANNARY OF TAVISTOCK

ONSIDERED as an item in the budget of Tavistock Abbey, the tin-mines were of only secondary and occasional importance. For a brief term in the fourteenth century the abbot held the stannaries in farm; and it is probable that from time to time succeeding abbots became shareholders in mining ventures, but of such transactions little record has survived. On the whole it must be said that the tin trade, like the cloth trade, was a business in which the abbey seldom intervened directly. To not a few of its tenants, on the other hand, and to those of many another lord, the industry was both a source of wealth and a factor which conditioned their relations with the rest of the community at almost every turn. As such it did become a matter of intimate concern to the monks of Tavistock, and no description of their economy would be complete without some notice of it.

Tin-mining is well known to be of great antiquity in the southwest. Long before any Englishman set foot in the neighbourhood of Tavistock, the inhabitants of Cornwall were busily exploiting the alluvial deposits of tin with which their land abounded. Diodorus, writing on the eve of the Christian era, describes the natives of Land's End as carrying blocks of tin at low tide in wagons to St Michael's Mount—he calls it Ictis—whence visiting Gallic merchants took it across the Channel and overland to Marseilles, presumably for shipment to the farther Mediterranean ports. At the time when this was written, the trade had already begun to fall off, deposits of tin having been opened in north-western Spain. Under Roman administration a new spell of activity began about the middle of the third century; and the export trade outlasted the decay of Roman rule in Britain, for the biographer of John the Almsgiver, patriarch of Alexandria, who died in 616 or thereabouts, refers to an Alexandrian seaman of that day who brought tin from Britain. Then darkness falls, and nothing more is heard of tin-working in the peninsula until the reign of Henry II.[1]

From the early Bronze Age down to the Roman period it was the deposits in the far west of Cornwall that were most extensively worked. Archaeologists have found some traces of mining activity in the country round Bodmin and St Austell, and a very few in east Cornwall, but no evidence at all of prehistoric tin-works in Devon. There is no reference to the trade in Domesday Book or in the one Pipe Roll that has survived from the reign of Henry I. When the curtain does at last go up in the middle of the twelfth century, it is in Devon that the tinners are found to be most active. It looks as if the rich deposits in the valleys of the Dartmoor streams had only just then begun to attract attention.

Either in consequence of this belated discovery, or from some other cause, the industry now entered upon a new phase, and the stannaries, or tin-mines (*minaria stanni*), began to find a place in official records. The word 'mine' here does not imply shaft-mining. In the twelfth century, and throughout the period with which this book is concerned, the ore was obtained by streaming. "A tin stream in accordance with the older usage of the term was not a stream of water but a bed of the detrital ore in the form of heavy black stones and sand. These beds varied in thickness from one to ten feet and in breadth from six feet to most of the width of a valley. They were usually fan-shaped, with the broader part lying on low ground or in a moorland vale, while higher up the hillside and corresponding to the handle of the fan was the parent lode from which in the course of time the tinstone in the bed had been carried down... These beds were found anywhere from the surface to a depth of thirty or forty feet." The early tinners contented themselves perforce with shallow workings. They first dug away the earth above the tin bed, and then dumped the sand and tin-stones into an artificial water-way constructed for the purpose, where it was stirred until the lighter waste or 'slime' had been washed away, leaving only the much heavier ore. The larger stones were broken down by hand on rocks, and the smaller were ground in a revolving hand-mill. The sand to which the stones were reduced in this laborious way was then washed, and the

[1] Hencken, *The Archaeology of Cornwall and Scilly*, pp. 162–201; Collingwood, *Roman Britain*, pp. 70, 231.

ore separated from the slime. It was now ready for smelting.[1]

The metal was extracted from the ore in two stages. A rough preliminary smelting took place near the mine, where a peat fire, with the ore built into its body, was kindled over a hole in the ground, and a comparatively low temperature served to reduce the metal. At this stage the tin became liable to a tax of half a crown a thousandweight in Devon, and five shillings a thousand-weight in Cornwall. Until this duty had been paid, the tin might not be put on sale, and then only in recognized market towns. Five places in the vicinity of Dartmoor are known to have possessed markets in the twelfth century. These were Lydford, Tavistock, Plympton, Chagford, and Ashburton.[2] We shall see that all five were destined to figure prominently in the stannary administration. It was in one or other of these towns that the second smelt-ing, or refining process, took place. The loss of weight caused by refining, the duty already paid, and the cost of carriage from the mine to the nearest market town, all helped to depreciate tin of the first smelting. To compensate for this depreciation, the scales were adjusted, and unrefined tin was weighed by a heavier stan-dard pound, which in Devon comprised eighteen ounces, and in Cornwall, where the duty was higher, eighteen and two-sevenths ounces.[3]

If the stream-work lay in private ground, the lord of the manor was entitled to a percentage of the tin, or its cash value, by way of toll.[4] Thus far his rights extended, but no farther. For custom decreed that the tinners might freely and peaceably, without

[1] Hencken, *op. cit.*, pp. 158 sqq.

[2] Lydford was one of the four pre-Conquest boroughs of Devon. Weekly markets were set up at Tavistock *circa* 1105 (*infra*, p. 197), and at Chagford, perhaps irregularly, soon afterwards (DCNQ XXIII, 1947, p. 21). There were burgesses at Plympton in 1195 (PRS XLIV, N.S. VI, p. 131), and burgesses imply a market. A grant by Roger de Nonant to Buckfast Abbey refers to the *forum* of Ashburton (DA LVI, 1924, p. 48). Okehampton had had a market in 1086, but it seems to have fallen into abeyance, and to have been revived in the second quarter of the thirteenth century, for in 1238 the men of Lydford objected to competition from Okehampton in terms implying that the mar-ket there was something new (PRO Assize Rolls, J.I. 1, 174, m. 39*d*).

[3] Worth, 'The Dartmoor Blowing House', DA LXXII, 1940, pp. 209, 247.

[4] Thus in 1177 and two following years the administrator of the earl of Devon's lands accounted for small sums received by way of customary dues for tin raised on the earl's Plympton estates (PRS XXVI, p. 9; XXVII, p. 16; XXVIII, p. 15).

hindrance from any man, dig for tin at all times and in all places, both on the royal moors and in the private lands of bishops, abbots, earls, and other lords. They might also divert streams of water, and dig for peat wherever and whenever fuel was required for smelting. These rights were guaranteed by customary law. In 1201 they were declared to be of ancient custom, and they had probably been exercised in Cornwall from time immemorial. As soon as mining began in Devon they would naturally be claimed by the tinners of that county as well.

The day-to-day practice of the trade was subject to a code of regulations imposed by the Crown and known as the assize of mines.[1] In taking the industry under their direct control the Plantagenet kings followed, consciously or unconsciously, a precedent set by the Roman administration;[2] and their control was all the more effective in that the counties of Devon and Cornwall at this period were deemed to be royal forests. Breaches of the assize of mines were punished by the justices of the forest who came down on circuit nearly every year.[3] In 1168 one of these judges imposed a fine of three marks on Guy de Bretteville "for his men of Sheepstor [Sitelestorra], because they have dug for tin in the king's forest against the rules"; and the lord of Brisworthy was fined twenty shillings for the same offence.[4] Brisworthy and Sheepstor are two moorland hamlets situated about seven miles south-east of Tavistock; and the culprits were perhaps guilty of digging after sundown, or without first staking out a claim: either of which proceedings would have been punishable under later regulations. In 1195 a castle was built at Lydford expressly for the custody of prisoners,[5] and its grim keep still testifies to the severity with which the stannary and forest codes were enforced.

In Cornwall the duty paid on tin of the first smelting was included in the miscellaneous revenues which made up what was called the farm of the county. This was in the hands of the sheriff, who paid a fixed yearly sum to the Exchequer and made his profit out of the surplus income. The fact that the stannary tax

---

[1] PRS XXXVIII, p. 169.   [2] Collingwood, *op. cit.*, p. 231.
[3] This was the rule, but in 1185 it was the justices in eyre who fined a group of Chagford tinners for illegal smelting (PRS XXXIV, pp. 160, 161).
[4] *Ibid.*, XII, p. 138.   [5] *Ibid.*, XLIV (N.S. VI), p. 126.

was treated in this way suggests that the proceeds were insignifi-
cant, and explains why nothing is said of the tin trade in Domesday Book. In Cornwall this state of affairs continued down to
1195.[1] A parallel arrangement may or may not have subsisted in
the neighbouring county. There is no evidence on this point, and
nothing to show why the twelfth-century revival received its first
impetus in Devon rather than in Cornwall, unless it was because
the alluvial deposits of the Devon valleys had been little if at all
reduced by prehistoric workings. Knowing, as we do, that the
Jews were taking an active part in the trade at the close of the
century, we may hazard a guess that that enterprising people, who
were tolerated chiefly because they made themselves financially
useful to the Angevin kings, may have taken the initiative in this
as in so many other commercial ventures. The old smelting
houses on Dartmoor were indeed traditionally known as Jews'
Houses.[2] All that can be said with certainty, however, is that
forty years before anything of the sort took place in Cornwall, the
mines of Devon were yielding a revenue considerable enough to
require separate administration.

At first this was entrusted to the sheriff, who in 1156 was paying
twenty-five marks yearly (£16 13s. 4d.) into the Exchequer on
account of "the new farm".[3] The amount was raised at frequent
intervals to keep pace with the growing output of the stream-
works. In 1161 it was increased to £20; in 1162 to £23 6s. 8d.;
in 1169 to £66 13s. 4d.; in 1171 to £80; and in 1194 to £100.[4] In
1169 the farm was taken over by a syndicate consisting of three
partners, William Bulzun, Alan Furneaux, and Joel of Ashburton.[5] The two last-named carried it on after William Bulzun's
death, and in 1187 Alan Furneaux was succeeded by his son
Geoffrey; but in the following year Joel of Ashburton, now the
senior partner, was convicted before the justice of the forest of
breaking the assize of mines.[6] The nature of his offence is not recorded. It was punished with the heavy fine of a hundred marks,

[1] PRS XLV (N.S. VII), pp. xx, 150.
[2] Worth, op. cit., p. 211. The formula used in the regulations of 1198 is:
"Non praesumat homo nec femina Christianus nec Judaeus . . ."
[3] The Great Rolls of the Pipe, ed. Hunter, pp. 48, 74.
[4] PRS I, p. 28; V, p. 4; XIII, p. 47; XVI, p. 25; XLIII (N.S. V), p. 171.
[5] Ibid., XIII, p. 47.
[6] Ibid., XXXVIII, p. 169.

which his son and heir was still paying off by slow instalments twenty years later.[1]

In 1195 a consignment of tin amounting to rather more than 254 thousandweight was shipped over to the king at La Rochelle, apparently for the purpose of adulterating the coin with which the Lion-Heart paid his troops.[2] This had been purchased at the cost of five marks a thousandweight. Two years later the Crown made a profit of £352 6s. 10d. on the purchase and re-sale of tin.[3] It was evident that the trade was flourishing enough to bear an increase of taxation, and also that it required more constant supervision than it was now receiving from Geoffrey Fitz Peter, who held the manor of Lydford with all Dartmoor in farm, and was also justice of the forest. Accordingly at the beginning of 1198 an experienced civil servant, William de Wrotham, was appointed warden of the stannaries, and, as such, first holder of an office which has continued in being down to the present day.

The new warden's first act was to assemble a jury of tinners in the county court at Exeter, and by their testimony to establish the facts of the duty on the first smelting and the system of weighing unrefined ore. The names of the jurors are interesting. They include tinners from Totnes, Plympton, and Ashburton, and the name which heads the list, Roger Rabi in the Exchequer transcript, may in all probability be identified with that Roger Rubi or Rubbi whose family gave its name to Rubbytown in Tavistock.[4] Having taken their sworn evidence, the warden proceeded to draw up a series of ordinances regulating the collection of the stannary dues. No one henceforward might retain possession of tin for more than a fortnight after the first smelting unless it had been weighed in the presence of three stannary officials and stamped with the royal mark as a sign that duty had been paid. Within thirteen weeks thereafter all tin was to be put into the second smelting, and again weighed and stamped. These operations were to be performed at Exeter or Bodmin, and also at a number of market towns designated from year to year by the

---

[1] PRS LXI (N.S. XXIII), p. 64. At that date £52 11s. 8d. was still owing, so that less than a quarter had been paid.

[2] Ibid., XLV (N.S. VII), pp. xix, 150.   [3] Ibid., XLVI (N.S. VIII), p. 8.

[4] Ibid., XXXI, p. 30; cf. XXVII, p. 17, and W. D Bdle 30, no. 4: grant, circa 1250, by Mariot Rubi of lands in Woodovis, near Tavistock, which she had inherited from Robert Rubi. Cf. also PND, p. 219.

warden. At the second smelting the tin now became liable to a new duty, imposed by William de Wrotham, of one mark per thousandweight in both counties; and stringent rules were laid down to prevent evasion of payment.[1]

The results of these measures must have been highly gratifying to the Exchequer. In the following year the new duty brought in £600 19s. 5d., over and above the farm of the tax on the first smelting, now fixed at one hundred pounds in Devon and two-thirds of that sum in Cornwall. Thus at one stroke the revenue had been more than quadrupled. In return the tinners received a notable extension of their privileges. By a charter dated the 29th of October 1201 king John not only confirmed their traditional right to dig for tin wherever they chose, but extended to all working tinners the legal status of tenants on royal demesne.[2] This meant that any serf who chose to engage in tin-streaming was henceforth exempt from pursuit by his lord. The lord's harvest might rot upon the ground for want of reapers, but only the warden of the stannaries could make a tinner leave his tin-work. By virtue of John's charter the warden was invested with civil and criminal jurisdiction over the tinners of both counties. He had his own courts and his own jails. Below him served a numerous band of stewards, under-stewards, bailiffs, treasurers, and clerks.

During the thirteenth century the warden frequently appears as lessee of the stannary revenues. In 1220 the Devon stannaries were farmed for two hundred marks, and those of Cornwall for one thousand, Cornwall having now regained the lead in production.[3] This predominance was never afterwards lost, but Devon continued to enjoy a more favourable rate of taxation. In 1243 we hear for the first time of the black rent, so called, of twopence a head paid by every digger of tin ore. Between that date and 1301, when it disappears, the receipts from this tax provide a useful key to the number of tinners actually at work in the county.[4] The "makers of white tin", that is to say those who brought the ore to be smelted and took away the finished product,

---

[1] *Liber Niger Scaccarii*, I, p. 360 sqq.

[2] Cartae Antiquae, 288; facsimile in Delabeche, *Report on the Geology of Cornwall, Devon, and West Somerset*, plate 13; cf. *Calendar of Charter Rolls*, I, p. 380.

[3] Lewis, *op. cit.*, p. 43.   [4] *Ibid.*, p. 267; see below, p. 187.

were compelled from 1288 onwards to pay a duty called white rent. This at first was paid in kind, at the rate of two pounds of refined tin per head, but by the close of the fourteenth century it had been commuted to a fixed charge of eightpence.[1]

At some time during the thirteenth century an improved method of smelting was introduced. Blowing-houses were erected, rude granite structures roofed with thatch. Here the prepared ore was put into a furnace. The fire was urged by the blast from a large pair of bellows actuated by a water-wheel. Afterwards the molten metal was ladled into granite moulds and cast into blocks weighing between one and two hundredweight. The particles of tin which the blast drove up into the thatch were recovered every few years by the simple though drastic process of burning down the roof. Remains of more than forty blowing-houses, of unknown antiquity, are to be found on Dartmoor at this day.[2]

The establishment of the new refining process made it unnecessary to fuse the metal twice, and the old taxes on the first and second smelting were abandoned. Their place was taken by the so-called coinage duty, charged on the finished metal. In Devonshire this duty was fixed at 1s. 6¾d. per hundredweight of one hundred and twenty pounds, and in Cornwall at four shillings. It was collected at certain towns appointed for the purpose. Thither came the tinners, having dispatched their metal in advance by packhorses or carts, while from London and the southern ports came intending purchasers, country chapmen, London dealers, pewterers' agents, and a sprinkling of Italian and Flemish traders. On the day of the coinage all assembled in a warehouse near the market-place. "An open space was roped off at the front, the king's beam was brought out and rectified by the controller and weigher, the weights were solemnly unsealed and handed to the weigher, the assay-master made ready his hammer and chisels, and the steward, controller, and receiver took their seats facing the beam. When all was in readiness, the porters brought out the blocks one at a time and placed them upon the scales. Each had been stamped with the private mark of the owner, and as the steward carried with him a register of these

[1] Lewis, pp. 141, 142, 187, 267, 268.
[2] For a full description of these remains, see Worth, *op. cit.*

marks no difficulty occurred in identification. The weight of each was shouted out by the weigher, and taken down by the three officials. The blocks, on leaving the scales, were taken in hand by the assay-master, who chiselled a small piece from a corner of each"—a coign: hence the name coinage applied to the whole process—"and rapidly assayed it to make sure that the metal was of the proper quality." If so, the controller with a blow from the hammer struck upon the block the royal arms, or later those of the duke of Cornwall, and a bill was made out showing the weight charged against each tinner, and the amount of coinage due from him. Not until this had been paid might the tin be put on sale.[1]

The earliest extant coinage roll of the Devon stannaries belongs to the year 1303, when eight coinages were held at Chagford, eight at Ashburton, and five at Tavistock.[2] As most of the stream-works lay on Dartmoor, these three towns were the natural market centres, and their position as such was recognized in a charter issued by Edward I in 1305. This charter fixed the coinage at the three towns above named, and the stannary prison at Lydford. At the same time it confirmed the tinners in all their ancient privileges.[3] But in one respect it fell short of John's charter. That instrument, which had been confirmed by Henry III in 1252, declared the stannaries throughout Devon and Cornwall to be royal demesne, and forbade any lord to implead a working tinner as his serf. Edward I limited this freedom to tinners "working in those stannaries which are our demesne", and left it to become a matter of fierce dispute whether a tinner working elsewhere than on Crown land was entitled to the same protection.

Another clause in this momentous charter exempted working tinners from "all tallages, tolls, stallages, aids, and other customary dues in towns, ports, fairs, and markets within the county of Devon". This the tinners boldly construed as exempting them from payment of all ordinary national taxes. Abbot Champeaux of Tavistock on one occasion went so far as to become their spokesman in this sense.[4] During Edward III's French cam-

[1] Lewis, p. 151.   [2] PRO E101, Bdle 260, no. 24.
[3] *Calendar of Charter Rolls*, III, p. 54.
[4] PRO Ancient Petitions, no. 7115; cf. *Calendar of Chancery Warrants*, I, p. 547.

paigns parliament voted frequent subsidies of a tenth and a fifteenth: a tenth of each tax-payer's personal estate in cities and boroughs and a fifteenth in rural districts. But from the very first year of the war the tinners refused to pay and went on strike; as the royal writ dolefully expresses it, "they desist from their work in the stannaries."[1] The Crown gave in, and for the remainder of Edward's reign contented itself with holding an inquiry whenever the subsidy was levied, to ascertain how many persons had passed themselves off as tinners merely to evade the tax. Thereafter the right of exemption seems to have been recognized as absolute.[2]

It was not to be expected that such ample privileges would endear the tinners to the rest of the community. In 1314 the "poor men of the county of Devon" complained that the tinners were destroying good farm land, including arable, wood, and meadow, as well as houses and gardens, at the rate of more than three hundred acres a year.[3] Four years later the tinners were accused of withholding the royalties due to the lords of the soil, blackmailing property-owners with the threat of mining in unaccustomed spots, and using violence to assert the jurisdiction of their courts.[4] In 1320 no fewer than ten different remonstrances were presented against them in parliament.[5] Another long list of grievances was drawn up in 1347;[6] and the agitation culminated in 1376 with two petitions introduced into parliament by the commons of Devon and Cornwall, praying for a more rigorous definition of the stannary privileges. The petitioners declared that not only working tinners but their employers claimed the freedom of the stannaries; that the warden was taking cognizance of pleas arising in every part of the county, as well as in the tinworks; that tinners prosecuted for felony and handed over to their warden for custody were allowed to run at large; and that debtors imprisoned in other jails were taken to Lydford by the warden and there treated so well that their lords could obtain no satisfaction from them.[7]

A commission of inquiry was appointed, and held one session

[1] CCR 1337–9, p. 585.   [2] Lewis, p. 165.
[3] *Rotuli Parliamentorum*, I, p. 297, no. 35, and p. 312, no. 95.
[4] Lewis, p. 94, quoting the Patent Roll of 12 Edw. II.
[5] *Rot. Parl.*, I, p. 382, no. 105.   [6] *Ibid.*, II, p. 190, no. 64.
[7] *Ibid.*, II, p. 343, no. LXXI, printed by Lewis, p. 242.

at Exeter under the presidency of the earl of Devon, but as the jurors were all chosen from the property-owning class their findings amounted to little more than an echo of the complaints already made.[1] They declared that before 1305, the date of Edward I's charter, mining operations had been confined within the bounds of the royal forest, as perambulated and recorded in 1240, but that under Edward II the tinners had begun to dig for tin and to divert streams in private grounds adjacent to the moor. This may have been true, but if so it was not because Edward's charter had widened the existing privileges; in this respect it had merely confirmed rights guaranteed by John's charter a century before. When the more easily worked deposits gave out, the tinners naturally opened up new stream-works further afield. The jurors were probably on surer ground when they declared that Edward's charter had brought about a great extension of activity on the part of the stannary courts. But these complaints bore little or no fruit. Had the financial interest of the Crown been less directly involved, the tinners might have appealed in vain to established custom and a succession of royal charters. As it was, the Crown upheld them against every attack.

In consequence, the lords of manors lying within the orbit of stannary privilege had to resign themselves to seeing their authority impaired and their revenues diminished. The loss was twofold. In the first place, their 'court perquisites', or profits of manorial justice, were reduced by the formidable competition of the stannary courts. These courts did not confine their attention to matters directly concerned with tin-mining: they adjudicated upon pleas of every description in which a tinner was either plaintiff or defendant. Their processes were summary— one litigant described the tin-court of Tavistock as a court "of quyke spede"[2]—and their verdicts were backed by the terrors of the Lydford dungeons. Naturally, therefore, they attracted a great deal of business from litigants in every walk of life, ecclesiastical and lay. Secondly, most of the working tinners were poor tenants of the servile class upon whose services their lords depended to some extent for the cultivation of their demesnes.

[1] According to Lewis, p. 97, the report of this commission has disappeared. A copy of it exists, however, in Bodleian MS. Rawlinson, B285, fo. 32.

[2] PRO Early Chancery Proceedings, File 999, no. 39.

Even if the lord did not require their labour, he expected them to pay the customary fee in lieu of service; but so long as they were engaged in digging for tin under the active protection of the Crown, he would find it no easy matter to exact either work or fee.

For some few lords, however, there were compensations; and the abbot of Tavistock was one of this more fortunate minority. Early in the reign of Henry I a weekly market had been set up at Tavistock. There merchants who came from afar to buy tin found an oasis in the midst of a commercial desert, a trading centre complete with stalls where they could purchase bread, fish, and meat. In the absence of any organized retail trade this was a great convenience. It gave Tavistock an advantage even over Chagford, where the tinners complained that the facilities for obtaining provisions were far from adequate.[1] Doubtless buyers and sellers alike brought their offerings to the shrine of St Rumon in the abbey church. Again, the growth of the industry must have intensified the demand for houses, thereby encouraging the abbot to develop the hamlet at his gate into an urban community. It is probably no accident that we first hear of burgages at Tavistock in 1185, just when the tin trade was most rapidly expanding.[2] Thus the diminution of court perquisites and labour dues was to some extent counterbalanced by an increase of revenue from burgage rents and market tolls. Edward's charter freed the tinners themselves from payment of toll, but, in fixing the coinage where it did, it conferred on Tavistock a privilege which, as we shall see, was greatly envied by one at least of the neighbouring towns.

From time to time the abbot intervened directly in the business of mining. In 1297, at the request of the Lord Treasurer, he consented to supervise the working expenses of the royal silver mine at Bere Ferrers.[3] Three years later he was appointed controller of all the silver mines in Devon and of one at Altarnun in Cornwall. The account rendered by him for the period 26 November 1307—26 January 1309 is still extant;[4] it provides a mass of interesting detail concerning the operation of the argentiferous

[1] PRO Ancient Petitions, no. 2098.
[2] Finberg, 'The Borough of Tavistock', DA LXXIX, 1947, pp. 129 sqq.
[3] PRO E101, Bdle 260, no. 18.
[4] CPR 1292-1301, p. 577; PRO E101, Bdle 261, no. 10.

lead mines in the parish of Bere Ferrers. In 1318 the government pledged the revenue from these mines to the abbot for three years in return for a loan of three hundred pounds, and shortly afterwards offered him an extension of the term if he would advance another four hundred pounds towards the expenses of the Scottish war.[1] In May 1319 the abbot was appointed warden of the Devon stannaries and keeper of the port of Dartmouth for ten years. Before the second year had run its course he bargained with the Exchequer for a lease of the revenues, which was granted to him at a yearly rent of one hundred pounds;[2] but the contract expired with the abbot's death in 1324. It had evidently been profitable for the abbey, for in the following year the prior and convent secured its renewal for seven years at an increased rent of £113 6s. 8d.[3] Their tenure, however, was to be anything but peaceful. Presently news reached them that the stannaries had been granted to Thomas de Shirigge during the king's pleasure. This seems to have been a mere oversight, and the order was rescinded nine days later.[4] But when another twelvemonth had elapsed, the stannaries were granted to Richard Calwar, the king's butler, for his lifetime. Again the order was revoked on petition of the prior and convent, though not so promptly as before; but a month later John Mautravers was appointed warden for seven years.[5] These contradictory grants reflect the administrative confusion of the interregnum under Roger Mortimer and the queen-mother Isabella.

About this time the London girdlers complained that members of their craft outside the city were damaging the trade by applying ornaments of pewter, lead, or tin to girdles made of leather, silk, wool, or linen; and they obtained an order prohibiting the use of base metals for this purpose. Thereupon the municipal authorities of Bristol and Coventry took steps to discourage their girdlers from coming to buy tin at Tavistock, Chagford, and Ashburton, as they had been wont to do. On hearing of this, the tinners lodged a protest; and the government, zealous as ever to uphold their interests, issued letters patent allowing the pro-

[1] CFR 1307–19, p. 384; CCR 1318–23, p. 59.
[2] CFR 1307–19, p. 399; ibid., 1319–27, p. 38.   [3] Ibid., p. 370.
[4] Ibid., 1327–37, pp. 13, 23; PRO Ancient Petitions, no. 500.
[5] CFR 1327–37, p. 83; PRO Ancient Petitions, no. 12893; CCR 1327–30, p. 291.

vincial girdlers to garnish their wares in the accustomed fashion until further notice.[1]

With a government believing itself competent to regulate manufacture and commerce down to the smallest detail; with its officials constantly besieged by the clamour of rival interests; and with success usually rewarding the man who knew how to pull the right string, the history of the tin trade at this period reads much like a forecast of industrial life at the present day. Unfortunately for Tavistock, just when a well-filled purse and an alert brain were more than ever needed, the abbey suffered itself to be rent by internal conflict. A disastrous vacancy, prolonged over three years (1324–7), wrecked the prosperity it had enjoyed during the long abbacy of Robert Champeaux, and, amid a succession of other misfortunes, laid Tavistock open to a plot which threatened its very existence as a stannary town.

The moving spirits in this intrigue were a group of Plympton burgesses. Towards the close of 1327 they got up a petition, asking that the coinage of tin might be removed from Tavistock to Plympton. They argued that Plympton was a maritime town, where the metal could be put on shipboard at small expense, whereas Tavistock lay so far inland that few merchants went there to buy tin, on account of the high cost of transport. They refrained from alluding to the fact that Tavistock lay nearer to the sea than Chagford, and that alone of the three stannary towns it had its own port on a navigable river. Their petition, unblushingly presented in the name of the tinners of Devon, induced the government to order an inquiry. The order was addressed to Roger Rodde, sheriff of Devon; and if the men of Plympton had not already made sure of this personage, they took steps to do so now. When we find among the jurors empanelled for the occasion such names as Hugh de Coleford, Roland de Apeldore, Walter de Langhiwish, and John Page of Wodeford, we know what to think of the proceedings, for Collaford, Applethorn, Langage, and Woodford are all in the immediate neighbourhood of Plympton. On the strength of their sworn verdict the sheriff reported that the proposed transference would be prejudicial neither to the Crown nor to any other party. Thereupon letters patent were issued ordering the coinage of tin to be removed from Tavi-

[1] CPR 1327–30, pp. 40, 367, 379.

stock, and constituting Plympton a stannary town in its place.[1]

This order, dated the 1st of March 1328, drew forth an emphatic protest from the tinners. They, or some Tavistock spokesman in their name, declared that any inquest touching the stannaries ought by rights to be held before the warden, and that it was derogatory to their franchise for such an inquest to be held by the sheriff, who had moreover packed the jury with burgesses of Plympton "and other outsiders" (*et de autres foreyne gent*).[2] The further stages of the affair are wrapped in obscurity; but the upshot was a compromise. Plympton became an additional coinage town, while Tavistock retained its old position. From this time onwards the four towns divided between them the stannary jurisdiction over the county of Devon. Their boundaries met at Crockerntor, a bleak spot in the very centre of Dartmoor. The Tavistock stannary comprised that part of Devon which lay west of a line drawn from Barnstaple to Crockerntor and thence to Plymouth. That of Plympton was bounded on the west by the Plymouth line and on the east by a line from Crockerntor to Modbury and Borough Island. That of Ashburton lay between the Plympton boundary and a line from Crockerntor to Teignmouth. All the rest of the county went to Chagford.[3]

Each of these four districts had a court of its own. The clauses in John's charter which placed civil and criminal jurisdiction over the tinners in the hands of their warden had made it necessary to establish these tribunals; and as early as 1243 the profits of the Devon courts were being paid into the Exchequer.[4] Cases were decided by a jury of tinners under the presidency of a steward appointed by the warden. Thirteen sessions were held annually, of which two were known as law courts. These met in the spring and autumn, and were supposed to be attended by every tinner in the district. Their procedure closely resembled that of the manorial courts leet. A grand jury of twelve tinners made presentments of criminal offences, appointed petty officers, and when necessary reaffirmed the customs of the stannary. The law courts also served as administrative centres. They provided

[1] PRO Inquisitions *ad quod damnum*, C143, File 194, no. 12; CPR 1327–30, p. 240.
[2] PRO *loc. cit.* [3] DCNQ XXII, 1942, p. 121.
[4] Lewis, pp. 90, 273, quoting Pipe Roll, 27 Hen. III.

N

the machinery for enforcing stannary assessments, verifying weights and measures, and proclaiming such royal ordinances or statutes of the realm as might affect the tinners.

The rolls of the Tavistock stannary court for the years 1374–5, 1396–7, and 1477–8 have survived.[1] They show the court dealing at one time with over ninety cases of debt, trespass, and assault. Defendants are attached by the seizure of their livestock or their pots and pans. Sometimes the bailiff is fined for neglecting to distrain; sometimes he is ordered to distrain more effectually. R. Hankford is prosecuted by the abbot of Buckland for killing two oxen. The steward commits him to jail at Lydford, and the bailiff is fined at each court until he takes him there. The abbot of Tavistock prosecutes Walter Maynard and John Jurdan for trespassing at Foghanger; at the next court they pay threepence each for licence to compound with the plaintiff. Reginald Strode is fined fourpence for trespassing on John Hikkewode's rye; Hikkewode denies that he stole apples from the other's garden. Laurence Chubbe and John Bradenige make so much noise that the whole business of the court is interrupted; the steward fines each fourpence.

The court shows itself extremely sensitive to any encroachment on its jurisdiction. It is always ready to hear complaints from tinners who have been impleaded in the manorial or forest courts, the consistorial court of Exeter, or the court of King's Bench. Sir Ralph Carmynow, accused of having impleaded John Mewy before the King's Bench, replies that he did not know Mewy was a tinner, and that the stannary courts exist to hear pleas arising within the county of Devon, whereas this plea arose out of a contract made at London, a place which, as he is careful to remind the court, lies outside the county of Devon. At a later session he pays for licence to compound. John Baggetorr has been charged with venville rent, and the bailiff of Dartmoor has distrained him for non-payment. He asks the court to decide whether or not his tenement is liable for this rent. Such a question would seem to be essentially one for submission to the forest court; but the plaintiff is a tinner, and therefore the stannary court is more than willing to adjudicate. Its verdict is that the bailiff who distrained him must pay a fine.

[1] PRO S.C. 2, Portfolio 168, nos. 33, 34, 35.

Lastly, there are the cases arising directly out of the tin trade. Several persons have claimed stannary privilege who are not genuine tinners. Their conduct is denounced as prejudicial to the franchise. The bailiff is fined 3s. 4d. because he has not taken the coinage hammer over to Chagford as he should have done. Henry Wymmeslond, who admits to having sold to Agnes Staunton, widow, of Buckland Monachorum, "two hundred and fourteen pounds of corrupt and deceitful tin, to the great prejudice of the king's people and to the damage of the said Agnes", is very properly consigned to Lydford.

It has already been remarked that the grand juries of the local stannary courts were called upon from time to time to declare the customs of the tin-works. In this function of theirs we may perhaps detect the germ of that remarkable institution, the stannary parliament.[1] According to some local writers, the tinners of Devon and Cornwall used at one time to meet in general assembly every seven or eight years. These gatherings are said to have taken place on Hingston Down, which would certainly have been a conveniently central rendezvous for the tinners of both counties; but no record of any such joint assembly has been found, and in point of fact the tinners of Devon and Cornwall were being treated as two distinct bodies as far back as 1198.[2] The surviving records of the stannary Great Courts, or parliaments, in Devon go back to 1494, and in Cornwall to 1588; and in origin these

[1] The word parliament appears to have been first used of these gatherings in 1533 (Pearce, *The Laws and Customs of the Stannaries*, p. 216). In 1574 it was adopted into the official style, which then ran: "The Great Court, or Parliament, of our Sovereign Lady Elizabeth" etc. Until then the assembly had been styled "The Great Court of our Sovereign Lord the King in his duchy of Cornwall". Lewis, p. 130 *n.*, gives a list of six recorded sessions, to which four more can now be added. The full list as at present known is: 1494 (*vide infra*), 1510, 1532, 1533, 1552, 1567 (Pearce, *op. cit.*, p. 256), 1574, 1600 (DA LXXXII, 1950, pp. 295 sqq.), 1687–8 (Bodleian Add. MS. C85, ff. 51, 52), and 1703 (*ibid.*, fo. 55). Mrs Bray states that a meeting took place in 1749 (*Traditions, etc.*, 1, p. 113), and it is certain that one was contemplated as late as 1786 (DCNQ XXII, 1942, p. 121).

[2] In 1571 an assembly of the Cornish tinners was held, somewhat anomalously, at Tavistock (Pearce, *op. cit.*, p. 154). It may have been formally opened on Hingston Down, which is on the Cornish side of the Tamar, and then adjourned for the convenience of the warden, just as the Devon parliaments were adjourned from Crockerntor to Tavistock in 1687 and 1703 (Bodleian Add. MS. C85, ff. 52, 55). Such a proceeding might well give rise to an erroneous tradition of joint meetings.

gatherings may not be much more ancient. They took place at no set times, being convoked by the warden or vice-warden whenever he thought fit. A writ addressed to the bailiffs of the four stannary courts directed them to summon all tinners, owners or sharers in tin-works, and labourers therein, to attend in person at the next meeting of their respective local court for the purpose of electing twenty-four jurors to represent them at the forthcoming Great Court. When this had been done, and the appointed day came, all ninety-six representatives assembled in the presence of the vice-warden at Crockerntor. No amenities awaited them at this inclement spot. They met there because Crockerntor was the central point where the bounds of the four stannaries converged.[1]

The earliest parliament of which the statutes have been preserved took place at Crockerntor on the 11th of September 1494, in the presence of Sir John Sapcote, vice-warden, and commissioners representing Prince Arthur, duke of Cornwall. Its most remarkable ordinance was one forbidding owners of landed property above the yearly value of ten pounds, ecclesiastics, foresters, and stannary officials to acquire any interest in tin works outside their own freeholds. It would be interesting to know what lay behind this curious enactment. Was it a genuine solicitude for the prosperity of the humbler tinners? Another statute, following a precedent set by the Exchequer of Pleas in Edward I's reign, debarred professional lawyers from pleading in any tin-court. A series of more conventional decrees required the bounds of new tinworks to be registered in the local stannary court, and insisted that all tin must be stamped with the trademark, similarly registered, both of its owner and of the blowing-house where it was smelted.[2]

These and all other statutes then in force were annulled by the Great Court at a meeting held on the 24th of September 1510. Lawyers were no longer to be excluded from the tin-courts, but

---

[1] This explanation was too simple for the older and more Celtically inclined local antiquaries. Polwhele decides that Crockerntor was the judgement-seat of his imaginary Cantred of Tamar, and has "scarce a doubt" that the stannary parliament inherited the powers of this "old British court".

[2] Statutes transcribed "from a record in the Treasury of the Exchequer" by Edward Smirke, afterwards vice-warden of the stannaries, and printed in Rowe, *Perambulation of Dartmoor*, p. 334.

they must plead in English. The regulations dealing with trade-marks and the marking of ore were re-enacted; but the chief pur-pose for which this parliament assembled was to impose fixed penalties for breaches of stannary law. In a series of thirty-seven chapters the immemorial customs of the trade were solemnly re-affirmed, and fines ranging from five to forty pounds were decreed against their contravention.

It was the third of these chapters that gave rise to the famous case of Richard Strode. Strode was himself a tinner: that is, an owner or part-owner of tin-works, not a working miner, for he came of a prosperous family seated at Newnham, in Plympton St Mary: and he represented the borough of Plympton in the West-minster parliament of 1512. It appears that two partners, William Rede and Elis Elforde, had started digging for tin on Strode's land. The Crockerntor parliament had just reaffirmed the right guaranteed to all the stannary men by Edward I's charter, "to dig in every place within the county of Devonshire where tin may be found", and had decreed that anyone obstructing this right should be liable to a fine of forty pounds. The partners, therefore, were within their rights in digging where they did. In order to rid himself of his unbidden guests without incurring the penalty appointed, Strode introduced a bill into the parliament of West-minster, to restrain mining operations in the vicinity of sea-ports, alleging that the harbours of Devon were being choked with refuse from the mines. The bill, though it never became law, aroused great indignation in the stannaries; and at the next law-day the under-steward, John Furse, caused Strode to be pre-sented at all four local courts for conduct subversive of the miners' liberties. The culprit was fined forty pounds in each court; but refusing to pay, was arrested "and imprysoned in a dongeon and a deepe pitte under the ground in the castel of Lid-ford ... the which prison", as he afterwards feelingly declared, "is one of the most annoious, contagious, and detestable places wythin this realme." To avoid being put in irons and fed on no-thing but bread and water, he was obliged to pay the keeper one mark and to promise him three more. After languishing there for some three weeks, he was released by a writ of privilege from the Exchequer, to which he had appealed, not as a member of parliament, but as a collector of the subsidy that parliament had just voted to the Crown. However, Strode clearly thought it well to secure himself against further attack. He therefore complained to the parliament of Westminster, and persuaded it to pass a statute not only annulling his condemnation in the stannary courts, but granting immunity to him and his associates for anything done or to be done by them in that or future parliaments.[1]

It may have been true that some harbours on the south coast were being damaged by rubbish from the mines; but if so, the matter could have been dealt with at Crockerntor, and in fact it was put on the agenda of the meeting that took place there on the 28th of October 1532, Sir Philip Champernoun being then vice-warden. In the preamble to its decree on the subject the Great Court states that it has been the custom, time out of mind, to bury gravel, sand, and rubble from the stream-works under grass, but that certain inhabitants of Dartmouth and Plymouth suppose the refuse to be washed down by the great floods into their harbours. It is therefore ordained that in future all rubbish from the mines shall be deposited in "old Hatches, Tipittes, miry Places, or other convenient Places" away from the main streams.[2]

Other statutes enacted at this session dealt with the upkeep of water-courses and the fees due to stannary officials. In the following year the Great Court met again, and provided appropriate penalties for various forms of sharp practice, such as tampering with juries, evading stannary assessments, and surreptitiously removing ore from the tin-works.[3]

Thus, in the three sessions of 1510, 1532, and 1533, the tinners' parliament had comprehensively re-stated the customary laws of their trade, and provided answers to most of the problems arising in its everyday practice. It was now desirable to make their ordinances widely known. Fortunately the most up-to-date means of publicity lay at hand, for in the course of this very decade the monks of Tavistock had set up a printing press, the first in the south-west and the seventh in all England. Here the statutes of

[1] 4 Hen. VIII, c. 8. The provisions of the act are limited to Strode himself "and every other of the person or persons afore specifyed": that is, those "other of this house" who had joined him in promoting a bill against the tinners. There is therefore no ground for regarding it as a corner-stone of parliamentary freedom, and it is misleading to say, as Halsbury does (*The Laws of England*, xxi, p. 782), that the Tudor and Stuart kings "chose to regard it" as a particular and not a general statute. A particular statute is just what it was.

[2] Pearce, *op. cit.*, p. 204.   [3] *Ibid.*, pp. 208 sqq.

the three most recent Crockerntor parliaments, together with the charter of Edward I, were printed in a small quarto of twenty-six leaves. The colophon runs:

> ¶ Here endyth the statutes of the stannary
> Imprented yn Tauystoke yᵉ XX. day of August
> the yere of the reygne off our soueryne Lord
> Kynge Henry yᵉ viii, the xxvi. yere.

—that is, in 1534. One would like to know how many copies of this booklet were printed. To-day, only one survives.[1]

The activities of the Crockerntor parliament at this period co-incided with, and were no doubt partly occasioned by, a notable expansion of output from the Devon mines. In the first quarter of the sixteenth century production stood higher than it had done at any time since the reign of Henry II, when the Dartmoor stream-works had produced more tin than all those of Cornwall put to-gether. From the returns of taxes paid during the years 1171–89, it has been estimated that the average annual output was then approximately 640 thousandweight. By 1243, when Cornwall had regained the lead, it had fallen to 74 thousandweight.[2] For the rest of the thirteenth century the number of tinners actually at work may be calculated from the returns of 'black rent', and may usefully be compared with the output of 'white tin' recorded in the Pipe Rolls.

TABLE XXIII

Yr ending Michael-mas	No. of working tinners	Output m. c. lb.	Yr ending Michael-mas	No. of working tinners	Output m. c. lb.
1243	149	74 4 72	1295	258	46 2 65
1288	300	81 7 12	1296	199	38 1 30
1289	308	82 6 3	1297	218	43 0 56
1290	323	82 7 84	1298	346	46 5 35
1291	450	87 7 85	1299	415	52 9 20
1292	457	86 7 70	1300	436	53 0 0
1293	453	86 0 79	1301	440	53 0 0
1294	334	56 8 0			

[1] In the library of Exeter College, Oxford, to which it was presented by Joseph Sanford (ob. 1774), a native of Topsham and one-time Fellow of Balliol.   [2] Lewis, p. 252.

The figures display noteworthy fluctuations, and suggest that many of the tinners were artisans or small husbandmen who eked out their livelihood by joining occasionally in the search for tin ore, as they might easily do, since it was a pursuit requiring no great fund of technical knowledge, and no equipment beyond a pick, a shovel, and perhaps a bucket for baling water out of the diggings. It will be noticed also that the increase of man-power in 1291 and 1299 was not attended by a proportionate increase of production. But we must always reckon with the possibility that some tinners may have evaded payment of their lawful dues.[1]

In 1303 some 90 thousandweight were coined at Ashburton, Chagford, and Tavistock, paying coinage duty as follows.[2]

Ashburton	£37 14s. 9¾d.
Chagford	29 17s. 6¼d.
Tavistock	2 11s. 8d.
	£70 4s. 0d.

So disastrous were the effects of the Black Death that in 1355 the coinage yielded nothing at all in Devon and less than £1,000 in Cornwall, whereas seven years before Cornwall alone had paid £2,500.[3] By 1371, however, the Devon stannaries had so far recovered as to bring in £52 5s. 9d.[4] In 1373 there were one hundred and fifty-one recognized tinners in the stannary of Tavistock, and their numbers were swollen by the addition of several persons, including Walter Langeford, M.P. for the borough, who had falsely claimed to be tinners in order to evade payment of the tenth and fifteenth.[5]

From the middle of the fifteenth century until the first quarter

---

[1] Lewis, p. 40, observes that "no explanation entirely satisfactory can be given of these irregular ebbs and flows in the tide of mining prosperity. The fact that the same phenomenon may be observed in the German tin districts throughout the Middle Ages suggests the hypothesis that a cause common to both was the capriciousness of nature in revealing the ore, especially the stream tin, which might be found in abundant 'pockets' for a limited number of years and then disappear almost entirely."

[2] PRO E101, Bdle 260, no. 24.

[3] Lewis, p. 156.   [4] Ibid., p. 260.

[5] For the numerical strength of the tinners in the borough of Tavistock see DA LXXXI, 1949, p. 184.

TABLE XXIV[1]

Date	Ashburton	Chagford	Plympton	Tavistock	Total	Total for year
	£ s. d.	£ s. d.	£ s. d.	£ s. d.	£ s. d.	£ s. d.
1381 Sept.	12 12 2¾	11 12 4	7 10 7½	35 3 11¾	66 19 2	
1385 May	1 18 10½	6 9 11¼	1 1 8½	1 17 0¼	11 7 6½	
Sept.	5 4 9¼	14 16 1	14 1 8¾	8 1 5¼	42 4 0¼	53 11 6¾
1394 June	3 5 11½	8 7 6½	5 2 0½	5 19 6½	22 15 1	
Sept.	8 0 9¼	9 5 11½	14 9¼	2 2 8	20 4 2	42 19 3
1398 May	6 14 4	10 9 3¼	6 1 7¼	5 3 3¼	28 8 5¾	
Sept.	11 12 4¼	17 18 9¾	5 13 3	4 6 11½	39 11 4½	67 19 10¼
1399 June	6 1 2¾	2 8 4¾	3 8 2¾	2 5 1	14 2 11¼	
1440 June		9 11¼		11 7¾		
1447 Sept.			10 13 1¾	13 16 10¼	80 19 1¼	
1449 June	3 3 11	6 7 1½	19 0	3 4 9½	13 14 10	
1450 June	5 18 1	6 7 4½	2 18 7¼	6 2 9½	21 6 10¼	
1456 June	4 14 4½	6 11 6¾	3 17 5	2 9 3¼	17 12 7½	
Sept.	17 15 3¾	32 1 3¼	6 4 11¾	14 10 8¾	70 12 3½	88 4 11
1463 June	7 9 9¼	5 17 5½	2 6 2½	8 6 8¼	24 0 1½	
Sept.	25 9 8¾	25 6 11¾	6 8 7½	25 16 4¼	83 1 8¼	107 1 9¾
1466 June	12 3 6½	12 0 9¾	2 5 10¾	11 8 7	37 18 10	
Sept.	35 9 2½	36 6 0	11 18 7¾	16 5 5¾	111 12 1	149 10 11
1470 June	25 1 2¼	9 5 0½	5 8 5	12 12 6¾	52 7 2½	
Sept.	41 8 3½	40 9 11	11 9 10	19 1 4½	112 9 5	164 16 7½
1487 June	21 4 10	16 17 6½	4 12 8¼	9 4 11¾	52 0 0½	
Sept.	48 3 7½	48 11 9½	5 3 4¼	37 7 7½	139 6 4¾	191 6 5¼
1493 June	28 16 9	26 4 1	7 15 3¾	23 1 10¼	85 18 0	
1511 June	55 18 10¾	22 15 0¾	18 7 11½	38 7 7¼	135 9 6¼	
1513 June	56 8 2¾	18 5 1	13 13 9½	27 4 8	115 11 9¼	
Sept.	65 13 7¼	33 11 6¾	17 14 8½	53 1 7	170 1 5½	285 13 2¾
1514 June		17 18 3¾			98 7 11	
1515 June					134 18 7½	
Sept.					234 1 0¾	368 19 8¼
1523 June	54 5 7¼	37 9 5	27 0 6½	39 6 2¾	158 1 9½	
Sept.	89 0 5¾	35 15 5½	19 1 9¾	66 7 4	210 5 1	368 6 10½

[1] This table has been compiled from PRO E101, Bdle 263, nos. 18, 20, 25; Bdle 264, nos. 3, 6; Bdle 265, nos. 7, 12, 14, 15, 19, 23; Bdle 266, nos. 5, 9, 10, 11, 17, 20, 21; Bdle 267, nos. 3, 6, 7, 15; Bdle 268, nos. 4, 5, 14; Bdle 271, nos. 4, 5. The details given for September 1466 are incomplete; the total is that given on the roll.

of the sixteenth the record of the industry is one of steady growth. Its progress is reflected in the coinage rolls. Each tinner carried his metal to the stannary town nearest to the mine,[1] there to have it coined and to pay duty on it at the standard rate of 1s. 6¾d. a hundredweight. The records of the coinage therefore illustrate the distribution of the trade between the four districts. In the beginning Tavistock leads; but in 1385 Chagford takes the first place, which it keeps until the middle of the fifteenth century, thereafter yielding to Ashburton, while Tavistock varies between second and third, and Plympton, after 1450, invariably lags far behind the other three. (Table XXIV.)

From 1400 to 1450 the average production was approximately 100 thousandweight a year. During the next half-century it rose to 194. A further steep rise took place in 1513, and the summit was reached in 1515 with a total production of 470 m. 5 c. 33 lb. As the price of tin then stood at about fourpence a pound, the gross value represented is just over £9,400. In 1523 the output again exceeded 470 thousandweight, the greater part of the tin being coined at Ashburton and Tavistock.[2]

On the two coinage rolls of 1523, which are more detailed than those of 1515, all ranks of society are represented.[3] The earl of Devon himself has three hundredweight of metal coined at Plympton. Names of well-known landed families—a Shilston, a Copplestone, a Prideaux, a Trevanion—mingle with those of tuckers, bakers, and tanners. We also find a number of parish guilds: All Saints, Bickleigh, St Edward of Holne, St George of Manaton, St Pancras of Widecombe, whose wardens either received gifts of metal or invested some of their funds in the tin-works. The largest producer is Elis Elforde, Strode's old antagonist, and the second is Richard Wavell. Elforde coins 6 m. 7 c. 21 lb. at Tavistock, and Wavell 6 m. 2 c. 79 lb. at Chagford. But these two have left most of their fellow-tinners far behind. Entries recording the coinage of a thousandweight or more at one time are as follows:

[1] Lewis, p. 149.

[2] *Ibid.*, pp. 252, 253. In Worth, *op. cit.*, p. 230, the statistics given by Lewis are expressed in the form of a graph. The figures given in the text for 1513, 1515, and 1523 are taken from documents in the PRO which Lewis did not consult (E101, Bdle 268, nos. 4, 5, 15, 16, and Bdle 271, nos. 4, 5).

[3] An abstract of these rolls is printed in DA LXXXI, 1949, pp. 173 sqq.

	June	September	Total
Chagford	16	11	27
Ashburton	21	27	48
Plympton	4	0	4
Tavistock	9	16	25
	50	54	104

As the total number of entries is 1177, this is less than ten per cent. It is clear that tin-mining was, in the main, the small man's trade. We have seen the tinners' parliament endeavouring in 1494 to keep it so. The big capitalist has already appeared on the scene, preceded, in all likelihood, by the group of shareholders employing hired labour; but there is still ample room for small working partnerships, and even for the lone adventurer toiling with pick and shovel at his own claim.

In 1470 John Dynyngton, abbot of Tavistock, empowered his attorney to dispose of "the third part of a tin-work in Bruggepole".[1] This transaction is unlikely to have been unique, but the surviving Tavistock muniments provide no other indication of a direct financial interest in the trade. Nevertheless the economy of Tavistock Abbey, and indeed of all Devon, was profoundly affected by the stannaries. The existence in the heart of the county of this ancient and elaborately organized industry, offering, with its extensive privileges and its peculiar jurisdiction, chances of enfranchisement to countrymen of the lowliest class, and of enrichment to all who cared to take a hand in it, explains many of the distinctive features in the social life of Devon from the twelfth century onwards.

[1] W. D Bdle 76, no. 5.

CHAPTER VIII

SEIGNORIAL REVENUES

HITHERTO our study of the Tavistock economy has advanced by slow steps through a series of detailed investigations. Attention has been concentrated in turn upon the land, the social structure, the technique of food production, and the paramount industries. These are all themes of cardinal importance; and all of them are strongly marked by local peculiarities. When we turn to those items in the Tavistock budget which may properly be classified as seignorial, the case is rather different. The profits of lordship on these estates did indeed exhibit some features of distinctively local character and interest, but in essence they differed not at all from corresponding profits in the midlands and elsewhere. It is therefore permissible to treat of them in more discursive fashion.

The lord of nearly every manor possessed monopolistic rights in cornmills, dovecotes, and game preserves. Henry I authorized the abbot of Tavistock to maintain warrens, and imposed a heavy fine upon anyone who should course a hare without the abbot's leave. His charter was confirmed by Henry II and later kings.[1] Deerpark Hill, between Taviton and Whitham, is the site of a park where the abbey once kept some forty head of game. Below, in Dolvin Wood, there was a rabbit-warren which, with "a little house within it called 'le lodge' ", was always kept in hand when the rest of that wooded hillside was let out on lease.[2] The abbey also had warrens at Plymstock and at Webworthy in Werrington. Occasional raids by poachers find mention in the court rolls; in 1463 an inhabitant at Werrington was fined threepence for keeping a greyhound bitch. There were times in the fourteenth century when the monks themselves kept hounds, to the sore displeasure of their bishop; and from sundry complaints in which they with many of their neighbours both ecclesiastical and lay were implicated, it appears that when the hunt was up, they

---

[1] Dugdale, II, p. 496.   [2] W. D Bdle 53, no. 175.

sometimes pursued the quarry far into the royal forest.[1] Red deer abounded in the Tavistock woods down to the middle of the eighteenth century, when the farmers complained so vehemently of damage to their crops that a pack of hounds was fetched all the way from Bedfordshire to end the nuisance.[2]

Pigeons were another source of damage. These greedy birds are said to consume their own weight in food every day, and they share the human preference for wheat over other cereal grains. In order to minimize the loss at seed-time, a quantity of wheat-chaff was regularly set aside at Werrington to feed the lord's pigeons in winter, even while the dovecote was farmed out. The Plymstock accounts record occasional sales of pigeons at a penny a pair, but the dovecote there must have been a small one, for in 1414 it was farmed out at 2s. 6d. a year, and after 1433 it disappears from the accounts. In 1356 the Werrington dovecote contained only one hundred and forty-nine birds. It was taken in hand about 1490, after having been farmed by the reeve of the manor for the previous hundred years at an annual rent of four shillings. At Tavistock a meadow named Averne-mead or Prior's Mead, with a dovecote in it, was assigned to the prior and leased out in 1477 at 3s. 4d. a year. This rent was for the meadow alone, but sixty years later the dovecote was included in a new lease and the rent went up to twelve shillings.[3] It seems evident that all these culver-houses, to use the local name, were small affairs; and some of them were privately owned. For example, the dower which Robert David, a leading Tavistock burgess, settled on his daughter in 1355 included "a park by Bannawell, with two granges there and a garden adjoining and one dovecote".[4] Again,

---

[1] They were accused of trespassing at Ermington in 1316, and of the same offence at Keyrbullok, a royal park near Stoke Climsland, in 1329 (CPR 1313–17, p. 499; 1327–30, p. 433). In 1335 and again in 1341 they were reported to have gone stag-hunting on Dartmoor (*ibid.*, 1334–8, pp. 214, 282; 1340–3, pp. 365, 439). At that time hounds ("*canes venanctici*") were being kept by abbot John de Courtenay and some lay members of his household, as well as by the prior and a monk named Thomas Coffyn. Bishop Grandisson forbade this in 1345, and renewed the prohibition three years later (*Reg. Grandisson*, pp. 997, 1071). His successor had to deal with a fresh and apparently final outbreak of stag-hunting in 1371 (CPR 1370–4, p. 172; *Reg. Brantyngham*, p. 312).
[2] Bray, *op. cit.*, I, p. 340. [3] W. D Bdle 39, no. 8; Bdle 53, nos. 142, 106.
[4] BM Add. Ch. 29074. This 'park', later known as Culver Meadow, is now the site of the Tavistock Union Workhouse. Another close, with a dovecote in

at the southern edge of Whiteborough Down there stood a circular dovecote of great antiquity, with stone walls over three feet
thick, and thirteen tiers of nest-holes, which belonged to the
freeholder of Gawton.[1] It seems clear that the abbot was not
unwilling to share the privilege with some of his free tenants.

In the matter of cornmills he could not afford to be so accom-
modating. The construction of a mill involved a considerable
outlay, and its repair was a frequently recurring item of cost. In
order to secure a fair return for this expenditure, nearly every
lord required his tenants to give up the use of hand-querns, to
take their corn to no other mill but his, and to pay for having it
ground by leaving behind, as toll-corn, a percentage of the grain
which might be anything from a tenth to a twenty-fourth, according to local custom. There are grounds for believing that in the
eleventh century cornmills were still a novelty in Devon, though
fairly numerous in counties further east. Of those recorded in the
Domesday of Devon more than half were situated east of the
Exe.[2] The abbot of Tavistock, however, had already taken the
initiative. Besides two mills at Askerswell, in Dorset, which
brought him in seven shillings a year, he had built one at Tavistock, on the south side of the great courtyard, for the domestic
use of the monastery; and his tenant Walter had one at Hatherleigh, or more probably at Broomford, worth sixpence a year. The
creation of a borough at Tavistock in the following century made
it necessary to provide a town mill outside the abbey precinct.
Hurdwick had its mill at Indescombe, the revenue from which
formed one of the sacristan's perquisites; and by the end of the
thirteenth century there were at least half a dozen cornmills up
and down the parish. They were all water-mills; in 1449 those in
the town were stated to grind eight quarters of any kind of grain
in twenty-four hours.[3]

---

it, known as Culver-park, lay between the abbey meadows and West Bridge;
it was acquired by the abbey in 1460 (W. D Bdle 2, no. 129).

[1] The remains can still be seen; they are described by Mr G. W. Copeland
in DA LXXV, 1943, p. 270.

[2] See above, p. 53, and Morgan, 'The Domesday Geography of Devon',
DA LXXII, 1940, p. 327. Mr Morgan suggests that other mills may have
existed besides those enumerated in Domesday. This may well be true, but
since the possibility is not confined to Devonshire, it cannot affect a conclusion drawn from the recorded distribution over England as a whole.

[3] W. D Bdle 33, no. 1.

The rule that every manor should possess its own mill was not invariable. Morwell seems never to have had one; and in 1322 the tenants of Roborough received permission to grind their corn at Whitsleigh mill.[1] On the other hand, so large a manor as Werrington required more than one. Here Penrose mill, which paid a rent of fourpence to the neighbouring manor of Penheale for its mill-stream, served the North Petherwin district, leaving Ham mill to deal with the corn grown nearer Werrington. The customary tenants of Burrington, Leigh, and Milton were responsible for cleaning out the mill-leat; those of Plymstock had to repair the sluice. Both at Leigh and at Milton Abbot the serf was bound to act as farmer of the mill when chosen by his fellows, but by the end of the fourteenth century Leigh mill had fallen into disuse and the custom had been superseded by an arrangement under which the tenants of both manors combined to pay the abbot thirty shillings a year for the use of Willesley mill, and undertook to keep it in repair at their own cost.

The practice of farming the mills out at a fixed rent and leaving the miller to make a profit from the toll-corn appears in the earliest surviving account rolls, and it became the rule again in the fifteenth century; but for about a hundred years after the Black Death the mills were kept in hand, and receipts from the sale of toll-corn figured regularly in the accounts. It is noteworthy that the farm was appreciably lower in the fifteenth century than it had been before the Black Death. For example, the farmer of Ottery mill in 1337 paid £3; his successor in 1461 paid only £1 11s. Ham and Penrose mills, which in 1298 had been worth £4 7s. 4d., and in 1350 £9 16s. 8d., were let in 1461 for 6s. 8d. and 14s. respectively. For Plymstock, which was pre-eminently a corn-growing manor, we have no comparable figures; but the following table shows the gross and net income from Pomphlett mill from 1392 to 1521. Here the receipts, down to 1481, represent sales of toll-corn, and thereafter a fixed rent, and the expenses are the cost of upkeep, or, after 1481, the portion of the cost borne by the abbot, who in such cases usually undertook to supply timber and thatching-straw, but left the miller to carry out the actual repairs.

[1] W. G Bdle 6, no. 40.

TABLE XXV
RECEIPTS AND EXPENSES:
POMPHLETT MILL, PLYMSTOCK

	Receipts			Expenses		Net proceeds		
1392	£2	3s.	5½d.		3s.	5d.	£2	0s.	0½d.
1397	£1	5s.	7d.		5s.	2½d.	£1	0s.	4½d.
1414	£2	18s.	8d.		nil		£2	18s.	8d.
1431	£2	12s.	7½d.		1s.	0d.	£2	11s.	7½d.
1432	£1	19s.	6d.		3s.	11½d.	£1	15s.	6½d.
1433	£2	18s.	5d.			9d.	£2	17s.	8d.
1442	£3	3s.	10d.		10s.	10d.	£2	13s.	0d.
1470	£4	14s.	4d.	£2	4s.	3d.	£2	10s.	1d.
1475	£4	5s.	8d.		11s.	2d.	£3	14s.	6d.
1477	£3	3s.	9d.		4s.	7d.	£2	19s.	2d.
1480	£2	10s.	2½d.		3s.	5d.	£2	6s.	9½d.
1481	£2	17s.	7d.		3s.	4d.	£2	14s.	3d.
1484	£4	0s.	0d.	£1	0s.	3d.	£2	19s.	9d.
1489	£4	0s.	0d.		nil		£4	0s.	0d.
1497	£4	0s.	0d.		nil		£4	0s.	0d.
1499	£4	0s.	0d.		nil		£4	0s.	0d.
1504	£4	0s.	0d.		16s.	1d.	£3	3s.	11d.
1521	£5	0s.	0d.	£1	11s.	6d.	£3	8s.	6d.

The use of water-power was not limited to cornmills. In 1291 the sacristan pays sixpence for the rent of a tanning mill near Parkwood, and Osmund the Smith fourpence for an edge-tool mill.[1] Both of these were converted into fulling mills late in the fifteenth century; but the same expansion of the cloth trade which dictated this change emphasized the clothworkers' demand for well-ground shears, and in 1494 the abbey granted William Drake a site between the Tavy and the Mill-brook on a forty-year lease for the building of a new edge-tool mill.[2]

At Plymstock the abbot had a cider press, which the tenants also used. When they did so they paid toll in kind. In 1475 four pipes of cider were brewed from the apples grown in the abbot's orchard, and the tenants contributed three pipes by way of toll. Another three, left over from the year before and now sufficiently matured, were shipped up the Tamar to Morwellham for con-

[1] W. D Bdle 84, no. 2.   [2] *Ibid.*, Bdle 53, no. 77.

sumption in the abbey. Receipts and expenses under this heading figure in the surviving accounts from 1392 to 1489, after which the orchard and press were farmed out at a yearly rent of 26s. 8d.

The income from mills and dovecotes accrued to the monks primarily because their command of labour and materials enabled them to construct and maintain the necessary buildings. Right of warren, again, would obviously have been worthless to them had they not owned woodlands and game-preserves. In all these cases property comes first, and privilege is brought in to reinforce it so that the owner may exploit his property to fuller advantage. On the other hand, one need not be the lord of a manor to extract profit from the ownership of land, and that on a considerable scale. Anyone—a parson, a neighbouring lord, a parish guild—might own land and draw an income therefrom by demising it to a tenant at a fixed yearly rent. 'Assized rents' constituted an important item in the monastic budget from the first, and loomed ever larger as time went on; but outside boroughs they formed no part of the seignorial revenue as such, and consideration of them must therefore be deferred until we come to deal with the management of the estate as a whole. At the other end of the scale, lordship could be entirely divorced from ownership. For example, it was quite possible for an individual to be lord of a hundred in which he possessed not an acre of land. In such a case his seignory consisted in the right to preside, through his steward, over the hundred court and to keep the profits of justice. The possession of markets, fairs, borough rents, and manor courts, partook of this character, for although in practice these things were associated with landownership, in theory they could be separated from it, and the income they brought in was essentially the fruit of seignorial privilege.

It was probably in 1105, and in return for a contribution to the funds he was busy raising for a campaign in Normandy, that Henry I authorized the monks to hold a weekly market in Tavistock on Fridays.[1] Hitherto Lydford had been the recognized commercial centre of the region between Dartmoor and the Tamar. It was a royal borough with its own mint, where silver pennies had been coined in every reign from Ethelred II to Edward the Confessor. Now, with a rival market already opened

[1] ETC iv.

o

at Okehampton, its burgesses might well look with a jealous eye on the commercial autonomy of Tavistock. That this was not established without a struggle may be inferred from the fact that the abbot soon found it necessary to procure another royal mandate, warning "all the barons of Devonshire" to let him "have his Tavistock market in peace". In 1116 the king issued a third writ, confirming the market-grant and adding a three-day fair, to begin yearly on the eve and to end on the morrow of St Rumon's principal feast: that is, from the 29th to the 31st of August.[1] Thereafter Lydford fought a losing battle, watching its trade slip away to the new market, which was far more conveniently placed.[2]

In 1220 the newly elected abbot William de Kernet gave the king two palfreys for the grant of a Thursday market and an annual fair on the 23rd and 24th of June at Hatherleigh.[3] In the following year he offered five marks for a Saturday market at Werrington "until the king should come of age".[4] The proximity of Launceston ruled out any hope of permanence here; and similarly Plymstock was far too close to the old-established Plympton market to cherish any commercial aspirations. The next abbot, John of Rochester, paid five marks for a three-day Michaelmas fair at Brentor.[5] Half a century then elapsed before any further application of the sort was made; but in 1286 the abbey obtained a Wednesday market at Denbury, with a fair originally meant to last three days but subsequently reduced to two, the 7th and 8th of September.[6] Finally, in 1501 abbot Banham secured the right to hold additional fairs at Hatherleigh from the 27th to the 29th of October, and at Tavistock from the 4th to the 7th of January.[7]

These grants entitled the abbot to levy toll from buyers and

---

[1] Dugdale, II, p. 496; for the date, see DA XLVII, 1915, p. 376.

[2] The Lydford burgesses tried to protect themselves by forming a merchant guild. In 1180 they were heavily fined for having done so without royal permission (PRS XXIX, pp. 93, 94). From 1195 onwards the Crown granted an annual allowance "for making the Lydford market as it used to be of old" (ibid., XLIV, N.S. VI, p. 125). In 1238 the revival of the Okehampton market was one of several grievances alleged by the traders of the older borough (PRO Assize Rolls, J.I. 1, 174, m. 39b).

[3] PRO Fine Roll, 4 Hen. III, pt 1, m. 2.   [4] Ibid., 5 Hen. III, pt 1, m. 5.

[5] Bodleian MS. Dodsworth xv, f. 138; CPR 1225–32, p. 481; CCR 1321–34, p. 74; Cal. Charter Rolls, I, p. 157.

[6] Cal. Charter Rolls, II, pp. 331, 352.   [7] Ibid., VI, p. 273.

sellers. At the present day the tolls of the Friday market at Tavistock are worth some £1,500 a year, but in the abbot's time they were subject to numerous exemptions. Burgesses of Tavistock were free of the local market, and the same liberty was claimed by all tenants of manors belonging to the ancient demesne of the Crown, as well as by the burgesses of chartered towns and members of privileged bodies like the Hospitallers. In 1354 the council of the duchy of Cornwall wrote to the lords of Tavistock, Plympton, Holsworthy, and Exeter-without-the-walls, reminding them that Liskeard was a free borough and requesting them to see that its burgesses were not compelled to pay toll.[1] Such claims must have given rise to frequent disputes and made the administration of the markets a vexatious business. When some inhabitants of South Tawton complained that they had been distrained for toll in the Tavistock markets and fairs, the abbot and convent replied that their bailiffs had been unaware that the strangers were tenants of ancient demesne.[2]

In 1472 the under-steward of the duchy of Cornwall, John Glyn, was murdered near Morval in that county at four o'clock in the morning of the 29th of August as he was setting out for the fair at Tavistock.[3] Evidently the original August fair had acquired a more than local importance. In 1535 the Tavistock market and two fairs were valued at one pound, and the Brentor fair at 6s. 8d.[4] Concerning the other markets there is little information. In 1393 the tolls at Hatherleigh amounted to no more than fourpence. Denbury fair dwindled to a single day; the portreeve's account for 1497 states that the proceeds were delivered to the abbot, but does not mention the amount. In later centuries this fair became a great event; it is said to have been established under the same name in Labrador by settlers from that part of Devon.[5]

In consequence of Henry I's market-grant Tavistock became, in the language of Old English law, a 'port'. The kings of Wessex had borrowed this word from the administrative terminology of the Carolingian realm to express, not a sea-port, but a trading centre. It is probable, though we have no record of the fact, that

[1] *Register of the Black Prince*, II, p. 68.
[2] In 1281. PRO Assize Rolls, J.I. 1, 186, m. 52, printed in DA xxxv, 1903, p. 507.
[3] *Rotuli Parliamentorum*, VI, p. 36.   [4] *Valor Ecclesiasticus*, II, p. 381.
[5] Worth (R.N.), *History of Devonshire*, p. 290.

the abbot soon found it necessary to appoint an official styled a *port-gerefa*, or port-reeve, whose function it was to collect the tolls, to authenticate by his presence the more important sales, and perhaps to settle any disputes which might arise.

The acquisition of a market did not lead necessarily to the foundation of a borough. Before this further and decisive step could be taken, some additional impulse was required. The impulse might proceed from above, prompting the lord to develop his property on urban lines, or from below, moving his tenants to insist upon their freedom from servile obligations; or both tendencies might be at work simultaneously. It has already been shown that the boom in the tin trade which began in the middle of the century supplied the abbot of Tavistock with a compelling motive just when some of his tenants were agitating for a reduction of their labour service.[1] But the origins of the borough remain obscure. All that can be said with certainty is that at some date between 1105, the year of the market-grant, and 1185, when we first hear of burgages at Tavistock, one of the abbots deliberately created an urban district on the right bank of the Tavy.[2]

Whatever degrees of freedom or unfreedom had characterized the inhabitants in the past, they now became portmen, free burgesses. They could be called upon to serve as portreeve or bailiff; they were bound to attend at the borough court and to grind their corn at the town mill, both of which belonged to the abbot; and they owed him a fixed rent for their tenements; but there was no longer any question of service in the fields, and the only remnants of customary labour service that still clung to them were the obligations to provide an occasional messenger between Tavistock and Plymstock and a bodyguard at funerals in the abbey church. From these two duties newcomers who took up building-sites were of course exempt. All burgage tenements could change hands by purchase, exchange, or inheritance, without interference from the abbot, except that he claimed a succession-duty of 2s. 6d. when a burgess entered upon his inheritance. If any seignorial charge was made in cases of ex-

---

[1] See above, p. 71.
[2] Finberg, 'The Borough of Tavistock, Its Origin and Early History', DA LXXIX, 1947, pp. 129 sqq.

change or purchase, the fact is not on record. In some boroughs, as at Bury St Edmunds under abbot Samson's charter of 1190, tenements acquired by purchase could be sold without restriction, but the sale of inherited tenements was not allowed. At Tavistock the "liberties and free customs" of the borough included a virtually unlimited freedom of sale.[1]

The opportunity of acquiring burgages on these conditions was no doubt grasped eagerly by the local handicraftsmen and smallholders. There is reason to believe that it appealed quite as strongly to the landowners and well-to-do ecclesiastics of the neighbourhood. Sir Reginald de Ferrers, lord of the neighbouring manor of Bere Ferrers, took a plot of ground "between the house of Osmar the smith and that of Semar the cobbler", and let it to one Laurence Colbert, who in turn conveyed it, still vacant, to an under-tenant, reserving an annual rent of tenpence. The knight of Crebor owned a tenement in the borough, upon which, in 1185, he created a rent-charge in favour of the Hospitallers. Robert, the parish priest of "Tavy"—that is, either Petertavy or Marytavy—an ecclesiastic who combined a distaste for celibacy with a shrewd appreciation of real estate, built a house at Tavistock and left it to his son; when the latter sold it *circa* 1222, it was worth five marks.[2]

The abbot took care to provide his new town with all necessary services. A cornmill was built just outside the monastery gate and supplied with power from a new leat called the Mill-brook, water being drawn off from the Tavy by means of a weir in Parkwood, about a mile away to the east. The borough boundary seems to have been purposely drawn across Parkwood in order to include the weir and the whole course of the Mill-brook within the burghal area. Further west, this area took in the arable, wood, and meadow which had supported the agricultural population of the original hamlet. The Fishlake, augmented by a tributary called the Buddle, flowed down Market Street and round to the abbey gateway in an open channel whence the inhabitants could help themselves to water. And finally, at the western extremity of the borough stood "the hospital of St Mary Magdalene of Tavistock", intended, like other establishments with the same

[1] DA LXXIX, p. 139.   [2] *Ibid.*, pp. 145 sqq.

dedication, chiefly for sufferers from the then prevalent disease of leprosy.[1]

Of this burghal area, covering some three hundred and twenty-five acres, less than half is built up even now. The residential and commercial quarter lay in the centre, radiating outwards from the abbey gate and the new parish church of St Eustace, but constricted by the surrounding hills. West Street led towards a ford over the Tavy, later known as Fitzford, which was superseded half way through the fifteenth century by a stone bridge.[2] Market Street and its continuation Bannawell ran northward up the valley of the Fishlake. To the east went Brook Street, most of which belonged to the sacristan, an official whose duties kept him much at home and whom it was therefore convenient to endow with burgage rents. Another stone bridge, on the site of the present Abbey Bridge, served the private needs of the monastery, but the town bridge, or "great bridge", as it is first called *circa* 1260, a narrow five-arched structure with cutwaters on either side, was built about two hundred and forty yards upstream.[3]

A surviving rent-roll calls up a picture of the town at the close of the thirteenth century: a picture which, however, does not include the sacristan's property. The date is 1291, and the burgages which then owed rent to the abbot consisted of one hundred and six messuages, fifty-three of which had gardens adjoining; twelve "tenements"; two "tenements with gardens"; and thirty-five detached "gardens, with liberty". In some cases a holding is divided into moieties, each paying half the original rent; but the "liberty" (of transfer, exemption from toll, and so forth) is then attached to one moiety, and the other is described as being "without liberty". Fifteen residents pay twopence each for having foot-

---

[1] The hospital is first mentioned in 1244 (PRO Assize Rolls, J.I. 1, 175, m. 11 *b*). It stood on the site of the tenements known lately as Old Workhouse Cottages.

[2] A charter dated 1460 refers to West Bridge as "le newbrig" (W. D Bdle 2, no. 129).

[3] TPR, p. 65. The Great Bridge was pulled down in 1764. Only one document known to me refers to the forerunner of the present Abbey Bridge. It is a letter, dated 26 August 1743, informing the steward of the Tavistock estate that the writer has been looking for some large moor-stones to repair a breach in the Mill-brook. "Hunsdon has taken several out by the riverside opposite to the Lower Abbey Gate" (i.e., the water gate) "that were formerly part of the ancient bridge there" (John Wynne to R. Butcher, W. Table 4 B, Drawer 1).

bridges across the Fishlake or the Mill-brook; and one "for an encroachment by the great bridge". Ten persons, three of them women, and all presumably non-resident, are charged twopence each "for liberty to buy and sell" in the borough. The total revenue is £7 8s. 4½d.[1] More than half the burgages pay rents of eightpence. The next commonest amounts are sixpence and fourpence. It seems probable that eightpence had at first been the standard burgage rent, as it was at Exeter, and that the smaller payments may represent partitions of the original holdings.[2]

At the time of the foundation of the borough, a burgage rent of eightpence compared favourably with the rent obtainable for a corresponding area of farm-land.[3] Very soon, however, it came to represent only a minute fraction of the site-value. Already, by 1222, a house in Tavistock is changing hands for £3 6s. 8d., exactly a hundred times as much as the burgage rent.[4] A further drawback was that the burgage rent was fixed. The value of house property might go up while that of money fell, but the abbot, and indeed his successors within living memory, would still receive no more than eightpence. It is true that there was nothing to prevent him from buying houses if he chose, or receiving them as gifts, or simply taking possession of one if a burgess died intestate leaving no heirs of his body. But in fact the abbot's income from the borough did remain almost stationary for two hundred years. This is established by a comparison between the rent-roll of 1291 and an account rendered at Michaelmas 1497. In that year the gross rental, £7 19s. 5½d., was reduced to £6 4s. because fifteen tenements were in hand, one was derelict, an unspecified number, with an aggregate rental of 5s. 9d., were lying vacant, and one or two, like that of the abbey laundress, and the vicar's house in St Matthew Street, were rent-free; but reliefs and other perquisites brought the net income up to £8 3s. 4d.

Both of the accounts just cited were rendered by the portreeve,

[1] W. D Bdle 84, no. 2.
[2] At Lydford the burgage rent was 4d. (*Dartmoor Preservation Assoc.*, I, p. 152). At Bradninch it was 6d.; at Barnstaple 8d. (average); and at Oke-hampton 1s. (Hemmeon, *Burgage Tenure in Mediaeval England*, pp. 67 sqq.).
[3] Ballard, *The English Borough in the Twelfth Century*, p. 18.
[4] It is interesting to compare this with the three pounds paid at about the same date for a shop in Bath, where the burgage rent was 6d. (Hemmeon, *op. cit.*, pp. 67, 81).

an officer who emerges into full daylight in the thirteenth century. He was appointed at the Michaelmas law-day by the abbot's
steward, who as a rule, although not absolutely bound to do so,
made his choice between two or more candidates put forward by
the jury of portmen. The burgess finally selected served for
twelve months, and rarely indeed held office for a second term,
his duties being as onerous, in their own way, as those of his rural
counterpart, the reeve. They were sweetened by an allowance of
two shillings from the abbot; and a garden in the borough was reserved for his use. Many charters show him witnessing convey-
ances of burgage tenements, but his main responsibility was to
see that the lord's urban dues were paid. As the highest elective
officer of the borough court he enjoyed a precedence of honour,
and sometimes no doubt of leadership, over his fellow-townsmen.
The portreeve who accounted in 1497, Richard Lybbe, is styled
prepositus, as usual, on the roll, but in a conveyance executed two
or three days earlier he is described as "mayor of Tavistock".[1]
This unauthorized use of the mayoral title, which had its parallel
in other Devon boroughs, and which occurs intermittently at
Tavistock between 1449 and 1556, amounted to nothing more
than a fitful and rather half-hearted attempt to dignify an officer
whose origin and essence lay in the service due from a tenant to
his lord. Not for him, whatever he might call himself, the power
and pre-eminence enjoyed by the chief magistrate of an incor-
porated borough.[2]

The foundation of the borough, while establishing a new
relationship between the abbot and the men of Tavistock, made
little difference to outside parties. Hence there was no need for
the abbot to seek royal confirmation of his act. Only in judicial
matters, when the justices in eyre came down to Exeter or the
sheriff went round Devon on his 'tourn', was there any contact
between the borough and the king's representatives. By 1238

[1] TPR, p. 81.

[2] An inquiry held in 1385 established that the prior of Plympton, as lord
of Sutton Prior, Plymouth, held a court at which a portreeve was elected by
a jury of twelve, and that the portreeve's function was to receive and account
to the prior for debts, amercements, fines, reliefs, court perquisites, and all
other profits accruing from the borough (DA xvi, 1884, p. 174). It was the
same at Hatherleigh (DA xxxviii, 1906, p. 303). At Ashburton the portreeve
and burgesses used a common seal (DA lvi, 1924, p. 57); but this seems to
have been exceptional.

Tavistock was one of eighteen Devon boroughs represented at the eyre not by delegations from the hundreds in which they were situated, but by their own burgesses. This privilege, which implied public recognition of its urban status, can hardly have been acquired without a royal grant, but no record of such grant has been preserved.[1]

In 1294 Edward I obtained from parliament a tax on personal property at the rate of a tenth in rural districts and a sixth in "cities, boroughs, and market towns". A higher rate of tax was destined to be one of the distinguishing marks of boroughs recognized as such by the Crown. In the following year, with a view to fresh taxation, the sheriffs were instructed to send up two knights from each county, two citizens from each city, and two burgesses from each borough, to attend a parliament at Westminster. The sheriff of Devon returned representatives of the shire, of the city of Exeter, and of five towns: Barnstaple, Totnes, Plympton, Tavistock, and Torrington. Thenceforth, with occasional interruptions, Tavistock was represented in parliament by two members until 1868. When the quotas of taxable capacity were fixed in 1334, it was placed fifth among the Devon boroughs, after Exeter, Plymouth, Barnstaple, and Dartmouth, Totnes being sixth and Torrington seventh. By 1445, when the quotas were revised, it had superseded Dartmouth in the fourth place; and it still held that position in the assessment of 1523.[2] As a stannary town, a thriving centre of the cloth trade, and a parliamentary borough, Tavistock easily escaped the obscurity and insignificance which characterized so many boroughs of seignorial creation.

The same can hardly be said of the two other market-centres, Denbury and Hatherleigh, to which the abbots of Tavistock conceded burghal "liberties and free customs". If the date of the market-grant is taken as the upper limit in each case, and compared with that of the earliest known document in which the place is styled a borough, the grant of burgality must have taken place between 1220 and 1374 at Hatherleigh, and at Denbury between

---

[1] It may have been purchased from John Lackland during the period, beginning in December 1189, in which he ruled Devon, Cornwall, and five other counties, as a quasi-independent palatinate.

[2] PRO Lay Subsidy Rolls, E179, Bdle 95, nos. 10, 99; Bdle 97, no. 186.

1286 and 1393. Both possessed burgage tenure, with their own
courts and portreeves, but they never achieved separate representation at the eyre, or the less enviable privilege of being taxed
above the rural rate. The borough of Hatherleigh included within
its boundary some four hundred acres of moor on which the
burgesses had rights of common, in this particular resembling the
not far distant borough of Great Torrington.[1] In 1394 its rents
amounted to £6 19s. 6d., those of Denbury at the same date being
£4 11s. 4½d.; and like those of Tavistock they remained almost
static until the Dissolution.

At Tavistock the borough court originally met in the open air,
among the shambles, or stalls upon which meat and fish were exposed for sale on market-days. In the local dialect these were
called shammels; and from the circumstance of its meeting in the
midst of them the court was known in the thirteenth century as
the Shammel-Moot.[2] Much later, on the eve of the Dissolution,
a Guildhall was built, probably by some such body as the Jesus
Guild to which all the leading inhabitants belonged;[3] and by then
the court had doubtless moved indoors. Its function was to transact such business, arising within the borough bounds, as would
have been dealt with at the manor court had no borough been
created. When the abbot divided the territory of the original
manor into a rural district called the manor of Hurdwick and an
urban district or borough of Tavistock, he also set up a court for
each, and in those two courts he thenceforth exercised the jurisdiction he had previously exercised in one.

On the right of the road that leads from Tavistock to Brentor,
where the parish of Tavistock Hamlets ends and Lamerton begins, there is a field marked on the nineteenth-century estate
maps as Forges Field. The name, originally Forches, indicates
that here, in accordance with the usage which decreed that such
work should be done at the manor boundary, the abbot had his
furcae, or gallows. It is a reminder that he once wielded powers of
life and death. How had this jurisdiction been acquired? And

[1] Alexander and Hooper, *History of Great Torrington*, pp. 9, 78.
[2] Finberg, *op. cit.*, p. 139.
[3] Similarly at Modbury there was a guild of St George, consisting of the
portreeve and commonalty of the borough (DA XVI, 1884, p. 178).

since no one does justice for nothing, what was it worth to the abbot?

The coercive power which an eleventh-century abbot, like any other slave-owner, could bring to bear on his servile dependants lost some, but not by any means all, of its force when they were transformed into serfs dwelling apart from the lord's hall and cultivating land on their own account. As a matter of convenience this power would be exercised within some sort of organic framework, such as that provided by periodical assemblies of the tenants in a 'hall-moot' under the presidency of an officer appointed by the abbot. The purpose of such meetings would be to regulate servile land-tenure in accordance with the custom of the manor, and perhaps also to deal, at least as a court of first instance, with the offences of delinquent serfs. Here, already in being, was an institution that might well in course of time attract within its orbit those free *ceorls* who had been used to owe the king certain dues in money or in kind: dues which the king had now made over to the abbot by including their farmsteads within the bounds of the abbot's 'book-land'. For purposes of justice and police, these franklins had been organized in hundreds and tithings. The hundred court took cognizance of their crimes and of disputes concerning property; the tithing, a territorial division of the hundred, was the police unit, responsible through its head-man or tithingman for the arrest of criminals. Cnut's law required every freeman above the age of twelve to join a tithing, in order that he might be held to good behaviour under the collective suretyship of all its members. It was a system of joint mutual responsibility for law and order; but who was to hold the franklins to it, and to supervise its day-to-day working?

There are scholars who believe that a clause like that in Ethelred II's charter which conferred upon the book-land of Tavistock immunity from ordinary taxes had the further effect of granting justiciary rights. Others hold that such rights could only be conferred by an express royal grant of 'sake and soke'. It is a question into which we need not enter here. Grants of sake and soke were dealt out lavishly to favoured churches by Edward the Confessor, and it would have been surprising indeed if such a prelate as Lyfing, who had been one of Cnut's chief ministers and to whom the Confessor was largely indebted for his throne, had omitted to secure any privilege that his own abbey still lacked. Hence we may be tolerably sure that if the abbot of Tavistock did not possess justiciary rights at the beginning of the century, he had acquired them by 1050.

The policy of the Norman kings gave a further impetus to this development. William I re-enacted the law requiring all freemen to be "in pledge". To ensure that it should not become a dead letter, the tithings were constantly reviewed. This periodical inspection, which the lawyers termed a view of frankpledge, was described in the homelier language of the peasants as a trimming.[1] It was a lucrative matter for the authority by whom it was conducted, since a penny was taken from each man newly sworn to the peace, and a penny or twopence at each trimming from every man already enrolled. This is the payment which figures in the accounts of so many south-western manors as *census, censura,* or *redditus censariorum.* It was always collected and paid into court at the Michaelmas trimming-day.[2]

If the abbot of Tavistock construed his sake and soke as empowering him, not only to view and trim the tithings, but also to do justice on delinquents, he was fully in line with the theory and

[1] Cf. Cam, *The Hundred and the Hundred Rolls,* pp. 126, 210.

[2] Miss Neilson, author of the classic treatise on *Customary Rents,* failed to grasp the connection between *censura* and the frankpledge system (*op. cit.,* p. 106). The connection is, however, established by numerous entries in the court rolls. For example, X is at law with Y because he did not put him in pledge with the lord and bailiffs of the hundred "pro redditu censario bene et fideliter solvendo" (Ogbear, 1342). The three Werrington tithings are instructed to have ready at the next court a list of all *nativi* over twelve years old so that they may pay *censura* according to the custom of the manor. At a subsequent court this is referred to as a *loquela* "concerning *nativi* and other servants not sworn to the peace" (1366). Again, X, being surety for Y, is "in mercy" for not having paid Y's *censura* (*ibid.,* 1384). At Hurdwick X is presented as being domiciled with Y "outside the assize of our lord the king". A note is added to the roll: "jur' cens'", and the name of his surety (1534). In the Lydford and Dartmoor accounts the payment is equated with *capitatio garcionum, advocacio,* and chevage, which last was the regular name for the head-money paid in connection with the view of frankpledge (*Dartmoor Preservation Assoc.,* I, pp. 10, 12, 16, 17, 21). *Censura* was in effect a poll-tax on tenants, children, servants, and all residents on the manor not themselves householders. Freemen and bondmen were both liable. A Werrington account refers in 1356 to free *censarii,* but somewhat later the twelve freemen of the manor jury pay twopence each under this head, perhaps by way of composition on behalf of all the free inhabitants. For the customs of Braunton, see DA xx, 1888, pp. 279, 280.

practice of the age. Probably every lord who was strong enough to exercise it now claimed a jurisdiction not limited to civil cases.[1] Further, the abbot now had feudal business to transact. After the introduction of knight service, he found himself at the head of an 'honour' or feudal complex of fifteen knights' fees, and was said to hold his lands 'by barony'. Everyone who has read Jocelin of Brakelond knows what contentious matters might come up for debate between the abbot and his knights. The court of Tavistock, therefore, in addition to its other attributes, now became a feudal court at which the abbot's military tenants presented themselves to do homage for their lands in Devon, Cornwall, and Dorset, and perhaps to wrangle over the garrison-duty they were supposed to perform by turns at Exeter, or the amount of scutage due from each.[2]

So long as the abbot held his barony by the service of fifteen knights, his feudal jurisdiction remained whole and indivisible. Not so the jurisdiction that he wielded as a landlord over his tenants, and as a local guardian of law and order. That could be divided, and passed on to others with the land itself. His military tenants now held courts, not only in Sheviock, Houndtor, Thornbury, and the other distant manors, but in those portions of Tavistock itself which they held of the abbot by knight service. Any civilian also could set up a court if he had tenants on his freehold. In 1348 one Richard de Lamburn granted a life-lease of a tenement and garden in Tavistock, reserving to himself a rent of 2s. 4d. and "suit of our court at Tavistock twice yearly when we shall hold court there".[3] The creation of new manors and courts in fact went on uninterruptedly all over England until 1290, when it was ended by the statute *Quia Emptores*. Long before that date the Domesday manor of Tavistock had been divided between the borough of that name and the manors of Hurdwick, Morwell, Ogbear, Parswell, and Cudlipptown.[4]

---

[1] Denholm-Young, *Seignorial Administration in England*, p. 87.

[2] ETC 1 is the only surviving document that refers to the obligation of castle-guard. On the Ramsey estates the business of knight service was regulated in the court of the honour; at St Albans the abbot used to convene special meetings of his knights (Chew, *The English Ecclesiastical Tenants-in-Chief and Knight Service*, p. 129).

[3] W. D Bdle 2, no. 131.

[4] Crebor and Taviton had been held by knight service, but their courts must have fallen into desuetude when the lands were reabsorbed into Hurd-

The growth of private jurisdiction entailed the gradual disintegration of the hundred court. As Vinogradoff has put it, the manorial court-leet—that is, a manor court which holds the view of frankpledge—is, "at bottom, a portion of the hundred court in private hands".[1] By the early years of the twelfth century the process had gone so far that the word hundred could be used, and was used even in royal charters, as synonymous with any kind of court. Confusion reached its height when the Exeter borough court was loosely styled "the hundred of the Exeter burgesses", and rural or suburban manors like Topsham, Cowick, Alphington, and Holcombe were also said to have their hundreds.[2] At the same time, the original hundreds properly so called, though depleted in vitality, were not allowed to die. Henry I decreed that they should meet at the same times and places as before the Conquest. They continued to be used for administrative purposes, such as the mustering of the militia and at a later period the assessment and collection of subsidies. From the reign of Henry II onwards their judicial business was periodically inspected by the sheriff, who came round every year on his tourn and presided at the great law-court or general meeting of the hundred.

A lord entitled to hold the view of frankpledge was exercising hundredal jurisdiction; but so long as the original hundred remained in other hands, he might be obliged to exercise it within the older framework. Maitland illustrates this by the custom of Brook in Kent, a manor belonging to the prior of Canterbury. When a thief was caught there he was taken to the local hundred court and judged by the hundred, unless he was one of the prior's men. If he was the prior's man the bailiff of Brook "craved the prior's court". His fellow tenants would then go apart and judge the accused, a few of the hundred-men going with them to act as assessors.[3] The emancipation of the manor from the hundred is

wick. The sacristan held a court for his own tenants (W. D Bdle 53, no. 109), and was therefore sometimes described as lord of the manor of Indescombe. A manor of Newton appears in the *Valor Ecclesiasticus* (II, p. 384) as a name for property in the west of the parish belonging to the prior and convent.

[1] *English Society in the Eleventh Century*, pp. 97, 214.
[2] Rose-Troup, 'Exeter Manumissions and Quittances', DA LXIX, 1937, p. 425; and cf. Henry I's reference to "the manor, church, and hundred of Legh", that is, Monkleigh in the hundred of Shebbear (*Montacute Cartulary*, Somerset Record Society, VIII, p. 120).
[3] Maitland, *op. cit.*, p. 97, from the Custumals of Battle Abbey.

thus a matter of degree; and we shall see that the Tavistock estates exhibit every stage of the process very clearly.

On each of his manors the abbot, like any other lord, held a
court in which he transacted domestic business with his tenants
and enforced the customs and by-laws of the manor. In the same
court, if the manor was one of those which he held as "pertaining
to his barony", he also exercised a quasi-hundredal jurisdiction,
with power to trim the tithings, to collect *censura*, to hear complaints against bakers and brewers who had contravened the
'assize of bread and ale', and to punish breaches of the peace. The
court is entitled simply *curia manerii*, except on the half-yearly
law-days, when it becomes *curia legalis manerii*. Of manors pos-
sessing such a court Plymstock is a typical example.[1] But Plymstock also formed a tithing in the hundred of Plympton, and was
never allowed to forget that fact. If summoned to the hundred
court, the tenants were bound to attend. At the very least they
must send their tithingman to meet the sheriff when he came
thither on his tourn. And any of them would have to answer in
the hundred court if sued in a personal action, unless the abbot
appeared and 'claimed his court'. The abbot himself owed suit to
Plympton; but well before the close of the fourteenth century he
had compounded for non-attendance by a yearly payment of two
shillings to the lord of the hundred.[2]

Privilege of a somewhat higher grade is exemplified in those
'free manors' or 'hundred-manors', as they were variously styled,
of which, apart from Tavistock itself, the abbot had three: Denbury, Hatherleigh, and Werrington. Before the Domesday inquest some nineteen square miles of Werrington belonged to the
Cornish hundred of Stratton, while the portion between the
Tamar and the Carey lay in the hundred of Black Torrington.
After its confiscatioñ by the Domesday commissioners it was
wholly annexed to Black Torrington, and in Devonshire it has
remained to the present day. Apparently its restitution to the
abbey was not accomplished without friction. That two changes

[1] In 1284-6 the abbot is described as holding Plymstock, Denbury,
Werrington, Hatherleigh, Abbotsham, Burrington, and Taviton as pertaining
to his barony (FA, pp. 317, 327, 329, 335, 340).

[2] He also paid threepence to the clerk for entering the payment on the
court roll. In the *Valor Ecclesiasticus* (II, p. 382) the sum is wrongly given as
2s. 4d.

of ownership in one decade should have unsettled the inhabitants was hardly surprising; and abbot Osbert dealt gently with their insubordination. Early in Henry II's reign his successor Walter, finding the position to some extent compromised by Osbert's leniency, obtained a royal writ commanding the tenants to render the same dues and services as had been customary before Osbert's time.[1] The writ is addressed "to the whole hundred of Werrington". Manifestly the abbot was claiming rights which to some extent ousted the jurisdiction of Black Torrington. The same term was used in connection with an incident that occurred in 1231, when the abbot, John of Rochester, arrested two men "at his hundred of Werrington" and imprisoned them at Tavistock. Presently the twelve jurors of the Werrington court arrived at Tavistock to bail them out, but were forthwith taken into custody themselves. On the following day "the whole of that hundred" came in force to get them released; a scuffle took place on the outskirts of the town, and a man was killed. His slayer was outlawed; the sheriff imposed a fine of six marks upon the men of Tavistock; and the hundred-jurors of Black Torrington did not forget to report the affair at the next session of the justices in eyre, which took place in 1238.[2] By that time an agreement had been concluded between the abbot and Hamelin de Wanford, who held Black Torrington hundred by charter from its hereditary lords. This settlement cost the abbot three marks; and the document which records it styles Werrington indifferently a manor, a hundred, or a manor and hundred. It provides that the men of Werrington, both free and unfree, shall have "all the liberties pertaining to the hundred-manors of Black Torrington which they used to have of old". They are to pay no trimming-dues to the hundred and are to be quit of attendance at its court except on three days of the year, namely, at the courts next after Michaelmas, St Hilary, and Easter, when the 'hundred-man' and three tithingmen of Werrington may attend for the whole manor. Distresses for recovery of debt are to be levied by the sergeant of Werrington in concert with the hundred-bailiff. In return for these concessions the abbot binds himself to pay five shillings a year to Hamelin and his successors.[3]

[1] Finberg, 'The Early History of Werrington', EHR LIX, 1944, p. 248.
[2] PRO Assize Rolls, J.I. 1, 174, m. 30d.   [3] W. D Bdle 65, no. 1.

A "trimming-rent" of 8s. 4d. paid every year from Hatherleigh, which lies in the same hundred, points to the existence of a similar agreement for that manor.[1] For Denbury the abbot made a concordat with the hundred-lord of Haytor, which cost him sixteen pounds; it was confirmed by Edward II in 1319. The abbot's right to "all pleas and attachments pertaining to a free manor" was recognized in return for a yearly payment of 6s. 8d. His tenants were to be represented at meetings of the hundred by four of their number, who however were to pay nothing and to take no part in the business of the court. His own attendance was limited to the three days called filling-days, clearly a local variant of trimming-days.[2] In pursuance of this agreement he was represented at the hundred court by his attorney until some time in the fifteenth century, when he compounded by paying sixpence to the lord and a halfpenny to the clerk for enrolling his release.

At Tavistock, the seat of his barony, the abbot himself possessed, from 1116 onwards, the status of a hundred-lord. By a clause in the same writ which gave Tavistock its August fair, Henry I decreed that "the hundred of Tavistock", meaning the abbot's court as then existing, should be "free and quit by itself, and not answerable or subordinate in any way to the hundred of Lifton".[3] This did not affect the portions of Tavistock which lay east of the Tavy: Cudlipp, Taviton, and Whitham, for they belonged to the hundred of Roborough;[4] but it detached from Lifton all the rest of the manor, and with it those others, Milton Abbot, Leigh, Holeyeat, Week, and Liddaton, which lay in the same hundred. Ottery alone remained to Lifton, perhaps because the abbey had not yet acquired it in full ownership. The area thus detached became an independent hundred of Tavistock in the full original sense of the word: one of the smallest in Devon, it is true, but still a recognized administrative district and unit of public jurisdiction.[5] For police work it was divided into eleven tithings. Four of these, namely, Chillaton, Youngcott, Week, and East

---

[1] *Valor Ecclesiasticus*, II, p. 381.   [2] CPR 1317–21, p. 353.

[3] Dugdale, II, p. 496.

[4] All the maps that I have seen place them in the hundred of Tavistock; but cf. FA, pp. 340, 355, 404, 449.

[5] In 1182 the sheriff accounts for one mark from Tavistock hundred "pro murdro" (PRS XXXI, p. 30).

P

Liddaton, policed the outside manors; the other seven were responsible for the rural area of Tavistock.[1]

Before long the abbot founded his borough, with its portreeve, Shammel-Moot, and other 'liberties'. In order to emphasize its freedom he removed the court of the manor, hundred, and barony to Hurdwick; or perhaps, as the abbey was accounted part of Hurdwick, it would be more correct to say that he instituted a new court of that name for the transaction of manorial, hundred-al, and feudal business. The court met twelve or thirteen times a year. Soon after Easter, and again at Michaelmas, it held a general session, and was then styled "the law court of the hundred and manor", to distinguish it from the intervening by-courts, which were known as "courts of the manor". The trimming and the sheriff's tourn were held at the Michaelmas law-court. By the second quarter of the thirteenth century, if not earlier, the proceedings were being formally enrolled.[2] The court had its gallows, as we have seen, at the northern boundary of Hurdwick. Nearer home, the borough was equipped with other penal apparatus: a clink, a pillory for male offenders, and a skelving-stool, as it was called, for ducking female termagants.[3]

In the actual administration of justice the abbot was little more than a sleeping partner. He took the profits, but left the execution of the work to his officials, who performed it under the general control of the sheriff.[4] In 1275 the men of Tavistock complained that the sheriff had been visiting them far too often, and that the liberties of the "free manor of Hurdwick" had been more than once infringed by the steward of Cornwall, the sheriff of Devon, and lesser officials acting under their orders.[5] Six years later the abbot was called upon to show his warranty for claiming a hundred court, a market, and a fair at Tavistock, and for keeping gallows, holding view of frankpledge, and enforcing the assize of

[1] See above, p. 52.

[2] There is a reference in the 1416 Extent of Hurdwick, m. 14, to the court roll of 33 Henry III. Unfortunately no rolls of earlier date than 1413 have survived.

[3] For the skelving-stool, which elsewhere was called a cucking-stool, see DCNQ xxii, 1946, p. 368, and xxiii, 1948, p. 218. It is sometimes associated with the enforcement of the assize of ale, on the ground that brewing was mainly a female occupation (*Select Pleas in Manorial Courts*, ed. Maitland, 1889, p. xxxviii).

[4] Cf. Cam, *op. cit.*, p. 142.   [5] *Rotuli Hundredorum*, I, p. 81.

bread and ale at Tavistock, Werrington, and Hatherleigh. The king's lawyers argued that no one could lawfully possess a hundred unless the Crown had granted it in so many words. They would have made short work of such vaguely worded documents as Ethelred II's charter, or even Henry I's writ, if the abbot had been so ill-advised as to produce them. It was safer to rely upon prescription. To a similar inquiry in 1238 the local jury had replied, somewhat inaccurately, that the abbot held the hundred by a tenure antecedent to the Norman Conquest, and without other warranty.[1] So, on this occasion, the abbot answered that the hundred was one of the appurtenances of his barony, that his market and fair had been held time out of mind, and that Hatherleigh and Werrington were situated in a private hundred where the king had nothing to gain or lose.[2] The plea of immemorial tenure was recognized as a valid answer in such cases;[3] and the plea of tenure by barony, when advanced by a churchman, amounted to the same thing, for no new ecclesiastical baronies had been created since the Conqueror's reign.[4] In 1290 it was settled that continuous possession of a liberty from before the coronation of Richard I should be a sufficient answer to the writ of *Quo warranto*. In the meantime Edward I had solemnly confirmed Ethelred's charter and those of Henry I and II.[5]

The abbot therefore kept his jurisdiction, not without some trouble and expense. It is on record that in 1322 his court sent a convicted cattle-thief to the gallows.[6] But the lord of a private hundred took risks if he hanged a man except in presence of the coroner. For his court was private only in the sense that he kept its profits and appointed its officers. It never ceased to be a unit in the national system of justice. This remained true even of those liberties which possessed 'return of writs': the privilege, that is, of executing royal writs by their own officials, to the exclusion of the sheriff and his bailiffs. The abbot of Tavistock did not enjoy this privilege until 1501, when Henry VII gave it to him by a charter which appointed him "the king's justice for

---

[1] *Testa de Nevill*, p. 1372.
[2] *Placita de Quo Warranto*, pp. 166, 170, 171.
[3] Cam, *Liberties and Communities in Medieval England*, p. 179.
[4] Chew, *op. cit.*, p. 10.
[5] On 10 September 1285 (*Cal. Charter Rolls*, II, p. 324).
[6] DCNQ XXIII, 1948, p. 186.

keeping the peace" in the hundred of Tavistock, with full powers of distraint and arrest, and with the right to hear all pleas, real, personal, and mixed; to determine pleas of debt, trespass, and contract; to keep the profits of such pleas; and to seize the chattels of convicted felons. Even so, the sheriff could still enter the hundred "in case of default by the said abbot and convent or their bailiff".[1] Only if he saw to it that the king's work was properly done could the franchise-holder feel secure in his liberty.[2]

The feudal history of the court is an almost complete blank. If the court rolls of the thirteenth century were extant, they would doubtless show this part of its business gradually dwindling as the system of knight service lost contact with the realities of war. As late as 1303 the abbot's knights, or some of them, took the field with Edward I in Scotland;[3] but the feudal army was mustered for the last time in 1385, and long before the end of the century the knights had compounded for non-attendance at the Hurdwick court by a yearly payment of two shillings each. Thereafter the court had nothing to do with them except to register the succession to their estates in order that the abbot might claim homage, fealty, and relief from the heir of a deceased knight, and profit by the occasional windfall of an heir succeeding while still a minor.[4]

From the eleventh to the thirteenth century the profits of jus-

[1] *Cal. Charter Rolls*, VI, p. 273.   [2] Cam, *op. cit.*, p. 192.
[3] *Cal. of Chancery Rolls, Various*, p. 378.
[4] These occasional profits may be illustrated from the history of the Dorset fees. In November 1292 John de Oskereswell died, leaving a son John, aged six, and three daughters. Three months later the abbot gave the custody of his estates, during the minority of the heir, to Alan Danus for a rent of ten marks a year, reserving to the widow her dower, and to himself the marriage of the heir. In 1374 another John of the same family died, leaving a son Roger under age. The abbot appointed Sir Thomas West custodian of his manors, for what consideration is not stated (W. D Bdle 34, no. 6). Roger died in 1417, without male issue. His widow purchased from the abbot the wardship and marriage of their only child Joan, then aged three (Memorandum endorsed on m.3 of the Extent of Hurdwick, 1416). Joan died six years later, when the court of Hurdwick gave orders for all the Askerswell estates to be taken into the lord's hand. After an interval of three years the court directed that Joan's next-of-kin should be distrained for homage and fealty. In 1522 the beadle was instructed to take seisin of Askerswell by reason of the death of Richard Grey, who had been seised of that and other manors by knight service as of the manor and barony of Hurdwick. On every occasion when the heir succeeded or came of age, the abbot collected a relief of five pounds for each of the two Askerswell fees.

tice may well have amounted to as much as a fifth of the manorial income. As the value of money fell, and private jurisdiction had to face increasingly efficient competition from the royal courts, this high proportion could no longer be maintained. The item *perquisita curie* in the bailiff's accounts is a gross figure made up of amercements inflicted by the court, *censura*, and succession duties in the shape of heriots and reliefs. To compare this figure with the gross total income, and to express the one as a percentage of the other, would be a simple enough task; but the result would be to a large extent misleading, for the accounts rendered by the bailiff or reeve merely show what the abbot ought to have received from his courts, not what he received in fact. It was the beadle, armed with an 'estreat' or list of names and amounts 'extracted' from the court roll, who set about collecting the money; and often he failed signally to lay hands on more than a fraction of the sum due. The year 1512 may be taken as a single instance. Had the bailiff's account alone survived, it would tell us that the proceeds of thirteen courts held at Hurdwick in that year amounted to £7 13s. 1d. But how much of this was really paid? By a rare chance the beadle's account is there to supply the answer. In the first place, the heirs of thirty-one deceased tenants have been fined sums varying between 2s. 6d. and 3s. 9d. "for homages and fealties not done, and for default in suit of court". Among them are the earl of Devon, Fulk Lord Fitzwarren, a knight, and several esquires: persons for whom the Hurdwick beadle may with reason feel himself to be no match. He therefore prays the abbot to write off their amercements, at a loss of £5 11s. 6d. Of the other debtors, one is away on the king's service; another's fine has been omitted from the estreats; over two more there is a discrepancy between the court roll and the estreats. When these and other excuses have been allowed, the abbot's income from this source has been reduced to £1 15s. 5d. So too with the nine small manors around Tavistock for which the steward holds a combined court.[1] One tenant is away in Spain with Lord Willoughby de Broke; several others claim to have been excused by the lord; and there is one who does not live

---

[1] Ottery, Ogbear, Morwell, Parswell, Petertavy, Holeyeat, Week, Foghanger, and West Liddaton.

on the manor. A nominal revenue of £3 1s. 9d. is thus brought down to 19s. 5d.

Such figures make it plain that the courts must sometimes have brought in scarcely enough to cover their expenses. By the fifteenth century they had indeed passed their heyday; but this does not mean that they had ceased to answer any useful purpose. Men were bound to their lord not only by material ties, but also by a sentiment of loyalty inherited from the remotest period of English history. To this feeling the court of the manor gave public and formal expression. On the great law-days the business of the lord with his tenants was conducted according to set forms; and when it was over the lord regaled them with a dinner. The festive impulse and the craving for ceremony were thus both satisfied. An institution which could answer these two abiding needs of human nature, and at the same time give body and form to sentiments deeply ingrained in the English character, was something more than an item in a balance-sheet; and in fact it still had several centuries of active life before it.

CHAPTER IX

THE MONASTIC ECONOMY

SINCE the abbey was not intended to be a profit-making enterprise, its accounts are not profit-and-loss accounts. With
one or two exceptions, all that have survived are manorial
compotus rolls. They begin by detailing the gross income of the
manor from rents, commuted labour services, court perquisites,
sales of grain and livestock, and other sources. Then, under the
heading of expenditure, are entered the costs of demesne farming, wages, purchases of grain and stock, miscellaneous expenses,
and any portion of the year's income that has already been paid
over to the abbey. The difference between the total income and
the sum of payments represents the liability of the manorial
officials at the date when the account is rendered.[1] On the back of
the roll a stock and grain account is usually added, and sometimes
also a statement of the services performed by the tenants. The
purpose of an account drawn up in this form is to reveal the
amount of cash owing to the lord, the quantity of grain stored in
his granary, and the numbers and description of his livestock.
No attempt is made to assess the value of the produce delivered to
the abbey or consumed on the spot; nor does the account state
what was done with the cash balance.

For a full view of the Tavistock economy we should need a
series of *compotus* rolls from all the manors, with the dockets of
the beadle, hayward, granger, and other subordinate officials, and
the accounts of all the monastic office-holders from the abbot
downwards. Even so, the data would need to be thoroughly
sifted and re-arranged before anything resembling a modern
balance-sheet could be drawn up. Lacking materials for such an
audit, we must content ourselves in this chapter with first piecing
together such information as can be gleaned concerning the
monks' liabilities, and then reviewing their system of management and the varying success with which they exploited their
assets.

[1] Cf. Denholm-Young, *Seignorial Administration in England*, p. 127.

I. LIABILITIES

The first charge against the endowments of any monastery is the livelihood of the monks themselves. Tavistock was never a large community. Perhaps its greatest numerical strength was attained in the first half of the twelfth century. This is known to have been the case in many houses,[1] but for Tavistock no figures are available until 1334, when eleven monks are said to be "the greater part" of the convent.[2] In 1391 thirteen are named besides the abbot.[3] Fourteen took part in the election of a new abbot in 1422, and again in 1447.[4] In addition there were usually one or two monks resident in the priory of Tresco, far away in Scilly, where they ministered to the islanders and kept an eye on the property of the house;[5] and from 1462 onwards the priory of Cowick formed another external cell. In 1495 the abbot and convent agreed to increase the number of resident monks from sixteen to twenty.[6] For the board of the proposed recruits the sum of twenty pounds a year was set aside from the rents of Cowick, and for their clothing the sheaf-tithe of Okehampton, valued at approximately £9 6s. 8d.[7] The cost of maintenance thus worked out at £7 6s. 8d. a head, which may be compared with the corresponding figures of £6 13s. 4d. allowed at Durham in 1235 and ten pounds at Bath in 1500.[8]

In 1429 the household staff consisted of twenty servants, including the washerwoman, who lived in a rent-free house outside the monastery. The combined wages of the staff at that date amounted to £22 1s. 4½d. In addition, the barber received a yearly fee of 6s. 8d. What with monks, lay servants, pensioners, and visitors, the resident population can seldom have numbered less than fifty persons.

A discourse addressed to a monastic house by bishop Bartholomew of Exeter (1162–84) implies that his audience was drawn

---

[1] Knowles, *op. cit.*, p. 425.   [2] *Reg. Grandisson*, p. 744.
[3] *Reg. Brantyngham*, p. 719.   [4] *Reg. Lacy*, pp. 51, 318.
[5] In 1345, on account of the war with France, they let the property look after itself and deputed a couple of secular priests to perform the religious duties (CPR 1343–5, p. 480). By 1367 they were back again in the isles (Oliver, p. 74).
[6] W. D Bdle 84, no. 51.
[7] This was the value in 1535 (*Valor Ecclesiasticus*, II, p. 384).
[8] Snape, *English Monastic Finances in the Later Middle Ages*, p. 168.

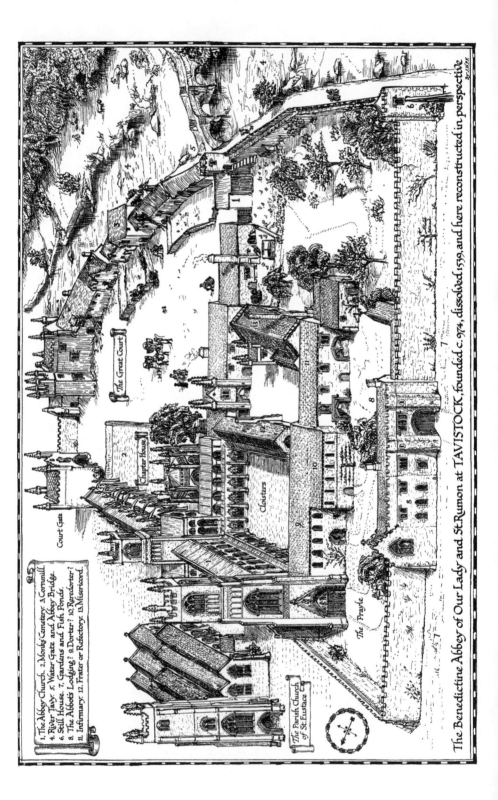

1. The Abbey Church. 2. Monks' Cemetery. 3. Cornwall.
4. River Tavy. 5. Water Gate and Abbey Bridge.
6. Still House. 7. Gardens and Fish Ponds.
8. The Abbot's Lodging? 9. Dortar? 10. Reredorter?
11. Infirmary. 12. Frater or Refectory. 13. Misericord.

Court Gate

The Great Court

Chapter House

Cloisters

The Frayle

The Parish Church of St. Eustace

The Benedictine Abbey of Our Lady and St. Rumon at TAVISTOCK, founded c. 974, dissolved 1539, and here reconstructed in perspective

By Inx

from every social class. In point of fact the monks came chiefly from the upper and middle ranks of society, with the sons of local merchant and yeoman families on the whole predominating.[1] All of them spent their first four or five years in the monastery training for priestly orders. They were men who had renounced the joys and escaped the sorrows of marriage, and dedicated themselves to a life of corporate liturgical observance. The daily and nightly service in the choir of the abbey church was their principal occupation; and at the heart and centre of it all was "that powerful thing they called their Mass".[2]

For its perfect celebration the liturgy demanded a worthy architectural setting. William of Malmesbury, who visited Tavistock before 1125, commends the beauty of the abbey church. It is unlikely that he would have done so if the early Norman abbots had been content, like bishop Osbern at Exeter, to keep up the buildings they had inherited from the Old English period, for William regarded this as a piece of antique simplicity on the bishop's part.[3] But the earliest direct references to building operations date from the second quarter of the thirteenth century, when the reconstruction of the church was taken in hand.[4] An Early English cloister arch, which backed on to the south wall of the nave, is to-day the only surviving fragment of the structure which bishop Stapeldon dedicated in 1318.[5] It must have been a splendid building. Bishop Grandisson, who was no mean judge of architecture, refers in 1348 to the "edificia pulcherrima" of Tavistock, but complains that some of them are badly in need of repair.[6] A bell-tower was begun at the western end of the church,

[1] Morey, *op. cit.*, p. 111. John de Courtenay, abbot from 1334 to 1349, was a son of Hugh, baron Courtenay of Okehampton, heir to the earldom of Devon. He was not a success; and the later abbots were all of comparatively modest origin.

[2] In 1419 and again in 1452 there was a shortage of priests, and the abbey was allowed to have some of its monks ordained at the age of twenty-two (*Calendar of Papal Letters*, VII, p. 126, and X, p. 589).

[3] *Gesta Pontificum*, p. 202.

[4] Indulgence granted by R., bishop of Salisbury (probably Robert Bingham, 1229–46), to all contributors towards the rebuilding of Tavistock Abbey (W. D Bdle 84, no. 1). Grant, *c.* 1250, by Agnes de Mewy, to the church of our Lady and St Rumon, in aid of its building work, of a burgage near the Mill-brook (*ibid.*, Bdle 2, no. 5).

[5] *Reg. Stapeldon*, p. 137.

[6] *Reg. Grandisson*, p. 1072. He had said the same thing ten years before

and was still under construction in 1373, when the dorter, rere-
dorter, refectory, and cloister were said to need rebuilding.[1] They
were still dilapidated in 1390, by which time the misericord, or
infirmary dining-hall, was also alleged to be in bad condition.[2]
Some years later an extensive work of reconstruction was begun.
Contributions towards the cost of repairing the church and Lady
chapel were solicited in 1420.[3] All the extant remains that are not
Early English belong to the fifteenth century. Court Gate, the
main entrance from the town, has Perpendicular additions, and
the abbot's lodging appears to have been entirely rebuilt at this
period: it was a handsome structure overlooking the gardens and
fishponds, and separated from the church and the western range
by a grass plot called the Prayle.[4]

An establishment on this scale must have provided much employment for stone-carvers, glass-workers, bell-founders, weavers, goldsmiths, and other handicraftsmen. Calligraphy and
bookbinding were doubtless practised by the monks themselves.
Their library, when Leland visited Tavistock, included commentaries on Aristotle's logic by Grosseteste and Kilwardby, a
medical treatise by Constantine the African, John of Cornwall's
Eulogium super Alexandrum Papam, and a Life of St Rumon.[5]
There had been no written life of the saint at the time of William
of Malmesbury's visit, but the deficiency had since been made
good by adapting a biography of the Breton saint Ronan, with
whom Rumon was now mistakenly identified.[6] A series of annals,
begun in the twelfth century and carried down to 1256, shows
that the monks of that period were taking an intelligent, if not
particularly well informed, interest in general as well as local
history.[7] Among the other books in their possession were a copy

(*ibid.*, p. 882), and a certain amount of new building was then undertaken by
the sacrist, Richard Ash, who became abbot in 1349 (W. D Bdle 53,
no. 137).

[1] *Reg. Brantyngham*, p. 313.   [2] *Ibid.*, p. 716.
[3] *Calendar of Papal Letters*, VII, p. 153.
[4] First mentioned in 1474 as "our conventual garden called le Prayell"
(W. D Bdle 53, no. 140); from *pratellum*, a small meadow.
[5] Leland, *Collectanea*, p. 152.
[6] Doble, *St Rumon and St Ronan* ('Cornish Saints' Series, No. 42), pp.
5 sqq.
[7] The manuscript may have been taken by a monk-student from Tavistock
to Gloucester College, Oxford. Thomas Allen, the mathematician and antiquarian, who resided at the college from about 1570, bequeathed it, with

of St Jerome's commentaries on Matthew and Daniel, written in
the middle of the twelfth century, and two eleventh-century
manuscripts of Ælfric's vernacular homilies. These last were
found at Tavistock in 1566 by Robert Farrar (or Ferrers), a
lawyer or steward employed by Francis, earl of Bedford. One of
them is now in the British Museum; the other, a magnificent
specimen of Old English calligraphy, was presented by the earl to
Matthew Parker, and by him to the University of Cambridge.[1]
On the evidence of this manuscript Parker asserted that the
Old English vernacular was cultivated at Tavistock to the very

other MSS., to Sir K. Digby; and Digby gave it to the Bodleian Library
(MS. Digby 81, ff. 67–88b). The annals are our chief authority for the succession of the early abbots. Apart from this and one or two local events which
they record, their historical value is not great.

[1] Mr Neil Ker informs me that the Jerome, which is now on loan at the
Colchester museum, bears on the verso of the front flyleaf an ex-libris
inscription in red ink, partly erased: "Liber ... marie de ... s ..." Sir
Frederic Madden, to whom it formerly belonged, read the missing name as
Tavistock. An inscription on the flyleaf of the Cambridge MS. (Ii.4.6) reads:
"Hunc codicem cum altero consimili reperit R. Ferrers, servus comitis
Bedfordie, in domo quondam cenobio de Tavestock in devinshire, anno
1566." The "alter consimilis" was identified by Wanley (Antiquae Literaturae Septentrionalis Liber Alter, p. 208) with BM Cotton Vitellius C.v., a
manuscript which is known to have been the property of Francis, earl of
Bedford (Smith, Catalogus Bibliothecae Cottonianae, p. 85). According to
Mr Ker, it was written c. 1000 and added to with the greatest care not very
much later. But for the damage it sustained in the fire of 1731, it would rank
as one of the most important of all Ælfric manuscripts. The Cambridge
volume is undamaged. On the lower margin of f. 602 is the autograph
inscription: "frannscus Comes Bedfordie, 1566," below which is added in
another hand: "dedit Matthaeo Cantuar 29° Decemb. Anno 1567 in camera
stellata." On f. 608 Ferrers has repeated his inscription, adding, after
"cenobio", the word "monacharum", a slip of the pen for "monachorum",
which led Parker to believe that Tavistock had been a nunnery.

The possession of these two important manuscripts links Tavistock
directly with the vernacular literary movement in which Ælfric took a leading
part. Ælfric's patron Æthelweard attested the foundation charter of Tavistock;
he was then, and remained until his death c. 998, ealdorman of a province
which included Dorset, Somerset, Devon, and Cornwall, and he was probably a frequent visitor to the abbey. The compilation of the famous Exeter
Book of Old English poetry dates from this period. On palaeographical
evidence the Exeter Book is believed to have been written between 970 and
990 in a remote south-western monastery (so Flower argues in the facsimile
edition, pp. 83–90); and the possibility that this monastery may have been
Tavistock deserves consideration. The connecting link between the abbey
and bishop Leofric, who took the volume to Exeter, might well have been
Lyfing, sometime abbot of Tavistock and Leofric's predecessor in the see of
Crediton.

last. It is doubtful whether he had any other grounds for the statement.[1] But the educational work of the abbey certainly began soon after its foundation and continued in one form or another till the end. In the eleventh century parents dedicated their children to the monastic life at a very early age, and sent them to be brought up in the cloister. After 1215 the formal 'offering' of young children was condemned by ecclesiastical decree, but boys continued to be sent to the monastic school. They were welcomed there because of the need to encourage possible recruits and to provide clergy for the impropriated churches. Whenever the bishop came to Tavistock he conferred the tonsure on a number of local boys. Some of these went on to priestly orders, but many more appear later as burgesses, portreeves, and members of parliament.[2] An instance of the encouragement given to those who were minded to serve in the ranks of the parochial clergy occurs in the almoner's account for 1386, when Roger Wylle, subdeacon, received an allowance of £1 6s. "in aid of his studies", and a further six shillings for clothing. Ordained deacon in 1390, he was presented two years later by the abbot and convent to the vicarage of Milton Abbot.[3] In 1523 the convent appointed an organist at a salary of four pounds, with free board and lodging, to train half a dozen choirboys.

Bishop Brantyngham refers to the course of regular instruction imparted to the junior monks by one or more novice-masters.[4] Those who displayed an aptitude for higher studies might subsequently proceed to the university. In 1291 a general chapter of the English Benedictines, at which Robert Champeaux, abbot of Tavistock, was present, appointed a committee to draw up statutes for Gloucester College, recently founded at Oxford as a common house of studies for the order.[5] Thenceforth Tavistock

[1] Preface to Asser's *Annales Rerum Gestarum Ælfredi Magni*, p. xiv. Parker's statement was repeated by Camden and others, with the result that the refectory at Tavistock, then still almost intact, became known as "the Saxon school".

[2] *Reg. Stapeldon*, p. 494; *Reg. Brantyngham*, pp. 777, 797, 823, 864; *Reg. Stafford*, pp. 425–67.

[3] *Reg. Brantyngham*, pp. 117, 884, 888. The cost of maintaining a student at the university was then about seven pounds a year (Snape, *op. cit.*, p. 106).

[4] *Reg. Brantyngham*, p. 313.

[5] *General and Provincial Chapters of the English Black Monks*, ed. Pantin, I, p. 130.

regularly maintained one scholar there at the expense of the
house. Occasionally the practice was interrupted when funds
were low, as in 1423–26;[1] but in all probability a fair proportion
of the senior monks at any given date would have taken university
degrees in theology or canon law.[2]

In the eyes of the monks and their contemporaries the cease-
less round of prayer and sacrifice they kept up in their great
church fulfilled a threefold purpose. It glorified God, sanctified
the monks themselves, and brought many graces to the rest of
mankind, living and dead. At the same time it expressed a charity
too abundant to operate by prayer alone. The poor must be
clothed and fed; and every traveller who knocked at the door
must be given a ready welcome. In the early days it was a common
practice for laymen in their declining years to enter a monastery
so that they might receive skilled medical attention in the infirmary while they lived and be remembered in the prayers of the
brethren after their death. At Tavistock the community undertook a special responsibility for lepers. They built a leper hospital at the western end of the borough, where half a dozen
patients of both sexes were housed under the care of a resident
warden, variously styled the master or prior of the Maudlin. The
hospital lay under the general superintendence of the convent
almoner, who paid a weekly pension of twopence to each in-
mate.[3]

[1] General and Provincial Chapters, II, pp. 22, 150, 172.
[2] Of the last two abbots, Richard Banham was a doctor of canon law and
John Peryn a bachelor of divinity (W. D Bdle 53, nos. 92, 203). Thomas
Hamlyn, monk-steward in 1533, and subsequently abbot of Athelney, was a
bachelor of canon law (Oliver, p. 46). For the academical career of Thomas
Richard, the Tavistock master-printer, see Appendix D.
[3] The bishops of Exeter more than once recommended the Maudlin to the
charity of the faithful (Reg. Brantyngham, p. 346; Reg. Stafford, p. 346;
Reg. Lacy, p. 776), and the example of bishop Bytton, who remembered it in
his will, was followed by other testators (Accounts of the Executors of Thomas,
Bishop of Exeter, p. 28; Reg. Stafford, pp. 385, 419). The hospital was also
endowed with lands and rents (TPR, pp. 80, 84, 85; PRO Inquisitions ad
quod dammum, C143, File 259, no. 10). A lease by Ralph Cornish, prior in
1478, is expressed as being granted by leave and consent of the abbot and of
the convent almoner, "rector of the said hospital" (W. B Bdle 117, no. 26);
but there were occasional bids for recognition as an independent body. Thus
in 1244 the "master" brought an action of novel disseisin against the abbot,
but failed to pursue it (PRO Assize Roll, J.I. 1, 175, m. 11b); and in 1529 the
prior complained to the court of Star Chamber of forcible entry by the abbot's

The half-dozen almonry accounts which have survived all date from the last two decades of the fourteenth century. They show that no great sums were bestowed in casual alms: only 28s. 9d. in 1381 and 24s. in 1390, besides a few shillings to brief-bearers, the authorized mendicants who travelled round each year in Lent. Food and clothing, on the other hand, were given away much more freely. Bishop Brantyngham refers in his injunctions to the custom of handing cast-off clothing to the chamberlain for distribution to the poor. He had previously forbidden the monks to send bread, ale, meat, and fish into the town, except by the hand of their almoner, but in 1387 he modified his ruling so far as to permit food to be sent by any monk to his poor relations. This was one of the restrictions which the monks refused to accept.[1] The custom that prevailed was for four or five monks at a time to dispense hospitality and to receive an extra allowance of bread for the purpose. Besides these daily gifts, there were formal distributions at regular intervals. In 1291 abbot Champeaux assigned the income from West Liddaton to the almonry, to be spent on shoes and clothing for the poor. These gifts were to be handed out in the cloister each year on All Souls' Day (November 2); and on an earlier page we saw the almoner buying nearly three hundred yards of cloth for the occasion.[2] At the same time he gave two shillings in cash to the lepers and nine shillings to the poor, with bread to the value of 5s. 6d. A smaller distribution of bread and money took place on Maundy Thursday; and on St James's Day (July 25) the almoner gave a breakfast and alms in cash to poor people at Ottery. But the most notable occasions were the obits of the four original benefactors, Ordulf, Ælfwynn, Lyfing, and Eadwig. To theirs a fifth name, Robert Champeaux, was added after his death in 1324. On these anniversaries the great bell was tolled, wine was served to the monks at dinner, and eight bushels of wheaten flour were baked into bread for the poor.

The manorial accounts tell their own tale of charitable gifts. Three quarters of oats from the demesne of Leigh are distributed

---

messengers (PRO Star Chamber Proceedings, Bdle xxix, no. 157). The hospital survived the Dissolution, and in 1585 was taken under the control of the parish vestry (TPR, p. 92).

[1] *Reg. Brantyngham*, pp. 313, 669, 717, 719.
[2] Dugdale, ii, p. 498; p. 152 above.

to the poor every Lady Day, and Plymstock sends a quarter of wheat annually to the friars minor of Plymouth. Two poor boys are fed and clothed at the abbot's expense, one of them being afterwards employed as a shepherd at Hurdwick. A sick plough-man is paid half wages until he returns to work after an absence of fifteen weeks.

With so many social obligations imposed upon them by the rule and spirit of their order, the monks can hardly be said to have turned their backs upon the world. Theirs was indeed a complex, busy, and expensive way of life. In the opening chapter an account was given of the churches and manors with which their benefactors had endowed them. Here we must note that each new benefaction automatically extended the range of liabilities. On every manor there were farm buildings and a court-house to be kept in repair; in every impropriated parish a church to be main-tained and staffed. Sometimes the monks were said to hold their endowments "in free and pure alms",[1] but this was never entirely true, and it became less and less so as time went on. Landowner-ship could not be divorced from secular obligations. Even in the Old English period the abbot was held responsible for seeing that his tenants contributed to the cost of bridges and fortifications and furnished their quota to the army in time of war. After the Norman Conquest the state multiplied its demands a hundred-fold.

We have seen how William I imposed on Tavistock a crushing burden of knight service. It was as if one of the least wealthy col-leges at Oxford or Cambridge to-day were ordered to find the whole pay of fifteen cavalrymen in perpetuity. In effect it cost the abbot over a dozen manors. But the mischief did not end there. As a system of national defence knight service broke down in the very hands of its author. Confronted in 1085 with a serious threat of invasion from Denmark, William found himself obliged to hire troops in large numbers from the continent and to billet them on his tenants in chief. His successors also employed mercenaries whenever they saw fit. Hence the commutation of service in the field for scutage. To ensure against defaults when active service was required, the tenant in chief endowed one or more super-numerary knights. If the king preferred to levy scutage, the ten-

[1] FA, pp. 402, 404, 451, 456.

ant in chief, assisted when necessary by the sheriff,[1] collected the money from all his knights, but paid into the Exchequer only so much as was due from his recognized quota. This arrangement enabled him not only to recover his expenses as a collector of war-tax, but even to make a profit; and in 1166 Henry II determined to bring it to an end. He required all his tenants in chief to state how many knights they had enfeoffed before 1135 and how many since. Abbot Walter of Tavistock replied that his "poor little house" had enfeoffed sixteen, one more than its quota, before that date, and that under Stephen's reign one and a half more knights' fees had been extorted from his predecessors.[2] By giving this information he exposed himself to the full rigour of the new policy. Hitherto he had been treated as liable only for the recognized fifteen fees;[3] but in 1168 he was charged with the full sixteen "of old feoffment". The other tenants in chief, both ecclesiastical and lay, were similarly charged, but the laymen were also debited with their fees "of new feoffment", and by a singular exception the abbot of Tavistock was treated in this respect as if he had been a lay baron.[4] He withheld payment on the sixteenth fee until the following year, and the debt on the new fees had to be carried forward until Walter and his successor were both dead.[5] In 1174 abbot Baldwin repudiated liability for more than fifteen, quoting Henry I's charter in support of his contention,[6] but two years later he gave way so far as the new fees were concerned,[7] and in 1180 he paid on the sixteenth fee of old feoffment.[8] No further scutage was levied until 1187, when the Crown abandoned the attempt to bring fees of new feoffment under contribution. Thereafter the abbots accepted sixteen fees as the standard assessment, though Baldwin's protest was renewed by his successor in the reign of John.[9]

---

[1] 1217: order to the sheriff of Devon to help the abbot of Tavistock distrain on his military tenants for scutage (*Rotuli Litterarum Clausarum* I, p. 373*b*).

[2] *Red Book of the Exchequer*, p. 250.

[3] PRS IV, p. 29; V, pp. 5, 6; *Red Book*, pp. 25, 30, 698.

[4] PRS XII, p. 128; *Red Book*, p. 43.

[5] PRS XIII, p. 50; XV, p. 99; XVI, p. 26; XVIII, pp. 100, 102; XIX, pp. 145, 147; XXI, p. 91; XXII, p. 60.

[6] Above, p. 12; PRS XXI, p. 93.   [7] *Ibid.*, XXV, p. 142.

[8] *Ibid.*, XXVI, p. 3; XXVII, p. 12; XXVIII, p. 11; XXIX, p. 90.

[9] *Ibid.*, XXXVII, p. 146; XLIII (N.S. V.), p. 171; LII (N.S. XIV), p. 223; LIX (N.S. XXI), p. 75.

From time to time a contingent of the Tavistock knights was
called up for active service, as in 1223, when some of them
fought in the Welsh expedition,[1] and the following year, when
they took part in the siege of Plympton Castle.[2] Meanwhile the
practice, begun by abbot Baldwin, of creating small freeholds to
be held by military service, was continued by his successors, particularly abbot Jordan. The tenant undertook to pay his share of
any scutage that might be levied; and as a rule the abbot, not
content with the casual profits of feudal overlordship, stipulated
also for a small yearly rent. The subdivision of knights' fees into
peasant holdings removed the system one stage further from the
realities of war. During the thirteenth century campaigns leng-
thened, equipment became more costly, and rates of pay went up.
Towards the close of Henry III's reign, therefore, a new principle was introduced. At the beginning of a campaign the tenant
in chief either proffered service from a reduced number of fees or
paid a fine at a rate previously determined by the Crown. In the
case of Tavistock the number of fees was reduced, for all purposes except that of scutage, from sixteen to one.[3]

In November 1276 nineteen abbots were summoned to provide service for an expedition against Llewellyn of Wales, but the
abbot of Tavistock was not among them,[4] and consequently he
neither sent his knights to the muster nor offered a fine instead.
Some two years later writs were issued for a retrospective collection of scutage, at the rate of two pounds the fee, and the abbot at
once paid on all sixteen fees.[5] In 1282 he proffered a fine of fifty
marks (£33 6s. 8d.) on one fee for another Welsh campaign,[6] subsequently procuring the order which entitled him to reimburse
himself by collecting scutage from his undertenants.[7] King
Edward lost nothing by this transaction; nevertheless, while
accepting the fine he demanded scutage as well, thus in effect
asking to be paid twice over; and in 1292 abbot Champeaux was

[1] Chew, *The English Ecclesiastical Tenants-in-Chief and Knight Service*,
p. 52.
[2] *Rotuli Litterarum Clausarum*, II, p.16.
[3] Chew, *op. cit.*, p. 32; *Parliamentary Writs*, I, pp. 228, 235.
[4] *Ibid.*, I, p. 196.   [5] Chew, *op. cit.*, p. 61.
[6] PRO Exch. L.T.R. Misc. Roll, E 375, Bdle 1, no. 13.
[7] An interval of three years elapsed before he obtained this order (*Calendar of Chancery Rolls, Various*, p. 367).

Q

subjected to a prosecution in the court of Exchequer. Because his predecessor had offered neither men nor money for the first Welsh campaign he was fined five marks, though custom decreed that without a summons no liability arose. A further charge was brought: namely, that in fining for his service in 1282 his predecessor had paid on one fee only, instead of on the full sixteen; but the abbot replied that this accorded with the precedent established in Henry III's reign, and he was therefore acquitted on this count. As for the second Welsh scutage, it continued to be charged against him in the Pipe Roll until his death, when it was written off as a bad debt.[1]

The practice of fining, varied by occasional service in the field, was continued during the Scottish war;[2] but the feudal host assembled for the last time in 1385. Thereafter knight service, though obsolete for all military purposes, survived as a mode of land tenure, with its odious concomitants of reliefs, wardships, and compulsory marriages, a running sore in the body politic, not finally removed until 1661. As fines and scutage receded into the background the government intensified its demands for subsidies and war-loans. In vain had Boniface VIII sought to end the scandal of war between Christian princes financed, more or less reluctantly, by the clergy on both sides. When the English churchmen, following Boniface's lead, refused to subsidize Edward I's continental war, he seized all their lay fees, those of Tavistock among the rest, and kept them until they gave way.[3] Thereafter neither Edward nor his successors encountered any serious ecclesiastical resistance to their bellicose enterprises. From time to time the abbot of Tavistock was called upon to act as a recruiting officer, as in 1322, when troops were needed for service against Thomas of Lancaster, and two years later for the defence of Aquitaine.[4] In the course of the Hundred Years' War

[1] Chew, *op. cit.*, pp. 61, 67, and 'Scutage under Edward I', EHR xxxvii, 1922, p. 331.
[2] The abbot gave service in 1303. He fined in 1290 and 1306 (*Cal. Chancery Rolls, Various*, pp. 374, 378, 387).
[3] 4 April 1297; order to the sheriff of Devon and Cornwall to deliver without delay to the abbot of Tavistock all his lay fees, with the goods and chattels found therein, which the sheriff took into the king's hand by virtue of the king's order to take into his hands all the lay fees of all the clergy (*ibid.*, p. 43).
[4] *Parliamentary Writs*, ii, part i, pp. 550, 664.

the government more than once ordered him to arm his tenants and station them in the neighbourhood of Plymouth to guard the coast against invasion.[1] By profession a man of peace, he was obliged to keep a store of arms, and the cost of furbishing the weapons in his armoury was one of the regular charges the monk-steward of the abbey had to meet.

By the introduction of knight service William I had transformed the abbot into a feudal baron. His successor introduced the theory of the vacant fief.[2] On the pretext that when the abbot died there was no one to discharge his feudal obligations, the king took the barony into his own hand until a new abbot was appointed. The longer the appointment could be postponed, the greater the profit to the royal Exchequer. After the death of abbot Baldwin in 1184 the abbacy remained void for some twenty months. During that time the custodians appointed by Henry II collected £103 14s. 8d. and disbursed £66 0s. 5d. in overhead expenses. The net profit to the Crown was thus £37 14s. 3d., over a third of the total income.[3] From a vacancy of three months in 1248 the Crown reaped one hundred marks.[4] Nine years later the abbey succeeded in limiting this liability. In return for payment of a sum agreed beforehand the monks were allowed to keep the property in their own hands during vacancies. The sum was raised in 1261 from twenty pounds to £33 6s. 8d.[5] Even these limited payments constituted a serious drain on the income of the house when vacancies occurred in rapid succession, as they did just at this time.[6] Finally in 1315 abbot Champeaux celebrated the thirtieth anniversary of his appointment by paying a hundred marks for a royal charter whereby custody of the existing temporalities was granted to the monks for all future voidances. The Crown was to be paid forty pounds for each vacancy of four months or less, and, if the vacancy should last longer, a further proportionate sum calculated at the rate of one hundred marks a year.[7]

From this grant of custody certain exceptions were made. The Crown did not relax its claim to feudal windfalls and ecclesiastical patronage. If a tenant holding by knight service died while

[1] CCR 1374–7, p. 497; 1381–5, p. 270; CPR 1401–5, p. 353.
[2] Knowles, *op. cit.*, p. 613.   [3] PRS xxxiv, p. 204; xxxvi, pp. xxii, 204.
[4] CPR 1247–58, p. 22.
[5] *Ibid.*, p. 560; 1258–66, pp. 22, 87, 219; CCR 1259–61, pp. 294, 447.
[6] *Ibid.*, 1261–4, p. 132.   [7] CFR 1307–19, p. 246.

the abbacy was vacant, his estate fell into the king's wardship.[1] If the vicar of an impropriated church died or resigned, the king nominated one of his own clerks to fill the place.[2] But if no benefice was available just then, the abbey had to pay the royal clerk a yearly pension until such time as they could themselves present him to one of their parish churches;[3] or the king might exercise the right of presentation the next time a benefice fell vacant, in some cases years after the new abbot had been elected.[4] Fitful attempts by the Church to prohibit clerks in holy orders from holding secular posts all came to nothing, for why should the government staff the civil service with laymen when by employing clerics it could pay them at the Church's expense? For the army, indeed, and for menial posts in the royal household laymen were indispensable; but here too the Church could be, and was, laid under contribution. From 1300 onwards there was always a retired servant of the Crown living at Tavistock: it might be some battered veteran of the French or Scottish wars, or a groom of the king's chamber, or even—a more welcome guest perhaps— the royal cook, sent down to receive free board and lodging in the abbey, with pocket money, until the end of his days.[5]

When a newly elected abbot did homage for his temporalities, he gave a palfrey to the earl-marshal.[6] There were other occasions on which high officials claimed their perquisites. The sheriff of Devon was entitled to an annual due known as Sheriff's Aid. This

---

[1] 8 November 1365: grant to John de Cary of the wardship of the lands which John de Brounford held by knight service of Tavistock Abbey on the day of his death in the time when the abbacy was void, not exceeding the value of five marks yearly, with the marriage of Nicholas, son and heir of the said John (CPR 1364–7, p. 185).

[2] 1224, Hatherleigh (CPR 1216–25, p. 435); 1270, Lamerton (CPR 1266–72, p. 420); 1447, Antony (CPR 1446–52, p. 54).

[3] CCR 1333–7, pp. 303, 310; CCR 1377–81, p. 501; CCR 1399–1402, p. 586.

[4] 1368, Milton Abbot (CPR 1367–70, p. 161); 1385, Burrington (CPR 1385–9, p. 10; Reg. Brantyngham, p. 94); 1398, Whitchurch (CPR 1396–9, p. 337; Reg. Stafford, p. 220), seventeen years after the last vacancy.

[5] Cal. Chancery Warrants, p. 115; CCR 1307–13, pp. 434, 444; 1313–18, p. 447; 1360–4, p. 258; 1392–6, p. 476; 1396–9, p. 61; 1402–5, p. 116; 1413–19, p. 202; 1422–9, p. 328; 1429–35, p. 114; L. & P. Hen. VIII, I, pt ii, p. 1429, §3408, no. 11; ibid., II, pt ii, p. 1223, §3929; ibid., IV, p. 1232, §2761, no. 15.

[6] W. D Bdle 84, no. 53.

was the payment which Henry II, at the council of Woodstock, proposed to divert into the royal treasury, leaving the sheriffs to find some less regular source of income: a plan which foundered on the opposition of the primate, Thomas Becket. It was levied at varying rates, and not all manors appear to have paid. On the Tavistock estates it occurs at Abbotsham, where it amounted to 7s. 9d., and at Hurdwick, where the tenants paid usually but not invariably at the rate of a halfpenny a ferling.[1]

In his baronial capacity the abbot had a place in the great council of the realm. Like the bishops, he was affected by the Conqueror's ruling that all prelates and magnates should be present thrice a year when the king wore his crown; and a charter drawn up on one such occasion was attested by Sihtric of Tavistock with other abbots.[2] The obligation, however, was a burdensome one, and the distance of Tavistock from the seat of government provided a ready excuse for evading it. In 1265 abbot Chubb was one of the exceptionally large number of heads of houses summoned to parliament at the instance of Simon de Montfort;[3] and abbot Champeaux received a writ of summons from Edward I in 1302.[4] Such writs were sent to the bishops and greater abbots as a matter of course. By the time of Edward II these prelates, with the more considerable lay barons and the earls, were beginning to regard the parliamentary summons as their right and to call themselves peers of the realm. For the rest of the clergy it was more convenient to deal with royal demands for money in their provincial synod or convocation. The abbot of Tavistock was invariably summoned to the convocation of Canterbury, and in 1332 a note was made that he was not one of the heads of houses who usually received a parliamentary writ.[5] So matters rested until 1514, when Henry VIII, who two years previously had created the abbot of Tewkesbury a peer of parliament, conferred the same dignity on abbot Banham of Tavistock, at the same time permitting him and his successors to compound

[1] *Valor Ecclesiasticus*, II, pp. 381, 384; W. D Bdle 84, no. 72.
[2] Davis, *Regesta Regum Anglo-Normannorum*, p. 6, no. 22.
[3] CCR 1264–8, p. 86.
[4] *Reports from the Lords' Committees touching the dignity of a Peer of the Realm*, III, pp. 144, 147, 150.
[5] *Ibid.*, IV, p. 409. Nevertheless he was summoned in 1349 (pp. 579, 582, 584).

for non-attendance by a payment of five marks for each parliament.[1]

From time to time the abbot of Tavistock was called upon to serve as a collector of subsidies.[2] The clergy might claim to be immune from secular taxation, but they could always be pressed for a gift or loan.[3] In 1294 Edward I went so far as to demand a moiety of their whole revenue. From the close of the thirteenth century until 1535 the basis of assessment was a valuation made in 1292 under the authority of Pope Nicholas IV, when the temporalities of Tavistock Abbey were estimated to yield an average net income of £72 10s. a year.[4] Some of the properties were heavily undervalued. For example, while £6 4s. was a reasonable figure for the borough of Tavistock, it is difficult to see how Werrington could be assessed at only £11 15s.

Compared with the demands of the secular power, those of the Church were not excessive. Heavy occasional taxes were indeed imposed on the clergy by papal authority, but nine-tenths of the proceeds went to the Crown.[5] The bishop of Exeter, in return for his assent to the impropriation of parish churches, required to be paid a yearly fee, amounting in 1535 to £3 6s. 8d.[6] The Benedictine order levied a triennial income tax at varying rates to defray the expenses of its general and provincial chapters. In 1414–17, when the rate was a halfpenny in the mark, the payment from

---

[1] L. & P. *Henry VIII*, II, pt ii, p. 1146, §2617, no. 27. Coke held that only a baron, or one holding land in barony, could be created a lord of parliament; and believing erroneously that the abbot of Tavistock lacked this qualification, he opined that Henry's grant was invalid (*Institutes of the Laws of England*, IV, p. 45).

[2] E.g. in 1294 (CPR 1292–1301, pp. 89, 173), 1384 (*Reg. Brantyngham*, p. 160), and 1440 (*Reg. Lacy*, p. 769).

[3] 1310, loan for the Scottish expedition (CCR 1307–13, p. 263); 1319, loan of four hundred pounds requested for the summer campaign against the Scottish rebels (CCR 1318–23, p. 59); 1332, subsidy requested for the marriage of the king's sister (CCR 1330–3, p. 592); 1347, loan of wool in aid of the war with France (CCR 1346–9, p. 269); 1415, loan of one hundred marks on the security of a silver-gilt tabernacle lately belonging to the duke of Burgundy (CPR 1413–16, p. 354).

[4] *Taxatio Ecclesiastica*, p. 153.

[5] "Of the total yield of tenths paid by the clergy of England and Wales at the papal order during the reign of Edward II the king received nearly 92 per cent. and the papacy eight." (Professor Lunt, quoted by Powicke, *The Reformation in England*, p. 12 n.)

[6] *Valor Ecclesiasticus*, II, p. 289.

Tavistock amounted to thirty-nine shillings, indicating an
assessed income of £208 for the three years, or £69 6s. 8d. a year,
which agrees closely enough with the valuation of Nicholas IV.
By 1492 it had gone up to 56s. 9d. at a penny in the mark on
£151 6s. 8d. a year.[1] To the central administration of the Church
the abbey contributed a small annual payment called procurations, intended to meet the expenses of the papal representatives.[2]
The ancient papal tax called Peter's Pence amounted to no more
than £9 5s. a year from the whole diocese of Exeter.[3] Towards
this Denbury contributed three farthings and the other Tavistock
parishes nothing at all. Finally, there was the *census* due to Rome
in token of immediate dependence on the papacy. The sum was
fixed at three *aurei*, equivalent to six shillings,[4] by Celestine III,
who in 1193 took the abbey and all its possessions under the
special protection of the Roman see, at the same time declaring it
wholly exempt from diocesan jurisdiction.[5] For some reason at
which we can only guess—it may have been royal opposition—
the abbey discontinued this payment at a very early date, or perhaps never made it at all, and therefore was not enrolled in the
official Roman list of *census*-paying monasteries.[6] The consequence was that its exemption lapsed.[7] From time to time an
abbot smarting under some particularly outrageous piece of episcopal tyranny would dwell wistfully on the memory of a lost

[1] *Chapters of the English Black Monks*, III, pp. 174, 178, 193.
[2] W. D Bdle 84, no. 71 (receipts from the collectors of procurations,
1331–1527). This payment often fell into arrears, as in 1373 (*Reg. Brantyngham*, p. 298), 1408–10 (*Reg. Stafford*, p. 346), and 1421 (*Reg. Lacy*, p. 440).
[3] *Reg. Grandisson*, pp. 360, 556.
[4] Lunt, *Financial Relations of the Papacy with England*, p. 640.
[5] Dugdale, II, p. 498; Oliver, p. 95.   [6] Lunt, *op. cit.*, pp. 110, 123.
[7] In 1261 Boniface, archbishop of Canterbury, carried out a visitation of
the abbey by his deputies (*Reg. Bronescombe*, p. 42), and eight years later
bishop Bronescombe assumed the right to depose abbot Chubb. Succeeding
bishops of Exeter regularly visited the abbey down to 1505. Professor Lunt
(*op. cit.*, pp. 109, 110) is therefore mistaken in believing that the exemption
was maintained until 1514. He is under the impression that the abbots had
their elections confirmed by the pope, but the only instance he adduces is the
wholly exceptional one of abbot Bonus, who was not elected at all, but
directly appointed by Pope John XXII. When Bonus appealed against the
fine imposed upon him by the English government, the precedents he cited
referred not to his predecessors, as Professor Lunt supposes, but to the
abbots of other monasteries who had been appointed in the same way
(PRO Ancient Petitions, no. 11954; CCR 1330–3, p. 14).

independence;[1] but no steps were taken until 1517, when abbot Banham, after an embittered contest with bishop Oldham, procured from Leo X a bull of complete exemption, subject to an annual payment of twenty shillings to the papal exchequer.[2]

II. THE ADMINISTRATIVE STAFF

From the foregoing recital it will be evident that the points of contact between the monastery and the outside world were very numerous. The duty of preventing such contacts from shattering the peace of the cloister lay primarily with the abbot. It was to him, as representative and head of the community, that Church and State addressed their calls. His office required long training as well as natural ability. Nearly always he had graduated through a series of lesser posts. Thus, to take one example from each of three centuries, Richard Ash, ordained deacon in 1321, and strongly recommended by bishop Grandisson for the office of *salsarius* in 1329, became precentor and sacristan in 1338, prior ten years later, and abbot in 1349; Thomas Crispyn, steward in 1429, was prior at the time of his election in 1442; and John Peryn, the abbot of the Dissolution, had been first cellarer, then steward.

From the twelfth century onwards each of the higher officials possessed an income of his own. Town rents to the value of £2 15s. 4d. were settled on the prior, or second in command, who however derived the greater part of his income from Abbotsham. The sacristan—or sexton, to give him his vernacular name—was endowed with burgage rents and land at Parswell, Kilworthy, and Indescombe. His revenue from these sources amounted in 1414 to £7 16s. 3½d., but he was also entitled to parish offerings and he probably had a share in the impropriated churches. Upon him rested the care of the abbey church and cemetery. The precentor looked after the library and choir; to him were assigned a couple of mills and the greater part of Taviton. A surviving account, which dates from the troubled epoch following the death of John of Gaunt, shows him in receipt of an income of £3 2s. 10d., out of which he spent 8s. 6d. on packing materials for removing

---

[1] Abbot Bonus did so in 1328, after receiving a series of contradictory mandates from bishop Grandisson, alternately enjoining and prohibiting the admission of novices (DCNQ XXII, 1946, pp. 343, 344).

[2] Oliver, p. 103.

precious manuscripts to a place of rural safety. A field on the left
bank of the Fishlake known as Sellars Close commemorates the
cellarer, who was in charge of the catering department. His average expenditure on the eve of the Dissolution was 32s. 4d. weekly.[1]
He was assisted by a garnerer (*granarius*) responsible for the supply of corn, and a *salsarius*, or purveyor of salted meat and fish.
The administrative prominence assumed by the *salsarius* at Tavistock was due to the fact that he served also as *medarius*, or purveyor of mead and other drinks, thus assuaging in one capacity
the thirst he provoked with his salted victuals in the other. He was
endowed with land at Newton and part of the Brentor sheaf-tithe.
Ottery, Ogbear, and West Liddaton belonged to the almoner,
with all the tithe-corn and tithe-hay from Ottery, and six 'hoops'
of beans for distribution to the poor in winter. Lastly there was an
officer variously known as steward of the abbot's lodging, receiver of the lord's rents, and steward of the abbey. His post may
have been created at the instance of bishop Grandisson, who in
1338 prescribed the appointment of a receiver-general to collect,
distribute, and conserve the rents and other income of the house.[2]
Thirty-five years later bishop Brantyngham instructed the abbot
to depute the administration of the temporalities to a committee
of three, namely, the steward, the cellarer, and the receiver-
general.[3] It seems that the first and third of these posts were subsequently amalgamated. In 1429 the steward accounted for the
following expenditure:

	£	s.	d.
Rent of Calstock fishery	10	0	0
Repairs to buildings	12	17	9
Servants' wages	22	4	8½
Ale purchased	30	6	9
Board allowance of monks	31	14	8
Personal allowances of monks and vicar of Tavistock	24	13	4½
Haymaking in the abbey meadow		10	2
Shoeing horses	2	0	9¼
Sundries	2	10	5
	£136	18	7¼

---

[1] Finberg, 'A Cellarer's Account Book', DCNQ XXIII, 1948, p. 253.
[2] *Reg. Grandisson*, p. 889. [3] *Reg. Brantyngham*, p. 314.

On the credit side he showed an income of £134 3s. 6¾d., derived from rents, the sale of corn-tithes, and parish offerings. It seems clear that he dealt with the non-manorial portion of the abbot's revenue, and had nothing to do with the income and expenses of the various departments. In 1535 the revenue of the prior and convent was returned as follows:

	£	s.	d.
Temporalities	33	1	1½
Spiritualities	27	5	4
	£60	6	5½

This represented 6⅔ per cent. of the total income.[1] All the rest was paid to the abbot and administered by him through local officials or the monk-steward. The functions of the monk-steward were thus entirely different from those of the lay stewards, five of whom were enumerated, with their yearly fees, in the valuation of 1535, as follows:

	£	s.	d.
The High Steward of the Abbey	3	6	8
The High Steward of the Liberties and Franchises of Tavistock[2]	3	0	0
The High Steward of Cowick	1	0	0
The Steward of Cornwood		13	4
The Steward of Abbotsham, Roborough, and Newton	1	0	0

Their duty was to preside over the manor and borough courts: a task requiring professional knowledge of the law. Thomas Reymond, who served as high steward of the abbey for several years before his death in 1418, was also recorder of Exeter from 1383, escheator of Devon in 1401, and six times a member of parliament.[3]

---

[1] *Valor Ecclesiasticus*, II, p. 384. In his *English Monasteries on the Eve of the Dissolution*, p. 272, Savine assigns the income of the prior and convent to an imaginary house of Augustinian hermit-friars. His figures for Tavistock Abbey are consequently worthless (DCNQ xxi, 1941, p. 348).

[2] i.e., the borough.

[3] He was elected M.P. for Barnstaple 1372, Tavistock, Dartmouth, and Barnstaple 1377, Plympton 1381, Exeter 1382, Tavistock 1384, and Exeter 1388 (DA lxxi, 1939, p. 155).

Next in importance to the stewards came the lay auditor. Incidental references in the account rolls allow us to see this officer going to Plymstock to draw up a new rental, or to Werrington to inspect the husbandry of the demesne; and it is clear that besides controlling the system of account he took an active part in estate management. In 1535 he was paid three pounds as auditor-general and one pound as auditor of Cowick. From time to time we hear of a surveyor (*supervisor*) of particular manors, who seems to have been usually a neighbouring landowner. He attended on law-days, kept an eye on the business of the manor, and was repaid any expenses he incurred in so doing. It is probable that the lay stewards, the auditors, and one or two of the senior monks, assisted on occasion by these representatives of the local gentry, constituted the abbot's council, a body to whose existence the documents make several passing allusions, without throwing any light on its work.

The lowest grade of the administrative staff consisted of the petty officers appointed locally for each manor. Generically they were known as bailiffs, a term which in its widest connotation included rent-collectors, beadles, grangers, reeves, and sergeants.[1] The rent-collector, sometimes called the gather-reeve, requires no definition. The beadle's task was to collect the *perquisita curie*, or revenue from the lord's courts. The granger conducted the operations of threshing and winnowing and accounted for supplies of grain. In the performance of these duties they were supervised by the reeve, who directed the husbandry of the demesne and yearly at Michaelmas rendered an account for the whole manor. All these were servile offices; as a rule they were filled by bondmen nominated by the jury of the manor court and sworn in by the steward. During their term of office the reeve and beadle paid no rent, and were excused from labour service; they might even be rewarded with gifts of cash or grain; but essentially their work was done as a form of the service due from bondmen to their lord. In this respect they differed from the sergeant (*serviens*), who was appointed directly by the lord and paid a regular salary to act as his local agent. With the gradual decay of servile obligation, the sergeant's responsibilities increased; he

---

[1] A Werrington account roll (1454) refers to the "redditus ballivorum, videlicet prepositi et ij bidellorum."

became known as the bailiff *par excellence*, and in some places by the end of the fourteenth century had virtually superseded the reeve.

In 1535 the salaries and wages of the administrative staff amounted in all to £29 4s. 6d., or approximately three per cent. of the total income.

III. THE EXPLOITATION OF ASSETS

Turning from this necessarily rapid sketch of organization and expenses to review the assets, we may pass over jurisdiction and its proceeds, which have been discussed in the preceding chapter. Nor is there much that need be added here to what has already been said concerning the spiritualities. As a rule parish glebes were converted into peasant holdings. For example, Thele, which in 1190 belonged to the abbot and convent as impropriators of Lamerton church, was occupied in 1387 by a tenant in free socage who rendered twelve pence yearly on St Rumon's Day for all service.[1] In this way it became indistinguishable from the surrounding freeholds. Tithes of stock were sold, or killed and eaten, or added to the manorial flocks and herds; the tithe of hay, at Werrington and possibly elsewhere, was converted into a rent-charge by the close of the thirteenth century; tithes of corn were usually sold on the ground. A series of episcopal decrees regulated the proportion of parish income that should go to the vicar. From time to time a storm would blow up, as when certain nameless "sons of iniquity" tried to prevent the parishioners of Tavistock from offering more than a penny at burials,[2] or a vicar of Burrington sought to evade liability for repairing the chancel;[3] but on the whole the administration of the spiritualities proceeded uneventfully.

Just as the rector drew part of his income in the form of tithe, a direct levy on the fruits of husbandry, so the lord of the manor might subsist partly on food-rents. One example of such a rent occurs in the Tavistock Domesday: we read there of four swine-

---

[1] Similarly at Stokenham in 1309 there were four free tenants called Parson's Men, holding between them two ferlings of land, evidently glebe, for which they paid a yearly rent, aid, and boonwork (DCNQ xxiv, 1950, p. 69).

[2] *Reg. Brantyngham*, p. 481.   [3] *Reg. Stafford*, p. 45.

herds at Burrington who render forty swine a year. Nothing is said in Domesday Book of any payment in kind from Plymstock, but in the last decade of the fourteenth century the tenants there paid food-rents amounting to more than seventy quarters of wheat a year, and five pounds of bees-wax, while the cash rents were only £2 11s. 4d. It will be remembered that when the abbot founded a borough at Tavistock, he reserved the right to send one or other of the original householders with a message to Plymstock whenever he wished to call up a supply of corn. Since the pre-eminent aptitude of the Plymstock soil for wheat-growing was thus recognized as far back as the twelfth century, it may be that the wheat-rents were more ancient still, and that the Plymstock husbandmen were paying them to the Old English royal house long before one of its members gave the manor to Tavistock Abbey. Rents in kind are obviously consistent with a primitive economy, but this one long outlasted the conditions of its origin. From 73 qrs 7 bus. in 1392 it rose by gradual slight increases to 79 qrs 5 bus., valued at £26 10s. 10d., in 1535, when the cash rents came to no more than £12 9s. 3d.; and it survived the Dissolution by half a century or more.[1]

If the Domesday returns could be taken literally, one would infer that in 1086 the abbey was keeping some livestock and growing a certain amount of corn on every one of its demesne manors. But in some cases the record may conceal an arrangement very generally adopted by monastic houses at the time. Under this plan whole manors were farmed out at a fixed annual rent. The *firmarius*, or farmer, ran the estate for his own profit, but undertook to leave the land and buildings in as good a state as he found them. The agreement was often made for the term of the farmer's life. It delivered the owners from the cares of management, and secured them an income, lower indeed than the

---

[1] In 1586 there were thirty-eight customary tenants on this manor. The average size of their holdings was fifteen to sixteen acres. One tenant paid two shillings for a house and half an acre. All the others paid a wheat-rent varying from one to forty bushels, and fifteen of them a cash rent in addition. The holder of two tenements and eighty acres of land paid £3 6s. 8d.; the other cash rents varied between one penny and two shillings. There were also fifty customary tenants of cottages newly erected, paying money only, usually one shilling each; and two tenants by indenture. The total income was £14 5s. 8½d., and 79 qrs 6 bus. of wheat.

value of the property, but measurable in advance and easy to collect.[1] In the twelfth century the monks of Tavistock farmed out the manor of Abbotsham in this way, as well as the three parochial benefices of the Sheviock fief, and perhaps other properties besides.[2] On the other hand, since agricultural expenses figure among the items of the account rendered by the custodians of the abbey in 1186, we may infer that some at least of the nearer demesnes were kept in hand. With the rise in prices that took place in the thirteenth century fixed incomes became a disadvantage, and the system of lifelong farms had to be modified. One expedient, which seems to have been adopted at Tavistock as at other monasteries, was to appoint monks of the house as *firmarii*. This plan should have secured for the abbey the profits which had formerly accrued to the outside farmers; but bishop Grandisson considered it unsatisfactory, and his successor forbade it altogether.[3] By the end of the fourteenth century the monk-farmers were transformed into monk-wardens, charged with a general superintendence of their particular manors; and these in turn were superseded by lay surveyors. Meanwhile a number of the outlying demesnes were being leased out either in parcels or entire. In 1302 the abbey granted all its property in Monk Okehampton to a tenant for life.[4] As a rule, however, leases were given for a term of years. Butworthy, the demesne of Cudlipptown, was leased for twenty years in 1301, and Burnshall, the barton of West Liddaton, for thirty years from 1317 to a tenant whose father had been holding it at will.[5] There is no indication that the demesnes of Abbotsham, Roborough, and Plymstock were ever taken in hand again, though the garden of the Plymstock court-house yielded a small revenue from sales of herbage. By the close of the fourteenth century the income from these manors and from Hatherleigh consisted almost exclusively of rents and the profits of jurisdiction. During the time covered by

---

[1] Knowles, *op. cit.*, p. 442.   [2] ETC xv, xxix.

[3] "Obedienciarum Officia et bona ad ea spectancia, que a longis, ut audivimus, retroactis temporibus, sub certis prestacionibus annuis fuerunt monachis nonnullis dicti monasterii, licet ad ampliores sufficerent, dimissa. . ." —*Reg. Grandisson*, p. 886. "Item statuimus et ordinamus quod nullus locus aut possessio per abbatem alicui de monachis suis tradatur ad firmam."— *Reg. Brantyngham*, p. 670.

[4] W. G Bdle 5, no. 19.   [5] *Ibid.*, D Bdle 53, nos. 16 and 223.

the extant records the maximum number of demesnes kept in hand appears to have been nine.[1]

If the monks wished to examine the financial results of their husbandry in any given year, they would consult, not the manorial *compotus* roll, which blended in one account the separate returns of three or four officials, but the docket of the particular official who managed the demesne in their behalf.[2] Sometimes this would be the hayward, sometimes the monk-warden, but normally it was the reeve or bailiff. Unfortunately very few of these purely agricultural returns have survived. It is, however, possible to construct a picture of the demesne husbandry in its financial aspect by abstracting the relevant items from the *compoti*. This has been done in Table XXVI (pp. 244 sqq.); but it must again be emphasized that the result is not strictly a profit-and-loss account.

It will be observed that while thirty-three accounts declare a favourable cash balance, as many as thirty-one show a deficit. A cash deficit, however, does not necessarily mean that the abbey was farming at a loss. To arrive at a true statement of profit and loss, we should have to take into account the produce consumed by the monks and by the household staff, as well as that given away to outsiders. Unfortunately, while the quantities thus disposed of may be stated in the *compoti*, the value at current market rates is not. We have therefore no means of estimating the value by reference to current prices. Nor are we ever told exactly how much of the produce delivered to the lord is used to feed the demesne staff. Again, when produce is given away, we very often have no clue whatever to its destination. The *compotus* will tell us that a bushel of wheat has been delivered to AB; but is AB an employee taking some of his pay in kind, or a poor man receiving alms, or a friend to whom the abbot is making a present? What is clear is that the true profit is often greater, and the true loss often less, than appears from the cash account. Indeed, the value of the

---

[1] Hurdwick, Morwell, Ottery, Week, Leigh, Milton, Werrington, Denbury, and Burrington.

[2] At Hurdwick this docket was called the *Onus Ballivi*. At Werrington, where grain sales were never included in the *compotus*, it would have been necessary to examine the granger's account as well as the bailiff's docket. For the method of estimating wainage, or the profits of agriculture, practised in Norfolk and elsewhere, see Denholm-Young, *op. cit.*, pp. 128 sqq.

TABLE XXVI

The third column gives the *Vadia Famulorum*, or wages of the permanent staff (bailiff, ploughmen, ploughboys, and shepherds). It does not represent the total cost of labour. The pay of the dairywoman and her assistants, as well as those of the thatcher, the sandman, and piece-workers, are entered under various other headings in the *compoti*. These and all other agricultural expenses declared as such, including repairs to ploughs, carts, and buildings,

Year	Manor	Wages			Other Expenses			Total Expenses		
		£	s.	d.	£	s.	d.	£	s.	d.
1298	Werrington	4	6	2	23	14	0¾	28	0	2¾
1332	Hurdwick	5	0	6½	8	10	8½	13	11	3
1335	Ottery	6	16	2½	6	1	6	12	17	8½
1336	,,	6	14	7½	7	4	9	13	19	4½
1337	,,	6	1	7½	5	13	3½	11	14	11
1342	,,									
1343	,,									
1344	,,									
1358	Burrington	2	18	10	4	19	2¼	7	18	0¼
1381	Ottery	7	18	2	14	9	10	22	8	0
1382	Week	4	9	3½	7	2	7	11	11	10½
1385	,,	2	12	4	2	0	10	4	13	2
1386	Ottery	7	11	8	17	9	10	25	1	6
,,	Werrington	4	10	11	9	6	8¼	13	17	7¼
1390	Ottery	7	17	5	12	15	11	20	13	4
1393	Denbury	4	7	4	6	10	3½	10	17	7½
1396	Ottery	4	19	4	16	16	5	21	15	9
1398	Hurdwick	11	5	10	21	17	3	33	3	1
,,	Werrington	5	7	7	10	13	8¾	16	1	3¾
,,	Leigh	4	8	10	11	1	8¼	15	10	6¼
,,	Milton	5	0	10	5	7	1	10	7	11
1412	Hurdwick	13	11	8	43	16	1¾	57	7	9¾
1413	Werrington	7	6	0	5	16	7¾	13	2	7¾
,,	Hurdwick									
1414	,,	13	14	11	22	11	0	36	5	11
1416	,,	13	5	10	27	5	3½	40	11	1½
1427	,,	13	1	1	22	5	3¾	35	6	4¾
1433	,,	8	4	8	11	10	7½	19	15	3½
1435	,,	9	7	0	9	19	0	19	6	0
1441	,,	6	18	8	5	6	5¼	12	5	1¼
1446	,,	11	3	1	16	0	9¼	27	3	10¼

FINANCIAL RESULTS OF DEMESNE HUSBANDRY

replacement of livestock, and purchases of seed-corn, are summed up in the fourth column. On the other side of the account we have, first, the *Vendicio operum*, or sums paid by the tenants from year to year in lieu of their customary labour services; and under SALES the total of the *Vendicio stauri, Exitus manerii, Vendicio bladi*, and miscellaneous *Vendicio super compotum*. (See p. 155 above.)

Works Commuted	Sales	Total Receipts	Cash Balance	Manor	Year
£ s. d.	£ s. d.	£ s. d.	£ s. d.		
3 9 3	4 0 11¾	7 10 2¾	−20 10 0	Werrington	1298
13 11	7 7 0¼	8 0 11¼	− 5 10 3¾	Hurdwick	1332
nil	4 13 5	4 13 5	− 8 4 3½	Ottery	1335
nil	7 3 3	7 3 3	− 6 16 1½	,,	1336
nil	5 8 3½	5 8 3½	− 6 6 7½	,,	1337
2 10	10 11 0	10 13 10		,,	1342
2 10	11 9 1½	11 11 11½		,,	1343
2 10	8 13 10¾	8 16 8¾		,,	1344
6 0	10 8 9¾	10 14 9¾	+ 2 16 9½	Burrington	1358
nil	29 13 3¾	29 13 3¾	+ 7 5 3¾	Ottery	1381
nil	10 13 3½	10 13 3½	− 18 7	Week	1382
nil	8 15 6	8 15 6	+ 4 2 4	,,	1385
nil	15 16 8	15 16 8	− 9 4 10	Ottery	1386
6 6 3½	14 17 7½	21 3 11	+ 7 6 3¾	Werrington	,,
nil	20 13 10½	20 13 10½	+ 6½	Ottery	1390
7 10	17 7 1½	17 14 11½	+ 6 17 4	Denbury	1393
nil	16 16 9½	16 16 9½	− 4 18 11½	Ottery	1396
17 1½	57 1 11	57 19 0½	+24 15 11½	Hurdwick	1398
6 10 8	24 4 8	30 15 4	+14 14 0¼	Werrington	,,
10 1	18 1 0¼	18 11 1¼	+ 3 0 7	Leigh	,,
13 1	20 2 3	20 15 4	+10 7 5	Milton	,,
5 3½	61 18 10¾	62 4 2¼	+ 4 16 4½	Hurdwick	1412
6 13 2½	22 14 6½	29 7 9	+16 5 1¼	Werrington	1413
4 6½	48 18 5½	49 3 0		Hurdwick	,,
4 9½	45 0 8	45 5 5½	+ 8 19 6½	,,	1414
4 9½	79 14 5½	79 19 3	+39 8 1½	,,	1416
5 5½	40 9 1	40 14 6½	+ 5 8 1¾	,,	1427
5 5½	35 5 6	35 10 11½	+15 15 8	,,	1433
5 5½	34 12 8½	34 18 2	+15 12 2	,,	1435
5 5½	9 1 8	9 7 1½	− 2 17 11¾	,,	1441
6 0½	17 17 6	18 3 6½	− 9 0 3¾	,,	1446

R

TABLE XXVI *(cont.)*

Year	Manor	Wages			Other expenses			Total Expenses		
		£	s.	d.	£	s.	d.	£	s.	d.
1450	Hurdwick	11	1	0	22	3	1½	33	4	1½
1454	Werrington	7	6	7	7	9	6	14	16	1
,,	Hurdwick	11	7	2	23	4	10½	34	12	0½
1458	,,	11	9	8	26	6	2½	37	15	10½
1460	,,	12	12	0	25	2	2	37	14	2
1461	Werrington	5	5	3	7	6	1¾	12	11	4¾
1463	Hurdwick	13	6	0	23	1	3¾	36	7	3¾
1464	,,	13	6	0	18	15	1¾	32	1	1¾
1466	,,	13	1	0	16	15	2⅜	29	16	2⅜
1470	,,	11	9	6	24	8	1	35	17	7
1471	,,	11	10	1	18	8	6	29	18	7
1473	,,	12	3	0	19	3	4	31	6	4
1475	,,	12	7	4	15	2	7	27	9	11
1477	,,	12	7	4	16	11	9	28	19	1
1480	,,	12	7	4	19	6	10½	31	14	2½
1482	,,	12	3	0	18	14	7½	30	17	7½
1489	,,	12	2	8	22	9	1½	34	11	9½
1490	,,	12	11	0	24	10	2¼	37	1	2¼
1491	,,	12	2	8	24	10	11½	36	13	7½
1492	,,	12	2	8	23	6	10	35	9	6
1497	,,	12	7	0	20	9	8½	32	16	8½
,,	Morwell	5	4	0	3	10	2	8	14	2
,,	Leigh	6	18	8	7	14	1	14	12	9
1498	Hurdwick	12	7	0	19	3	4¼	31	10	4¼
1499	Werrington	6	18	8	9	15	11	16	14	7
c.1500	Leigh	6	18	8	9	13	7½	16	12	3½
1502	Hurdwick	12	6	0	22	2	7½	34	8	7½
1504	,,	12	6	0	22	15	8½	35	1	8½
1505	,,	12	10	0	22	17	11½	35	7	11½
1508	,,	10	12	4	29	9	6¼	40	1	10¼
1509	,,	11	18	9	27	19	2¾	39	17	11¾
1513	,,	11	4	4	29	11	1¾	40	15	5¾
1516	,,	11	5	8	29	8	3	40	13	11
1517	,,	9	9	0	31	15	10	41	4	10
1522	,,	12	10	2	29	14	3	42	4	5
1524	,,	9	11	0	20	4	9¾	29	15	9¾
1537	,,	9	19	0	30	2	6	40	1	6
1538	,,	9	6	8	28	7	2½	37	13	10½

FINANCIAL RESULTS OF DEMESNE HUSBANDRY

Works Commuted	Sales	Total Receipts	Cash Balance	Manor	Year
£ s. d.	£ s. d.	£ s. d.	£ s. d.		
nil	40 5 3½	40 5 3½	+ 7 1 2	Hurdwick	1450
6 5 10¼	9 0 0¼	15 5 10½	+ 9 9½	Werrington	1454
nil	36 11 1	36 11 1	+ 1 19 0½	Hurdwick	,,
nil	47 1 8	47 1 8	+ 9 5 9½	,,	1458
nil	44 13 8¾	44 13 8¾	+ 6 19 6¾	,,	1460
6 3 6¾	13 15 10	19 19 4¾	+ 7 8 0	Werrington	1461
nil	23 9 11¼	23 9 11¼	−12 17 4½	Hurdwick	1463
nil	25 1 3½	25 1 3½	− 6 19 10¼	,,	1464
nil	25 7 0	25 7 0	− 4 9 2⅜	,,	1466
nil	20 7 8	20 7 8	−15 9 11	,,	1470
nil	25 12 5	25 12 5	− 4 6 2	,,	1471
8	29 5 2	29 5 10	− 2 0 6	,,	1473
nil	26 1 6½	26 1 6½	− 1 8 4½	,,	1475
8	28 9 6¼	28 10 2¼	− 8 10¾	,,	1477
8	29 14 2	29 14 10	− 1 19 4½	,,	1480
8	27 9 3	27 9 11	− 3 7 8½	,,	1482
8	34 16 4½	34 17 0½	+ 5 3	,,	1489
8	35 14 11	35 15 7	− 1 5 7¼	,,	1490
8	36 17 6	36 18 2	+ 4 6½	,,	1491
8	33 16 11	33 17 7	− 1 11 11	,,	1492
1 0	33 17 2¼	33 18 2¼	+ 1 1 5¾	,,	1497
nil	7 16 4¼	7 16 4¼	− 17 9¾	Morwell	,,
18 9	20 19 11	21 18 8	+ 7 5 11	Leigh	,,
1 0	28 8 8¼	28 9 8¼	− 3 0 8	Hurdwick	1498
?	6 2 6½	?	?	Werrington	1499
18 9	16 1 4	17 0 1	+ 7 9½	Leigh	c.1500
5	33 5 3¾	33 5 8¾	− 1 2 10¾	Hurdwick	1502
2 2	37 0 7¼	37 2 9¼	+ 2 1 0¾	,,	1504
1 9	29 18 5¾	30 0 2¾	− 5 7 8¾	,,	1505
1 9	38 3 2	38 4 11	− 1 16 11¼	,,	1508
nil	37 17 7	37 17 7	− 2 0 4¾	,,	1509
1 0	37 15 3	37 16 3	− 2 19 2¾	,,	1513
1 1	39 4 1	39 5 2	− 1 8 9	,,	1516
1 1	42 6 0	42 7 1	+ 1 2 3	,,	1517
1 1	42 0 7	42 1 8	− 2 9	,,	1522
1 7	36 10 3½	36 11 10½	+ 6 16 0¾	,,	1524
1 0	41 13 10	41 14 10	+ 1 13 4	,,	1537
1 0	41 7 7	41 8 7	+ 3 14 8½	,,	1538

food consumed at home and given away to friends, if we but knew it exactly, would often counterbalance the cash deficit and transform a seeming loss into a profit.

Sales of produce have been analysed in a previous chapter, so far as the accounts admit of such analysis.[1] The 'sale of works' recorded in the sixth column does not by any means tell the full tale of commutation, any more than the wages of the permanent staff represent the full cost of labour. From the very beginning the monks had required a certain amount of work from their tenants, freeholders included; but there had probably never been a time when they did not take some sort of payment in lieu of service if the labour was not needed in a particular year.[2] At the close of the eleventh century their demesnes were still being cultivated mainly by slaves, with occasional assistance from the tenants. Within two or three generations of Domesday the process of transforming the Tavistock slaves into economically self-supporting serfs, begun perhaps well before the Conquest, was rapidly completed. Emancipation seems to have been granted on fairly easy terms. Many Devonshire lords, both ecclesiastical and lay, continued to demand week-work from the descendants of their former slaves, but no trace of such an exaction has been found on the Tavistock estates. Perhaps the manors were too big for it; a serf living at Troswell, six miles from Werrington, could not possibly have brought his oxen once a week to the demesne and back. The lord who had resolved to plant out his slaves would set aside a portion or portions of the manor as bond-land (*terra nativa*), to be held at his pleasure but on terms that rapidly solidified into the 'custom of the manor'. The serf paid *census*, tallage, and in many cases a money rent. Unlike the slave, whose service to the lord had been a matter of personal obligation and indefinite in quantity, the serf rendered labour-dues that were regulated by custom and attached to his tenure rather than his personal status.[3]

---

[1] P. 156 above.

[2] In 1297 it was stated that the tenants of Ottery St Mary, a manor belonging to the dean and chapter of Rouen, paid nothing when their services were not required on the demesne. ("De serviciis consuetudinariorum et hydariorum nichil, quia omni anno excolunt dominicum domini; et licet non excoluerint dominicum, nil dare tenentur pro hujusmodi servicio secundum consuetudinem manerii."—PRO Ministers' Accounts, S.C. 6, Bdle 1125, no. 5.) I know of no parallel to this custom on other Devon manors.

[3] The custom of the manor was not inviolable. In 1309 bishop Stapeldon

The bond-land of Tavistock, which lay between the Lamerton road and the valley of the Lumburn, is mentioned as late as 1317.[1] By that time, however, the relative economic positions of the abbot and his bondmen had undergone a notable change. Prices having risen, the bondman found himself able to offer his lord a premium as well as a yearly rent for any holding that chanced to become vacant. By the second half of the thirteenth century we find the abbot converting bond-land into tenements held by lease. Thus in 1288 the abbot and convent "demise and let to farm all their land of La Doune"—that is, Downhouse, near Tavistock—"which Richard Cola formerly held of them in villeinage", to Peter de Doneslond for twenty-three years, at an annual rent of twelve shillings payable on St Rumon's Day, with one pound of pepper and one pound of cummin to the *salsarius*, reserving suit to the court of Hurdwick on law-days, and suit to Crowndale mill.[2] In nearly every case a lease of this kind is granted in consideration of a premium or entry fine, the amount of which may or may not be stated in the document.[3] Often the lord stipulates for a small payment, called a farleve or farleu, at the expiry of the term. Sometimes a proviso is inserted authorizing the lessee to surrender the lease whenever he thinks fit, taking the year's crop and his livestock with him; but in that case he must pay whatever farleu would have become due had the lease run out. This word farleu, which occurs in scores of Devonshire leases, has baffled the compilers of the Oxford English Dictionary; but its context in these early Tavistock leases reveals that it is just a legal variant of the military 'furlough', meaning 'leave to fare' or to go away.[4]

In 1339 the abbot and convent announced their intention of demising 890 acres of arable, 418 acres of meadow, and 460 acres of pasture in Tavistock, Hatherleigh, and Werrington, a house in Exeter, and 86 acres of arable and meadow in their Cornish

compelled his serfs at Paignton to accept an increase of labour-dues (*Reg.*, p. 310).

[1] W. D Bdle 30, no. 3.   [2] *Ibid.*, Bdle 53, no. 27.

[3] In 1301 the tenants of Staverton, a manor belonging to the dean and chapter of Exeter, complained of excessive entry fines, and declared that in the past such fines had been customarily assessed in the manor court (*Reg. Stapeldon*, p. 379).

[4] DCNQ XXIII, 1948, p. 133.

estate of Antony, to tenants for life or for a term of years. The premises were then valued at only forty shillings, but were expected to yield ten pounds a year or more under lease.[1] For the remainder of the fourteenth century leases were given for terms varying from twenty to fifty years. Thereafter forty years became the regular term. Of one hundred and fifty-four extant Tavistock leases granted between 1400 and 1517, only thirty-one are for terms other than forty years. The corresponding figure for Werrington is twelve out of ninety-four. In 1517 the abbot began to give leases not for a term of years but for the lifetime of the lessee and of two other persons nominated by him. This was the system of three-life leases which later became general in the south-west and persisted down to the nineteenth century. The conditions of tenancy were published in the manor court, and a week or two later an indenture reciting the entry on the court roll was drawn up and sealed by the steward, or at Werrington by the surveyor. With this document in his possession, the leaseholder could style himself a copyholder.[2] Entry fines differed widely in amount, being sometimes less than one year's rent and sometimes two or three times as much. In almost every case the fine would be the outcome of a bargain which took account of the value of the premises, the lessee's expectation of life, and other relevant circumstances. After abbot Banham's death in 1523, leases by copy of court roll were discontinued, and ordinary indentures of lease took their place, though new tenancies were still regularly proclaimed in court. Three-life leases continued to be the rule at Werrington and to predominate at Tavistock, where however leases for a term, usually forty years, enjoyed a partial return to favour.[3]

[1] PRO Inquisitions *ad quod damnum*, C143, File 251, no. 8. The Tavistock land was not a compact block; it consisted of holdings at Morwell, Newton, Bowrish, Downhouse, Stilesweek, Ottery, Indescombe, Taviton, Whitchurch, and Hurdwick.

[2] On the manors belonging to the prior and convent, leases by copy of court roll had been granted a century before this date.

[3] The history of Crowndale, reputed birthplace of Sir Francis Drake, may be given here as typical. In the middle of the fourteenth century one Richard Lamborn obtained a lease from the abbot and convent at four pounds a year. His son-in-law, William Gylys, was in occupation in 1387. Gylys was followed in 1396 by Stephen Brounyng, who took a lease for thirty-five years at the same rent, subsequently assigning it to John Strode. The next occupant was Henry Drake, who appears to have entered on the premises in 1441 with

The bondman who can persuade his lord to grant him a lease is transformed at once from a customary tenant, holding at the lord's will by the custom of the manor, into a conventionary tenant, holding by deed; and, as the prior of Otterton noted in 1260, he is apt thenceforth to consider himself a free man.[1] At first an effort will be made to keep him in his place. A distinction will be drawn between the servile and the free conventionary, and a clause will be inserted binding the former to discharge the various manorial offices as in the past, and to perform the same labour services as "other tenants of the same condition". But the lord who has condescended to bargain with one who is legally his property will find it impracticable, in the long run, to keep up these invidious distinctions.

How far the process had been carried by the end of the fourteenth century appears from a survey of Hurdwick drawn up in 1387. Fifty-eight tenants are there classified as freeholders, twenty-two as leaseholders, and nineteen as tenants-at-will. In addition, there are seventy-one whose tenure is not specified, but from other sources it is clear that some at least of them were freeholders. Three of the tenancies-at-will became leaseholds a year or two later; and by 1416, when the manor was surveyed

a forty-year lease. In September 1481 a new lease was granted to Simon Drake, to run for forty-six years at £4 3s. 4d. In 1519, while Simon was still in occupation, abbot Banham accepted an offer of £13 6s. 8d. for the reversion, which he sold to John Drake, to be held during John's lifetime and the lives of his wife and son. This agreement, which provided for an increased rent of £4 6s. 8d., took effect in 1528. After the Dissolution, John, Lord Russell, who had stepped into the abbot's place, exacted from Drake a fine of £6 13s. 4d. for a new lease on the same terms. This was dated 8 October 1546 (Eliott-Drake, *The Family and Heirs of Sir Francis Drake*, I, p. 5). John Drake died in 1566, and his widow was then admitted as tenant; but in the following year her son died, and a new reversionary lease for three lives was sold to Roger Upcott, who entered upon the premises after her death in 1571. The rent was still £4 6s. 8d., and it remained stationary for another century and a half, though the enhanced value of the farm was doubtless reflected in higher entry fines. In 1706 Hugh Pyne gave five hundred and forty pounds for a three-life lease at the old rent. The premises were then said to comprise 157 acres 2 roods 32 poles customary measure. Pyne's lease ran out in 1778, and in the following year the farm was rack-rented for the first time, at eighty pounds a year, on a fourteen-year lease, without entry fine. By 1803 the rent had gone up to £114 10s., and the acreage, in statute measure, was set down as 191 acres 3 roods 24 poles.

[1] "Nativus qui tenet aliquam terram per cartam incontinenti dicit se liberum" (Oliver, p. 254).

anew, five more had been similarly converted. A survey of Leigh and Milton dated 1411 can be analysed as follows:

Freeholds	29
Leaseholds	9
Tenancies-at-will	28
Unspecified	1

In the western half of Werrington there were only fifteen tenants-at-will in 1486, as against fifty-four leaseholders.

Although servile tenure was now visibly on the wane, boon-works in many cases were still performed, even by free tenants. Harvest works especially could ill be spared when labour was becoming more and more costly. In the chapters on demesne husbandry particulars have been given of the rates for some forms of piecework, and of the wages paid to sandmen, shepherds, and dairywomen. These were supposed to be part-time workers, though in practice many of them were employed all the year round, as were also the *famuli*, the permanent staff recognized as such, whose cash wages are summarized in the third column of Table XXVI (pp. 244 sqq.). The rise in the weekly wage-rates of the *famuli* can be shown at a glance.[1]

TABLE XXVII
WEEKLY WAGES

	Bailiff	Ploughman	Ploughboy	Shepherd
1298	6d.[2]	3½d.	3d.	3d.
1334		4d.	3½d.	
1358				4d.
1373		6d.	4d.	6d.
1380		7d.	5½d.	
1381	7d.			
1385		8d.	6½d.	
1386	8d.			
1387			7d.	7d.–8d.
1390	9d.			
1414			8d.	
1538	9d.	8d.	8d.	7d.–8d.

[1] The wages of the permanent staff were very generally supplemented by allowances of food.

[2] At this date he was still known as the *serviens*, or sergeant.

A parallel movement took place in the cost of piecework. The rates for threshing and winnowing, two of the most important operations, may be quoted here as typical.

TABLE XXVIII

COST OF THRESHING AND WINNOWING
PER QUARTER

Year	THRESHING			WINNOWING	
	Wheat	Rye	Oats	Wheat & Rye	Oats
1298		3d.		$\frac{1}{4}$d.	$\frac{1}{4}$d.
1332	3d.	2$\frac{1}{2}$d.		$\frac{1}{4}$d.	$\frac{1}{4}$d.
1380	4d.	4d.	1$\frac{1}{2}$d.	$\frac{1}{2}$d.	
1416	4$\frac{1}{2}$d.	4d.	2d.	1d.	$\frac{1}{3}$d.
1435	5d.	4d.	2d.	1d.	$\frac{1}{3}$d.
1454	6d.	5d.	2d.	2d.	$\frac{1}{3}$d.
1471	7d.	6d.	3d.		
1482	8d.	6d.	3d.		
1491	7d.	6d.	3$\frac{1}{2}$d.		
1538	7d.	6d.	3d.		

Sheep-shearing, on the other hand, remained constant at a penny a score from the end of the thirteenth until the middle of the fifteenth century or even later. And since the outlay on pastoral husbandry was always lower than that required for cereal cultivation, one way of parrying increased labour costs was to convert arable into pasture. In point of fact the Hurdwick accounts do testify to marked reductions in the acreage under crops between 1433 and 1446, and again from 1473 to 1491, accompanied on each occasion by enlarged sales of livestock, wool, and dairy produce.[1] At Werrington the ploughland dwindled progressively and with scarcely an interruption over the whole period covered by the accounts; but there was no corresponding increase of pastoral receipts or multiplication of the sheep-flock. On the whole, the Tavistock records disclose nothing like that wholesale change from agriculture to sheep-farming which in other parts of England raised such an outcry in the early Tudor period.

What they do show is a steady growth of the 'assized' or fixed rents paid in cash. We have seen that food-rents prevailed at

[1] Cf. pp. 102, 156, 157 above.

Plymstock to the last. It may be that such rents had once been a ubiquitous feature of the Tavistock economy, but the paucity of early documents leaves this a matter of surmise. It is equally probable that the monks had always collected a certain amount of money from tenants who paid some or all of their rent in cash. From the fourteenth century onwards money rents grew ever more important as leases were granted of land withdrawn from servile tenure, of freeholds acquired by purchase or otherwise, and of demesnes let out in parcels or entire.

The Werrington records illustrate the whole process very clearly. In 1298 the assized rents of this manor amounted to £29 9s. 8d. By 1350 they had gone up to £34 14s. 3½d., and a note in the margin of the account directs that the twenty pounds collected from the serfs in tallage, locally called their aid or gift, shall in future be entered with the assized rents. This was done, but the aid still figures as a distinct item down to 1486, when it ceases to be named as such. In 1356 the ancient compulsory ploughing service, the *arura debita*, is all sold at the customary rate. Thirty years later it appears as "a rent called need-earth". By the close of the fourteenth century the rents have gone up to £57 12s. 4½d. Transport service outside the manor is now rarely performed, and by 1450 it is invariably commuted, though still only from year to year. At the same time the custom of designating three candidates for the office of reeve, and taking money from the two who are not sworn in, becomes fossilized in its turn.

TABLE XXIX

FINES FOR RELEASE FROM THE OFFICE OF REEVE
AT WERRINGTON

1365	40s.	0d.	26s.	8d.	Total £3	6s. 8d.
1368	60s.	0d.	40s.	0d.	£5	0s. 0d.
1384	60s.	0d.	40s.	0d.	£5	0s. 0d.
1385	45s.	0d.	38s.	4d.	£4	3s. 4d.
1395	53s.	4d.	42s.	4d.	£4	15s. 8d.
1398	46s.	8d.	46s.	8d.	£4	13s. 4d.
1413	50s.	0d.	50s.	0d.	£5	0s. 0d.

The payments had been quite substantial, and it would seem that the candidates, instead of being left to find the whole amount themselves, were assisted by a contribution from their fellow-serfs. By 1452 this arrangement has been superseded by a 'reeve-rent', paid by all the customary and conventionary tenants at a fixed rate of 1s. 2⅝d. a ferling. At the same date an item of 19s. 9¾d. appears under the heading *Opera arentata*. It represents the labour services due from twelve tenements, now permanently commuted. By 1450 the assized rents have gone up to £67 3s. 4¼d., by 1500 to £88 14s. 5⅞d., and by 1532 to £113 18s. 7d.

The Hurdwick accounts disclose a parallel progression. Commuted works here are not styled *Opera arentata*, but are said to be "abrogated by the lord's charter", meaning an indenture of lease, which comes to the same thing. The remaining works are either exacted or sold from year to year as in the past; but from 1450 onwards the bailiff has orders not to sell them without express permission from the abbot. The bailiff is the employee who in earlier days was called the sergeant. At Hurdwick and the other manors round Tavistock he now shoulders, for pay, the responsibilities formerly incumbent on the reeve as a matter of servile obligation; and by the close of the fourteenth century the annual account for the whole manor is rendered in his name. Here too the assized rents are doubled in less than a hundred years.

1332	£26 16s. 11d.	+ tallage	£3 0s. 4¼d.	=	£29 17s. 3¼d.
1347	£25 13s. 1d.	,,	£10 9s. 7d.	=	£36 2s. 8d.
1398	£48 1s. 5¼d.				
1412	£60 5s. 9d.				
1433	£62 10s. 2¼d.				

The upward movement of rents at Plymstock has already been described. For Burrington, Denbury, Leigh, and Hatherleigh it is epitomized in Table XXX below. The pace was not everywhere uniform. On some manors indeed no upward trend is visible: thus, Morwell appears to have remained stationary from 1414 to 1497, and Roborough from 1375 to the Dissolution. At Hurdwick the figure attained in 1433 is repeated down to 1522, after which rents disappear from the bailiff's account.[1] But the general ten-

[1] It is most unfortunate that the valuation of 1535 gives only an aggregate rental of two hundred and thirty-one pounds for Hurdwick, Milton, Week, Holeyeat, Antony, and scattered properties elsewhere. This figure may or may not include some income from Scilly; if it does not, the islands were altogether omitted from the valuation.

dency on the abbey manors during the century and a half preceding the Dissolution was for rents to increase. Here and there the process was halted for a time; but so far as can be seen, it was nowhere even temporarily reversed.[1]

TABLE XXX

GROWTH OF ASSIZED RENTS

	Burrington	Denbury	Leigh	Hatherleigh
1358	£8 19s. 4½d.			
1393		£7 7s. 6½d.		
1398			£3 5s. 6¾d.	
1408	£11 6s. 5d.			
1410				£19 14s. 3d.
1456				£20 1s. 9d.
1471	£11 9s. 8¾d.			
1497	£11 10s. 9¾d.	£15 3s. 7½d.	£5 5s. 4½d.	
1535	£15 7s. 1½d.	£17 4s. 3½d.		£24 4s. 4d.

By the middle of the fifteenth century the portion of the Hurdwick demesne lying between the Fishlake and the Wallabrook had been leased out in four or five parcels. The barton land of Burrington was leased out in its entirety at some date between 1358 and 1382. By 1410 that of Hatherleigh had gone the same way. Milton Abbot was already broken up. It is more than likely that when the abbot and convent took over the Cowick properties in 1462, they found the demesnes had been leased out by the previous owners, and they showed no disposition to put back the clock.[2] By 1497 Denbury had been partitioned among three or four leaseholders, and only four bartons remained in hand. These were Leigh, Morwell, Hurdwick, and Werrington. Three years

---

[1] Professor M. M. Postan, who has examined the fifteenth-century accounts of some four hundred and fifty manors, declares that "over four hundred show a contraction of land in the hands of tenants, and a corresponding fall in rents" (*Economic History Review*, IX, 1939, p. 161). He reserves the detailed evidence for publication in a forthcoming book on manorial profits. When this work appears, it will probably reveal to what extent, if at all, Devonshire participated in the recession he describes. *Prima facie* the Tavistock manors would seem unlikely to have been a unique exception.

[2] Cf. Morgan, *The English Lands of the Abbey of Bec*, pp. 113–15. The barton of Christow was certainly leased out by 1464.

later abbot Banham granted a forty-year lease of Werrington barton, with all its livestock and equipment, and with the ser-vices of the tenants, to John Clotworthy, his bailiff there, at a yearly rent of three pounds and thirty-two quarters of wheat. All the cheese made in the dairy was to go to the monastery as before. The abbot also reserved to himself the use of the manor-house and the right to employ the farm animals for purposes of trans-port during building operations. He undertook to continue pay-ing the bailiff's wages, at the current rate of thirty-nine shillings per annum, and to give anything up to twenty shillings apiece for two stall-fed oxen.[1] In 1501 he granted a similar lease of Morwell barton, with the port-dues of Morwellham, for twenty years, at £5 12s. and six quarters of wheat.[2] By 1535 Leigh was in a ten-ant's hands, and only Hurdwick retained its traditional function as the home-farm. In that year rents made up five-sixths of the income from temporalities: in all, £618 9s. 7½d. out of a gross total of £731 18s. 4⅛d.[3]

Recent historians have done full justice to the monastic "high farming" of the thirteenth and early fourteenth centuries.[4] When we read how Michael of Amesbury added sixteen new plough-teams to those at work on the demesnes of Glastonbury (1235–52); how Geoffrey of Crowland improved the waste lands of Peterborough (1299–1320); and how the great Henry of Eastry conjured huge profit from those of Christ Church, Canterbury (1285–1331), the decision of so many later heads of houses to abandon husbandry seems by contrast to betoken loss of energy and lack of enterprise. It is however only fair to remind ourselves that agriculture is not a function of the monastic life as such. To combine the spirit of liturgical devotion with an anxious watch on corn-yields and the price of wool is no easy feat, and the more intent a man is on spiritual things, the less will be his inclination to attempt it. Other critics, again, find it positively reprehensible that the monks should have settled down in the position of mere

[1] W. D Bdle 73, no. 112.
[2] *Ibid.*, Bdle 53, no. 193. At about the same date he leased the islands of Scilly, with their churches and chapels, to William Trewynnard for seven years.
[3] *Valor Ecclesiasticus*, II, pp. 381–4.
[4] Knowles, *The Religious Orders in England*, pp. 32 sqq.; Smith, *op. cit.*, p. 143.

rentiers. But an abbey like Tavistock was burdened, as we have seen, with multifarious obligations to the State and to society at large; and it was the plain duty of the monks to apply whatever system of management would best enable them to fulfil those obligations. To practise husbandry, if they could do it with success, was one way of making both ends meet, but it diverted attention from prayer and study, and may at times have made bad blood between them and their neighbours. As a rule, the laity has always preferred competitive buying and selling to remain in lay hands.

The available figures are too scanty to determine whether the outlying demesnes were being run at a loss when the monks finally resolved to lease them out. In taking this step they complied with the fashion of the time. It may well be that they were actuated as much by a desire to simplify their administration as by hopes of increased revenue. The endless petty peculation of the manorial officials could only be checked by active supervision. Besides exposing them to all the fluctuations of the market, demesne husbandry involved continual small disbursements. By handing the demesnes over to a lessee they secured for themselves a sure income, removed a number of possible irritants, and freed themselves for tasks more in keeping with their vocation.

The process described in these pages is thoroughly familiar to students of manorial history. All over England lords were leasing out their demesnes and resigning themselves to the gradual relaxation of manorial discipline. But the pace of change was not uniform, and in Devon, that stubbornly conservative shire, it was noticeably slower than in regions further east. The monks of Christ Church, Canterbury, had leased out all but one of their demesnes by 1411, a full century before their brethren of Tavistock.[1] As late as 1532 the reeve of Plymstock was fined for neglecting to distrain a *nativus* whose son and daughter had gone to live outside the manor. It was the reeve of Werrington, not the hired bailiff, in whose name account was rendered to the last. Boonworks continued to be performed or redeemed. In 1500 the Werrington tenants whose works had not yet been commuted paid £7 2s. 11½d. in lieu of service; at Hurdwick in 1497, the

[1] Smith, *op. cit.*, p. 200.

latest year for which an account of works is extant, twenty-nine tenants gave a day's ploughing, twenty-one helped to gather in the wheat and rye, eighteen harvested the oats, and fourteen carried the crops home. On some of these manors tenants' works long survived the Dissolution.[1]

Looking back over the long history of Tavistock Abbey, we find it chequered by three distinct phases of economic stress. The first occurred towards the close of the eleventh century, when the Norman Conquest, as we have seen, transformed the abbot into a feudal baron, and at the same time deprived him of nearly half his lands. Yet the ensuing hundred years, notwithstanding the encroachments of lay magnates, the disturbances of Stephen's reign, and the increased feudal assessment, witnessed some notable constructive effort. Parishes were organized, and churches built. Three massive bays of early Norman work in the church of North Petherwin suggest that a pre-Conquest building was enlarged at the beginning of the century. Other signs of architectural activity are the late twelfth-century baptismal fonts that still remain at Abbotsham, Burrington, Denbury, and Plymstock. On the secular side, the abbot enlarged his jurisdiction, developed his property in the Scilly Isles, and established a borough outside the monastery gates.

Then, in 1225, a complaint of poverty is heard, accompanied by a charge of negligence on the part of recent abbots.[2] The cry goes up again, with greater urgency, in the third quarter of the century, when strangers are brought in to fill the abbatial office for which no local candidate will stand.[3] Henry de Northampton, cellarer of St Saviour's, Bermondsey, appointed abbot in 1257, tried with no great success to cope with the burden of debt.[4] He was followed by a monk of St Swithun's, Winchester. In 1262 John Chubb was elected abbot of the nearly bankrupt house.[5]

---

[1] In 1555 a Werrington serf paid the customary fine on his daughter's marriage. The word *nativus* appears in the court rolls for the last time in 1558. The leaseholders among whom Leigh barton was divided in 1725 were each entitled to so many days' ploughing, harrowing, reaping, and carriage from the tenants of the neighbouring farms, or to payment instead at a few pence more than the rates current in 1497.

[2] ETC LVII, LVIII.   [3] *Reg. Bronescombe*, p. 265.

[4] CPR 1247–58, p. 602; CCR 1256–9, p. 313.

[5] CCR 1261–4, p. 132.

Before long he was at odds with some of the monks, and also with bishop Bronescombe, who accused him of wasting the property: a charge that might with greater justice have been levelled against the bishop's own subordinates.[1] There may have been maladministration; it is certain that the value of money had dropped, and that civil disorder helped to make a difficult situation worse. An entry in the liturgical calendar of the abbey provides a succinct comment on the government of Henry III as viewed at Tavistock:

August 4: St Simon de Montfort.[2]

In the end Bronescombe deposed the abbot, to the great indignation of the countryside.[3]

Under the next abbot, Robert Colbern, the monastery entered upon a period of slow recuperation, though a new obstacle arose in 1279. By the Statute of Mortmain enacted in that year no monastic house could recover any of its lands which had been alienated, or acquire any new estate, without first submitting to a special inquest, and then, if successful, paying for a royal licence. Funds were still low when Colbern died, after fifteen years of office. His successor, Robert Champeaux, elected in 1285, cherished an ambition to be ranked with the 'founders' or chief benefactors of the house; and in the course of his thirty-nine years' rule he fully earned the title. To him was due the recovery of Ogbear and West Liddaton. He raised the value of the arable round Tavistock by consolidation and enclosure. His mining ventures have been related on an earlier page. At different times he took up leases of the Calstock fishery, the borough of Lydford, and the chase of Dartmoor.[4] He it was who secured the impropriations of Antony and Burrington, and the charter limiting the rights of the Crown in future voidances. We have seen him taking part in the foundation of a Benedictine house of studies at Oxford. He completed the reconstruction of the abbey

---

[1] See above, p. 23.   [2] DA xviii, 1886, p. 478.

[3] Three juries in the hundreds of Shebbear and Black Torrington made no secret of the fact that their sympathies lay wholly with Chubb (*Cal. Miscellaneous Inquisitions*, i, p. 129). A jury from Denbury took the same line (PRO Assize Rolls, J.I. i, 186, m. 26).

[4] For the fishery, see p. 162 above. For Lydford and Dartmoor, of which he took five-year leases in 1319, CPR 1317–21, pp. 406, 424.

church and the building of Tavistock parish church, both of which were dedicated in 1318.[1] He regulated the ceremonial of anniversaries and burials, and obtained bishop Stapeldon's consent to the establishment of a chantry at Whitchurch, under an archpriest and three assistant priests, each of whom was to offer Mass daily for the abbot and all the faithful, living and dead. It is expressly stated that the abbot's name is placed first because his exertions had so greatly enlarged the resources of the house.[2] The claim was amply justified. Soon after his election he had been compelled to borrow some two hundred pounds; when he died he left over twelve hundred in the treasury.

His death in 1324 was followed by a disputed election, a costly appeal to the Holy See, and the appointment of Bonus, a stranger from Aquitaine. Before long the new abbot fell foul of bishop Grandisson. He proved unequal to the difficult situation in which he found himself, and after a struggle over the impropriation of Whitchurch in which the abbot certainly had right on his side, Grandisson deposed him.[3] The masterful bishop then appointed his own cousin, John de Courtenay. Four years later it was found that Courtenay had borrowed from London and Florentine merchant bankers sums amounting to thirteen hundred pounds.[4] Thereupon Grandisson appointed a receiver-general, allowed the abbot eighty pounds a year to support himself and his monk-chaplain, and bade him lodge till further notice "in some decent place" outside the monastery. For the maintenance of the other monks he allowed one hundred pounds a year. The surplus revenue was to be used for paying off debts.[5] In 1345 the bishop complained that the reeve of Leigh and Milton had rendered no account, and that the abbot was keeping a pack of hounds.[6] Three years later there are fresh reports of maladministration: tithes are being sold well below their true value, buildings are dilapidated, and the abbot is mortgaging or selling

[1] *Reg. Stapeldon*, pp. 136, 137.
[2] *Ibid.*, pp. 402–5. The project was to have taken effect on the death of James Fraunceis, then rector of Whitchurch; but Fraunceis lived on till 1331, by which time obstacles had arisen which prevented it from being realized.
[3] Finberg, 'The Tragi-comedy of Abbot Bonus', DCNQ XXII, 1946, pp. 341–7.
[4] CCR 1337–9, pp. 109, 112, 117.
[5] *Reg. Grandisson*, pp. 886, 889.   [6] *Ibid.*, p. 996.

S

the property of the house.[1] Within another twelvemonth Courtenay was dead, a victim probably of the great pestilence, and his
successor was reported to be too ill to do fealty for his temporalities.[2]

How far was Grandisson justified in imputing all the trouble,
as he did, to folly and mismanagement? We search his registers in
vain for any mention of rising costs, any awareness of the prevailing economic trend. What we do find is that nearly every
monastic house in the diocese was in financial difficulties at this
time. Totnes and Launceston are said to be on the verge of ruin;
Plympton, Bodmin, and Frithelstock are all in debt; St Michael's
Mount is maladministered; the monks of Barnstaple, Tywardreath, and St James's, Exeter, have barely enough to support
life.[3] Either as cause or effect, at several of these houses demoralization has set in. But if the language of the episcopal chancery is
to be taken literally we must postulate a simultaneous administrative collapse in all of them: which seems improbable. It was
easier to blame an abbot or prior for incompetence—and in-
competent some of them doubtless were—than to seek and find a
remedy for deep-seated economic ills. Years after the plague had
visibly impoverished many through no fault of their own, bishop
Brantyngham, without waiting to see the accounts, proclaimed
his suspicion that abbot Langdon of Tavistock was a bad man-
ager, and appointed a committee to look after the temporalities.[4]

In 1352 it was stated that revenue had fallen away and rents
depreciated to something like half their former value.[5] The gift of
the manor of Week and the final impropriation of Whitchurch
were the first steps towards recovery. A flexible system of land-
leasing brought its harvest of entry fines. Rents were raised, and
the demesnes showed good returns in cash. By the turn of the
century the shadow of insolvency had passed.

In the course of the next hundred years three abbots made their
mark as administrators. John Mey, elected in 1402, distinguished
himself by his resolute assertion of ancient rights. It was probably under his direction that the great register of Tavistock was

---

[1] *Reg. Grandisson*, pp. 1050, 1057.   [2] *Ibid.*, p. 71.

[3] *Ibid.*, pp. 1074 (Totnes), 837 (Launceston), 231, 620 (Plympton), 980,
1009 (Bodmin), 925 (Frithelstock), 813 (St Michael's Mount), 289 (Barnstaple), 695 (Tywardreath), 305 (St James's).

[4] *Reg. Brantyngham*, p. 314.   [5] W. D Bdle 47, no. 11.

compiled.[1] This volume is unhappily not extant now, but there is other evidence of abbot Mey's researches. He bought up old charters, made the tenants produce their title-deeds, procured a certified copy of the Tavistock Domesday, and drew up a series of unprecedentedly detailed manorial extents.[2] On one notable occasion he exercised the right of a lord to seize his serf's chattels. The motive was not to oppress the serf but to obtain redress from a third party. A certain Nicholas Tregodek of Launceston, whom he sued for trespass before the King's Bench, entered no defence and was consequently outlawed, but managed to buy the royal pardon, and no doubt congratulated himself on having baffled the abbot's pursuit.[3] But the abbot's opportunity came when Nicholas Joy, a Werrington serf by origin and a merchant by trade, returned from Brittany with a hundred and sixty quarters of bay salt, which he unloaded at the port of Landulph, on the Tamar. Joy was known to have purchased the salt for Tregodek, whether or not the latter had—as he afterwards asserted—advanced twenty pounds towards the purchase. As soon as the cargo was landed, the abbot confiscated it and sold it off at ten shillings a quarter, leaving his discomfited opponent to petition the court of Chancery in vain.[4] Mey resisted any attempt to convert a servile tenure into freehold, but continued the policy of leasing bondland to conventionary tenants. Before his death he set on foot the reconstruction of the abbey church. After twenty years of office he left the administration on a thoroughly sound footing.

John Dynyngton, who ruled the monastery from 1451 to 1490, decided to petition the Holy See for the insignia of a mitred abbot.[5] It was he who obtained from Edward IV the grant of the

[1] It ran to 400 pages and more. In 1698 White Kennett made a note in his copy of the *Monasticon*, which is now in the Bodleian, to the effect that the cartulary was written about the time of Henry IV. William Wotton (1666–1726) consulted it when drawing up a list of the abbots for Browne Willis (DA LXXV, 1943, p. 245), and according to Anstis, Matthew Hutton (1639–1711) saw it about five years before his death (BM Stowe MS. 1044, fo. 49). Since then it has disappeared.

[2] A bundle of early fourteenth-century deeds relating to Pixon is endorsed with a note that abbot Mey gave twenty shillings for these charters (W. D Bdle 23, no. 5).

[3] CPR 1416–22, p. 352.

[4] PRO Early Chancery Proceedings, C.1, File 45, no. 43, and File 74, no. 18.

[5] CPR 1452–61, p. 431.

Cowick properties. This donation he succeeded in making good
against the provost and fellows of Eton, to whom Cowick had
been assigned by Henry VI.[1] Much rebuilding took place in
Dynyngton's time. His next successor but one, Richard Banham
(1492–1523), enlarged the numbers of the community. This
abbot's triumphs, in securing for the abbey exemption from
diocesan control, and for himself a seat in the House of Lords,
have already been told. When Cardinal Morton's commissary
visited Tavistock just after Banham's election he found nothing
worse to report than habitual negligence on the part of the bell-
ringer.[2] A generation later the ancient house gave striking proof
of its ability to move with the times by importing from France
matrices for two founts of type and establishing the first printing
press in the south-west. From this press issued in 1525 a handsome quarto edition of *The Consolations of Philosophy*, translated
from the Latin of Boethius.[3] In these closing decades the sun-
shine of prosperity and peace was clouded only by tidings from
afar portending a general onslaught on the monastic order.

[1] Morgan, *op. cit.*, p. 134.   [2] *Tudor Studies*, p. 62.
[3] See Appendix D, 'The Tavistock Printing Press'.

CHAPTER X

THE DISSOLUTION

ONE day in 1536 John Peryn, thirty-ninth abbot of Tavistock, sitting at table, remarked to a guest: "Lo, the king sends about to suppress many houses of religion, which is a piteous case. And so did the cardinal in his time, but what became of him and what end he made for his so doing, I report me unto you; all men know." It was the year following that in which More, Fisher, and the London Carthusians had forfeited their lives for passive resistance to the break with Rome. Since then parliament, with a backward glance at the precedent set by Wolsey, had passed an act suppressing all monasteries endowed with less than two hundred pounds a year. One former monk of Tavistock was already at large, having been ejected from his monastery and pensioned in accordance with the act. This was Thomas Richard, prior of Totnes, the printer of the Tavistock Boethius, "a man of good vertuus converssacyon" according to Sir Piers Edgcumbe, who knew him well.[1] It must have been clear to many that the attack on the greater houses would not be long delayed.

Abbot Peryn had apparently mistaken his audience. The visitor to whom he spoke at once called the whole company to witness; and John Amadas, a gentleman-at-arms who by royal letters patent had been quartered on the abbey, hastened to report the indiscreet words by letter to Thomas Cromwell.[2] Cromwell passed the letter on to the king, and a note was made to keep the abbot under observation. Presently the abbot and Amadas both received orders to accompany the king's expedition into Lincolnshire, where the populace, enraged by recent events and especially by the dissolution of monasteries, was up in arms against the government.[3] Before the order could take effect, however, the Lincolnshire rebels were dispersed by the local gentry. Several

---

[1] Oliver, p. 240. Thomas Richard subsequently became rector of St George's, Exeter.

[2] L. & P. *Hen. VIII*, x, p. 509, §1221.   [3] *Ibid.*, xi, p. 261, §670.

churchmen, including the abbots of Kirkstead and Barlings, were executed for their part in this abortive rising.

The next eighteen months must have been a nightmare of uncertainty and dread. In January the abbot was reported to be seriously ill.[1] However, he recovered, and in May sent Cromwell a "fee" of ten marks.[2] Cromwell was conducting what would nowadays be called a war of nerves, and he managed it so skilfully that in the end the greater monasteries fell with very little bloodshed.

At Tavistock, meanwhile, a number of the tenants were doing their best to secure themselves by getting their leases renewed. No proffered entry fine would be refused at a time when ready money was going to be more obviously useful than ever. It was afterwards alleged that some of these leases were antedated.[3] Life pensions were settled on some of the household servants and on various friends, but there is no sign of any wholesale dispersal of assets, an annuity of £6 13s. 4d. to Richard Peryn, clerk, being the only grant that smacks of possible nepotism.[4] The account rendered by the bailiff of Hurdwick at Michaelmas 1538 shows the home-farm still in full working order. The only deviation from its immemorial routine was that the lambs' wool, instead of being sold as usual, was all made into shirts and blankets for the labourers.

The end came five months later. On the 14th of February 1539 the abbot of Dunkeswell surrendered his monastery to the king's representatives. By the 22nd Polsloe, Canonsleigh, and Hartland had taken the same course; and within the next eight days Tor, Launceston, Buckfast, Buckland, Bodmin, Plympton, and St Germans were all dissolved. Then on Monday, the 3rd of March, the royal commissioner, Dr John Tregonwell, arrived at Tavi-

---

[1] L. & P. *Hen. VIII*, xiii, pt i, p. 4, §9.   [2] *Ibid.*, xiv, pt ii, pp. 319, 323.

[3] W. D Bdle 53, no. 219 (Ottery, 20 September 1537), and Bdle 73, no. 81 (Penrose mill, Werrington, 20 January 1538) are both endorsed with a note stating that they were found to have been sealed within twelve months of the Dissolution. No other examples have come to light.

[4] In 1545 the sum of forty-eight pounds was distributed in varying amounts between nineteen annuitants, among whom are recognizable the ex-organist, the former steward of Cornwood, some household servants, the Crown pensioner John Amadas, and his son William. This was in addition to the pensions of the dispossessed monks (PRO Ministers' Accounts, S.C. 6, Henry VIII, 7303).

stock. Despite recent alarms, the community was even now at full numerical strength. Twenty monks assembled with the abbot in their beautiful octagonal chapter-house, and took their places for the last time in the accustomed stalls, "arched overhead with curious hewn and carved stone". Here they signed and sealed the deed of surrender.[1] Two houses only, Ford and Newenham, now remained; and with their dissolution later in the same week monastic life in Devon came to a full stop.[2]

Orders were now given to dismantle the shrine of St Rumon, to convey its gold, silver, and jewelled ornaments to the Tower of London, to sell the fittings of the church and monastery, and to strip the lead from the roof. Six bells weighing something like half a ton each were sold for £50 10s. 6d. The wardens of the parish church paid £5 6s. 8d. "to the kyngs visitours" for paving-stones, choir-stalls, candelabra, and three tabernacles, besides 7s. 6d. "for the exchaunge of a cope in the abbey", and twopence "for carynge oute of stones and bones oute of the churche yarde", which adjoined the abbey and was evidently littered with its débris.[3]

The commissioners brought with them a warrant signed by Cromwell, appointing pensions for the abbot and his brethren. The abbot received a hundred pounds a year: a comfortable figure, yet not so generous as the hundred and twenty pounds allotted to the prior of Plympton and to the abbot of the far less wealthy house of Buckfast. The prior of Tavistock received ten pounds; the subprior and the prior of Cowick eight pounds each, and the other monks £6 13s. 4d., £6, £5 6s. 8d., and £2 according to their age and seniority.[4] These pensions were payable during

[1] PRO E322, no. 236; *Eighth Report of the Deputy Keeper*, Appendix II, p. 44.
[2] The numerical strength of the chief Devon monasteries at this date was as follows: Plympton 18, Tor 15, Ford 13, Buckland 12, Buckfast 10. There were 17 nuns at Canonsleigh and 13 at Polsloe. To these numbers must be added the abbot, abbess, prior, or prioress in each case (Burnet, *History of the Reformation*, IV, p. 246).
[3] TPR, pp. 16, 17.
[4] Two names, John Androw and Richard Eustes, which figure on the deed of surrender, are not included in the pension list. The name which follows theirs, John Bonyfant, is entered in the pension list as "Richard Bonyfote, *nil.*" All three were perhaps novices or postulants. On the other hand, two monks, John Wele and John Peke, whose names are missing from the deed of surrender, were allotted pensions of two pounds each.

the lifetime of the recipients or until such time as they could be presented to ecclesiastical benefices; but they were taxed at a specially high rate, they sometimes fell into arrears, and the officials through whose hands they passed deducted something for their fees.[1] The abbot lived on in Tavistock for another ten years, according to tradition in a house at the top of the hill in West Street. His will refers to featherbeds best and second-best, fustian blankets, silver spoons, gilt goblets, a silver-gilt ewer and basin, and a herd of cattle out at Crebor.[2] The picture it evokes is one of cushioned ease, far removed in spirit from the grim circumstances in which Colchester, Reading, and Glastonbury saw their last abbots die.

For three months after the surrender all the possessions of the abbey lay in the king's hand. But the government had now decided to set up a Council of the West, with jurisdiction over Devon, Cornwall, Somerset, and Dorset. The object was to suppress the disaffection known to be rife in consequence of the religious changes, and to provide facilities for the local administration of justice. Four sessions were to be held in the year, at Dorchester, Wells, Exeter, and one other town farther west. After some initial hesitation, Tavistock was chosen for the fourth meeting-place; and John, first baron Russell, was appointed president of the council.[3] Descended from a line of petty Dorset squires, Russell was one of the new men who had risen to eminence by adroit service to the Tudor monarchy. At this date he possessed an estate in lands and offices valued at some five hundred and fifty-six pounds a year.[4] But none of this property lay in Devon or Cornwall, and as a whole it was insufficient to sustain

[1] A. G. Dickens, 'The Edwardian Arrears in Augmentations Payments and the Problem of the Ex-Religious', EHR LV, 1940, pp. 384-418, an admirable study, only marred by the writer's almost morbid anxiety not to be classed as a "sentimentalist". For the equivalent modern values, one authority multiplies the pension figures by twenty (Rowse, *Tudor Cornwall*, p. 190), another by thirty (Baskerville, *English Monks and the Suppression of the Monasteries*, p. 296).

[2] PCC 11 Coode, quoted in DA XLVI, 1914, p. 139, where it is suggested that the pensions were at first heavily reduced; but this is due to a misunderstanding of the account rendered for an incomplete year.

[3] The council was discontinued after five years of life. Its records have disappeared (Skeel, 'The Council of the West', in *Transactions of the Royal Historical Society*, Fourth Series, IV, 1921, pp. 62 sqq.).

[4] Scott Thomson, *Two Centuries of Family History*, pp. 168-70.

the quasi-viceregal dignity now conferred upon him. Accordingly on the 4th of July 1539 the king by letters patent granted him the site of Tavistock Abbey and the greater part of its possessions, temporal and spiritual. Hatherleigh, Abbotsham, Roborough, the isles of Scilly, the Tamar fishery, and a house at Exeter were not included; but in lieu of these the king was pleased to give him the rich manor and rectory of Blackawton, the site of the Dominican friary at Exeter, the rectories of Dunkeswell and Awliscombe, and the site of Dunkeswell Abbey with nearly six thousand acres of its former lands. Thus, with landed estates in the east, south, and west of Devon, Russell acquired a vested interest in the suppression of two considerable monasteries be-sides Tavistock and Dunkeswell, for Blackawton had belonged to Tor and its rectory to Plympton. So far as can be ascertained by comparing the items of the grant with the valuation of 1535, the gross value of his new property was approximately £1,050 a year.[1]

Edmund Burke, at odds long afterwards with Russell's de-scendant, exclaimed that the family fortune rested on a series of grants "so enormous as not only to outrage economy, but even to stagger credibility".[2] The grant of 1539 was certainly conceived on a handsome scale, all the more so as the majority of those who acquired monastic property bought it from the Crown at current values, whereas this was bestowed on Russell as a gift, "in con-sideration of his good, true, and acceptable service". But to any-one who reads the royal verbiage through to the end, it becomes apparent that the gift was subject to considerable drawbacks. In the first place, it was to be held of the Crown in chief by the ser-vice of two knights' fees: that is to say, by feudal tenure, with all its oppressive concomitants, including that most detrimental of all feudal incidents, prerogative wardship, which entitled the king to take possession not only of the Tavistock estates, but of all Russell's other property, whether ancestral or newly acquired, whenever it passed by inheritance to a minor, and to put the heir's marriage up for sale in a highly competitive market.[3]

---

[1] The letters patent are printed in full by Oliver, pp. 104–8.
[2] Burke, *Letter to a Noble Lord*, 1796 (*Works*, 1826, VIII, p. 35).
[3] Cf. Hurstfield, 'The Greenwich Tenures of the Reign of Edward VI', in *The Law Quarterly Review*, January 1949, pp. 72 sqq., especially p. 75.

Secondly, the act of 1536 had provided that in granting away monastic property the Crown should always reserve a tenth of the annual value. A paper drawn up while the grant to Russell was under consideration estimated the tenth at £72 1s. 3d.[1] This calculation, however, was made when the "Landes to be graunted unto him by the Kings grace Highnes" had reached a total yearly value of £725. By the time the letters patent were drafted this total had been increased by some fifty per cent., as we have seen; but the tenth, instead of being raised proportionately, was fixed at virtually four times the original figure. The effect was to saddle Russell and his heirs with a perpetual fixed rent-charge of £284 5s. a year. Of this sum thirty-six pounds was charged on Tavistock, Hurdwick, the small manors in and adjacent to the hundred of Tavistock, and Antony, which, with the rectory, vicarage, and advowson of Tavistock, were to be held as one knight's fee. The other lands and churches formed the second fee and bore the remainder of the charge. Thus the Crown retained a sort of debenture on the property for rather more than a quarter of its current annual yield.[2]

It seems probable that the rent-charge was deliberately fixed as high as this to compensate the Crown for the loss of the capital sum that would have accrued to it had the property been disposed of by the usual process of bargain and sale. Moreover the grant purported to take effect from the previous Michaelmas. The first payment thus fell due three months after Russell took possession, and well before he was able to meet it. There are several indications that the king's trusty servant found himself at this juncture in urgent need of ready money. By Michaelmas 1540 he was in debt to the Crown for the whole of the first two years' rent.[3] Perhaps that is why the Lady Anne, his wife, was reduced to borrowing a hundred marks from the ex-abbot.[4] To one speculator Russell sold, for twenty-eight pounds, the right to demolish

[1] Scott Thomson, *op. cit.*, p. 171.
[2] The rent was paid regularly down to 1784, when the trustees of the Bedford estate bought it in, together with a fee-farm rent of £34 8s. 1d. issuing out of the manor of Heathfield and one of seven pounds issuing out of Yarcombe rectory. For these three rents the trustees paid £6,500.
[3] PRO Ministers' Accounts, S.C. 6, Henry VIII, 7300, 7301.
[4] "*Item*, I lent unto my lady Russell by thands of Leonarde Bosgrove 66 li. 13s. 4d." (Schedule of outstanding debts appended to the abbot's will, DA xlvi, *loc. cit.*).

the church and monastery of Dunkeswell.[1] To another, the John Servington who had bought up the Tavistock bell-metal, he leased out Hurdwick barton. The abbot's lodging appears to have been let to Dorothy, widow of the fourth baron Mountjoy, who in March 1541 obtained the bishop's licence to have church services performed within the abbey precinct.[2] Meanwhile Russell's agents turned their attention to the rank and file of the tenants. They scrutinized current leases in the hope of detecting legal flaws. Where possible, they invoked the statute which had just annulled all leases made within the year before the Dissolution. By this and other forms of pressure or cajolery they induced the tenants one by one to give up their indentures and to pay entry fines for new leases embodying somewhat less favourable terms. At the Hurdwick law-court held on the 15th of March 1540, John West, the surveyor deputed by Lord Russell to attend to this business, issued the first batch of new grants, nineteen in number, in return for entry fines totalling £40 15s., of which £22 16s. 8d. was paid on the spot. A note in the margin records that one tenant flatly refused to pay his fine. Several of the old leases, for which fines had already been paid to the abbey, are extant and can be compared with those granted on this occasion.[3] The tenant of one close near the borough seems to have been evicted, but most of the new lessees were already in occupation, holding leases from the abbey for three lives or sixty years. Their rents were not put up; in two cases they were even reduced. But in every case the term was shortened to two lives, usually those of the tenant and his wife if she should outlive him and not marry again. The governing principle evidently was to collect as much ready cash as possible, and to prepare the ground for a fresh harvest of entry fines in the not too distant future.[4]

---

[1] DA XLVI, p. 148.   [2] Oliver, p. 93.

[3] A schedule of the 1540 leases is annexed to the Hurdwick court roll (W. Table 2, C2). The corresponding pre-Dissolution leases are in W. D Bdle 53, which by some inexplicable oversight remains in the Bedford estate office, Bloomsbury, though the cognate documents have nearly all been removed to Woburn.

[4] Some rents however may have been increased. In 1522, as we have seen, the Hurdwick rents totalled £62 10s. 2¼d. But John West, Russell's agent, consulted abbot Mey's original extent of the manor, erased the summary of rents he found on the last membrane, and rewrote it, giving a new total £71 7s. 3⅝d., to which he appended his signature. At the foot of the roll

From the example of the Drakes of Crowndale, already quoted, it would seem that the process of surrender and re-grant was carried on at Hurdwick for the best part of a decade, and that few tenants, however long established, succeeded in escaping.[1] Unless we are prepared to believe that Hurdwick was singled out for special treatment, we must suppose that parallel action was taken on the other manors. Russell, it need hardly be said, was astute enough not to antagonize his new tenants more than he could help; but he was himself in the grip of higher powers. No doubt his agents did their best to convince the tenants of his fundamental goodwill. It may however be doubted whether the tenants were easily or quickly reconciled. The abbey had not been suppressed in response to any wish of theirs. Even less did they desire the overthrow of those familiar observances that centred on their parish church. Tavistock was to receive many benefits from Russell's descendants, but these lay in the far future. The townsmen's thoughts, of course, are not on record; but an incident that befell not long afterwards allows us to see plainly enough what the authorities believed them to be thinking. In 1548 riots on a considerable scale broke out in Cornwall, and a royal commissioner who came down to enforce the destruction of sacred images was killed. When these disturbances had been put down, the ringleaders were hanged, drawn, and quartered, some at Launceston, one, a priest, at Smithfield, and one nameless

---

appears an intermediate figure, £70 3s. 7¼d., which may represent the total as it stood just before Russell and West came on the scene.

[1] Above, p. 250 n. John Drake, the Crowndale tenant, was father of Edmund and grandfather of Francis Drake, the great seaman. Camden states that Francis, son and heir of John Russell, stood godfather to the future admiral. If so, we may perhaps infer that a measure of condescension was employed to procure or soften the renewal of the Crowndale lease. It is at any rate certain that this renewal preceded by two years, and therefore was unconnected with, Edmund's flight from his native county. He was a shearman by trade. In April 1548 he and an accomplice waylaid a man at Petertavy and robbed him of his purse. Nine days later Edmund stole a horse and fled. He was indicted for these robberies, but his friends managed to obtain his pardon (CPR 1547–8, p. 290). Perhaps that is why his father had to borrow money from the ex-abbot, and was still in debt to him when the abbot made his will in the following year. Early in Elizabeth's reign, when marriage no longer precluded men from priestly orders, Edmund became vicar of Upchurch, Kent. He gave his children to understand that he had quitted Devon to avoid persecution as a Protestant; and in due course the admiral passed this tale on to Camden.

"traytor of Cornwall" on Plymouth Hoe. The municipal authorities of Plymouth, acting presumably on orders from above, then paid one John Mathewe a shilling "for Carying a quarter of the traytor to Tavystoke".[1] With this grisly object before their eyes, the people of Tavistock were left to meditate at leisure on the hazards of a too militant conservatism.

A year later, on the introduction of the new English prayer-book, a flame of revolt lit the peninsula from end to end. It was not an organized insurrection, but a spontaneous outbreak, beginning with the populace and presently joined by several men of wealth and position. With an army four thousand strong the rebels laid siege to Exeter. Against them stood Russell, at the head of a mixed force consisting partly of local levies, partly of German and Italian mercenaries. As the money sent him by the Privy Council did not suffice, he laid the parish churches of Devon under contribution. The men of Tavistock had had their warning: they paid £13 6s. 8d. "for the charge of XX men to serue the Kyngs majestie in the commocyon tyme".[2] One parishioner, John Prideaux, was afterwards arrested on suspicion of complicity in the rebellion, but discharged on payment of a recognizance.[3] There is no need to tell how the revolt was crushed, and its leaders executed: among them Robert Welsh, vicar of St Thomas by Exbridge, who had been presented to his vicarage by the abbot and convent of Tavistock in 1537.[4] This priest was gibbeted from the summit of his church tower, with "a holy-water bucket, a sprinkle, a sacring bell, a pair of beads, and such other popish trash hanged about him" in mockery. He is described as going to his death "very patiently". For us the main point of interest lies in the demands presented by the rebels, or, as they styled themselves, "the Commoners of Devonshyre and Cornwall in diuers Campes by East and West of Excettor". After rejecting the new English service "because it is but lyke a Christmas game", and demanding the restoration of the Mass and all the ancient rites, they went on:

"Item we wyll that the halfe parte of the abbey landes and Chauntrye landes, in euerye mans possessyons, how so euer he

---

[1] Worth (R.N.), *Calendar of the Plymouth Municipal Records*, p. 115.
[2] Rose-Troup, *The Western Rebellion of 1549*, p. 508.
[3] *Ibid.*, p. 500.   [4] *Ibid.*, pp. 292, 293.

cam by them, be geuen again to two places, where two of the chief Abbeis was with in euery Countye, where suche half part shalbe taken out, and there to be establyshed a place for devout persons, whych shall pray for the Kyng and the common wealth, and to the same we wyll haue al the almes of the Churchè boxe geuen for these seuen yeres."[1]

This was evidently a considered scheme. Its adoption, as Mr Rowse has not failed to observe, would have involved the restoration and re-endowment of half a dozen monasteries in the south-west, including Tavistock and Glastonbury.[2] The monks of Tavistock had been ejected from their home without any chance of appealing to the popular verdict; but it seems clear that many of their neighbours and tenants would have been glad to see them back. It was only after the collapse of the revolt that steps were taken to provide educational facilities in place of those which had vanished with the Dissolution. In 1551 two parishioners, William Poynter and William Grills, took the initiative. They persuaded Russell, now earl of Bedford, to obtain royal letters patent establishing two new yearly fairs at Tavistock, and to grant the profits thereof, as also of the existing Michaelmas fair which had lately been removed from Brentor to Tavistock, to a select vestry headed by themselves. The revenue was to be applied "towards and for the charitable aide releef supportacion assistance and comfort of the poore people inhabytant and dwelling within the precincte of my said Towne, and towards and about such necessary affaires and doeings as shall bee most beneficial and profitable for the whole body and commonwealth of my said Towne of Tavistock". Among these "necessary affaires and doeings" was the engagement of a schoolmaster, who makes his first appearance in the churchwarden's account two years later.[3] The earl's share in the transaction was almost entirely passive. It was the parishioners who "sustayned the costs and charges of xxij *li.* for and about thobtaining of the foresaid two fayres", and their leaders, Poynter and Grills, have accordingly the best right to be

[1] Rose-Troup, *op. cit.*, p. 221.   [2] Rowse, *op. cit.*, p. 272.
[3] The item of fifty shillings paid quarterly to the "scholemaster" has been regrettably omitted from Worth's *Calendar* (TPR, p. 22), though the 6s. 8d. spent on glazing "the Sowth wyndow in the Schole howse" is included.

considered as the founders of Tavistock Grammar School.[1] The earl allowed them to use his name and granted them a two-hundred-year lease of the fairs, with licence to build at their own expense a market-house in the high street "where the Crosse now standeth" and to apply the income thereof "to such godly uses and behoofes as are before specified".[2]

Thus, while the possessions of the abbey were shared between the Crown and a non-resident grandee, its responsibilities for education and the relief of poverty were taken over by the parish. As for hospitality, the act of 1536 had enjoined the new owners of the smaller monasteries to keep "an honest continual house and household in the same site or precinct"; but as this neither did nor could apply to Tavistock, travellers now had to pay for such entertainment as the local inns provided, while the hungry applied to the churchwardens.

In retrospect, the monks of Tavistock appear as a community for whom the extremes of praise or blame would be alike out of place. If no feats of heroic sanctity are ascribed to them, neither are any really lurid scandals. Every now and then, as we peruse their record, we catch the rumble of a bygone storm; a flash of wrath lights up the darkness, and we perceive, without surprise, that unregenerate human nature is once more having its fling. Some of the monks are quarrelling with the vicar, or giving private dinner-parties, or writing letters without the abbot's leave, or exchanging gossip with the townspeople over a tankard of ale at Court Gate. In several thousand words of thunderous

---

[1] In 1562 Grills took an active part in recovering some parish lands (TPR, p. 27, where the following item has been omitted: "Payed unto Wyllyam Grylls in parte payment of xiij *li*. vj*s*. xj*d. ob*. which was awed unto hym by the parisshe before, the some of iiij *li*. vj*s*. xj*d. ob*."). He also increased the endowment of the almshouse (*ibid.*, p. 32).

[2] W. D General Evidences, Bdle 1, no. 8. When the lease expired in 1753, the duke of Bedford took the fairs and market-house back into his own hands and allowed the salaries of the master and under-master to become a charge on the estate. He and his successors thenceforth acted as patrons of the school. The position however was anomalous, and in 1889 the ninth duke declined to appoint a new headmaster, but handed £20,000 to the Charity Commissioners in order that a new school might be established under a properly constituted board of governors. The present school was opened accordingly in 1895.

Latin the bishop calls them to order; then silence returns until the next outbreak.[1] From these episcopal monitions we infer that a high standard of personal conduct and corporate observance was taken for granted, and that few lapses went unremarked. From other documents we gather that their administration was usually efficient, and their agriculture, though perhaps not superior to that of other Devonshire landowners, as good as the best in England at the time. If the final impression is one of mediocrity, it may fairly be called a golden mediocrity.

In suppressing the English monasteries, Cromwell and his agents attacked, and so far as they could destroyed, a way of life which has never ceased to attract recruits and to cast its spell over many whose own vocation lies outside the cloister. John Aubrey was not alone in looking back wistfully to the "convenience of religious houses" and thinking it "fitt there should be receptacles and provision for contemplative men".[2] Within the memory of persons now living great sums have been expended in re-establishing such "receptacles" within the national Church.[3] Outside it such communities as Downside, Ampleforth, and Buckfast demonstrate the continued vitality of the Benedictine ideal. Many who see no value in liturgical prayer can appreciate the opportunities the cloister provides for study and meditation. The monks of Tavistock did not, like those of St Albans, earn remembrance by leaving to posterity a series of great chronicles, or like those of Peterborough by producing superlatively beautiful manuscripts. But they enriched Tavistock with architecture more splendid than it is ever likely to see again, and during half a millennium exhibited to all who cared to see it the spectacle of an ordered existence in which room was found for leisure, reading, and hospitality. When at last their abbey fell, no comparably civilized institution took its place.

[1] For an unexplained but presumably not unprovoked assault on the vicar, see *Reg. Brantyngham*, p. 565. For private dinners, *ibid.*, p. 312, and *Reg. Grandisson*, p. 997; private letter-writing, *Reg. Brantyngham*, p. 313; gossip at Court Gate, *ibid.*, p. 670. The lowest stage of demoralization in the history of the abbey was perhaps reached during the interregnum that followed the death of Robert Champeaux; cf. Finberg, 'Prelude to Abbot Bonus', in DCNQ xxiii, 1948, pp. 184 sqq.

[2] Powell, *op. cit.*, p. 138.

[3] Between 1906 and 1913 over sixty thousand pounds was subscribed for the foundation of the community now settled at Nashdom (Anson, *The Benedictines of Caldey*, p. 194).

ABBOTS OF TAVISTOCK

For a more detailed list, giving dates of *congé d'élire* and restitution of temporalities where they are known, with references, see DCNQ XXII, 1943, pp. 159 sqq.

1	(Name unknown)	*c.* 975 – ?
2	Ælfmær	*c.* 990 – ?
3	Lyfing	*c.* 1009–1027
4	Ealdred	1027–*c.* 1043
5	Sihtric	*c.* 1043–1082
6	Geoffrey	1082–1088
7	Wymund	*c.* 1091–1102
8	Osbert	*c.* 1107–1131
9	Robert of Plympton	1131–1146
10	Robert Postel	1147–1155
11	Walter	1155–1168
12	Godfrey	1168–1173
13	Baldwin	1174–1184
14	Herbert	1186–1200
15	Andrew	1200–1202
16	Jordan	1203–1220
17	William de Kernet	1220–1224
18	John of Rochester	1224–1233
19	Alan	1233–1248
20	Robert of Kidknowle	1248–1257
21	Henry of Northampton	1257–1259
22	Philip Trenchfoil	1259–1260
23	Alfred	1260–1262
24	John Chubb	1262–1269
25	Robert Colbern	1270–1285
26	Robert Champeaux	1285–1324
27	Bonus	1327–1333
28	John de Courtenay	1334–1349
29	Richard Ash	1349–1362
30	Stephen Langdon	1362–1380
31	Thomas Cullyng	1381–1402
32	John Mey	1402–1422
33	Thomas Mede	1422–1442
34	Thomas Crispyn	1442–1447
35	William Pewe	1447–1450
36	John Dynyngton	1451–1490
37	Richard Eme	1491–1492
38	Richard Banham	1492–1523
39	John Peryn	1523–1539

APPENDIX B

THE FOUNDATION CHARTER OF THE ABBEY

THE charter given to the abbey by Ethelred II in 981 is a fine specimen of the hybrid vocabulary and turgid style in which the draftsmen of the period indulged. In its original form it is no longer extant; but it was laid before Edward I in 1285 and confirmed by him on the 10th of September in that year, when a far from accurate copy was entered on the Charter Roll (13 Edw. I, m.3). In the following notes the symbol *a* refers to this enrolment. A second and even less accurate transcript was enrolled in 1348 (=*b*). This was printed from Charter Roll 22 Edw. III, m.27, with a few emendations, but still in a highly corrupt form, by Dugdale (II, p. 495), whose version (=*c*) has been reproduced by Kemble and Thorpe. Dugdale also printed an excerpt (=*d*) from the *Fundationis Historia* prefixed to the fifteenth-century register of Tavistock (above, p. 263 *n.*). The archaic language of this narrative suggests that the compiler transcribed it from a much earlier source. For textual purposes it is of the greatest value, including as it does a long passage quoted from the charter which appears to be more trustworthy than either of the enrolled versions. The reconstructed text which follows is based on a collation of *a*, *b*, *c*, and *d* with other charters of the period.

$\underset{X}{P}$ VNIVERSITATIS CREATORE IN ETERNVM REGNANTE ac iusto moderamine cuncta creata, visibilia et inuisibilia,[1] miro ineffabilique modo gubernante: ego ÆTHELRED, anglice nacionis, ceterarumque gencium triuiatim[2] intra ambitum britannie insulae degencium, regie dignitatis solio ad tempus, Christi mundi redemptoris gracia, subtronizatus basileus, a quodam milite, auunculo videlicet meo, qui secundae regeneracionis vtero, innouante gracia, ineffabiliter editus nobili ORDULF[3] pollens floret onomate, humili deuocione conpunctus, subnixis deposcens precibus efflagitare Domini[4] conpunctus gracia beniuolus

---

[1] et inuisibilia et inuisibilia *a*.
[2] For a discussion of this adverb, with examples, see *Crawford Charters*, p. 111.
[3] Ordule *ab*.
[4] Deum *c*.

ceperam,[1] vt arcisterium cui nobile[2] ATTAVISTOCA fulget vocabulum,
vbi mater eius[3] fraterque, aua videlicet mea et auunculus, ceterique
nostre posteritatis prosapies[4] mausoleis somate[5] tumulati, tuba huius
caduce vite clangente vltima, terciam resurreccionis natiuitatem, ani-
ma[6] corpori Deo faciente in ictu oculi mirabiliter associata, diem iudi-
caturi vel iudicandi prestolantur extremum: vt ibi loco celebri, domino
nostro Iesu Christo eiusque genitrici semperque virgini MARIAE dedi-
cato, monachos non seculares set regulares, in omnibus sancte regule
obtemperantes preceptis, licenter constitueret fiscisque naturalibus
deuotus locupletaret. Eius igitur votis applaudendo voti compos an-
nui,[7] et quod fide[8] catholica poposcerat ammodum libens tripudi-
ansque concessi. Admiranda namque eius fidei constancia. Nam illo in
tempore quo prefatus miles, Sancti Spiritus gracia conpunctus, ad
legitimos monachorum vsus, ad eterne vite lucrum, hoc construxerat
coenobium, ceteri quique, infidelitatis neuo turpati,[9] loca sancta dissi-
pantes, sancte religionis monachos insipidi, me impote nolenteque,
infantili adhuc, vt ita dicam, etate vigente, atrociter veluti pagani ad
perpetuum sui dampnum fugabant.[10] Eius igitur beniuolencie con-
gaudens, meorum optimatum vsus consilio, libertatis priuilegium pre-
fato loco, sancte Dei genitrici semperque virgini MARIAE dicato, magna
animi alacritate tripudians concedo. Et secundum patroni nostri beati

[1] ceperat abc. Some emendation is necessary to provide this involved
sentence with a main verb. For ceperam, cf. K600 (III, p. 142): "ego Eadgar...
intra mei pectoris arcano . . . obnixe rimari ceperam," and Vita Oswaldi
(Hist. Church of York, ed. Raine, I, 434), "coepit non desistere coeptis" [!].
The meaning seems to be: "I, Ethelred . . . had begun to urge . . . Ordulf
my uncle . . . to complete his foundation at Tavistock." It should be remembered that the words are put into the mouth of a boy-king in his early
teens. In the next sentence Ethelred speaks of himself as "voti compos".
[2] nocibile Attauistoce b, notabile c. [3] eiusque ab. [4] procapes ab.
[5] sonomate ab. [6] affla ab. [7] animi c. [8] fides c.
[9] Cf. K610 (III, p. 155): "canonici omni viciorum neuo deturpati".
[10] It is noteworthy that in this reference to the anti-monastic disturbances
that occurred under Edward the Martyr, Ethelred is made to speak as if he
himself had been the rightful king ever since his father's death. One is
reminded of William the Conqueror's attitude towards the reign of Harold.
It is known that Edward was elected in the face of strong opposition, but the
reasons for the opposition have been variously stated. According to one early
account, he was an ill-conditioned youth who had made himself personally
objectionable by his violence of speech and behaviour (Vita Oswaldi, p. 449).
But his father's private life before his marriage with Ælfthryth had been
irregular, and the suggestion advanced by Robertson (Historical Essays,
p. 176) that the so-called martyr was the offspring of a handfast connection,
and therefore of questionable legitimacy, deserves more attention than it has
received.

BENEDICTI tradicionem, post obitum abbatis qui nunc sancto presidet loco,[1] abbas ex eadem eligatur[2] congregacione qui dignus sit tali fungi officio; aliorsum vero minime, nisi culpis promerentibus inibi inueniri nequiuerit qui aptus sit animabus lucrandis. Quod si hoc, quod absit, miserabiliter euenerit, de alio noto et familiari monasterio vnanimi fratrum consilio eligatur cuius vita probabilis, sapiencia predita cultuque religionis fulgida, fidelibus clarescat. Finitis namque diebus beniuoli et laudabilis viri qui specialis lucri copia sanctum dapsilis ditauerit[3] locum, laicorum nemo ipsius loci dominium presumens sibi vsurpet. Rura[4] vero que ab eo [,vel a sua coniuge, vel a suis parentibus vel amicis] DOMINO NOSTRO IESU CHRISTO eiusque genitrici semperque virgini MARIAE, ob eterne vite[5] remuneracionem, concessa sunt vel concedenda, [haec sunt:[6] Tavistok, Midelton,[7] Hatherleghe, Berliton,[8] Leghe, Dunecheni,[9] Chuvelin,[10] Lankinhorn, haec a viro. Haec vero a coniuge: Hame,[11] Werdgete,[12] Orlege,[13] Anri,[14] Rame, Savyok,[15] Pannastan,[16] Tornebiri,[17] Colbrok, Lege, Wlsithetun,[18] Clymesland. Haec] nec abbas, nec alicuius persone homo licenciam habeat pro pecunia vendendi vel gratis concedendi vel mutandi, set eterno Deo maneat imperpetuum quod ei concessum vel concedendum

---

[1] The name of this first abbot is unknown. The next sentence but one ("Finitis", etc.) suggests that he was nominated by Ordulf, and this is borne out by the *Fundationis Historia* ("abbatem ordinauit"). For a similar exercise of founder's privilege by Æthelmær at Eynsham, cf. K714, p. 340.

[2] ligatur *b*.

[3] ditauerat *abcd*. But grammar demands the emendation. The extent of the Tavistock endowment is not yet determined: see p. 281, *n*. 1 below.

[4] Rex *abc*; Rura *d*.   [5] ab eterno vsque *abc*.

[6] This and the former bracketed passage occur only in *d*, where they are embedded in a word-for-word quotation from the charter. That is one reason for holding that they are part of its text; another is that such lists of possessions are a regular feature of monastic foundation charters: cf., among others, K581 (Ramsey), 710 (Burton), 714 (Eynsham).

[7] Milton Abbot.   [8] Burrington, the Domesday Bernintona.

[9] Dunethem *d*, but this is Dugdale's misreading. The Domesday spelling is Donecheniv, and the place is either Downeckney in Treneglos or Downinney in the neighbouring parish of Warbstow.

[10] Possibly Killinch *alias* Cavelynch near Denbury; the geographical sequence however points to Cornwall.   [11] Abbotsham.

[12] Worthygate in Parkham, the Domesday Wrdieta. Dugdale reads: Werelgete.

[13] Orleigh in Buckland Brewer.

[14] Auri *d*, another misreading, for Annery in Monkleigh.   [15] Sheviock.

[16] Panson in St Giles on the Heath.   [17] Thornbury.

[18] Apparently Wulfsige's *tun*, and therefore perhaps Woolston in West Alvington, the Domesday Ulsistona; but there are also Woolstons in Cornwall, one near Marhamchurch, the other between Pensilva and St Ive.

est.[1] Regum vero munimine deinceps ipse locus Domino protegente tueatur, ipsiusque loci abbas, regi[2] deseruiens, gregem sibi commissum dirocheo,[3] id est duplici pastu,[4] foueat. Sit igitur prefatum monasterium omni terrene seruitutis iugo liberum, tribus exceptis, rata videlicet expedicione, pontis, arcisve restauracione. Si quis vero tam epilempticus philargirie seductus amencia, quod non optamus, hanc nostre munificencie dapsilitatem ausu temerario infringere temptauerit, sit ipse alienatus a consorcio sancte Dei ecclesie, necnon et a participacione sacrosancti corporis et sanguinis Iesu Christi filii Dei, per quem totus terrarum orbis ab antiquo humani generis inimico liberatus est, et cum Iuda Christi proditore sinistra in parte deputatus, ni prius hic digna satisfaccione humiliter penituerit quod contra sanctam Dei ecclesiam rebellis agere presumpserit, nec in vita hac practica veniam, nec in theorica requiem apostata optineat vllam, set aeternis baratri incendiis trusus cum Anania et Saphira iugiter miserrimus crucietur. Anno dominice incarnacionis DCCCCLXXXJ, indictione IX, scripta est haec carta, hiis testibus consencientibus quorum inferius nomina caraxantur.

✠Ego ÆTHELRED[5] REX TOCIVS BRITANNIE PREFATAM DONACIONEM CVM SIGILLO SANCTE CRVCIS CONFIRMAVI.

✠Ego DVNSTAN[6] Dorobernensis ecclesie Archiepiscopus eiusdem Regis beniuolenciam consensi.

✠Ego Ælfthryth,[7] eiusdem Regis mater, hanc donacionem confirmaui.

✠Ego Oswald Archiepiscopus triumphalem tropheum agiae crucis impressi.[8]

[1] Cf. supra, "concessa sunt vel concedenda." This expression probably implies that Ordulf reserved to himself a life interest in some of the estates, as did his contemporary Æthelmær when founding Cerne Abbey (K656).

[2] Deo d. The corresponding passage in the Ramsey charter has also been tampered with; as printed, it reads: "regi deo soli seruiens" (K581, p. 109).

[3] This curious word is the title given to a set of quatrains by Prudentius in the oldest manuscripts of that poet's works. It is there accompanied by the gloss "duplex refectio". The editors of Prudentius have one and all treated it as a scribe's error. Of several possible emendations, that proposed by Aldus— dittocheum, from διττός and ὀχή—is now generally received. Ducange mentions no other instance of dirocheum outside these two contexts. It must, however, have been current some little while before this charter was drawn up, for it occurs in a Winchester document of Edgar's reign (K610, III, p. 154). Prudentius wished to signify that his theme was taken from both Testaments, the Old and New; but in these charters the twofold nourishment is spiritual and temporal (cf. K581, p. 109).

[4] pasto abc. [5] ADED a. [6] DUPSTAN b, omitting ego.

[7] Alfdryd eiusdem mater a; Alydryd b, which adds a second cross at the end of her line.

[8] impensi a; b omits ego.

✠Ego Æthelweald Wintaniensis[1] ecclesie Episcopus predictum donum consensi.

✠Ego Ælfstan Londoniensis ecclesie Episcopus consignaui.

✠Ego Æthelgar Episcopus[2] tropheum agiae crucis imposui.

✠Ego Ælfstan Episcopus[3] iubente Rege signum crucis infixi.

✠Ego Ælfstan Episcopus[4] consensum prebui figens crucem.

✠Ego Athulf Episcopus[5] crucis modum manu propria subscripsi.

✠Ego Ælfric Episcopus.[6]	✠Ego Ælfheah Episcopus.[7]	✠Ego Æscwig Episcopus.[8]
✠Ego Æthelsige Episcopus.[9]	✠Ego Wulfsige Episcopus.[10]	
✠Ego Ælfhere Dux.[11]	✠Ego Æthelwine Dux.[12]	✠Ego Beorhtnoð Dux.[13]
✠Ego Æthelweard Dux.[14]	✠Ego Æthelmær Dux.[15]	✠Ego Eadwine Dux.[16]
✠Ego Ælfweard minister.[17]	Ego Æthelweard min.[18]	Ego Beorhtweald min.[19]
Ego Ælfsige min.[20]	Ego Beorhtnoð min.[21]	Ego Ælfsige min.[22]

[1] Ego Ædeluuold Pictaniensis *a*; Ædeluuold Pictauiensis *b*; Etheluuoldus Wyntoniensis *d*.

[2] of Selsey; Ayelgar *ab*; Ethelgar *d*.

[3] of Rochester; Elstanus Cridiatonensis *d*.

[4] of Ramsbury; Ethelstan *d*.   [5] of Hereford; Ayulf *a*, Æyulf *b*, Athul *d*.

[6] of Crediton; Celfric *b*, Aluric *d*.   [7] of Lichfield; Celsheah *b*, Elfeac *d*.

[8] of Dorchester; ærþig *a*, Cerpis *b*, Cerdic *c*, Escui *printed as* Estin *d*.

[9] of Sherborne; ædelrige *a*, Cedelrise *b*, Ædelric *c*, Ethelsi *d*.

[10] of Cornwall; þulfrige *a*, yulfr. *b*, Wulfr. *c*, Wlsi *d*.

[11] of Mercia; Alfherie *a*, Ælrherie *b*, Alchere *c*. After Edgar's death he led the party whose quasi-heathen conduct is so feelingly contrasted (*supra*, p. 279, ll. 12–18) with Ordulf's piety. The opposition, now in power, cannot resist this dig at him.

[12] of East Anglia; Aþelþine *a*, Æyelþine *b*.

[13] of Essex; Bvyrihtnod *a*, Rvyrihtnod *b*.

[14] of the western shires; Aædelþearid *a*, Acedelyecirid *b*, Athelbriht *c*.

[15] of Hampshire; Aædelmœr *a*, Acedelmoer *b*.

[16] of Sussex; Aedþine *a*, Aeadyine *b*. The same half-dozen ealdormen, in the same order, attest a charter of the preceding year (K626).

[17] Aælfþearid *a*, Acelfyeard *b*, Athelweard *c*. Signs in the previous and following years (K624, 632).

[18] ædelþearid *a*, oedelyearid *b*; signs in 983 (K636).

[19] beorihtyold *a*, Beorcthtyold *b*; signs in 980 and 982 (K624, 632).

[20] ælfrige *a*, Celfrise *b*, Ælfric *c*; signs in 980 and 982 (K624, 632).

[21] byrihtnod *a*, Byrightnod *b*.

[22] ælfrige *a*, Celfrise *b*, Ælfric *c*; perhaps Æthelsige, who signs in 982 and 984 (K633, 641).

Ego Ordhelm min.[1] Ego God min.[2] Ego Ælfsige min.[3]

Ego Leofwine min.[4] Ego Leofric min.[5] Ego Ælfmær min.[6]

Ego Godwine min.[7] Ego Ælfwine min.[8] Ego Ælfric min.[9]

Kemble stigmatized this charter, and Plummer, presumably on the strength of Kemble's asterisk, dismissed it as "spurious".[10] It is, however, well known that many charters doubted by Kemble are genuine. This one was accepted as authentic by Thorpe, and also, apparently, by W. H. Stevenson.[11] None of these authorities had seen any but Dugdale's version of the text.

The date, 981, is consistent with the presence among the signatories of Æthelgar, who became bishop of Selsey in the previous year, of Ælfstan, bishop of Ramsbury, who died later in the year of issue, and of the two ealdormen Æthelmær and Eadwine, who both died in 982. It is in no way inconsistent with what is known of the other witnesses. There are thirty-four of these, besides Ethelred and his mother. We have seen that twenty-nine are verified by contemporary documents, and that there is nothing questionable about the remaining five. Nor is there anything doubtful in the substance of the charter. It confers no extravagant favours, merely the usual franchise; and its language is characteristic of such documents. In 997 the monastery was burnt down by Danish raiders, and the original charter may then have perished in the flames. This was what happened at Exeter, "diruto monasterio a paganis et crematis priuilegiis quae antiqui reges concesserant."[12] If so, the version which has survived may be a *bona fide* reproduction, written out from memory as soon as things had settled down again after the raid. On the other hand, it is equally probable that the monks found time to remove the precious document before the fire. But all this is mere surmise. As the charter now stands, there seems to be no reason for doubting its authenticity.

---

[1] oridelm *ab*; a thegn so named occurs *c*. 975, *Lib. Elien.* II, 19.

[2] A Goda *minister* who occurs *c*. 975 (Birch, *Cart. Sax.* 1308) may perhaps be identifiable with this witness and with the Devonshire thegn Goda who fell in combat with the Danes (A.S. Chron. 998). But instances of *God* as a man's name are to be found in Searle's *Onomasticon*.

[3] Variants as before.

[4] Leofþine *a*, Leofyine *b*; signs in 980 and 983 (K624, 639).

[5] Leofruc *ab*; signs in 980 and 982 (K624, 1278).   [6] ælmæri *a*, Celmær *b*.

[7] Signs in 980 and 984 (K624, 641).

[8] ælfþine *a*, Celfyine *b*; signs in 984 (K641).

[9] ælfruc *a*, Celyruc *b*; signs in 980 and 982 (K624, 632).

[10] K629 (III, p. 182); *Two Saxon Chronicles*, II, p. 179.

[11] Thorpe, *Diplomatarium*, p. 267; *Crawford Charters*, p. 122, and cf. *ibid.* p. x.   [12] K729.

THE ABBEY BUILDINGS

THE abbey church was extremely narrow in proportion to its width. Its dimensions were recorded in 1478 by William Botoner of Worcester, as follows:

Nave	60 paces long	
Choir	42	,, ,,
Retro-choir	24	,, ,,
Lady Chapel	12	,, ,,

With a total length of one hundred and thirty-eight paces, the church was only twenty-one paces wide, the width of the nave being fourteen and that of the single (northern) aisle seven paces.[1] Excavations carried out in 1914 determined the position of the south wall, which backed on to the cloister arch standing in the present churchyard. The wall was 41½ inches thick. On the side nearest to the parish church its plaster covering remained, with an ornamental pattern stencilled in black, red, and yellow. The excavation was carried down about seven feet until it reached the original floor-level, revealing an area covered with tiles, mostly of red and white clay, five inches square. These floor-tiles can still be seen by lifting an iron trapdoor in the churchyard. The designs, of early fourteenth-century date, include: a lion in a central ring, surrounded by fishes swimming; a bishop vested, with hand upraised in benediction; a serpent-like creature with a large head; a single fish; and what appears to be a shield of arms. A second excavation, carried out in 1920, uncovered the north wall of the church, the position of which is now indicated by a stone beside the churchyard path.

The excavations were conducted by Lady Radford, who wrote a paper on the subject, first published in 1914.[2] Lady Radford also made a careful study of the documentary evidence and of the eighteenth-century estate maps preserved in the Bedford Office. From the data thus collected Mr C. A. Ralegh Radford prepared a ground-plan of the site as a whole, which was printed with a revised version of Lady Radford's paper in the Transactions of the Exeter Diocesan

---

[1] DA XVIII, 1886, p. 480; cf. Alford, *Abbots of Tavistock*, p. 171.
[2] DA XLVI, 1914, pp. 119 sqq.

Architectural and Archaeological Society.[1] I gratefully acknowledge Mr Radford's kind permission to make use of his work. The drawing at p. 221 of this book is in all essential features based on his plan; it differs only in regard to the position of the misericord and of the abbot's lodging.

The ruins of the abbey church remained standing from the Dissolution until 1670, or thereabouts. They were finally demolished to provide materials for a schoolhouse, which was built on the site of the western tower.[2]

The arch now remaining in the churchyard stood in the north walk of the cloisters, and a small drain near it, revealed by the excavations of 1914, suggests that it may have been the *lavatorium* or washing-place of the monks. Browne Willis, writing in 1718, says: "The Scite of the Cloysters is visible, and measures about forty-five Paces in length; the East side opened into the Chapter-House, which was a neat Pile, being exactly octangular, and comprising thirty-six Stalls most beautifully arched overhead." The south wall of the chapter-house was uncovered when some drains were being laid near the Bedford Office; and some of its floor-tiles were dug up in 1830.[3]

Parallel with the abbey church and adjoining the south cloister stood a range of vaults and cellars, and above them the frater, or main refectory. In a lease of 1691 this great hall is described as "the Saxon School". It had acquired that name in consequence of the legend started by Matthew Parker, that Anglo-Saxon literature was studied at Tavistock until the Dissolution.[4] With the remains of the cloisters and chapter-house, the frater was pulled down between 1716 and 1725 by Jacob Saunders, a rich Presbyterian who held the site on lease from the duke of Bedford.[5] On the foundations of the frater Saunders proceeded to build himself "a pompous dwelling house", the present Bedford Hotel. In the course of this work he dug up an ancient stone sarcophagus containing two thighbones of unusual length. Tradition associates the longer of the two with Childe Ordulf, an eleventh-century benefactor of the abbey, noted for his gigantic stature, whose vast tomb is described by William of Malmesbury as one of the sights of Tavistock. Ordulf seems to have been entombed in the cloister, as was the founder of Burton Abbey. His broken effigy, according to Browne Willis, lay for some time under the remaining cloister arch,

---

[1] XV; republished as a booklet, Exeter, 1929.
[2] Browne Willis, *History of the Mitred Parliamentary Abbies*, I, p. 170; DA xlvii, 1915, p. 385.
[3] Bray, *Traditions etc. of Devonshire*, II, p. 110.
[4] Above, p. 223.   [5] DA xlvi, p. 151.

285

to which in consequence the townsmen gave the name "Childe's Tomb" or "Ordulf's Tomb".[1]

The great kitchen must have stood at the east or west end of the frater. It is described by Prince as "a large square room open to the roof, which was in timber so geometrically done that even architects did admire the curiosity thereof."[2] The normal plan of a Benedictine monastery placed the kitchen, buttery, storerooms, and cellars on the western side of the cloister, and the dormitory, with the adjacent rere-dorter or "necessary house", in the eastern block. But this arrangement might in certain cases be reversed, and there are grounds for believing that it was so at Tavistock. The eighteenth-century estate maps show a stream of water running alongside the former western range. This was the original outflow of the Fishlake. By the first quarter of the twelfth century the monks were utilizing it for purposes of sanitation. The presence of this rivulet supplied ample reason for placing the dorter and rere-dorter in the western range. Two artificial channels were drawn off at its entrance to the precinct, one to feed the stewpond, the other to drive the abbey mill, which at some date before 1086 was built on the site of the present Guildhall.

The eastern range appears to have been prolonged southward as far as the precinct wall, in order perhaps to accommodate the bakehouse, brewhouse, and other offices.

The infirmary buildings are first mentioned in 1348, when bishop Grandisson urged the abbot to dine with the brethren in the refectory, "or at least in the adjoining building commonly called the misericord".[3] At Tavistock as at other Benedictine houses the misericord, a dining-hall originally reserved for the use of the sick, came in process of time to be used by the abbot and most of the community, who dined there far more often than in the frater. This building survived the Dissolution, and from 1691 until the present day has been continuously used as a place of worship, at first by Presbyterians but latterly by Unitarians. In 1755 the timber roof was covered over with a plaster ceiling, towards the cost of which the duke of Bedford gave thirty pounds, the nonconformist trustees in return surrendering an "Old Building projecting out Northward from the North side and West end"—probably the infirmary chapel.[4] In 1845 the stone pulpit in the north wall of the misericord was removed, and a new entrance was made by inserting a granite archway into the east end. The original

[1] DA LXXVIII, 1946, pp. 272 sqq.; Bray, op. cit., II, p. 53. For the burial of Wulfric, the founder of Burton, "in claustro monasterii sui sub arcu lapideo juxta ostium ecclesiae", see Dugdale, III, p. 47.
[2] Worthies of Devon, p. 619.   [3] Reg., p. 273.
[4] John Wynne: A New Survey of the Borough of Tavistock, p. 43.

north entrance was then walled up. The approach to it lay through a porch which can still be seen in the yard of the Bedford Hotel; it has a groined stone ceiling, with armorial roof-bosses, above which is a chamber formerly approached by a circular stone staircase. In 1883 this room was described as having "a handsome oak roof with tre-foiled principals, now much decayed".[1] The main hall of the infirmary adjoined the west end of the misericord, and formed a prolongation of the western range. In the eighteenth century it was used as a ball-room.[2]

The abbot's lodging appears from bishop Brantyngham's injunctions to have stood at the westernmost extremity of the whole precinct: an eligible situation, facing the meadows, fishponds, and orchard.[3] This building was leased out by the second earl of Bedford, and at the beginning of the seventeenth century was occupied as a private residence by the father of Serjeant Maynard.[4] In 1642 it was attacked by Hopton's Cavaliers, who tore up the serjeant's papers, "cut his beds in pieces, casting abroad the feathers, and pulled down part of the roof of his house".[5] The building then fell into a slow decay. Its remains, consisting of a vaulted gateway between two massive towers, can still be seen in the front garden of the vicarage. The southern tower is traditionally known as Betsy Grimbal's Tower. In the time of the abbey it may have been called Blessed Grimbald's, after a ninth-century scholar-saint of that name who was much honoured in Benedictine houses.[6]

From time to time there is mention of buildings which cannot now be precisely located, such as New Cotehele ("la Nywecotehele"), named in 1352 as adjoining a garden called Sexton's-hay; a room somewhere on the ground floor called the Prior's Chamber; and another on the first floor "above the high vault". There was also a "chicken court" of which the cellarer had charge.[7]

The bones which from time to time have been dug up at the east end of the Plymouth road indicate that the monks' graveyard occupied its usual position near the chapter-house and eastern range. A line of wall which cannot now be traced separated it from the great courtyard.

The precinct wall ran from the west end of the church round to the abbot's lodging, enclosing a grass court known as the Prayle. From the

[1] *Journal of the British Archaeological Association*, xxxix, 1883, p. 188.

[2] Bray, *op. cit.*, ii, p. 114.   [3] *Reg. Brantyngham*, p. 670.

[4] Pole, *Collections towards a Description of the County of Devon*, p. 340.

[5] Contemporary news-letter, cited DA xlvi, p. 150.

[6] Bray, *op. cit.*, ii, p. 111.

[7] W. D Bdle 53, no. 137; *Reg. Lacy*, pp. 52, 320; DCNQ xxiii, 1948, p. 254.

abbot's lodging it continued to a two-storey building on the river bank traditionally known as the Still-House, perhaps because the herb-garden lay between it and the infirmary. This building, described in 1832 as very ruinous, was repaired in 1884.[1] From the Still-House the crenellated precinct wall ran along the river bank to the point where the prolongation of the eastern range terminated at the Water Gate. The latter, a four-centred arch of granite, about eight feet wide, gave access to the abbey bridge; it was taken down in the last century.[2]

Between the Water Gate and Court Gate stretched a line of buildings including the abbey mill and a turreted house which may have been the almonry or guest-house.[3] These faced on to the great court-yard. Court Gate, the main gateway of the abbey, is a two-storey building, which, with the turreted house just mentioned, was restored by John Foulston in 1824. Since 1829 it has been the home of the Tavistock Library. For more direct access to the abbey church, a passage led from Market Street under and through the tower of St Eustace's, which stands on four arches and was formerly open to pedestrians. The parish graveyard lay between the two churches, and in bishop Brantyngham's time extended eastward nearly to Court Gate.

The site was markedly affected by the building of the present Abbey Bridge in 1764. In order to provide convenient access to this bridge, Bedford Street was widened at the expense of the parish churchyard. The roadway now traversed the site of the choir and Lady chapel. Alterations yet more drastic followed in the second quarter of the last century, when the new Plymouth Road was driven straight over the site of the cloisters and chapter-house, both road and churchyard being made up to a higher level.

Since 1924 the remains of the abbey have been scheduled as ancient monuments under the protection of the Ministry of Works.

ICONOGRAPHY

The earliest representation of the buildings known to me is that given on a diagrammatic map of Dartmoor, drawn in the late sixteenth century, and now in the Royal Albert Museum at Exeter. A reduced reproduction was printed in DA v, 1872, p. 512. On this map the roofless condition of the abbey church is plainly indicated, but the other details are not clearly expressed.

The following is a list of the principal modern illustrations:

[1] Bray, *op. cit.*, II, p. 153; Alford, *op. cit.*, p. 175.
[2] Bray, II, p. 109; cf. p. 202 *n.*, above.
[3] In 1519 John Amadas was described as "dwelling at Court Yatte" (*Select Cases in the Court of Requests*, p. 23).

1716. TAVISTOCK ABBY IN THE C: OF DEVON.
A sketch by Edmund Prideaux, now in the possession of the Prideaux family. The abbey from the south-east, showing the frater, not yet dismantled, and the roofless octagonal chapter-house. Reproduced in *Trans. Exeter Diocesan Architectural and Archaeological Society*, xv, plate xv.

1734. THE WEST VIEW OF TAVISTOCK-ABBY, IN THE COUNTY OF DEVON.
Engraved by Samuel and Nathaniel Buck. Showing Court Gate, the turreted house near it, and the infirmary buildings, the latter in a highly artificial grouping. Reproduced *ibid.*, plate xvii.

1741. THE SOUTH EAST PROSPECT OF THE TOWN OF TAVISTOKE IN THE COUNTY OF DEVON.
Drawn by Charles Delafontaine and engraved by R. Parr. A bird's-eye view of the whole site, showing the new house built by Jacob Saunders on the site of the frater. Reproduced *ibid.*, plate xvi.

1807. ORDULPH'S TOMB [the cloister arch in the churchyard].
REMAINS OF TAVISTOCK ABBEY, DEVON [Court Gate and adjacent buildings].
Drawn by Samuel Prout; engraved by J. Greig; published in *The Antiquarian and Topographical Cabinet*, ii, 1808.

1810. THE GATEWAY AT TAVISTOCK ABBEY, DEVONSHIRE.
Court Gate. Drawn by J. Nixon; engraved by S. Rawle; published as frontispiece to Vol. LVIII of *The European Magazine*.

1811. An engraving published by T. Palser after an etching by Samuel Prout, showing the Water Gate, precinct wall, and new Abbey Bridge. Reproduced in DCNQ xxiii, 1947, p. 118.

1820. REMAINS OF TAVISTOCK PRIORY (*sic*), DEVONSHIRE.
Court Gate and adjacent buildings. Engraved by John Coney. Dugdale, ii, p. 489.

1830. TAVISTOCK ABBEY, DEVONSHIRE.
The same buildings after restoration. Drawn by T. Allom; engraved by S. Fisher.

1830. BETSY GRIMBALD'S TOWER, etc.
An engraving published in the *Gentleman's Magazine*, c, p. 489.

1866. INTERIOR OF THE ENTRANCE PORCH, and walled-up doorway leading into the misericord. Drawn by E. Appleton; printed in DA i, 1862–6, part v, p. 124.

The drawing at p. 221 of the present work has been made by J. H. P. Finberg. It gives a bird's-eye view of the whole site, reconstructed in

accordance with Mr Radford's ground-plan. Buildings now destroyed
have been depicted so far as possible by analogy with those which have
survived, but the architectural details are of course imaginary. By way
of contrast, an aerial photograph is appended, showing the present
aspect of the site.

APPENDIX D

THE TAVISTOCK PRINTING PRESS[1]

THE art of printing had been practised in England for nearly
half a century before Thomas Richard set up a press at Tavistock. It was, however, confined to half a dozen centres: West-
minster (1477), Oxford (1478–86, 1517–18), St Albans (1479–86),
London (1480), York (1509–16), and Cambridge (1521). The demands
of the English market were still met chiefly by importation of books
printed abroad. About 1505 an edition of Stanbridge's *Vocabula*,
printed at Rouen, was published by Martin Coffin, an Exeter stationer
and bookbinder, who some years later issued a *Catho cum Commento*,
also printed at Rouen. Coffin has a good claim to be regarded as the
first publisher in the south-west, but he never took the final step of
setting up his own press.

Thomas Richard, monk of Tavistock, was ordained subdeacon in
March 1502, at Exeter, and priest in September of the following year.
In 1507 he was admitted as a student at Gloucester Hall, Oxford. For
the next eight years he studied logic, philosophy, and theology. In
1510 he was appointed proctor for abbot Banham at a chapter of the
Benedictine order then about to be held at Coventry. He graduated
B.D. on the 28th of June 1515.[2]

It is possible that the idea of establishing a press at Tavistock was
suggested to him by his friend Robert Langdon (1483–1548), of
Keverell in St Martin's-by-Looe, Cornwall, who certainly inspired
the choice of the first book to be printed there; but there are no
grounds for believing that Langdon financed the undertaking.

---

[1] This account of the press is condensed, with some additions and cor-
rections, from Lady Radford's Presidential Address on 'Early Printing in
Devon', DA LX, 1928, pp. 51 sqq.

[2] The statement that he took a Cambridge degree of B.D. in 1517 is declared by Venn to be erroneous (*Alumni Cantabrigienses*, III, p. 450).

THE SITE OF THE ABBEY AT THE PRESENT DAY

Matrices for two founts of type were purchased, with a number of stock woodcuts, French in style. In the smaller founts two V's were used instead of W, and when the V's ran short, one only, as in vhen, vhether, vherfore. On this ground Professor A. W. Pollard held that the type also was of French origin; he argued that no German or Dutch typefounder would have omitted to provide a W.

The establishment of the press coincided with the departure from Oxford of John Scolar, a printer who brought out five books there under his own imprint in 1517 and the following year, after which he left the city. Nothing more is heard of him until 1528, when he found employment at Abingdon and printed a breviary in the abbey there.[1] It can be no more than a conjecture, though a plausible one, that he spent some of the intervening years at Tavistock. His technical experience would be of great value, and Thomas Richard, who probably met him at Oxford, may conceivably have utilized it as the monks of Abingdon did later.

The first book known to have issued from the press was *The Consolation of Philosophy*, translated from the Latin of Boethius. *Circa* 1478 Caxton had printed Chaucer's translation of this famous and beloved work; but Chaucer's, like the earlier rendering by Alfred the Great, was all in prose, whereas the original consisted of alternate prose and verse. To satisfy the demand for a metrical rendering, with annotations, John Walton, a canon of Osney, had made a new translation in 1410, which remained unprinted until Robert Langdon persuaded his friend to undertake an edition at Tavistock. As only seven copies now survive, the edition was probably not large. The book is a small quarto of 272 pages, measuring 176 × 130 mm. "The title-page has a woodcut of God Almighty crowned, with an orb and cross in his left hand, the right being raised in benediction. The figure is enclosed in a diamond; the corners that make the outline square are filled with emblems of the four evangelists. Outside this square appear four detached borders containing flowers, foliage, birds, and a singularly large and handsome snail. The whole of these woodcuts are French."[2] At the foot of the page appears the title

The Boke of comfort called in laten
Boetius de Consolatione philosophie
Translated in to englesse tonge.

---

[1] Gordon Duff, *The English Provincial Printers*, p. 100. Mr E. P. Goldschmidt, however, in a letter to the *Times Literary Supplement*, June 9, 1950, gives reasons for believing that Scolar's publications were printed for him by Wynkyn de Worde.
[2] Lady Radford, *loc. cit.*, p. 65.

Then follow the Prefatio Translatoris and the Prologue, after which comes the text, then the Cognomen Translatoris followed by the colophon.

> Here endeth the boke of comfort called
> in latyn Boecius de consolatione Phie.
> Enprented in the exempt monastery of
> Tauestok in Denshyre. By me Dan
> Thomas Rychard monke of the sayd
> Monastery / To the instant desyre of
> the ryght worshypful esquyer Mayster
> Robert Langdon. Anno d. M D xxv.
> Deo Gracias.

After this comes a woodcut of Langdon's arms, followed by the name Robertus Langdon.[1]

In February 1528 Thomas Richard left the abbey to become prior of Totnes, but the type and press remained at Tavistock. According to Joseph Sanford, "Mr Granger, who was formerly Schoolmaster of Lescard, saw a Latin Grammar, called the Long Accidence, which was printed at Tavistocke, and was then in the possession of Mr Piper of Lescard."[2] No copy of this grammar has been found. The author of the *Long Accidence* was John Stanbridge, whose *Vocabula*, as we have seen, had been published at Exeter by Martin Coffin. An edition of the *Long Accidence* was printed by Wynkyn de Worde in 1520 or thereabouts. At present it must remain an open question whether Mr Granger saw the Exeter *Vocabula*, or Wynkyn de Worde's *Long Accidence*, or an edition of the last-named printed at Tavistock, all copies of which have disappeared.

The only other production known to have issued from the press was *The Statutes of the Stannary* (1534), the contents of which have been described in Chapter VII.[3] It is a quarto of 52 pages, untrimmed, measuring 210 × 145 mm., which was probably the size of the Boethius before the binder trimmed its margins. The type is the larger of the two employed in the Boethius. The title-page is embellished with a woodcut of the royal arms, which is repeated on two later pages; and a woodcut representing the martyrdom of St Andrew faces the colophon. The composition is better than the press-work. Folios 20 v. and 22 are both a line short, the missing line coinciding in each case with a

---

[1] The copy in the library of Exeter College, Oxford, is not perfect, as Lady Radford states; it lacks two leaves, R vi and R viii.

[2] *Remarks and Collections of Thomas Hearne*, VII, p. 15.

[3] Page 187. A fuller description is reprinted from Cotton's *Typographical Gazetteer* in DA *loc. cit.*, p. 69.

lacuna in the text; and the last three lines of fo. 24 do not make sense. All three passages have been corrected in manuscript by a contemporary hand.

A certain amount of ephemeral printing—notices and the like—may have been carried out between 1525 and 1534. The equipment of the press appears then to have passed into the hands of a family named Williams, possibly through William Williams, a monk of the abbey who was present at the surrender in 1539 and drew a pension of six pounds for some years after.[1] He was probably a kinsman of Adam Williams, steward of Cornwood in 1535, and of the Philip Williams to whom the abbot and convent in 1537 granted an annuity of 26s. 8d. with free board and lodging in a house next to the Guildhall. In 1567 one John Williams, clerk, chaplain to the mayor of Exeter, made a will bequeathing "my printinge with the matrice and the rest of my tooels concerning my presse" to a cousin of his, also named John Williams. What use he made of them, if any, is not known; but no more books were printed in Devon for another century and a half.

---

[1] In the pension-list of 1539 he is misnamed John.

U

LIST OF SOURCES

1. MANUSCRIPT

PUBLIC RECORD OFFICE
  Ancient Petitions.
  Assize Rolls, Devon.
  Charter Rolls.
  Court of Requests, Proceedings in the
  Court Rolls, General Series.
  Early Chancery Proceedings.
  Exchequer Accounts, Various.
  Fine Rolls.
  Inquisitions *ad quod damnum.*
  Inquisitions *post mortem.*
  Lay Subsidy Rolls.
  Ministers' Accounts.
  Star Chamber Proceedings.
  Surrenders of Religious Houses.

BRITISH MUSEUM
  Additional Charters.

BODLEIAN LIBRARY, OXFORD
  MS. Digby 81 (Annals of Tavistock).
  MS. Rawlinson B285.
  Additional MS. C85.

ROYAL SOCIETY, LONDON
  Classified Papers, Vol. X.

WOBURN ABBEY MUNIMENT ROOM
Table 2:
B2. Hatherleigh and Roborough court rolls.
B3. Burrington court rolls.
C1. Hurdwick court rolls.
C2. Hurdwick court rolls.
C3. Hurdwick court rolls.
D1. Werrington court rolls.
D2. Werrington court rolls.
D4. Ottery, etc., court rolls.

D5. Hatherleigh and Denbury account rolls.
D6. Plymstock court rolls.

Table 4:
A1. Hurdwick and Ottery account rolls.
A2. Werrington account rolls and rentals.
    Cellarer's account book.
    Tavistock addenda.
A3. Russell cartulary of Tavistock.
    Tavistock Abbey White Book.

II B. D Bdles 2–41.
II C. D Bdles 42–69.
II D. D Bdles 70–83.
II E. D Bdle 84.
II F. G Bdle 1.
II G. G Bdles 2–5.
II H. General Evidences, Devon, 1.
II J. General Evidences, Devon 2.
      B Bdle 117, nos. 1–39.
II K. Devon Acquittances.
II L. Devon Miscellanea.

BEDFORD OFFICE, TAVISTOCK
    The Manor of Hurdwick and Scite of the Abbey: a survey taken by
    Humphry Smith, 1726.
    A New Survey and Valuation of His Grace the Duke of Bedford's
    Lands in the Borough of Tavistock, by John Wynne, 1753.
    Estate maps and plans.

BEDFORD OFFICE, LONDON
    D Bdle 53 (Tavistock leases, 1288–1538).
    D Bdle 73 (Werrington leases, 1304–1538).

2. PRINTED

The list which follows is not an exhaustive bibliography; its purpose is
confined to giving fuller particulars of the books and articles to which
reference has been made in the footnotes.

Account of the Executors of Richard, bishop of London, 1303, and of
    the Executors of Thomas, bishop of Exeter, 1310, ed. W. H. Hale
    and H. T. Ellacombe. London (Camden Soc., 2nd series, 10), 1874.

U*

ALEXANDER, J. J.: Presidential Address, 'The Saxon Conquest and Settlement', DA LXIV, 1932, pp. 75–112.

—— and HOOPER, W. R.: The History of Great Torrington in the County of Devon. Sutton, Surrey, 1948.

ALFORD, D. P.: The Abbots of Tavistock. Plymouth, 1891.

ANSON, P. F.: The Benedictines of Caldey. London, 1940.

ASHLEY, W.: The Bread of our Forefathers. Oxford, 1928.

ASSER: Annales Rerum Gestarum Ælfredi Magni, ed. F. Wise. Oxford, 1722.

BALLARD, Adolphus: The Domesday Inquest. London, 1906.

—— The English Borough in the Twelfth Century. Cambridge, 1914.

—— (ed.): British Borough Charters, 1042–1216. Cambridge, 1913.

—— and TAIT, J. (edd.): British Borough Charters, 1216–1307. Cambridge, 1923.

Barnstaple Records, Reprint of the, ed. J. R. Chanter and T. Wainwright. 2 vols. Barnstaple, 1900.

BASKERVILLE, G.: The English Monks and the Suppression of the Monasteries. London, 1937.

BENNETT, H. S.: Life on the English Manor. Cambridge, 1937.

BIRCH, W. de G. (ed.): Cartularium Saxonicum. 3 vols. London, 1885–93.

BRASH, R. R.: The Ogam Inscribed Monuments of the Gaedhil in the British Isles. London, 1879.

BRAY, Mrs A. E.: Traditions, Legends, Superstitions, and Sketches of Devonshire on the Borders of the Tamar and the Tavy, illustrative of its Manners, Customs, History, Antiquities, Scenery, and Natural History, in a series of letters to Robert Southey, Esq. 3 vols. London, 1838.

BURNET, G.: History of the Reformation of the Church of England, ed. N. Pocock. 7 vols. Oxford, 1865.

CAM, H. M.: The Hundred and the Hundred Rolls. London, 1930.

—— Liberties and Communities in Medieval England. Cambridge, 1944.

Cambridge Economic History of Europe from the Decline of the Roman Empire, The, ed. J. H. Clapham and Eileen Power. Vol. I, The Agrarian Life of the Middle Ages. Cambridge, 1941.

CAREW, R.: A Survey of Cornwall, ed. Dunstanville. London, 1811.

CARUS-WILSON, E. M.: 'The Aulnage Accounts: A Criticism', Economic History Review, II, 1929, pp. 114–23.

—— 'An Industrial Revolution of the Thirteenth Century', *ibid.*, XI, 1941, pp. 39–60.

CHADWICK, H. M.: Studies on Anglo-Saxon Institutions. Cambridge, 1905.

Chancery Rolls, Various, Calendar of. London, 1912.

Chancery Warrants, Calendar of, 1244–1326. London, 1927.

Chapters of the English Black Monks, Documents illustrating the activities of the general and provincial, ed. W. A. Pantin. 3 vols. London (Camden Soc., 3rd Series, 45, 47, 54), 1931–7.

Charter Rolls, Calendar of, 1226–1516. 6 vols. London, 1903–27.

CHEW, H. M.: The English Ecclesiastical Tenants-in-Chief and Knight Service. Oxford, 1932.

Chief Elements used in English Place-Names, The, ed. A. Mawer. Cambridge, 1930.

CHOPE, R. Pearse (ed.): Early Tours in Devon and Cornwall. Exeter, 1918.

—— 'The Early History of the Manor of Hartland', DA xxxiv, 1902, pp. 418–54.

Chronicles of the Reigns of Stephen, Henry II, and Richard I, ed. R. Howlett. 4 vols. London (Rolls Series 82), 1885–90.

CLAPHAM, Sir John: A Concise Economic History of Britain from the earliest times to 1750. Cambridge, 1949.

Close Rolls, Henry III, 1227–72. 14 vols. London, 1902– .

Close Rolls, Calendar of, 1272–1447. 40 vols. London, 1900–37.

COKE, E.: Institutes of the Laws of England. 5 vols. London, 1797.

Collectanea Topographica et Genealogica. 8 vols. London, 1834–43.

COLLINGWOOD, R. G., and MYRES, J. N. L.: Roman Britain and the English Settlements. Oxford, 1945.

Crawford Collection of Early Charters and Documents, The, ed. A. S. Napier and W. H. Stevenson. Oxford, 1895.

CULLUM, J.: History and Antiquities of Hawsted, Suffolk. London, 1784.

CUNNINGHAM, W.: The Growth of English Industry and Commerce. 3 vols. Cambridge, 1903.

Dartmoor Preservation Association Publications, 1. A Short History of the Rights of Common upon the Forest of Dartmoor and the Commons of Devon. Report of Mr Stuart A. Moore to the Committee, and Appendix of Documents. Plymouth, 1890.

DAVENPORT, F. G.: The Economic Development of a Norfolk Manor, 1086–1565. Cambridge, 1906.

DAVIS, H. W. C. (ed.): Regesta Regum Anglo-Normannorum. Oxford, 1913.

DELABECHE, H. T.: Report on the Geology of Cornwall, Devon, and West Somerset. London, 1839.

DENHOLM-YOUNG, N.: Seignorial Administration in England. Oxford, 1937.

Devon & Cornwall Notes & Queries. 23 vols. (in progress). Exeter, 1900–

Devon Feet of Fines. Vol. I, 1196–1272, ed. O. J. Reichel. Exeter, 1912. Vol. II, 1272–1369, ed. O. J. Reichel, F. B. Prideaux, and H. Tapley-Soper. Exeter, 1939.

Devonshire Association for the advancement of Science, Literature, and Art, Reports and Transactions of the. 81 vols. (in progress). 1863–

DICKENS, A. G.: 'The Edwardian Arrears in Augmentations Payments and the Problem of the Ex-Religious', EHR LV, 1940, pp. 384–418.

DOBLE, G. H.: Saint Rumon and Saint Ronan. 'Cornish Saints' Series, No. 42. Long Compton, 1939.

—— A History of the Church and Parish of St Meubred, Cardynham. 'Cornish Parish Histories' Series, No. 6. Long Compton, 1939.

Domesday Book, Liber Censualis vocatus. 4 vols. London (Record Commissioners), 1783–1816.

Domesday Studies, ed. P. E. Dove. 2 vols. London, 1888–91.

DOUGLAS, D. C.: The Social Structure of Medieval East Anglia. Oxford, 1927.

DUFF, E. Gordon: The English Provincial Printers, Stationers, and Bookbinders to 1557. Cambridge, 1912.

DUGDALE, W.: Monasticon Anglicanum, ed. J. Caley, H. Ellis, and B. Bandinel. 6 vols. in 8. London, 1817–30.

EKWALL, E.: Studies on English Place-Names. Stockholm, 1936.

ELIOTT-DRAKE, Lady: The Family and Heirs of Sir Francis Drake. 2 vols. London, 1911.

ELLIS, Sir Henry: General Introduction to Domesday. 2 vols. London (Record Commissioners), 1833.

Episcopal Registers of the Diocese of Exeter, The, ed. F. C. Hingeston-Randolph. 10 vols. London and Exeter, 1886–1915, comprising:
The Registers of Walter Bronescombe (1257–80), Peter Quivil (1280–91), and Thomas de Bytton (1292–1307). 1889.
The Register of Walter de Stapeldon (1307–26). 1892.
The Register of John de Grandisson (1327–69). 3 vols. 1894–9.
The Register of Thomas de Brantyngham (1370–94). 2 vols. 1901–6.
The Register of Edmund Stafford (1395–1419). 1886.
The Register of Edmund Lacy (1420–55). 2 vols. 1909–15.

Exeter Book of Old English Poetry, The. Facsimile edition. London, 1933.

Exeter City Records, Report on the. London (Historical MSS. Commission), 1916.

Feudal Aids, Inquisitions and Assessments relating to, 1284–1431. 6 vols. London, 1899–1921.

FINBERG, H. P. R.: 'The Friars of "Towestoke"', DCNQ XXII, 1942–6, p. 348.
'A Domesday Identification', *ibid.*, p. 95.
'Bounds of the Devon Stannaries', *ibid.*, p. 121.
'Abbots of Tavistock', *ibid.*, pp. 159–62, 174–5, 186–8, 194–7.
'Ancient Demesne in Devonshire', *ibid.*, p. 178.
'The House of Ordgar and the Foundation of Tavistock Abbey', EHR LVIII, 1943, pp. 190–201.
'Church and State in Twelfth-Century Devon', DA LXXV, 1943, pp. 245–57.
'The Early History of Werrington', EHR LIX, 1944, pp. 237–51.
'Pirate Gore in Scilly', DCNQ XXII, p. 250.
'Morwell', DA LXXVII, 1945, pp. 157–71.
'St Rumon', DCNQ XXII, p. 331.
'The Tragi-comedy of Abbot Bonus', *ibid.*, pp. 341–7.
'The Skelving-Stool', *ibid.*, p. 368.
'Drake's Weir, Tavistock', *ibid.*, p. 369.
'Childe's Tomb', DA LXXVIII, 1946, pp. 265–80.
'A Farmer's Lease in 1402', DCNQ XXIII, 1947–9, p. 50.
'Some Early Tavistock Charters', EHR LXII, 1947, pp. 352–77.
'The Borough of Tavistock', DA LXXIX, 1947, pp. 130–53.
'The Devon-Cornwall Boundary', DCNQ XXIII, p. 104.
'What is a Farleu?', *ibid.*, p. 133.
'Prelude to Abbot Bonus', *ibid.*, p. 184.
'The Manor of Roborough', *ibid.*, p. 241.
'A Cellarer's Account Book', *ibid.*, p. 253.
'The Meaning of Barton', *ibid.*, pp. 326, 363.
'Lydford Castle', *ibid.*, p. 386.
'The Open Field in Devonshire', Antiquity, XXIII, 1949, pp. 180–7.
'The Customs of Stokenham', DCNQ XXIV, 1950, p. 69.

Fine Rolls, Calendar of, 1272–1445. 17 vols. London, 1911–37.

FREEMAN, E. A.: History of the Norman Conquest. 5 vols and index. Oxford, 1867–79.

GALBRAITH, V. H.: Studies in the Public Records. London, 1948.

Gover, J. E. B., Mawer, A., and Stenton, F. M.: The Place-Names of Devon. 2 vols. Cambridge, 1931–2.

Gras, N. S. B.: The Early English Customs System. Cambridge (Mass.), 1918.

—— and E.C.: The Economic and Social History of an English Village. Cambridge (Mass.), 1930.

Gray, H. L.: English Field Systems. Cambridge (Mass.), 1915.

Great Roll of the Pipe, The, for the Second, Third, and Fourth Years of the Reign of King Henry the Second, 1155–8, ed. J. Hunter. London, 1844.

Halsbury, Earl of: The Laws of England. 31 vols. London, 1907–17.

Hearne, Thomas: Remarks and Recollections, ed. C. E. Doble and others. 11 vols. Oxford Historical Society, 1885–1921.

Hector, J. M.: Introduction to the Botany of Field Crops. 2 vols. Johannesburg [1936].

Hemmeon, M. de W.: Burgage Tenure in Mediaeval England. Cambridge (Mass.), 1914.

Hencken, H. O'N.: The Archaeology of Cornwall and Scilly. London, 1932.

Historians of the Church of York, ed. J. Raine. 3 vols. London (Rolls Series 71), 1879–94.

Hodgkin, R. H.: History of the Anglo-Saxons. 2 vols. Oxford, 1939.

Hoskins, W. G.: 'The Reclamation of the Waste in Devon', Economic History Review, XIII, 1943, pp. 80–92.

Hurstfield, J.: 'The Greenwich Tenures of the Reign of Edward VI', Law Quarterly Review, 1949.

Inquisitions post mortem, Calendar of. First Series. 11 vols. London, 1906–35.

Kemble, J. M. (ed.): Codex Diplomaticus Aevi Saxonici. 6 vols. London, 1839–48.

Kennett, White: Parochial Antiquities. 2 vols. Oxford, 1818.

Knights Hospitallers in England, The, ed. L. B. Larking. London (Camden Soc., 1st Series, 65), 1857.

Knowles, Dom David: The Monastic Order in England. Cambridge, 1949.

—— The Religious Orders in England. Cambridge, 1948.

Kosminski, E. A.: 'The Hundred Rolls of 1279–80 as a source for English Agrarian History', Economic History Review, III, 1931, pp. 16–44.

Leland, J.: Collectanea, ed. T. Hearne. 6 vols. London, 1774.

Lennard, R.: 'English Agriculture under Charles II', Economic History Review, IV, 1932, pp. 23–45.

Letters and Papers, Foreign and Domestic, Henry VIII, ed. J. S. Brewer, J. Gairdner, and R. H. Brodie. 22 vols. in 35. London, 1864–1932.

LEVETT, E.: Studies in Manorial History. Oxford, 1938.

—— The Black Death on the Estates of the See of Winchester. Oxford, 1916.

LEWIS, G. R.: The Stannaries. Cambridge (Mass.), 1924.

Liber Niger Scaccarii, ed. T. Hearne. 2 vols. London, 1774.

LUNT, William E.: The Financial Relations of the Papacy with England to 1327. Cambridge (Mass.), 1939.

MACALISTER, R. A. S.: Corpus Inscriptionum Insularum Celticarum. Vol. I. Dublin, 1945.

MAITLAND, F. W.: Domesday Book and Beyond. Cambridge, 1907.

MALMESBURY, William of: see William.

MARSHALL, William: The Rural Economy of the West of England. 2 vols. London, 1796.

Medieval Latin Word-List, ed. J. H. Baxter and Charles Johnson. Oxford, 1934.

Miscellaneous Inquisitions, Calendar of. 3 vols. London, 1916–37.

Montacute and Bruton Cartularies, Two (Somerset Record Society, 8), 1894.

MOREY, Adrian: Bartholomew of Exeter, Bishop and Canonist. Cambridge, 1937.

MORGAN, F. W.: 'The Domesday Geography of Devon', DA LXXII, 1940, pp. 305–31.

MORGAN, M. M. : The English Lands of the Abbey of Bec. Oxford, 1946.

NEILSON, N.: Economic Conditions on the Manors of Ramsey Abbey. Philadelphia, 1899.

—— Customary Rents. Oxford, 1910.

OLIVER, G.: Monasticon Dioecesis Exoniensis. Exeter and London, 1846.

ORWIN, C. S. and C. S.: The Open Fields. Oxford, 1938.

PAGE, F. M.: The Estates of Crowland Abbey. Cambridge, 1934.

Papal Letters, Calendar of, 1198–1471. 12 vols. London, 1894–1933.

Parliamentary Writs and Writs of Military Summons, with Records and Muniments relating to Suit and Service to Parliament. 2 vols. London (Record Commissioners), 1827–34.

Patent Rolls, Calendar of, 1216–1553. 60 vols. London, 1901–29.

Pipe Roll Society, Publications of the. 62 vols. (in progress). London, 1884–

Place-Names of Devon, The: see GOVER.

Placita de Quo Warranto. London (Record Commissioners), 1818.

POLE, Sir William: Collections towards a Description of the County of Devon. London, 1791.

POLLOCK, F., and MAITLAND, F. W.: History of English Law. 2 vols. Cambridge, 1911.

POOLE, A. L.: Obligations of Society in the Twelfth and Thirteenth Centuries. Oxford, 1946.

POUNDS, N. J. G.: 'Lanhydrock Atlas', Antiquity, XIX, 1945, pp. 20–6.

POWELL, Anthony: John Aubrey and his Friends. London, 1948.

POWER, E.: The Wool Trade in English Medieval History. Oxford, 1941.

—— and POSTAN, M. M. (edd.): Studies in English Trade in the Fifteenth Century. London, 1933.

POWICKE, F. M.: The Reformation in England. Oxford, 1941.

RADFORD, Lady: Tavistock Abbey. Exeter, 1929.

—— Presidential Address, 'Early Printing in Devon', DA LX, 1928, pp. 51–74.

RANDALL, H. J.: History in the Open Air. London, 1936.

Red Book of the Exchequer, The, ed. H. Hall. 3 vols. London (Rolls Series 99), 1896.

Register of Edward the Black Prince, The. 4 vols. London, 1930–3.

REICHEL, O. J.: The Hundreds of Devon. Issued in ten parts by the Devonshire Association, 1928–38, with index volume 1942.

Reports from the Lords' Committees touching the Dignity of a Peer of the Realm. 5 vols. London, 1820–9.

Reports of the Deputy Keeper of the Public Records, Annual; Eighth Report, London, 1847.

ROBERTSON, E. William: Historical Essays in Connexion with the Land, the Church, etc. Edinburgh, 1872.

ROBO, E.: Mediaeval Farnham. Farnham, 1935.

ROGERS, J. E. Thorold: The History of Agriculture and Prices. Vols. 1 and 2. Oxford, 1866.

ROSE-TROUP, F.: The Western Rebellion of 1549. London, 1913.

—— 'Exeter Manumissions and Quittances of the Eleventh and Twelfth Centuries', DA LXIX, 1937, pp. 417–45.

Rotuli Chartarum in Turri Londinensi asservati, 1199–1216. London (Record Commissioners), 1837.

Rotuli Hundredorum. 2 vols. London (Record Commissioners), 1812–18.

Rotuli Litterarum Clausarum in Turri Londinensi asservati, 1204–27. London (Record Commissioners), 1833–44.

Rotuli Parliamentorum. 8 vols. London, 1783–1832.

ROWE, S.: A Perambulation of the Antient and Royal Forest of Dartmoor. Plymouth, 1848.

ROWSE, A. L.: Tudor Cornwall. London, 1941.

Royal Historical Society, Transactions of the. 72 vols. (in progress). London, 1872–

SALTMARSH, J., and DARBY, H. C.: 'The Infield-Outfield System on a Norfolk Manor', Economic History, III, 1935, pp. 30–44.

SAVINE, A.: English Monasteries on the Eve of the Dissolution. Oxford, 1909.

SCOTT THOMSON, G.: Two Centuries of Family History. London, 1930.

SEARLE, W. G.: Onomasticon Anglo-Saxonicum. Cambridge, 1897.

Select Cases in the Court of Requests, ed. I. S. Leadam (Selden Society, 12), 1898.

Select Pleas in Manorial Courts, ed. F. W. Maitland. London (Selden Society, 2), 1889.

SKEEL, C.: 'The Council of the West', Trans. Royal Hist. Soc., Ser. IV, vol. iv, 1921, pp. 62–80.

SMITH, R. A. L.: Canterbury Cathedral Priory. Cambridge, 1943.

SMITH, T.: Catalogus Librorum Manuscriptorum Bibliothecae Cottonianae. Oxford, 1696.

SNAPE, R. H.: English Monastic Finances in the Later Middle Ages. Cambridge, 1926.

STENTON, F. M.: Anglo-Saxon England. Oxford, 1943.

STUBBS, W.: Select Charters and other Illustrations of English Constitutional History. 9th ed., revised by H. W. C. Davis. Oxford, 1913.

TAIT, James: The Medieval English Borough. Manchester, 1936.

Taxatio Ecclesiastica Angliae et Walliae, auctoritate Papae Nicholai IV. London (Record Commissioners), 1802.

Testa de Nevill (The Book of Fees). 3 vols. London, 1921–31.

THORPE, B.: Diplomatarium Anglicum. London, 1865.

Tudor Economic Documents, ed. R. H. Tawney and E. Power. 3 vols. London, 1924.

Tudor Studies, ed. R. W. Seton-Watson. London, 1924.

Two Saxon Chronicles, ed. J. Earle and C. Plummer. 2 vols. Oxford, 1892–9.

Valor Ecclesiasticus, temp. Henrici VIII auctoritate regia institutus. 6 vols. London (Record Commissioners), 1810–34.

VANCOUVER, Charles: General View of the Agriculture of the County of Devon. London, 1813.

VENN, J., and J. A.: Alumni Cantabrigienses. 7 vols. Cambridge, 1922–47.

Victoria County History of Cornwall, ed. W. Page. Part 8: The Cornwall Domesday. London, 1924.

Victoria County History of Devon, ed. W. Page. Vol. I. London, 1906.

VINOGRADOFF, P.: Villainage in England. Oxford, 1892.

—— The Growth of the Manor, London, 1905.

—— English Society in the Eleventh Century. Oxford, 1908.

WALTER OF HENLEY: Husbandry; with an anonymous Husbandry, Seneschaucie, and Robert Grosseteste's Rules, ed. E. Lamond and W. Cunningham. London, 1890.

WANLEY, H.: Antiquae Literaturae Septentrionalis Liber Alter. Oxford, 1705.

WESTCOTE, T.: A View of Devonshire in 1630, with a Pedigree of most of its Gentry, ed. G. Oliver and Pitman Jones. Exeter, 1845.

WILLIAM OF MALMESBURY. Gesta Pontificum, ed. N. E. S. A. Hamilton. London (Rolls Series, 52), 1870.

—— Gesta Regum, ed. W. Stubbs, 2 vols. London (Rolls Series 90), 1887–9.

—— Vita Wulfstani, ed. R. R. Darlington. London (Camden Soc., 3rd Series, 40), 1928.

WILLIS, Browne: An History of the Mitred Parliamentary Abbies and Conventual Cathedral Churches. 2 vols. London, 1718.

WORTH, R. H.: 'Prehistoric Tavistock', DA LXXIX, 1947, pp. 125–8.

—— 'The Dartmoor Blowing-House', DA LXXII, 1940, pp. 209–50.

WORTH, R. N.: A History of Devonshire. London, 1886.

—— (ed.) Calendar of the Plymouth Municipal Records. Plymouth, 1893.

—— (ed.) Calendar of the Tavistock Parish Records. [Plymouth], 1887.

YOUATT, W.: Sheep. London, 1837.

INDEX

Granger, 239
Grantchester, 114n.
Grendon, Tavistock, 45, 52
Grenoven wood, 132
Grento, 9, 14
Grey, Richard, 216n.
Grills, William, 274, 275n.
Grosseteste, Robert, 222
Grundy, G. B., quoted, 29n.
Guildhall, Tavistock, 206, 286, 293
Guilds, parish, 190, 206
Gulworthy, Tavistock, 42, 52, 79, 162, 163, 166n.
Gurdet, William, 14
Gylys, William, 250n.
Gytha, countess, 6, 10

Halberton, field names in, 38
Hall-moot, 207
Hamlyn, Thomas, abbot of Athelney, 225n.
Ham mill, 195
Hams, South, 86
Hannaborough, Hatherleigh, 14, 87n.
Harford Bridge, 41, 43n.
Harold, king of England, 6
Harris, William, of Radford, 164
Harrowing, 81, 109, 132
Hartland, 69, 266
Harton, 73
Harvesting, 82, 96, 129, 259
Hasworthy, Tavistock, 14, 42, 44, 45, 46, 52
Hatches, salmon, 160, 163–5
Hatch-silver, 46, 83, 161
Hatherleigh, 2, 3, 5, 9, 11, 58, 59, 87, 135, 194, 211, 213, 215, 242, 249, 255, 256, 269, 280; borough, 73, 87n., 204n., 205, 206; church, 22, 23, 24, 25, 26n., 232n.; demesne, 86, 87n.; market and fairs, 198, 199, 205; riots at, 23, 88n.
Hatherleigh Moor, 87n., 206
Hawkwell, Somerset, 28
Hawstead, Suffolk, 114
Hayles, Glos., 61
Haytor, hundred of, 213
Heathfield, manor of, 270n.
Heathfield, Tavistock, 3, 40, 43, 45, 46, 47, 48, 52, 68, 88, 92, 106, 131

Hecfelda, 3
Hecklake, 16n.
Hedgebanks, 50, 54
Heifers, 129
Helen, St, island, 15
Hemyock, 98n., 106
Hencken, H. O'N., quoted, 29n.
Hengham, Chief Justice, 56n.
Henry I, king of England, 12, 15, 168, 178, 192, 197, 199, 210, 213, 215, 228
Henry II, 16, 168, 187, 192, 212, 215, 228, 231, 233
Henry III, 23, 89, 175, 229, 230, 260
Henry VI, 264
Henry VII, 215
Henry VIII, 233
Herbage, sales of, 131, 150, 158, 242
Herbert, abbot of Tavistock, 17, 21, 23, 24, 161, 277
Heriots, 130, 132, 217
Highland zone of Britain, 29, 41
Hingston Down, 88, 164, 183
Hoeing, 109
Hoggasters, 129
Hoggets, 129, 132
Holcombe, 210
Holeyeat, manor of, 16, 17, 213, 217n., 255n.
Holland, John, duke of Exeter, 130
Holme, St Benet's abbey, 7n.
Holne, 190
Holsworthy, 133, 199
Honiton, 96n., 98n., 151
Honour of Tavistock, 209, and see Barony
Horrabridge, 41
Horses, 129, 131, 132, and see Packhorses
Horton abbey, 4, 5, 8n.
Hoskins, W. G., 34n., 51n., 69n.
Hospitallers, 129n., 199, 201
Houndtor, Manaton, 5, 9, 14, 59, 209
Hugo (knight), 9, 14, 58
Hulham, 104
Hundred courts, 55, 197, 207, 210, 211–16
Hunting, 192, 193, 261
Huntingdon, countess of, 130
Hurdwick, 17, 47, 80, 81, 82, 83, 161, 194, 206, 208, 209, 214, 216, 217, 227, 233, 249, 250n.,

For EU product safety concerns, contact us at Calle de José Abascal, 56–1°,
28003 Madrid, Spain or eugpsr@cambridge.org.

www.ingramcontent.com/pod-product-compliance
Ingram Content Group UK Ltd.
Pitfield, Milton Keynes, MK11 3LW, UK
UKHW042148130625
459647UK00011B/1233